The Harmony Guide to Knitting

THE HARMONY GUIDE TO
KNITTING
Techniques and Stitches

Edited by Debra Mountford

Harmony Books / New York

Copyright © 1992 by Lyric Books Limited

Published by Harmony Books, a division of Crown Publishers, Inc., 201 East 50th Street, New York, New York 10022. Member of the Crown Publishing Group. Originally published in three separate volumes under the titles **The Harmony Guide to Knitting Stitches Volume One, The Harmony Guide to Knitting Stitches Volume Two,** and **The Harmony Guide to Knitting Techniques.**

HARMONY and colophon are trademarks of Crown Publishers, Inc.

Manufactured in Belgium

Library of Congress Cataloging-in-Publication Data

The Harmony guide to knitting : techniques and stitches / edited
    by Debra Mountford. — 1st ed.
        p.   cm.
    Includes index.
    1. Knitting.   I. Mountford, Debra.
    TT820.H273 1992
    746.9'2—dc20   91-36891
                                                    CIP

ISBN 0-517-58848-X

10 9 8 7 6 5 4 3 2 1

First Edition

Contents

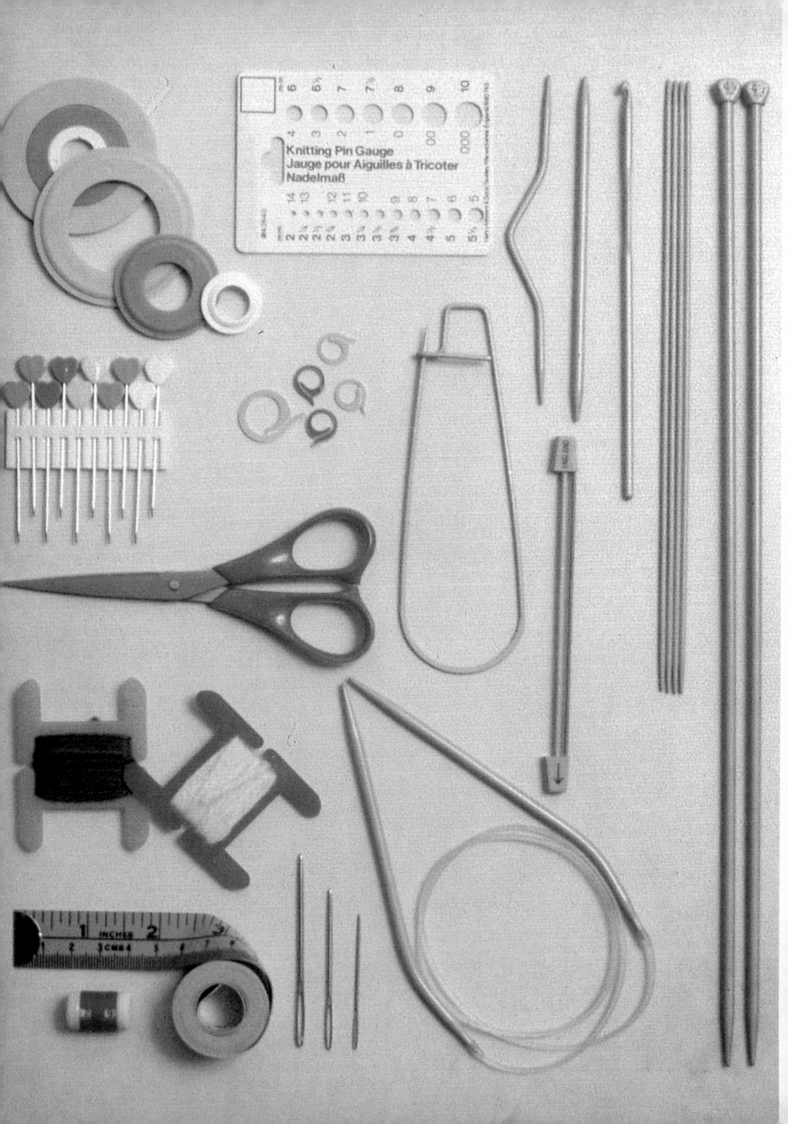

Introduction

In *The Harmony Guide to Knitting* we have brought together the answers to many of the questions that arise when knitting, and added hundreds of stitch patterns. There is information here for everyone from the beginner to the most experienced knitter. For instance have you tried our recommendation of mattress stitch for joining your garment pieces together? - See page 26. And had you realised the enormous variety of patterns you can make with just the help of a Cable needle? - See pages 84-118.

I am sure you will find a browse through the book interesting. We have also included a generous library of pattern stitches, written in easy-to-follow language. These include everything from basic knit and purl patterns to the most intricate cable and lace patterns.

Although much of the information in this book is directed towards hand knitting you will find a lot to interest you here even if you are mainly a crocheter or a machine knitter!

Happy Knitting,

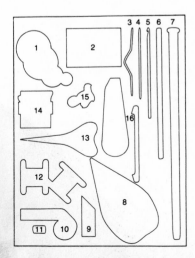

Debra Mountford

Series Editor

1. Pompon making discs. 2. Needle Gauge. 3. U-Bend Cable Needle. 4. Standard Cable Needle. 5. Crochet Hook. 6. Set of Four Double Pointed Needles. 7. Knitting Needles. 8. Circular Knitting Needle. 9. Sewing Needles. 10. Tape Measure. 11. Row Counter. 12. Bobbins. 13. Scissors. 14. Dressmaker's Pins. 15. Markers. 16. Stitch Holders.

Working from a Pattern

Understand your Pattern

Before starting to knit any pattern always read it through and check the points highlighted below. Even if you are inexperienced this will give you an idea of how the garment is structured. The styles of writing and presentation vary depending on who publishes the pattern, but the general format is common throughout the knitting trade. If you are working from a leaflet, all the following information should be included. A knitting book or a pattern in a magazine will also contain all the information but some may be given on a separate page at the beginning or end of the publication.

Measurements/Sizes

Most knitting patterns give instructions for a range of chest or bust sizes. Always work to your actual chest or bust measurement, as the designer will have decided how much 'ease' should be included in the design, and will have calculated the instructions accordingly.

However, if the garment illustrated appears too baggy for your taste, knit a smaller size - or likewise, make a larger size if you prefer garments with a lot of room. The amount of 'ease' - how much extra room there is in a garment over and above the bust/chest size - is not standard and can vary from no allowance at all for a fitted sweater to 20 cm (8 inches) or more for a loose-fitting chunky casual sweater.

Most patterns give a 'finished measurement' for each of the various sizes, so you will know how much ease has been allowed for. The photograph will show whether the design is meant to be fitted or loose-fitting. Some patterns also have measurement diagrams which give the shape and measurements of each of the pattern pieces.

Patterns which are given in a range of sizes have instructions for the smallest size printed first, followed by the other sizes in brackets or parentheses, for example 'Cast on 26(28-30-32) sts'. This instruction gives information for 4 sizes at the same time. To avoid confusion go through the pattern beforehand and underline or circle all the instructions for the size you are making. Take special care if the sizes have been separated to give a particular instruction. For example, say a pattern states '**1st(4th) sizes only:** Cast off 15(20) sts, work to end'. For the 1st size, follow the instructions outside the brackets, and for the 4th size follow the instructions within the brackets. For any other size, these instructions do not apply. Always look for the headings which apply to the size you are making.

Materials

This heading gives a list of all the materials required for making the garment including amounts of yarn (according to the size being made), needles, buttons and any other haberdashery items/notions.

Tension/Gauge

It is most important to check that your tension is correct by making a swatch BEFORE YOU BEGIN. Remember that

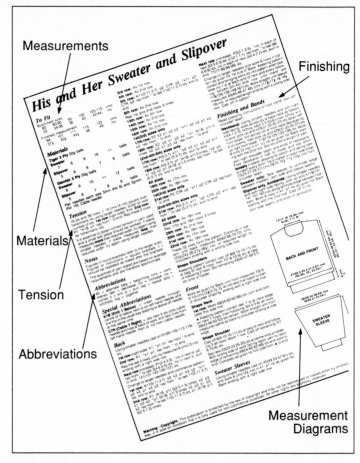

Labels: Measurements; His and Her Sweater and Slipover; Finishing; Materials; Tension; Abbreviations; Measurement Diagrams

the needle sizes quoted in the materials section are not necessarily the needles you will require to achieve the correct tension. Use whichever needles are correct for you, bearing in mind that if there are other needle sizes quoted (for ribbed edgings), these needle sizes should be adjusted accordingly (see table on page 10).

Abbreviations

These are used for many of the repetitive words and phrases which occur in the instructions in order to save valuable space. The most common abbreviations are given in the following paragraph. Not all publications have exactly the same abbreviations, but a lot of them are fairly standard and the jargon will soon become familiar.

Alt = alternate; **beg** = beginning; **cm** = centimetres; **dec** = decrease; **inc** = increase; **k** = knit; **KB1** =knit into back of next stitch; **p** = purl; **PB1** =purl into back of next stitch; **psso** = pass slipped stitch over; **rep** = repeat; **sl** = slip; **st(s)** = stitch(es); **st st** = stocking stitch; **ssk** = slip, slip, knit; **tog** = together; **tbl** = through back of loops; **yb** = yarn back; **yf** = yarn forward; **yfrn** = yarn forward and round needle; **yo** = yarn over; **yon** = yarn over needle; **yrn** = yarn round needle.

A list of all general abbreviations used in this book are given on page 189. If an individual pattern stitch has any unusual stitches these have been given as Special Abbreviations.

Garment Instructions

Actual working instructions are written in such a way that they should be self-explanatory. If metric and imperial measurements are given, always work either in inches **or** centimetres throughout, **not** a combination of both.

Asterisks, brackets or parentheses are used to indicate the repetition of a sequence of stitches. For example: *k3, p1; rep from * to end. This means knit three stitches, then purl one stitch alternately to the end of the row. It could also be written: [k3, p1] to end.

Asterisks and brackets or parentheses might be used together in a row: *k4, p1, [k1, p1] 3 times; rep from * to end. Part of the instruction is placed in brackets or parentheses to denote that these stitches only are to be repeated three times before returning to the directions immediately after the asterisk.

When repeating anything, make sure that you are doing so for the correct number of times. For example: [k1, p1] twice = 4 stitches worked, but *k1, p1; rep from * twice more = 6 stitches worked in all.

You may come across the phrase 'work straight' or 'work even'. This simply means continue without increasing or decreasing the number of stitches on the needle, keeping the pattern correct as established.

If you encounter the figure 0 within an instruction, for example k2(0-1-2), this simply means that for **that particular size** no stitches are worked at that point.

Always keep a note of the number of rows worked for each piece. This ensures that side seams match and can be joined row for row, and that sleeves are the same length as each other. You may find that a pattern tells you to work until the front is a particular number of rows shorter than the back before shaping the neck and this is much easier to calculate if you know exactly how many rows have been worked in the back and front.

When you put your knitting aside, always mark where you are on the pattern. You may think that you will remember, but it is better to be safe than sorry, especially if a difficult stitch is involved.

Finishing

It is best to read through this section of the pattern beforehand in case it requires a technique or finishing touch which is unfamiliar. This paragraph will also tell you whether to press your work or not according to the type of yarn or stitch used. In fact many patterns will refer you back to the ball band on the yarn. You will also be told to sew up the garment in a certain order. Always stick to this order as sometimes various processes (such as embroidery) are easier to work at a certain stage, or sections fit together more logically than would appear at first glance. Seams may also have to be joined before certain sections are knitted, for example neckband, front bands, etc. Types of seam are not always mentioned as this can be a matter of preference. If you are unsure which seam to use see page 26 for further guidance. Always check the measurements of each piece of knitting and see if there are any mistakes in the stitch pattern before sewing up. After completion, turn the garment inside out to make sure all loose ends have been secured.

Yarns

'Yarn' is the general term used for strands of fibre which are twisted (spun) together into a continuous thread. It encompasses both natural (wool, cotton, etc.) and synthetic fibres as well as plain or fancy finishes and varying thicknesses and textures. It is the main requirement for any knitted garment, since nothing can be produced without it.

The range of yarns available is virtually endless, and new spinning techniques are constantly being evolved to produce new effects. Detailed below are the various weights of the 'standard' (or plain) yarns and their uses, as well as the main yarn sources and the most common methods of producing fancy yarns.

Yarn Thickness or Weight

Yarns vary enormously in thickness (or weight) from very fine to very bulky, each yarn being more suited to a certain type of knitting. Over the years a series of 'standard' weights have been established which are described below from the finest through to the heaviest. However, the yarns available in each group are by no means identical, and the terms used merely signify a similarity in tension/gauge when knitted. Fancy yarns may also be available in these thicknesses, but extra care should be taken to ensure that the correct tension/gauge is achieved.

2 ply and 3 ply Until the 1950's these yarns were widely available, and many early knitting patterns can still be found (some have even been republished in recent years). Nowadays, however, very few people have the time, patience or skill to work with the very fine yarns and they are now generally used for baby's garments and very fine work such as lacy shawls. These yarns are only available in a limited range of colours, often only white.

Customary tension/gauge range over stocking stitch - 28 to 32 stitches to 10 cm (4 inches) in width.
Needle size range 3 1/4mm to 2 3/4mm (USA 4 to 2).

4 ply (USA Fingering, Australia/NZ 5 ply) Again popular for baby's clothes, but also used for adult's garments by the knitter who is prepared to spend a little longer completing a garment. 4 ply is very effective for lacy garments and Fairisles, and greater detail can be achieved in motif or picture knitting than in the thicker yarns. 4 ply is also very popular for crochet and machine knitting. Available in a wide range of colours, 4 ply may be bought on cones as well as in balls.

Customary tension/gauge range over stocking stitch - 28 to 30 stitches to 10 cm (4 inches) in width.
Needle size range 3 1/4mm to 3mm (USA 4 to 3).

Double Knitting (USA Sportweight, Australia/NZ 8 ply) By far the most popular of the standard yarns, double knitting can be used for baby's, children's and adult's garments. Designs for double knitting range from light and lacy to plain and classic and to heavily textured and cabled garments. Double knitting is available in a vast range of colours, and can be plain, brushed (fluffy), tweed effect or a variety of other finishes.

Yarns

Customary tension/gauge range over stocking stitch - 22 to 24 stitches to 10 cm (4 inches) in width.
Needle size range 4mm to 3³/4mm (USA 6 to 5).

Aran or Triple, (USA Knitting Worsted, Australia/NZ 12 ply) Aran or Triple is generally used for heavily textured and cabled garments. Originally available only in a natural (cream shade) pure wool, many spinners are now introducing a wider range of colours for fashion aran knits, and also using synthetic fibres for economy. A traditional aran knit in wool is extremely warm and durable.

Customary tension/gauge over stocking stitch - 18 stitches to 10 cm (4 inches) in width.
Needle size range 5¹/2mm to 5mm (USA 9 to 8).

Chunky (USA Bulky, Australia/NZ 14 ply) Quick to knit on large needles, chunky is very popular especially with beginners. Chunky is generally used for loose-fitting, outdoor sweaters and jackets, and can be plain or brushed. Most basic and current fashion shades are available, although the range is not as wide as in double knitting.

Customary tension/gauge over stocking stitch - 14 stitches to 10 cm (4 inches) in width.
Needle size 6¹/2mm (USA 10¹/2).

1 ply This is a misleading term sometimes used to describe the very finest cobwebby yarns. There is no such thing as a '1-ply' yarn except if it is a single filament - see under synthetics. The twisting of 2 or more threads together gives the yarn its strength. These very fine yarns referred to as 1-ply do not in fact fit into any standard. There are some fine Shetland yarns mistakenly called 1 ply; these are often used to knit 'wedding ring' shawls, so-called as they are soft and fine enough to be pulled through a wedding ring.

Yarn Sources

The fibres from which yarn is spun can be of animal, vegetable or synthetic origin. The following are the most popular types that you will come across, although fibres are often combined, either for reasons of economy, or to exploit the best qualities of each. The ball band should always give the percentage content of each fibre used. Natural (animal or vegetable) fibres are generally more expensive than synthetic but are also superior in quality. If many hours are to be spent producing a garment, a cheap, inferior yarn can prove to be a false economy.

Animal

Wool has always been the most popular fibre for hand knitting. It is hard-wearing, and very warm and comfortable to wear because of its ability to absorb moisture. It is also very pleasant to work with as it has excellent elasticity and produces a smooth, even fabric. However, great care must be taken when washing a wool garment as changes in temperature or over vigorous handling can cause shrinkage and felting which cannot later be rectified. Nowadays wool can be treated during the spinning process to make it less likely to shrink when washed.

Sheep are specially bred for wool production, Australia being the world leader. Wool can be spun into any yarn weight, although for reasons of economy it is often com-

bined with a synthetic fibre to produce the thicker yarns.

Mohair is a light, fluffy, extremely warm and luxurious fibre that comes from the Angora goat (the name denotes the area of Turkey - Ankara - where the goats originated). The main areas of production today include South Africa and Texas, but a lot of the spinning is done in the UK. As it is a very delicate fibre, mohair is usually spun with other fibres to strengthen it. Always check the ball band for the percentage content, as mohair can vary from as little as 5% to over 80% of the total yarn content, and this is generally reflected in the price. Although a ball of mohair may appear expensive, because of its lightness only a few balls may be required to knit a garment, thus making the price more acceptable. Because of its 'firm' type of fluffiness mohair is often spun to a very fine core yarn but can be knitted at the same tension/gauge as a much thicker yarn as the 'hairy' fibres give the fabric stability.

Angora comes from the angora rabbit and is principally produced in China. The luxurious silky hairs are very short and slippery and therefore difficult to spin without adding wool or synthetic fibres. Production is very limited, which makes angora one of the more expensive yarns available. It is therefore rarely used for an entire garment, but more usually as a trimming or detail together with another yarn. Beware also if you are an allergy sufferer, the short hairs are prone to shedding and can cause a miserable reaction. Angora yarns are generally produced in 4 ply or double knitting weights.

Alpaca is a luxury yarn spun from the long fine woolly hair of a type of llama that is found in Bolivia and Peru. It has a soft feel with a slight hairiness, but is not as light and fluffy as mohair. Because each individual hair is comparatively long, Alpaca is sometimes used to make men's suitings, producing a luxurious material with a slight sheen. It most often occurs in knitting yarns as a small percentage added to other fibres for a particular effect.

Cashmere is perhaps the most luxurious fibre known to man. Taken from the hair of a goat found in Tibet and Central Asia, cashmere is far softer than mohair or alpaca and also less hairy. Cashmere is often combined with wool to make the yarn stronger, and also more economical. It is sometimes combined with silk to give a yarn of the utmost luxury. China is the world's leading manufacturer of cashmere yarn.

Silk is the strongest and lightest of the natural fibres. It is produced from the cocoon of the silkworm in the form of a continuous filament, and because of its strength can be spun into very fine yarns. Silk is extremely receptive to dyes and produces yarns in the richest range of colours. Silk is a very heavy yarn and is often used in conjunction with other fibres such as wool to give greater elasticity.

Vegetable

Cotton is a fairly inexpensive fibre produced from the 'bolls' of the cotton plant grown chiefly in the USSR, USA, China and India. It is a non-allergic fibre with excellent absorbency and washing qualities. Originally spun into fine yarns for lacy crochet work, cotton is now available in thicker weights, double knitting being the most popular for hand knitting. Cotton is often spun into fancy yarns such as boucle, and may be combined with other fibres to give greater elasticity or warmth. As cotton on its own does not have much elasticity, great care must be taken to maintain an even tension to produce a smooth fabric. Ribbed welts may tend to become baggy, but this can be overcome by using shirring elastic in the ribbing.

Linen is a very heavy fibre obtained from the flax plant. It is strong, extremely durable and absorbent, but less receptive to dyes than cotton. Pure linen has even less elasticity than cotton and is therefore impractical for hand knitting as the garment would be heavy and lifeless. Most branded linen yarns are mixed with other fibres to produce a more versatile yarn.

Synthetics

Nylon, acrylic and viscose (rayon) are all included in a range of man-made fibres under the general term of synthetics.

Theoretically viscose (rayon) is not a synthetic fibre - but it **is** man-made. It is derived from a cellulose base, originally wood or other vegetable sources, but it is chemically treated to form a man-made liquid which is spun into filaments. These are then used in a similar way to synthetically derived filaments and spun as required.

100% synthetic yarns are strong and hard-wearing but lack many of the finer features of natural fibres. The feel of natural fibres is pleasanter than that of man-made yarns, although synthetics can be spun to imitate the look of a natural yarn at a fraction of the cost. Synthetic yarns are also lighter than natural yarns, and therefore less yarn would be needed to knit a garment in a 'high-bulk' acrylic yarn than in a wool yarn for example. Several synthetic yarns may be spun together to create varying effects, and these methods are constantly changing and updating to produce even more unusual yarns. However, synthetics are best used in conjunction with natural fibres to exploit the better qualities of the natural yarns while making the yarn more economical and possibly more hard wearing.

Spinning

Spinning is the term used to describe the transformation of raw fibres into usable yarn.

All yarn starts off either as a continuous filament (silk produced by a silkworm or synthetic fibre produced by an imitation silkworm!) or as staples varying in length from about 3-4 cm (1½ inches) to 12 cm (4 or 5 inches). Obviously wool is a staple fibre, the lengths of the staple varying quite considerably depending on which part of the fleece they come from. Cotton and linen are also staple fibres as they are made from the fibrous seed cases of the fruiting plant. In every case these staples have to be cleaned and straightened out sufficiently to enable them to be twisted together to form a usable yarn. The continuous filament fibres, such as silk and synthetics, are twisted together to form a much smoother, shinier yarn which is in fact much stronger. Quite often the synthetic, continuous filament is cut into short lengths to form imitation staples, which are then twisted together to copy the effects of wool, cotton or other natural fibres.

Buying Yarn

Yarn is most commonly sold ready wound into balls of specific weight. Some yarn, particularly if it is very thick, may also be sold on a coiled hank or skein and must be wound up into a ball before you begin knitting. Yarn manufacturers (spinners) wrap each ball with a paper band on which certain information is printed. The ball band states the weight of the yarn and its composition. It also gives instructions for washing and pressing and often states the ideal tension for the yarn with the recommended needle sizes that have been used to achieve this.

Dye Lot Number

Also given on the ball band is the shade number and a dye lot number. It is important that you use yarn of the same dye lot for a single project. Different dye lots vary subtly in shading which may not be apparent when you are comparing two balls of yarn, but the variations in shade will be very noticeable in a finished piece of knitting.

Always buy sufficient yarn to complete the garment, making sure they are of the same dye lot, or ask the store to keep some of the yarn for you until it is required. Many stores will also give refunds or credit for unused yarn, providing the same dye lot is still in stock. If you run out of yarn and cannot buy any more in the same dye lot, contact the spinner to see if there is any more available. Alternatively, use the different dye lot for the edgings only, or work 2 rows alternately from each ball so that the change in shade is less noticeable. If you are likely to make the garment longer than the pattern instructions state, buy one or two extra balls to allow for this.

Always keep one ball band as a reference. The best way is to pin it to the tension swatch and keep them together with any left-over yarn and spare buttons or other trimmings. You can always check the washing instructions and you will also have materials for repairs.

Choosing and Substituting Yarns

It is not always necessary to heed the warnings about only using the yarn stated on the pattern instructions. Of course, it is always best to try and obtain the correct yarn, but if this proves difficult then it is possible to substitute another yarn as long as the tension/gauge corresponds **exactly** with that given in the pattern. Check the details on the ball band of the substitute yarn or buy one ball to begin with to knit a tension swatch.

Tools and Equipment

Remember that the type of yarn should be suitable for the style of the garment - for example a fluffy yarn is not the best choice for an Aran sweater where the stitches should be clearly defined. It is fairly easy to find equivalents for standard plain yarns (see page 7), but be wary of very fancy yarns where the original appearance of the fabric and tension would be very hard to match.

With any substitution you will find that the amount of yarn required may vary from that given in the pattern even though the ball may be of the same weight. The weight of each yarn per metre is different, therefore the length in metres in a 50 gram ball differs from yarn to yarn. A lightweight, synthetic yarn could go twice as far as a cotton or wool yarn which tend to be heavy.

Tools and Equipment

Your pattern will tell you what basic tools are required (size of needles, amount of yarn, etc), but there are several other items which may be needed to complete the garment. Although they may not be used for every project, you will probably require most of the following items at some stage.

Pairs of knitting needles. These range in size from 0 to 25 (see conversion table), and it is useful to have several sizes in order to knit up and compare tension swatches. Needles are available in plastic, wood, bamboo, steel or alloy, and whichever you use makes no difference to the tension or quality of the knitting. They are also available in various lengths, so use one which will hold the required number of stitches comfortably - stitches can easily fall off an overcrowded needle! Check that needles have nicely rounded points and are straight - blunt, bent or scratched needles all reduce the speed and efficiency of knitting.

Circular and double-pointed needles. These are used for knitting tubular, seamless fabric or for knitting flat rounds (such as circular shawls and table cloths). Circular needles consist of two short needles joined by a length of flexible nylon of varying lengths. Your pattern will usually tell you what length is required to accommodate the number of stitches comfortably, the shorter lengths are used for sleeves, neckbands, etc, and the longer ones are used for larger areas. Circular needles can also be used as a pair of needles, turning at the end of each row, wherever you have a large number of stitches such as on a baby's shawl. Circular needles are not usually marked with the needle size so keep them in their packet when not in use. If you are not sure of the size, use a needle gauge.

Double-pointed needles are available in sets of four or six. They are often used to knit neckbands and can be used as an alternative to circular needles wherever there is a small number of stitches which may be too stretched on a circular needle. Double-pointed needles are also used for knitting seamless socks, gloves and berets.

Cable needles. These are short, double-pointed needles which are used for holding stitches to the back or front of the work when moving stitches for an Aran or Cable pattern (see page 35). They are generally available in three sizes so use whichever holds the stitches comfortably - one which is too thick will stretch the stitches, while a thin one may slip out of the stitches. Cable needles with U-bends to hold the stitches are easier to use than the traditional straight ones (see picture on page 4).

Stitch holders. These resemble large safety pins and are used to retain stitches which will be required later, for example across a pocket where the edging is done after the front is completed. Alternatively, thread a length of contrasting yarn through the stitches, slip them off the needle and knot both ends of the contrast yarn together. Slip the stitches back onto a needle before knitting the edging.

Row counter. This is a cylindrical device with a dial used to record the number of rows knitted. Slip the row counter onto the end of the needle before starting to knit and turn the dial at the end of each row.

Tape measure. This is essential for measuring the length and width of the knitting, as well as checking tension pieces (although a ruler is more accurate for this).

Wool sewing needle. This should be blunt-ended with a large eye for easy threading. Do not use a sharp pointed needle as this will split the yarn when joining seams - a round end will slip easily between the stitches.

Crochet hooks. These are useful for picking up dropped stitches (see page 48). Keep a selection of sizes depending on the thickness of the yarn being used. A crochet hook can also be used for casting off (see page 20). Many baby's sweaters have crochet edgings around the neck opening.

You will also require **dressmaker's pins,** preferably long ones with coloured heads which will not disappear in the knitting. These are used for pinning seams, blocking and marking tension swatches. **Safety pins** make ideal stitch holders when only a small number of stitches is involved. They can also be used for holding dropped stitches, and for marking button spacing. A small, sharp **pair of scissors** is also an essential requirement. A **needle gauge** may be useful for checking or converting needle sizes.

Knitting Needle Conversion Chart																			
Canadian & UK Sizes	000	00	0	1	2	3	4	5	6	7	8	9	10	11	12	13	14	15
Metric Sizes (for UK)	10	9	8	$7\frac{1}{2}$	7	$6\frac{1}{2}$	6	$5\frac{1}{2}$	5	$4\frac{1}{2}$	4	$3\frac{3}{4}$	$3\frac{1}{4}$	3	$2\frac{3}{4}$	$2\frac{1}{4}$	2	$1\frac{3}{4}$
US Sizes	15	13	11		$10\frac{1}{2}$	10	9	8	7	6	5	4	3	3	2	1	0	—

Crochet Hook Conversion Chart																			
	Steel								Aluminium										
UK Sizes	6	5	4	3	$2\frac{1}{2}$	2	1	2/0	14	12	11	9	8	7	6	5	4	2	1/0	2/0	3/0
Metric Sizes	0.60	0.75	1.00	1.25	1.50	1.75	2.00	2.50	2.00	2.50	3.00	3.50	4.00	4.50	5.00	5.50	6.00	7.00	8.00	9.00	10.00
US Sizes	14	12	10	—	6	4	1	1/0	B	C	D	E	F	G	H	I	J	K	—	—	P

First Steps
Holding the Needles

Before casting on stitches you must get to grips with the needles and yarn. At first they will seem awkward to hold, but practise will soon make these manoeuvres familiar. Use a double knitting (USA Sportweight, Australia/NZ 8 ply) yarn and a pair of 4mm (USA 6) needles to practise with (see conversion table opposite).

1. Hold the **right needle** in the same position as a pencil. For casting on and working the first few rows the knitted piece passes between the thumb and the index finger. As the knitting grows slide the thumb under the knitted piece, holding the needle from below.

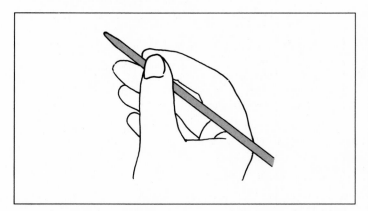

2. The **left needle** is held lightly over the top. If the English method of knitting (a) is preferred (see below) use the thumb and index finger to control the tip. If the European method (b) is used, control the tip with the thumb and middle finger.

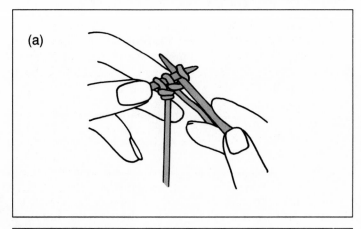

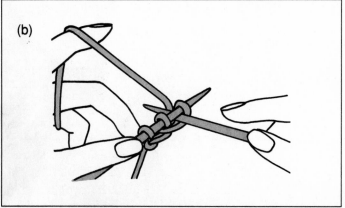

Holding the Yarn

The yarn may be held either in the right hand (English method) or the left hand (European method). Although both methods are explained here, the English method is illustrated throughout the rest of this publication.

There are various methods of winding the yarn round the fingers to control the tension on the yarn and so produce even knitting. In time you might develop a favourite way, but first try one of the popular and effective methods shown here.

Method 1

Holding the yarn in the right or left hand, pass it under the little finger of the other hand, then around the same finger, over the third finger, under the centre finger and over the index finger. The index finger is used to pass the yarn around the needle tip and the yarn circled around the little finger creates the necessary tension for knitting evenly.

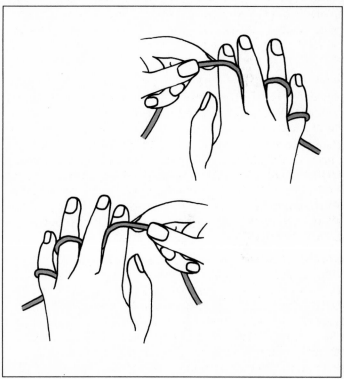

Method 2

Holding the yarn in the right or left hand, pass it under the little finger of the other hand, over the third finger, under the centre finger and over the index finger. The index finger is

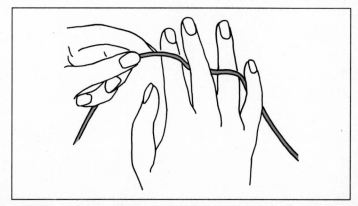

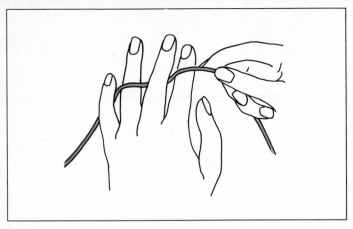

used to pass the yarn around the needle tip and tension is controlled by gripping the yarn in the crook of the little finger.

Making a Slip Knot

A slip knot is the starting point for almost everything that you do in knitting and is the basis of all casting on techniques.

1. Wind the yarn twice around the first two fingers of the left hand as shown, then bend the fingers so that the two loops are visible across the knuckles.

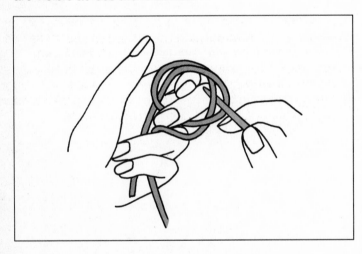

2. Using a knitting needle in the right hand, pull the back thread through the front one to form a loop.

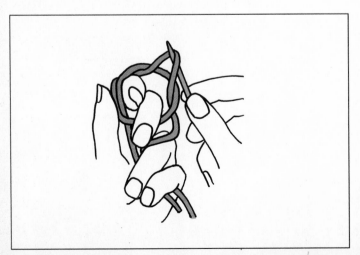

3. Release the yarn from the fingers and pull the two ends to tighten the loop on the needle. This forms the first stitch.

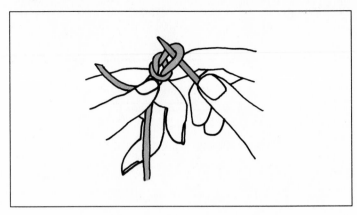

Casting On

Casting on is the term used for making a row of stitches as a foundation for knitting.

It is useful to know a few of the most popular ways of casting on as each method serves a different purpose according to the type of edge, or fabric, that you require. It is important for beginners to practise casting on until a smooth, even edge can be achieved.

Thumb Method

This method requires only one needle and is used for a very elastic edge or when the rows immediately after the cast-on stitches are worked in garter stitch (every row knitted).

The length of yarn between the cut end and the slip knot is used for making the stitches. You will learn to assess this length by eye, according to the number of stitches required, but as a general rule the length of yarn from the slip knot to the end of the yarn should be about 3 or 4 times the required finished width.

1. Make a slip knot the required length from the end of the yarn (for a practice piece make this length about one metre or one yard). Place the slip knot on a needle and hold the needle in the right hand with the ball end of yarn over your first finger. Hold the other end in the palm of your left hand. *Wind the loose end of the yarn around the left thumb from front to back.

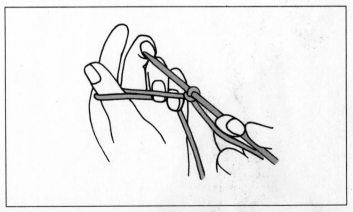

First Steps

2. Insert the needle upwards through the yarn on the thumb.

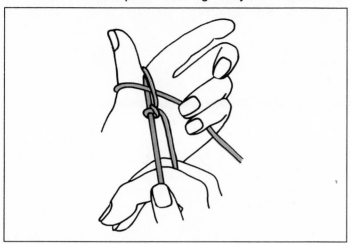

3. Take the yarn over the point of the needle with your right index finger.

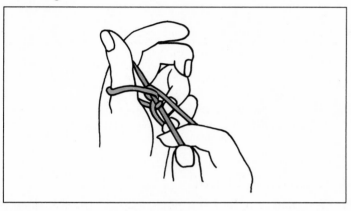

4. Draw the yarn back through the loop on the thumb to form a stitch.

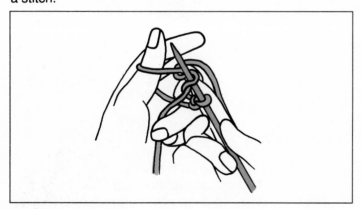

5. Remove the yarn from your left thumb and pull the loose end to tighten the stitch. Repeat from the * until the required number of stitches has been cast on.

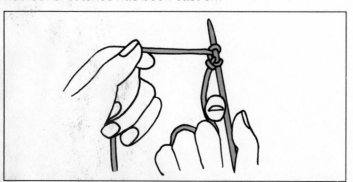

Finger and Thumb Method

This again requires only one needle and gives the same effect as casting on thumb method. Once mastered, this technique is extremely quick and efficient and produces a very even cast on edge. If you find the edge is too tight, hold two needles in the right hand instead of one as this will give you a looser edge.

1. Make a slip knot about 1 metre (1 yard) or the required length from the end of the yarn and place it on a needle held in the right hand.

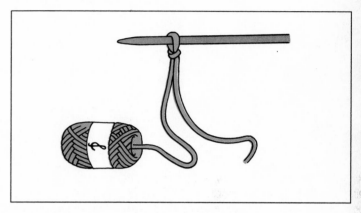

2. Wind the cut end of the yarn around the left thumb from front to back. Wind the ball end of the yarn around the index finger of the left hand from front to back as shown. Hold both ends of the yarn in the palm of the left hand. *Insert the needle upwards through the yarn on the thumb, down through the front of the loop on the index finger, then back down through the front of the loop on the thumb.

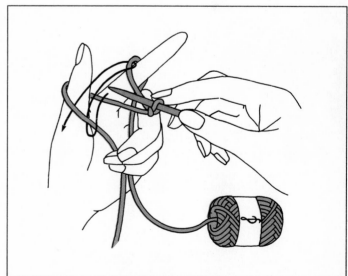

First Steps

3. Pull the yarn through, thus forming a loop on the needle.

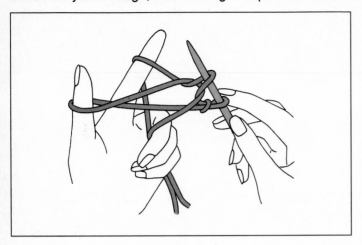

4. Remove the thumb from the loop, then re-insert it as shown, using the thumb to tighten the loop on the needle.

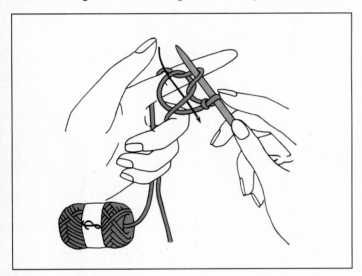

Repeat from the * until the required number of stitches has been cast on.

Cable Method

This method requires the use of two needles, and gives a very firm, neat finish that is ideal as a basis for ribbing or any other firm stitch.

1. Make a slip knot near the cut end of the yarn and place it on the left-hand needle.

2. Holding the yarn at the back of the needles insert the right-hand needle upwards through the slip knot and pass

the yarn over the point of the right needle.

3. Draw the right-hand needle back through the slip knot, thus forming a loop on the right-hand needle. Do not slip the original stitch off the left-hand needle.

4. Insert the left-hand needle from right to left through this loop and slip it off the right-hand needle. There are now two stitches on the left-hand needle.

5. Insert the right-hand needle between the two stitches on the left-hand needle. Wind the yarn round the point of the right-hand needle.

6. Draw a loop through and place it on the left-hand needle as before.

Repeat steps 5 and 6 until the required number of stitches has been made.

First Steps

Basic Stitches

It is essential to know two important stitches - **knit** and **purl** - as they provide the basis of most knitted fabrics. The **knit** stitch is the easiest to learn. Once you have mastered this, move on to the **purl** stitch which is slightly more complicated, but you need a combination of both of these stitches to make most of the basic fabrics.

How To Knit

1. Hold the needle with the cast on stitches in the left hand. With the yarn at the back of the work insert the right-hand needle from left to right through the front of the first stitch on the left-hand needle.

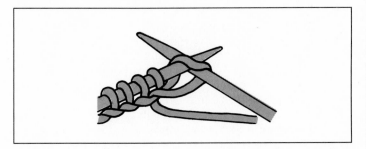

2. Wind the yarn from left to right over the point of the right-hand needle.

3. Draw the yarn back through the stitch, thus forming a loop on the right-hand needle.

4. Slip the original stitch off the left-hand needle.

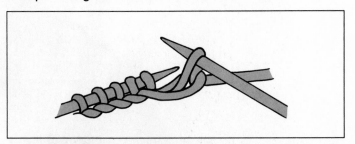

To knit a row, repeat steps 1 to 4 until all the stitches have

been transferred from the left needle to the right needle. Turn the work and transfer the needle with the stitches on to the left hand to work the next row.

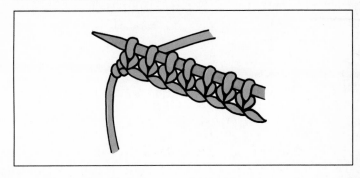

How To Purl

1. With the yarn at the front of the work insert the right-hand needle from right to left through the front of the first stitch on the left-hand needle.

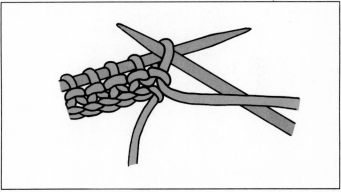

2. Wind the yarn from right to left over the point of the right-hand needle.

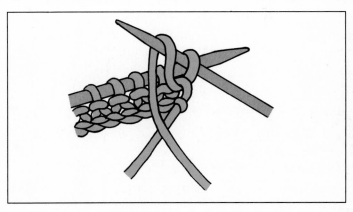

3. Draw a loop through onto the right-hand needle.

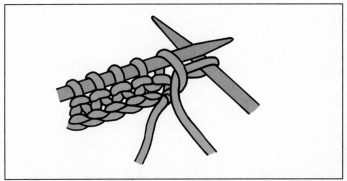

15

First Steps

4. Slip the original stitch off the left-hand needle.

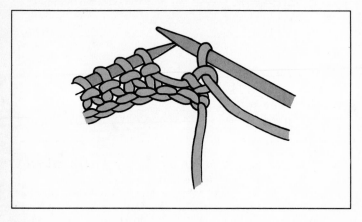

To purl a row, repeat steps 1 to 4 until all the stitches are transferred to the right-hand needle, then turn the work and transfer the needles to work the next row.

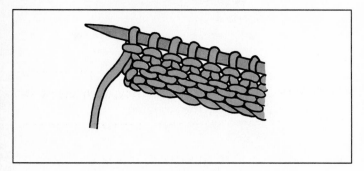

Slipped Stitches

It is often necessary to slip a stitch from one needle to the other without actually working it. This can be used in shaping or within a stitch pattern, and is very easy to work.

To slip a stitch knitwise (sl 1 knitwise)

Insert the right-hand needle into the front of the next stitch on the left-hand needle from left to right, then slip the stitch from the left-hand needle onto the right-hand needle without knitting it.

To slip a stitch purlwise (sl 1 purlwise)

Insert the right-hand needle into the front of the next stitch on the left-hand needle from right to left then slip the stitch from the left-hand needle onto the right-hand needle without purling it.

Unless otherwise stated, the yarn should be kept in the same place as it was for the last stitch worked. If the last stitch worked was a knit stitch, the yarn should be kept at the back and carried behind the slipped stitch. If the last stitch worked was a purl stitch, the yarn should be kept at the front and carried across the front of the slipped stitch. If this does not apply, the pattern instructions will tell you to bring the yarn forward or take the yarn back. If a pattern does not tell you whether to slip a stitch knitwise or purlwise, slip the stitch in the same way as the rest of the row is worked (knitwise on a knit row or purlwise on a purl row).

Working into the Back of a Stitch

This is a technique which is used to twist a stitch.

To knit into the back of a stitch (KB1) insert the right-hand needle from right to left into the **back** of the next stitch on the left-hand needle, wind the yarn around the point of the right-hand needle and draw a loop back through the stitch, dropping the stitch off the left-hand needle.

To purl into the back of a stitch (PB1) from the back insert the right-hand needle from left to right into the **back** of the next stitch on the left-hand needle, wind the yarn around the right-hand needle and draw through a loop, dropping the stitch off the left-hand needle.

Basic Fabrics

Using the two basic stitches - knit and purl - you can practise making some easy fabrics that occur frequently in knitting. In fact it will be a lot easier to understand complicated pattern stitches if you realise that a knit stitch and a purl stitch are one and the same thing but formed on opposite sides of the fabric. In both cases you are pulling a new stitch (loop) through an old one. In the case of a knit stitch you drop the old loop off the needle away from you to the back of the work. In the case of a purl stitch you drop the old loop off the needle towards you to the front of the work.

Garter Stitch

This stitch is often referred to as 'plain knitting' because every row is knitted. This produces a reversible fabric with raised horizontal ridges on both sides of the work. It is thicker and looser than stocking stitch. One of the advantages of garter stitch is that it does not curl so it can be used on its own, or for bands and borders. The same effect is achieved by purling every row, although this is slower to work.

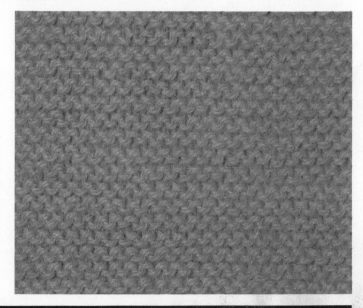

Stocking Stitch (st st)

Stocking Stitch is the most widely knitted fabric. It comprises alternate knit and purl rows. With the knit side as right side it makes a flat, smooth fabric that tends to curl at the edges and needs finishing with bands, borders or hems where it is not joined to another piece with a seam. As it is a plain fabric, evenness in knitting is important because any irregularities will be highlighted.

Reverse Stocking Stitch (rev st st)

This is the same as stocking stitch but with the purl side of the fabric used as the right side. At a distance it may look like garter stitch, but the ridges in reverse stocking stitch are much closer together and not so distinct. This fabric is often used as a background to cabled fabrics, thus making the cables more pronounced.

Single Rib (k1, p1)

This is formed by alternately knitting a stitch, then purling a stitch to give unbroken vertical lines on each side of the work. It makes a very elastic fabric that is mainly used for borders such as welts, neckbands and cuffs. When used as an edging, rib is generally worked on a smaller size needle than the main body of the garment to keep it firm and elastic.

1st row (right side):
1. Knit the first stitch.

2. Bring the yarn forward to the front of the work between the needles and purl the next stitch.

3. Take the yarn to the back of the work between the needles and knit the next stitch.

Repeat steps 2 and 3 until all stitches are transferred to the right-hand needle.

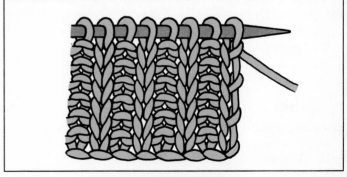

First Steps

For an odd number of stitches, this would be written as follows:

1st row (right side): K1, *p1, k1; rep from * to end.

2nd row: P1, *k1, p1; rep from * to end.

Repeat these 2 rows.

Always ensure that stitches which are knitted on one row are purled on the following row and vice versa. If an odd number of stitches is cast on, the right side rows will always begin and end with a knit stitch, while the wrong side rows begin and end with a purl stitch. If an even number of stitches is cast on every row will begin with a knit stitch and end with a purl stitch.

Note: If you are knitting in the round, with the same side of the work facing all the time, then a knit stitch will always be knitted and a purl stitch purled. It is better in the round always to work with an even number of stitches for rib. This note applies to all rib stitches in rounds.

Double Rib (k2, p2)

Double Rib is a popular variation of the single rib. This type of rib usually requires a multiple of four stitches plus two extra (e.g. 22 stitches).

1st row (right side):

1. Knit the first two stitches and bring the yarn forward to the front between the needles.

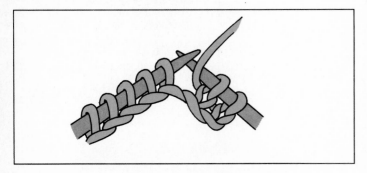

2. Purl the next two stitches and take the yarn to the back.

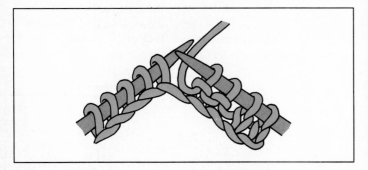

Continue in this way until all stitches are transferred to the right-hand needle ending with two knit stitches. This would be written as follows:

1st row (right side): K2, *p2, k2; rep from * to end.

2nd row: P2, *k2, p2; rep from * to end.

Repeat these 2 rows.

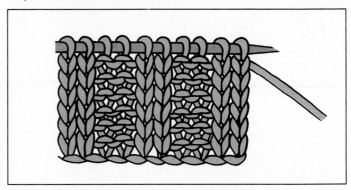

As with single rib, always purl stitches that were knitted on the previous row and vice versa. If the right side row begins and ends with two knit stitches, the wrong side row will begin and end with two purl stitches.

There are many rib patterns that involve varying numbers of knit and purl stitches. The more stitches that you work in one stitch before changing to the next, the looser and less elastic the rib.

Moss Stitch

This is a very basic textured stitch. It is made up of alternate knit and purl stitches but instead of following one another to form single rib, the stitches are staggered. Stitches that are knitted on one row will also be knitted on the following row, and stitches that are purled will also be purled on the following row. Thus if an odd number of stitches is cast on, every row will begin and end with a knit stitch. The fabric is firm, non-curling and reversible, and is often used for front bands or collars for example.

For an odd number of stitches, the instructions would be given as follows:

1st row: K1, *p1, k1; rep from * to end.

Repeat this row.

Tubular or Invisible Method of Casting On

This is a special method of casting on for single rib that gives a rounded edge, like a hem, but without the additional bulk of a double fabric. Use it for a professional finish when the edge of the work is a focal point.

Method 1

1. For an odd number of stitches add one stitch to the total number required, then divide this number by two. For an even number of stitches, divide the total number by two and increase one stitch when the cast on edge is complete. Using contrast yarn and any of the above methods, cast on this number of stitches. Purl one row, then knit one row. Break off the contrast yarn.

2. Change to the main yarn and work four rows in stocking stitch, beginning with a purl row.

3. **Next row:** Purl the first stitch, *using the point of the right-hand needle pick up the first loop of main yarn that shows through the contrast yarn 4 rows below, transfer the loop to the left-hand needle and knit it, purl the next stitch; repeat from * to the end of the row when the number of stitches will be one less than twice the number cast on.

4. Remove the contrast yarn by pulling the working end tightly to draw up the stitches. Cut the yarn and spread out the work. Continue in this way until all the contrast yarn has been removed. Continue in single rib, starting with a right side row.

Method 2

For abbreviations see page 6.

1. For an odd number of stitches add one stitch to the total number of stitches required, then divide this number by two. For an even number of stitches divide the total number by two and increase one stitch when the cast on edge is complete. Using a length of contrasting yarn and any of the above methods cast on this number of stitches then break off the contrast yarn.

2. Join in the main yarn and work as follows:

1st row (right side): K1, *yf, k1; rep from * to end. The required number of stitches is now on the needle (less one stitch for an even number).

2nd row: Sl 1 purlwise, *take yarn back, k1, bring yarn forward, sl 1 purlwise; rep from * to end.

3rd row: K1, *bring yarn forward, sl 1 purlwise, take yarn back, k1; rep from * to end.

4th and 5th rows: As 2nd and 3rd rows.

6th row: P1, *k1, p1; rep from * to end.

Continue in single rib, starting with a right side row. Carefully unpick the contrast yarn from the cast on edge.

Casting Off

There is one simple and most commonly used method of securing stitches once you have finished a piece of knitting - casting off. It is important to remember that the cast-off edge should have the same 'give' (elasticity) as the rest of the fabric. Always cast off in the same stitch as the pattern unless directed otherwise. If your cast off edge tends to be tight use a size larger needle. For casting off seams together see page 28.

Casting off Knitwise

Knit the first two stitches. *Using the left-hand needle lift the first stitch over the second and drop it off between the points of the two needles. Knit the next stitch and repeat from the * until all the stitches have been worked from the left-hand needle and one stitch only remains on the right-hand needle. Cut the yarn (leaving enough to sew in the end) and thread the cut end through the stitch on the needle. Draw the yarn up firmly to fasten off the last stitch.

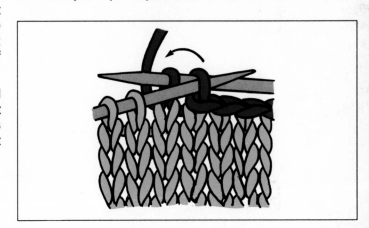

Casting off Purlwise

Purl the first two stitches, then *using the left-hand needle lift the first stitch over the second and drop it off the needle. Purl the next stitch and repeat from the *, securing the last stitch as described above.

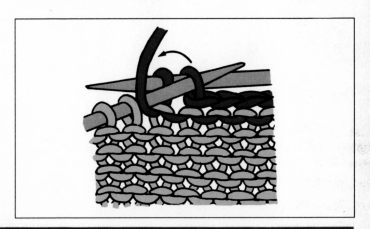

First Steps

Casting off in Rib

Always work the stitches as though you were working a row in rib, casting stitches off as you go along. For single rib knit the first stitch, purl the second stitch and lift the first stitch over the second and off the needle. Knit the next stitch and pass the first stitch over the second and off the needle. Continue in this way until one stitch remains on the right-hand needle, then fasten this stitch off as given before. For double rib or any other variation work in a similar way knitting the knit stitches and purling the purl stitches. Rib should normally be cast off fairly loosely to keep the cast-off edge elastic.

Pattern Repeats or Multiples

For abbreviations, see page 6.

Most stitch patterns, unless they are completely random or worked in separate panels, are made up of a set of stitches which are repeated across the row, and a number of rows which are repeated throughout the length of the fabric. If a pattern is symmetrical (for example a diamond pattern), it is important that each row begins and ends in the same way to 'balance' the row. In other words, if a pattern begins 'k3, p1, k5' it should end 'k5, p1, k3'. For a lace pattern, a row which begins with 'k2tog, yf', should end with 'yf, sl 1, k1, psso', as the decrease should be in the opposite direction (see next page). This ensures that when seams are joined, the pattern is symmetrical on either side of the seam. However, this rule does not apply to non-symmetrical patterns, for example diagonal patterns which cannot begin and end in the same way.

A pattern repeat within knitting instructions is contained either within brackets or parantheses, or follows an asterisk (*). The extra stitches outside the brackets or before the asterisk are the stitches required to balance the pattern. To work out the number of stitches in a pattern repeat, simply add together the stitches within the brackets or after the asterisk (i.e. the stitches which are to be repeated). For a lace pattern **either** count a yarn forward increase as one stitch and a knit two together as one stitch **or** count the knit two together as two stitches and do not include the yarn forward increase.

To work out the minimum number of stitches required to knit a tension piece or swatch, ascertain the number of stitches in the pattern repeat and add on the number of extra stitches at the beginning or end of the row. Extra pattern repeats can be added if needed.

Shaping

A knitted fabric can be shaped to make it narrower or wider by decreasing or increasing the number of stitches on the needle. Other methods of shaping are achieved by turning in the middle of a row so that one side of the material is longer than the other.

The most usual methods of decreasing and increasing stitches are given below. These can be used for shaping armholes, necklines, side seams, etc., as well as increasing or decreasing across a whole row, for example after a ribbed welt. They can also be used for decorative effect such as in lacy stitches (see pages 119 to 156).

Decreasing One Stitch

The simplest method of decreasing one stitch is to work two stitches together.

On a knit row insert the right-hand needle from left to right through two stitches instead of one, then knit them together as one stitch. This is called knit two together **(k2tog)** and on the right side of the work the decrease slopes towards the right.

On a purl row insert the right-hand needle from right to left through two stitches instead of one, then purl them together as one stitch. This is called purl two together **(p2tog).** Where this is worked on the wrong side row, the decrease slopes towards the right on the right side of the work.

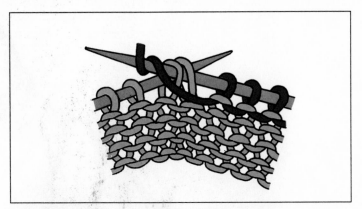

It is often necessary to create a slope towards the left, either to balance a right slope (for example on opposite sides of a raglan) or in decorative lace stitch patterns.

On a knit row there are three basic ways of creating this effect.

Method 1

1. Slip the first stitch onto the right-hand needle in a knitwise direction but without knitting it, then knit the next stitch.

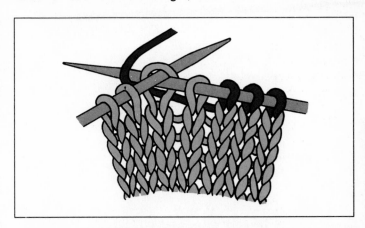

2. Using the left-hand needle lift the slipped stitch over the knitted stitch and off the needle. This is called slip one, knit one, pass slipped stitch over **(sl 1, k1, psso).** Some patterns abbreviate this whole process as **skpo.**

Method 2

This is worked in a similar way to k2tog, but the stitches are knitted through the back of the loops, thus twisting the stitches. Insert the right-hand needle from right to left through the back of the first two stitches, then knit them together as one stitch. This is called knit two together through back of loops **(k2tog tbl).**

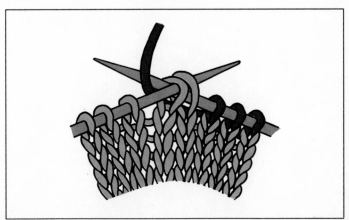

Shaping

Method 3

Slip the first and second stitches knitwise, one at a time onto the right-hand needle, then insert the left-hand needle into the fronts of these two stitches from the left, and knit them together from this position. This is called slip, slip, knit (ssk).

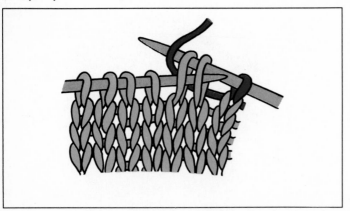

On a purl row the stitches are purled together through the back of the loops, which is a little awkward to work. From the back insert the right-hand needle from left to right through the back of the first two stitches, then purl them together as one stitch. This is called purl two together through back of loops (p2tog tbl).

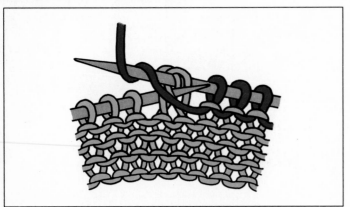

Decreasing Two Stitches

It is often necessary to decrease two stitches at the same point. The following methods are generally worked on right side rows, and all create different effects.

To create a slope towards the left, work as follows:
1. Slip the first stitch onto the right-hand needle without knitting it, then knit the next two stitches together as one stitch.

2. Lift the slipped stitch over the second stitch and off the needle. This is called slip one, knit two together, pass slipped stitch over (sl 1, k2tog, psso).

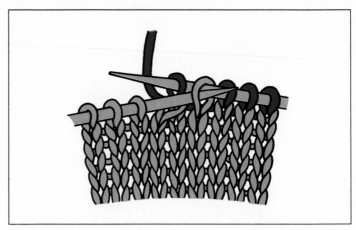

To create a right slope insert the needle knitwise into the first three stitches and knit them together as one stitch. This is called knit three together (k3tog).

For a vertical decrease (where the centre stitch remains central) work to 1 st before centre st and continue as follows:

1. Insert the right-hand needle into the first two stitches as if to k2tog, then slip them onto the right-hand needle without knitting them.

2. Knit the next stitch, then lift the two slipped stitches over the knit stitch and off the needle. This is called slip two together, knit one, pass two slipped stitches over (**sl 2tog, k1, p2sso**).

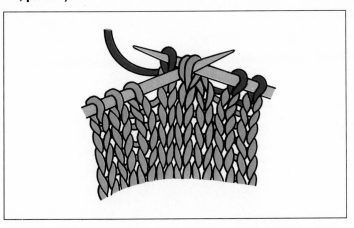

On a purl row the most usual method of decreasing two stitches is to work to 1 st before centre st, then purl three together (**p3tog**). This is worked in the same way as p2tog, but insert the needle through the first three stitches instead of two.

Increasing

The most usual method of increasing is to work twice into a stitch.

On a knit row work into the front and back of a stitch as follows: knit into the stitch, then before slipping it off the needle, twist the right-hand needle behind the left-hand one and knit again into the back of the loop then slip the original stitch off the left-hand needle. There are now two stitches on the right-hand needle made from the original one.

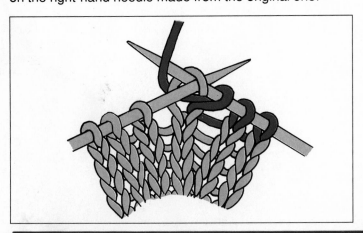

On a purl row the method is similar. Purl into the front of the stitch, then purl into the back of it before slipping it off the needle.

Making a Stitch

Another form of increasing involves working into the strand between two stitches and is usually called 'make one stitch' (**M1**). Insert the right-hand needle from front to back under the horizontal strand which runs between the stitches on the right and left-hand needles and insert the left-hand needle from front to back. Now knit or purl through the **back** of the strand to twist the new stitch so as to prevent the small hole that would otherwise form.

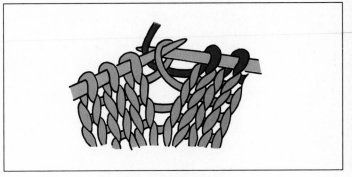

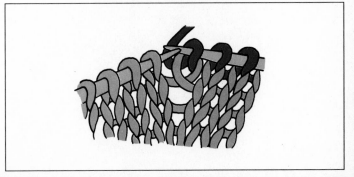

Shaping

Eyelet Methods of Increasing

Another method of increasing is to make an extra loop between two stitches which is knitted or purled on subsequent rows. This forms a hole in the material and is used as a decorative feature. Lace stitches are made in this way and the required position of the hole in the fabric affects the way in which the yarn is wound around the needle. Whether the increase is preceded or followed by a knit or purl stitch, the yarn is always taken around the needle in an **anti-clockwise** direction.

For USA readers all the following methods would be referred to as yarn over **(yo)** but the method of working would be the same.

A hole between two knit stitches Bring the yarn forward as if to purl a stitch, but then knit the next stitch taking the yarn over the top of the needle to do so. This is called yarn forward **(yf or yfwd)**.

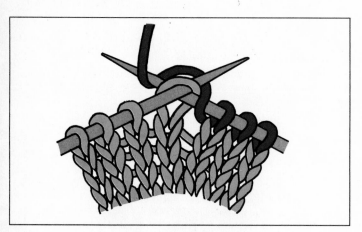

A hole between two purl stitches Take the yarn over the top of the needle, then between the needles to the front again before purling the next stitch. This is called yarn over needle **(yon)**.

A hole between a knit and a purl stitch Bring the yarn forward as if to purl, then over the needle to the back, then between the needles to the front again before purling the next stitch. This is called yarn forward and round needle **(yfrn)**.

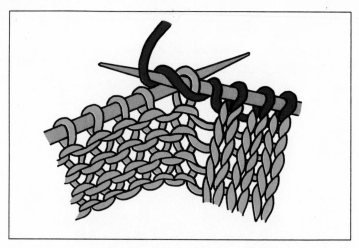

A hole between a purl and a knit stitch Instead of taking the yarn back between the needles ready to knit the next stitch, take it over the top of the right-hand needle and knit the next stitch. This is called yarn over needle **(yon)**.

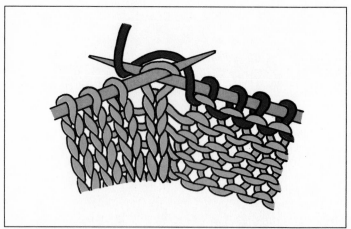

It is sometimes necessary to create a larger hole within a lace pattern, and this is done by making two extra loops instead of one. This is normally worked between two knit stitches. Bring the yarn forward to the front, over the needle and round to the front again, then over the needle to knit the next stitch. This is normally referred to as **[yf] twice**.

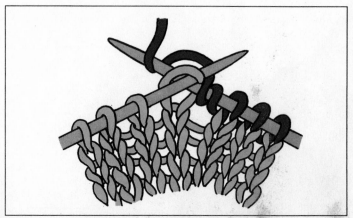

Increasing Twice into a Stitch

It is sometimes necessary to make 3 stitches where there was only one stitch before. This often happens where an increase is required in rib or where a large number of stitches is increased across a row. There are three usual methods of doing this, although a pattern will tell you which method to use.

Method 1

Knit into the front of the stitch, bring the yarn forward and purl into the same stitch, then take the yarn back and knit the same stitch again before slipping the original stich off the left-hand needle. This is called work (knit one, purl one, knit one or k1, p1, k1) into the next stitch.

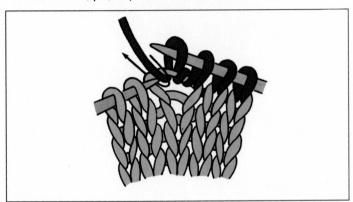

Method 2

This method makes a small hole in the work. Knit into the front of the stitch, bring the yarn forward then knit into the stitch again, taking the yarn over the top of the right-hand needle. This is called work (knit one, yarn forward, knit one or k1, yf, k1) into the next stitch.

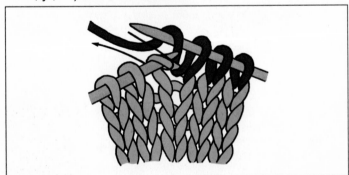

Method 3

This is usually used in stocking stitch as the stitch is knitted into three times. Knit into the front of the stitch, then into the back, then into the front again before slipping the stitch off the left-hand needle.

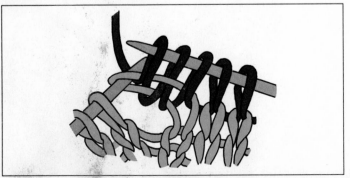

Joining in New Yarn

Always join in a new ball of yarn at the start of a row wherever possible. As a general guide, for a stocking stitch or fairly plain fabric, you can estimate whether there is sufficient yarn remaining in the old ball to complete a row of knitting. Lay the knitting flat and see if the yarn reaches at least three times across the width - that is the length you need to finish a stocking stitch row. For a heavily patterned or textured garment if in doubt join in the new ball at the start of the row to avoid the frustration of running out of yarn in the middle of a row and having to unpick the stitches worked. If you are sure you have enough for one row, but are unsure if it is enough for two, tie a loose knot halfway along the remaining length of yarn. Work one row, then if the knot has not been reached you will know there is sufficient to work another row.

To make a perfect join at the edge of the work, simply drop the old yarn and start working the row with the new yarn. After a few stitches, tie the old and new ends in a loose knot. The ends can be darned into the seam at a later stage. If it is impossible to avoid joining in the middle of a row (for example in circular knitting - see page 33), just drop the old yarn leaving sufficient length to sew in, pick up the new yarn leaving sufficient length and continue knitting with it. After

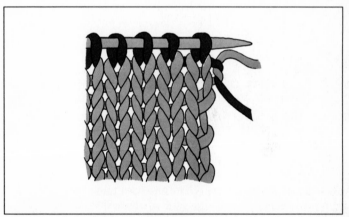

a few more rows have been completed, the ends of yarn should be darned in to secure them.

Securing Ends

An end of yarn simply woven around the stitches will soon work itself loose once the garment is worn. To secure the end properly, weave the yarn loosely around a few stitches, then double back on the woven-in end splitting those stitches already worked. Use a sharp needle (easier for splitting the yarn) rather than the blunt-ended needle necessary for seaming. Make sure the yarn is not pulled tightly as it will distort the knitting. Stretch the fabric before fastening off the yarn to loosen the woven in end. Make sure also that the woven in end is not visible from the right side.

Never tie knots in the yarn as these will almost invariably come undone or work their way through to the right side. Any knots found in the yarn should also be undone.

Sewing Up

The time spent on putting together a garment should never be underrated - too often a well-knitted garment can be ruined and made to look unprofessional by a lack of care and by rushing the final stages. A better appearance can be gained by blocking and pressing the separate pieces before sewing them together.

Some patterns indicate in the 'making up' or 'finishing' section the type of seam to use for various parts. If you are only told to 'join seams', then you have a choice. The seams described here are suitable for a variety of situations on most garments, but the mattress stitch is the most versatile and gives the best finish when worked carefully.

If possible, it is best to use the yarn that you have been knitting with for the seams. With very thick or heavily-textured yarn, or yarn which breaks easily you will need to use a finer, smooth yarn in a toning colour. Check that it can be washed in the same way as the original yarn.

It is always better to use a new length of yarn for sewing up, rather than the end used for casting on or casting off as the seam is then easier to undo if a mistake is made. You will find it easier to sew up a knitted garment if the pieces are laid flat on a table, rather than on your lap.

Mattress Stitch Seam

This seam is also known as **ladder stitch seam, running stitch seam** or **invisible seam.** It is the seam that the professionals use wherever possible and if you practise working it from the beginning you will find that it is an easy method for obtaining a perfect finish. Even if you have always used a backstitch or oversewn seam, try this method and you will be surprised how easy it is and how much better the seams look and feel. Mattress stitch should be worked either one whole stitch or half a stitch in from the edge depending on the neatness of the edge and the thickness of the fabric. It can even be worked on shaped edges - as you are working from the right side, it is easy to see where you are and to keep the seam neat and even.

When starting off, leave a long end which can be secured by running it back along the edge when the seam is completed. If the seam needs to be undone simply pull this end, thus drawing the yarn through the stitches.

Joining stocking stitch fabric or patterns on a stocking stitch background

1. With the right side facing you, lay the two pieces to be joined flat and edge to edge. Thread a blunt-ended needle with yarn and insert the needle between the edge stitch and the second stitch on the first row. Pass the needle under two rows, then bring it back through to the front.

2. Return to the opposite side and, working under **two** rows at a time throughout, repeat this zigzag action always taking

the needle under the strands that correspond exactly to the other side, and going into the hole that the last stitch on that side came out of, taking care not to miss any rows.

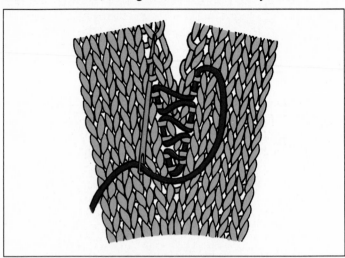

The secret of good mattress stitching is to keep the seam elastic without allowing it to stretch too much. The best way to do this is to work loosely for approximately 5 cm (2 inches) then pull the thread very firmly so that the stitches are held together quite tightly. Now stretch the seam slightly to give the required amount of elasticity, then continue with the next section of the seam.

The finished seam is almost impossible to detect on the right side and leaves only a small neat ridge on the wrong side. If only half a stitch is taken in (working through the centre of the edge stitch rather than between the two edge stitches) the ridge on the wrong side will be even smaller. This method is recommended for thicker yarns, providing the edge stitch has been worked firmly and neatly.

Note: If you work a slipped stitch at the beginning of every row (as recommended in some printed patterns) you should always work mattress stitch one whole stitch in from the edge.

Joining reverse stocking stitch fabric or background

When the purl side of the fabric is the right side, you may find that you achieve a better effect by working under **one** row at a time rather than the two rows as described for stocking stitch.

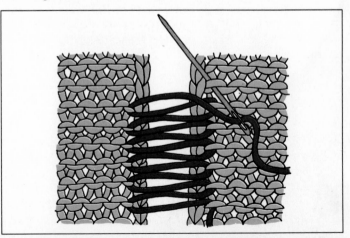

Joining single rib

When joining two ribbed sections together, it is best to take in only half a stitch on either side, so that when the two pieces are drawn together one complete knit stitch is formed along the seam. This should be a consideration when deciding whether or not to work the first stitch of the row as a slipped stitch.

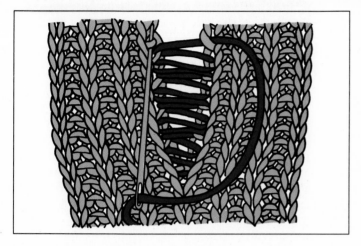

Joining two cast off edges

Two cast off edges can be joined together using mattress stitch so that the seam is matched exactly stitch for stitch.

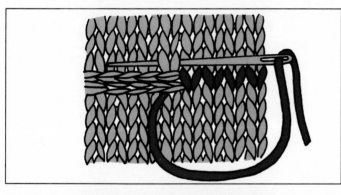

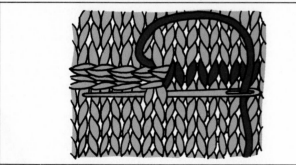

Joining two sections of different tensions

When joining together two pieces where the number of rows may be different, for example joining a ribbed front band to a stocking stitch or patterned front, work as follows: Lay the two pieces side by side, then using safety pins pin together at the lower and top edge stretching the ribbing slightly (unless otherwise stated), taking the edge stitch of each

piece. Pin again halfway between the two pins, then halve these distances again. Continue in this way until there are sufficient pins to keep the edges together, then join the two edges working under one or two rows as necessary and removing the pins as you go along.

Use this method also when joining a cast off edge (such as the top of a drop shoulder sleeve) to a side edge. Make sure that both edges lay flat, and work under one or two rows or stitches as necessary, making sure the seam retains its elasticity. In the case of a shaped sleeve heading, it is better to start at the centre and work downwards at either side.

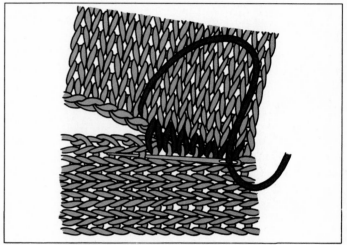

Backstitch Seam

This seam is really only suitable for lightweight yarns - double knitting at the heaviest. The seam is thicker and less elastic than mattress stitch and shows more definitely as a seam on the right side. It is also difficult to undo as each stitch has to be individually unpicked. Keep the seam allowance as narrow as possible - one stitch in is the maximum, and half a stitch will help to minimise the bulk.

1. Pin the pieces with right sides together, matching pattern for pattern and row for row, and thread a blunt-ended needle with yarn. At the start of the work, take the needle round the two edges thus enclosing them with a strong double stitch ending with yarn at front.

2. Insert needle into work just behind where last stitch came out and make a short stitch. Re- inset needle where previous stitch ended and make a stitch twice as long. Pull the needle through.

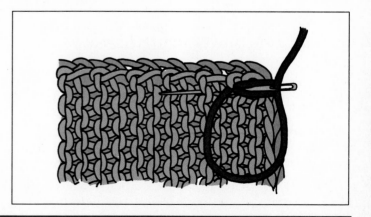

Sewing Up

3. Put the needle back into the work where the previous stitch ended and make another stitch the same length as the one before.

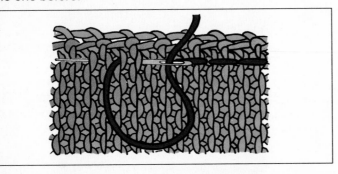

Repeat step 3 to make a continuous line of stitches of equal length on the side of the work facing you. On the reverse side the stitches form a straight, but slightly overlapping line. Remember to keep the seam fairly elastic by not pulling the stitches too tightly. Check after every few stitches that the seam is not too tight in relation to the knitted fabric.

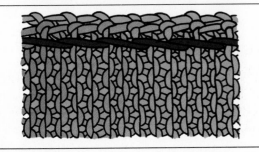

Flat Seam

A flat seam is a method of **oversewing** or **overcasting** which when opened out is completely flat. It can be used for joining ribbed sections of a garment such as welts and cuffs and for attaching buttonbands and collars where flatness and neatness are essential.

1. Lay the two pieces with right sides together, matching the edges exactly. Pin the work a few stitches in from the edge to allow room for your left index finger between the two fabrics. Thread a blunt-ended needle with yarn and insert the needle from back to front through the two thicknesses as close to the edge as possible. Pull the thread through and repeat this action, making two or three stitches in the same place to secure the yarn at the beginning of the seam. Take short stitches through both thicknesses as shown, working close to the edge.

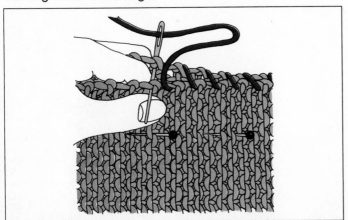

The finished seam opens almost flat and there should be no trace of the stitches on the right side. Be careful with the amount you take into the seam - a whole edge stitch will produce a lumpy seam which will not lie flat.

Casting off Seams Together

To avoid using a sewing needle to join two cast off edges, providing there is the same number of stitches in each section, the two pieces can be cast off together. This gives a very neat edge, and can also be very time saving. Leave the stitches on a spare needle at the end instead of casting them off, then use either of the following two methods to join the pieces together.

Method 1

Place the two pieces with right sides together, then using the same size needle as was used for the main part of the knitting *knit together the first stitch from the front needle with the first stitch from the back needle. Repeat from the * once more (2 stitches on the right-hand needle). Pass the first stitch over the second to cast off. Continue in this way until all the stitches are cast off, then fasten off the last stitch in the usual way.

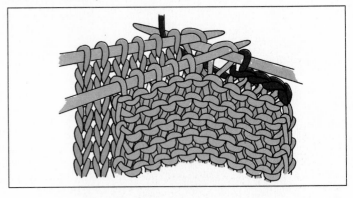

Method 2

Place the two pieces with right sides together, then using the same size needle as was used for the main part of the garment, pull the first stitch on the back needle through the front stitch. Lift the stitch on the front needle over this stitch and off the needle. Continue in this way until all stitches are transferred to the right-hand needle. Slip stitches back on to left-hand needle, if necessary and then cast the stitches off in the usual way.

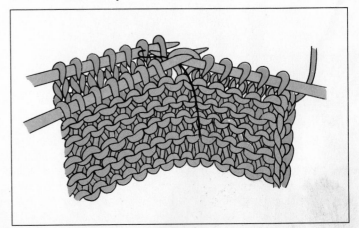

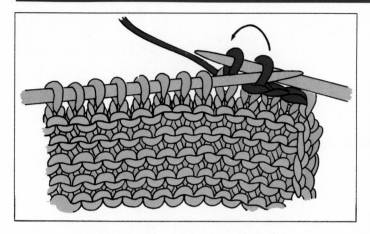

Slip Stitch Seams

This method of seaming is generally used when one piece is sewn on top of another, such as pockets, hems and neckbands, and ensures that the pieces lie completely flat. Where possible, match the pieces stitch for stitch and row for row, and keep the seam fairly loose. Using a sharp-pointed needle slip stitch the piece in place working as close to the edge as possible, splitting the stitches of the main part with the sewing needle if necessary to avoid the seam showing on the right side. It may help to run a line of contrasting thread in the main piece to mark the side of pocket.

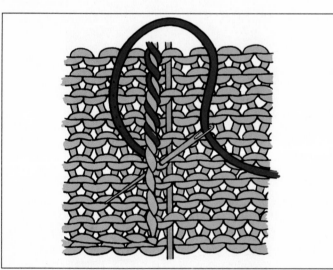

Grafting

This is an invisible method of joining two pieces of knitting either with the stitches on or off the needles, by exactly duplicating a row of knitted stitches. This method of joining is easiest to use for basic fabrics such as stocking stitch, garter stitch and rib as it becomes very involved when grafting two pieces of patterned fabric together. It is mainly used for joining seams which are not cast off (e.g. shoulder seams) and for repairs and alterations to the length of existing garments.

A variation of grafting can also be used to join a row of stitches to a side edge of a piece of knitting, for example at the top of a drop shoulder sleeve.

Carefully lay the pieces to be joined close together, with the stitches on each piece corresponding to those opposite and the right sides facing you. Thread a blunt-ended wool or tapestry needle with the knitting yarn.

Grafting Stocking Stitch

1. Beginning on the right hand side, bring the needle up through the first stitch of the lower piece from back to front, then through the first stitch of the upper piece from back to front. Bring it down through the first stitch of the lower piece from front to back and bring it up again through the next stitch to the left from back to front.

2. *On the upper piece, pass the needle down from front to back through the same stitch it came up through before and bring it up from back to front through the next stitch to the left. If working with stitches still on the needles slip them off one by one as they are secured.

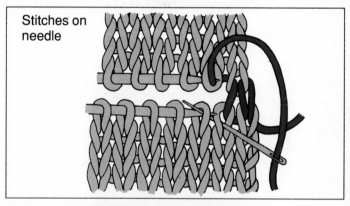

Stitches on needle

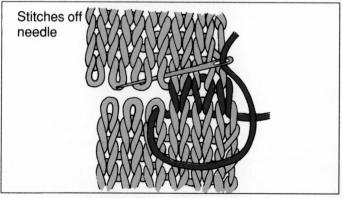

Stitches off needle

3. On the lower piece, take the needle down from front to back through the stitch it came up through before and bring

Grafting

it up through the next stitch to the left from back to front.

Repeat from * to the end, keeping the tension the same as the knitted fabric. Weave in the loose ends at the back of the work when completed, or run them into a seam if possible.

Grafting Garter Stitch

In order to keep the garter stitch correct, make sure one section has ended with a right side row, and the other has ended with a wrong side row (ridge).

Beginning on the right-hand side, follow the arrow on the diagram, thus forming a ridge on the upper piece to imitate a row of garter stitch. Take care not to twist the stitches and to keep the tension the same as the knitted fabric.

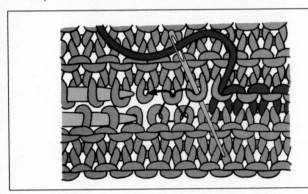

Grafting Single Rib

This is a little more complicated that joining stocking stitch or garter stitch, and requires a great deal of patience to produce a perfect result. There are two methods of joining single rib, the first is used when joining two pieces which are worked in the **same** direction, the second is used for joining two pieces worked in opposite directions.

Method 1

This method is used when the ribbing has been cut across, and both pieces are worked in an upwards direction. Both pieces should be left on the needle to avoid twisting the stitches and the stitches should be slipped off one or two at a time as required. Follow the direction of the arrow in the diagram, thus duplicating a row of rib. Take care that the grafting is worked at the same tension as the ribbing.

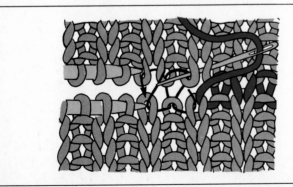

Method 2

This method is used to join two pieces of ribbing worked in opposite directions.

1. Using double-pointed needles slip the knit and purl stitches of each piece onto separate needles (4 needles in all).

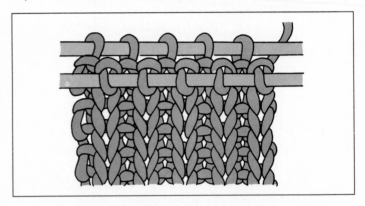

2. With the right side facing graft the knit stitches together as given for stocking stitch, keeping the grafted stitches fairly loose.

3. Turn the work so that the wrong side is facing and graft the remaining stitches in the same way.

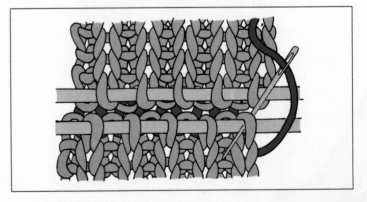

Although this method does not exactly duplicate a row of ribbing, it is a useful technique to avoid the bulk of a seam, and may be used to join vertical borders at the back neck for example.

Grafting a Row of Stitches to a Side Edge

This is a method of combining grafting with mattress stitch (see page 26), where one set of stitches is left on the needle (for example at the top of a sleeve). This method produces a soft, elastic seam and reduces the bulk of a cast off edge. Follow the direction of the arrows on the diagram taking one stitch from the needle and one or two rows from the side edge as necessary to keep both pieces flat. Do not pull the yarn too tightly as this may pucker the seam.

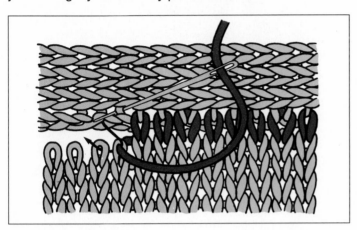

Working Two Sets of Stitches Together

This technique may be used to hold a pocket in position for example, or can be used as a decorative technique to attach separate knitted shapes onto a garment.

The stitches from the extra piece to be knitted in should be held on a spare needle of the same size or smaller. To attach the piece on a **right side** row, work to the position of the piece to be knitted in, hold the spare needle in front of the main piece if it is to be attached to the right side (or behind if it is to be attached to the wrong side) with the right side facing you, and the first stitch level with the first stitch on the left-hand needle.

To **knit** the stitches together, work as follows: *Insert the right-hand needle knitwise through the front of the first st on the front needle then through the front of the first stitch on the back needle. Wind the yarn around the right-hand needle from left to right and draw a loop through both stitches slipping them both off the needles at the same time.

Repeat from the * until all the stitches have been knitted from the spare needle, then continue across the remaining stitches on the left-hand needle.

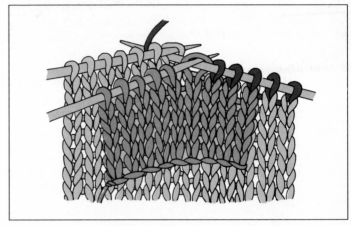

To **purl** the stitches together insert the needle purlwise through the front of the first stitch on the back needle, then through the front of the first stitch on the front needle, then purl the two stitches together slipping both stitches off the needle at the same time.

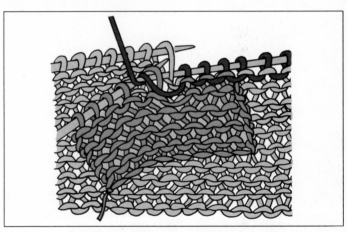

To attach the piece on a wrong side row, hold the spare needle in front of or behind the main piece with the wrong side facing you and work as given above.

Picking up Stitches along an Edge

Once the main body of the knitting is complete it is often necessary to add an edging or border to neaten the edge and prevent the fabric from curling. This can either be done by sewing a separate piece (for example a ribbed border) to the edge of the fabric, or by picking up stitches along the edge. The technique of picking up stitches along an edge is usually referred to as 'pick up and knit' or 'knit up', as stitches are made with new yarn rather than the loops of the

Picking up Stitches

main fabric. These are then worked in the appropriate stitch (usually ribbing), or simply cast off to give a very narrow border (sometimes called 'mock crochet'). As this technique is often used as a feature on a garment, great care must be taken to ensure that the stitches are divided evenly along the length of the fabric, and also that they are picked up **either** through a whole stitch **or** half a stitch throughout to produce a clean, unbroken line along the edge. To pick up the stitches only one needle is required, usually one or two sizes smaller than was used for the main fabric. The needle is held in the right hand, while the main body of the fabric is held in the left hand. After all the stitches have been picked up, turn the work and transfer the needle to the left hand, thus the first row worked will be a **wrong side** row.

The number of stitches to be picked up along an edge is given with the pattern instructions. This has been calculated so that the edging lays correctly according to the length of the edge being used. Therefore, if any alteration is made to the length of the garment, the edging may not sit properly if the same number of stitches is picked up. In this case the number of stitches picked up would have to be increased or decreased accordingly.

If the stitches are picked up across a row of stitches (cast on or cast off edges), they can be picked up stitch for stitch if the number of stitches is the same in the border and the main fabric. If the number of stitches is not the same, or if the stitches are picked up along a side edge (for example the front edge of a cardigan) or a shaped edge (such as a V-neck), you will probably find that not every stitch or row needs to be worked into, but this will depend on the tension of the main fabric and the number of stitches to be picked up for the edging.

To calculate how to pick the stitches up evenly, lay the edge to be used straight and measure the length of the edge. Place a pin at the halfway point at right angles to the edge of the fabric, then halve these distances again and again, so that the length is divided into eighths. Divide the given number of stitches by eight and pick up approximately this number in each section, checking that the total number of stitches has been picked up at the end. Always make sure that the first and last stitches at either end are worked into to avoid a gap forming.

Working along a cast-on/cast-off edge With the right side of the work facing you, insert the point of the right-hand needle from front to back under **both** loops of the cast on or cast off edge of first stitch, wind the yarn around the needle as though knitting a stitch and draw a loop through to form a new stitch on the needle. Continue in this way along the edge for as many stitches as required.

Working along a side edge With the right side of the work facing you, insert the point of the right-hand needle from front to back between the first and second stitch of the first row (working one whole stitch in from the edge). Wind the yarn round the needle and draw a loop through as though knitting a stitch to form a new stitch on the right-hand needle. Continue in this way, along the edge for as many stitches as required. Alternatively, if the yarn is very thick work through the centre of the edge stitch, thus taking in only half a stitch and reducing the bulk.

Working along an edge with held stitches Some edges, such as a crew neckline, often involve a combination of working across stitches on a holder, say at the centre front neck, and picking up stitches along an edge, in this case the front neck slopes. When you reach the stitches on a holder slip them onto another needle then **knit** across them onto the right-hand needle. To prevent a hole forming at the beginning or end of held or cast-off stitches, knit up a stitch from the loop **between** the stitches at these points.

Picking up stitches with the wrong side facing It is sometimes necessary to pick up stitches along an edge with the wrong side facing, so that the ridge is not visible on the right side of the work. This is done by picking up and **purling** the stitches. With the wrong side of the work facing, insert the right-hand needle through the edge of the fabric from **back to front,** wind the yarn around the needle and draw the loop through, thus forming a stitch on the right-hand needle. Continue in this way until the required number of stitches is on the needle.

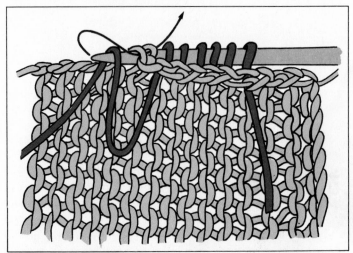

Circular Knitting or Knitting in the Round

This form of knitting produces a seamless fabric. Stitches cast on and knitted in the round continuously on a circular needle (twin-pin) or set of 4 needles without shaping will produce a tubular fabric. A few stitches cast on and worked in the round with suitable increases will form a Hat shape, a seamless circle or a polygon. This effect can also be achieved by casting on a large number of stitches and decreasing to the centre.

Until the end of the 19th century almost all knitting was worked in the round, and today many traditional garments are still constructed in this way. Norwegian and Icelandic designs are nearly always knitted on circular needles. For a jacket, two rows of machine stitching are worked close together at the centre front. The knitting is then cut between these two lines and the edges are finished off with braid or binding, or a crochet or knitted edging. Traditional guernsey sweaters are knitted in such a way that there are no seams at all to be joined.

Today, the most common use of circular knitting is in the working of neckbands and armbands. These are knitted after the side and shoulder or raglan seams have been joined, thereby avoiding a seam in the edging. However, there are also many other items which are best worked in the round on circular or double pointed needles. Circular shawls, table cloths and dressing-table mats start with a few stitches and by employing eyelet methods of increasing (see page 24), delicate lace patterns are created. However, as the mathematics required to ensure that the finished item lays completely flat are quite complicated, it is best to work them from a tried and tested pattern!

Hats and berets are frequently worked in the round, casting on at the lower edge and decreasing in to the centre with regular decrease rounds. The shape of the top of the hat is governed by the number of stitches decreased in a round, and the number of rounds between each decrease round.

Many patterns are available for socks and gloves worked in the round on sets of 4 needles. These are ideal for circular knitting as seams are often bulky and uncomfortable in such small items.

Another use for circular and double pointed needles is the working of yokes on sweaters or jackets. A sweater yoke would normally be worked in the round, while a jacket yoke would be worked backwards and forwards in rows, using a circular needle to accommodate the large number of stitches. A yoke can be worked from the neck downwards, casting on at the neck and increasing outwards in the relevant pattern, changing to longer circular needles as the stitches are increased. The stitches are then divided up for the back, front and sleeves with a cast on for the underarm gusset. The remainder of the garment is then worked downwards either in rows or rounds. Alternatively, the back, front and sleeves are worked before the yoke and the stitches are left on lengths of yarn. The yoke is then knitted up from these stitches (leaving a few stitches unworked for the underarm gusset), decreasing up to the neck and changing to shorter circular needles or sets of 4 needles as the stitches are decreased. The increases or decreases of a yoke are cleverly worked into a pattern, often fairisle, so that the pattern repeats are smaller at the neck edge and larger at the lower edge. For knitters who are less ambitious many specialist shops sell yokes already knitted, so that only the body and sleeves need to be worked.

There are many advantages to working in the round. It is much quicker since the knitting is never turned at the end of each row. The right side of the work is always facing you and **every** row is knitted when working in stocking stitch. The number of rows worked for the back and front will always be the same, and there are far fewer seams to join.

Colour and texture patterns are easier too. By looking at the right side all the time you can see how the pattern is developing. For Fairisle designs the colour not in use is always at the back of the work and colours are always in the correct position at the start of a round when they are next needed, thereby avoiding breaking off the yarns.

Many patterns can be adapted for circular knitting by simply casting on the back and front stitches together. Remember to reverse the instructions for the wrong side rows (i.e. knit instead of purl and vice versa). The work will have to be divided at the armholes and worked in rows as the pattern instructions. For the sleeves, cast on the number of stitches stated and join into a ring, working the increases at the underarm edge (i.e. the beginning and end of each round). Remember when working in rib that the same stitches are knitted and purled on every round.

Using a Circular Needle (or Twin Pin)

A circular needle has two pointed ends joined by a length of flexible nylon of varying lengths. A circular needle makes the manipulation of a large number of stitches easier to cope with. Always choose the correct length of needle according to the number of stitches (see table) - it is better to have a lot of stitches on a shorter needle as you can always push the stitches together, but too few stitches will be stretched and will not fit around the circumference of the needle. If you are working a sweater yoke where the number of stitches is decreasing, remember to check how many you end up with. You may have to buy a shorter length needle, or change to a set of four needles, to cope with the reduced number of stitches.

Tension-Stitches to		Minimum number of stitches required for various needle lengths						
1 inch	10 cm	40cm 16ins	50cm 20ins	60cm 24ins	70cm 28ins	80cm 32ins	100cm 40ins	120cm 48ins
3	12	56	69	81	95	109	136	160
3½	14	64	79	93	109	125	156	184
4	16	72	89	105	123	141	176	208
4½	18	80	99	117	137	157	196	232
5	20	88	109	129	151	173	216	256
5½	22	96	119	141	165	189	236	280
6	24	104	129	153	179	205	255	303
6½	26	112	138	164	192	220	275	327
7	28	120	148	176	206	236	294	350
7½	30	128	158	188	220	252	314	374
8	32	136	168	200	234	268	334	398
8½	34	144	178	212	248	284	353	421
9	36	152	188	224	262	300	373	445

Circular Knitting

To start work cast on to one of the points the number of stitches required, then spread them evenly along the complete length of the needle.

At this stage it is **vital** to check that the cast-on edge is not twisted before you join the circle of stitches into a ring. If it is twisted you will end up with a permanently twisted piece of material which cannot be rectified without cutting.

The first stitch that you work in the first round is the first cast-on stitch. To keep track of the beginning/end of the rounds make a slip knot in a short length of contrast-coloured yarn and place it on the needle as a marker, known as slip marker (see page 47), at the start of a round. Slip it from one needle to the other at the beginning of every round.

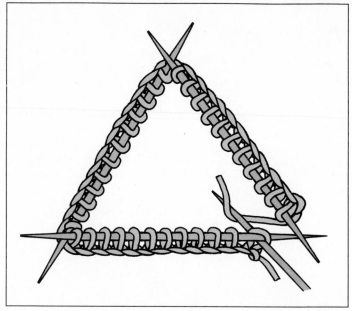

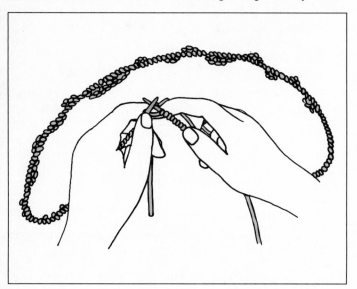

Always draw the yarn up firmly at the changeover point to avoid a ladder forming between the needles. Alternatively, the changeover points can be altered by working one or two stitches from the next needle on each round. To keep track of the beginning and end of a round, insert a contrast coloured marker as given for circular needles.

Although double pointed needles are usually available only in sets of four or six, any number of needles may be used, and many more may be required for a large number of stitches if a circular needle is not available.

Moss Stitch in Rounds

This is an interesting formation because the fabric consists of alternate knit and purl stitches placed one above the other, as when worked on 2 needles (see page 18), but has to be worked on an even number of stitches to achieve an all-over effect. This means that the beginning of the round must be clearly marked and a round that is worked *k1, p1; repeat from * to end, has to be followed by a round starting with a purl stitch. If an odd number of stitches is used, it is possible to work k1, p1 continuously without making a note of where the beginning or end of the round is placed. However, the changeover point of the round will be marked with two knit or two purl stitches which are actually the beginning and end of the round and spoil the continuous effect of the material (see diagram).

Using a Set of Four Needles

This is the best method to use if you have only a few stitches. Divide the total number of stitches by three and cast that number on to each of three of the needles (the fourth one is the working needle). Form the three needles into a triangle - taking care that the stitches are not twisted - by drawing up the last stitch to meet the first cast-on stitch.

Use the fourth needle to start knitting. Knit the stitches from the first needle onto the fourth needle and as each needle becomes free it then becomes the working needle for the next group of stitches.

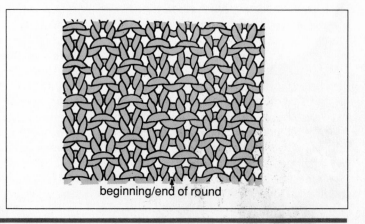

beginning/end of round

Aran Knitting

Traditional aran garments are composed of a combination of various cable, twist and bobble panels, using simple texture stitches to fill in the background areas. These garments were originally knitted in wool in a natural off-white shade. Although this is still the most popular yarn for knitting aran garments, 'aran-type' yarn is now available in a wide range of colours and even tweed effects, and may be composed of wool, synthetic yarn or a combination of both.

Aran style knitting has always been popular for outdoor garments because of its warmth and durability. Some Aran patterns are slow to knit and should not be attempted by inexperienced or impatient knitters!

Cables and Twists

Cables are not necessarily restricted to traditional aran garments and can be used in many other ways. They can be worked in single panels on plain garments, as all over patterns or single motifs, or in conjunction with lace or colour knitting. They can also be worked in any yarn thickness or texture.

Cabling or twisting stitches is simply a method of moving stitches across the material, or crossing one set of stitches over another. The following pages give details of how to work the basic cables, twists and bobbles which occur frequently in knitting. However intricate a cable panel may appear, the basic techniques still apply.

It is important to remember that all cables pull the fabric in, like a rib, and the tension will be much tighter than a flat fabric. Allowance is made for this in pattern instructions with increased stitches across the top of the welt corresponding to the position of the cables.

If you wish to add a cable or aran panel to a stocking stitch sweater you need to calculate the extra stitches required as follows:

1. Knit a piece of the cable panel with a few stitches extra in the background fabric at either side. The swatch should be a minimum of 5 cm (2 inches) in length, or at least one complete pattern repeat if it measures more than this.

2. Mark the edges of the cable panel with pins (inside the extra background stitches) and measure the distance between the pins without stretching.

3. Calculate how many stitches in the background fabric would be required to produce the same width as the cable panel, then subtract this number from the number of stitches in the cable panel to find the number of stitches to be increased. For example, say the cable panel contains 36 stitches and measures 15 cm (6 inches). The background stitch is stocking stitch with a tension of 18 stitches to 10 cm (4 inches). To produce 15 cm (6 inches) of stocking stitch, 27 stitches would be required. The cable panel has 9 stitches more than this, therefore an extra 9 stitches would have to be increased to allow for the cable panel and maintain the same width. These stitches should be increased above the welt across the stitches to be used for the panel.

Usually cables are shown in textured relief - the stocking stitch cable stitches are emphasised by a reverse stocking stitch background. A special cable needle is required to hold the stitches during the twisting process. It is short, double-pointed and the same thickness as the main needles (or slightly finer). Look for the cable needles that have a bend in the centre so that the stitches do not slide off.

For examples of cable panels using the techniques detailed below, see page 42.

Basic Cables

Basic cables are based on the concept of a rope. One set of stitches is held at the back or front on a separate needle while the following group is knitted, then the held stitches are knitted thus giving a crossover, twisted effect either to the right or left. The number of stitches contained in a rope cable varies, but four, six and eight are the most common.

Working a Basic Cable

C4B (Cable 4 Back)

Here the cable panel consists of four stitches in stocking stitch against a reverse stocking stitch background.

1. On a right side row, work to the position of the cable panel and slip the next two stitches onto the cable needle.

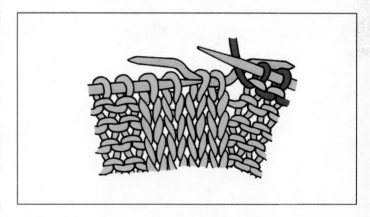

2. With the stitches on the cable needle held at the **back** of the work, knit the next two stitches from the left-hand needle.

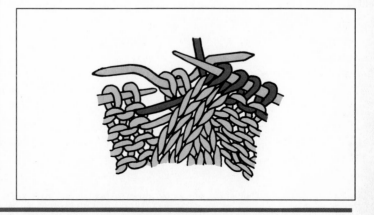

Types of Knitting

3. Now knit the two stitches from the cable needle to produce the crossover.

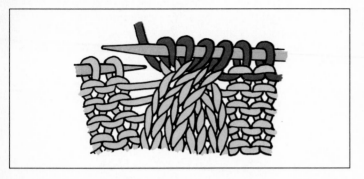

Leaving the first set of stitches at the back of the work produces a cable that twists to the right.

C4F (Cable 4 Front)

1. On a right side row, work to the position of the cable panel and slip the next two stitches onto the cable needle, leaving it at the **front** of the work.

2. Working behind the cable needle, knit the next two stitches from the left-hand needle.

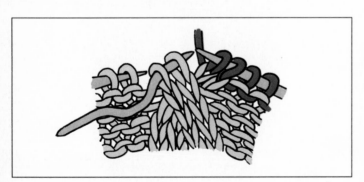

3. Now knit the two stitches from the cable needle to produce a crossover to the left.

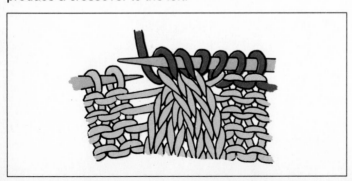

Leaving the first set of stitches at the front of the work produces a cable that twists to the left.

Working C4B or C4F on every sixth row creates a cable that looks like this.

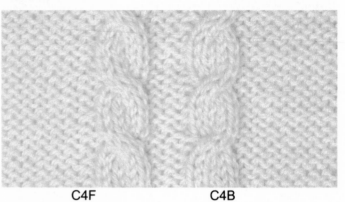

C4F   C4B

C6B or C6F
(Cable 6 Back or Cable 6 Front)

This is worked in the same way as C4B or C4F but working on a panel of six stitches in stocking stitch and holding three stitches on a cable needle at the back or front of the work, knitting the following three stitches, then knitting the three stitches from the cable needle.

C8B or C8F
(Cable 8 Back or Cable 8 Front)

Worked over a panel of eight stocking stitch stitches, hold the first four stitches on a cable needle at the back or front of the work, knit the following four stitches, then knit the stitches from the cable needle.

Generally speaking, the more stitches that are contained in a cable, the less frequently the stitches would be crossed. While C4B can be worked on every 4th or 6th row, C8B would be worked on every 8th, 10th or 12th row.

A combination of C4B and C4F can be used to create a plait effect either facing upwards or downwards. The following plaits are worked over six stitches in stocking stitch on a background of reverse stocking stitch.

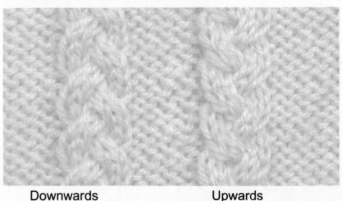

Downwards   Upwards

Downwards Plait

1st row (right side): C4F, k2. **2nd row:** P6.

3rd row: K2, C4B. **4th row:** P6.

Repeat these 4 rows.

Upwards Plait

1st row (right side): C4B, k2.

2nd row: P6.

3rd row: K2, C4F.

4th row: P6.

Repeat these 4 rows.

Plaits can be made thicker by crossing six or eight stitches over, but the total number of stitches in the plait must be a multiple of three.

Cable Variations

Once you have mastered the use of a cable needle to cross stitches over, you will find that there is an infinite variety of effects which can be created. Cables can be used to make diamonds, lattices, figures of eight and many other variations. The following techniques are used frequently in aran knitting to create more intricate panels than the basic rope cables.

In this book the terms 'cross' and 'cable' refer to crossing knit stitches over knit stitches. The term 'twist' is used where knit stitches are crossed over purl stitches (or vice versa)

Twisting Stitches

Many cable patterns involve two or more stitches travelling across a background fabric in a diagonal direction either as a lattice pattern or as part of a more intricate cable design. Altering the direction of a column of stitches requires a 'twisting' technique using a cable needle. The most common twists are T3B (Twist 3 Back) and T3F (Twist 3 Front). Two stitches in stocking stitch are moved across a reverse stocking stitch background by crossing them successively over 1 purl stitch on alternate rows. The number of stitches in a twist can vary according to the pattern being worked (for example, three stitches in stocking stitch can be moved across two stitches in reverse stocking stitch) but the technique always remains the same.

T3B (Twist 3 Back)

1. On a right side row, work to one stitch before the two stocking stitch stitches. Slip the next stitch onto a cable needle and leave it at the back of the work.

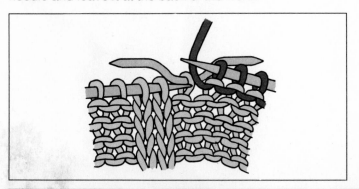

2. Knit the next two stitches on the left-hand needle.

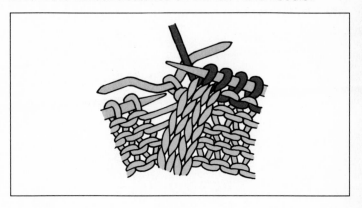

3. Now purl the stitch on the cable needle to produce a twist to the **right.**

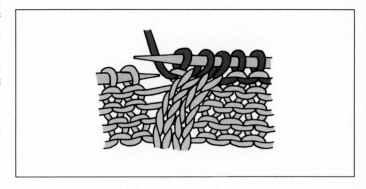

T3F (Twist 3 Front)

1. On a right side row, work to the two stocking stitch stitches. Slip these two stitches onto a cable needle and leave them at the front of the work.

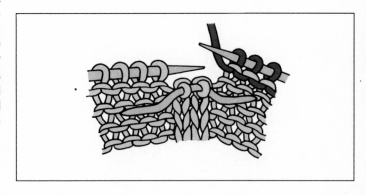

2. Purl the next stitch on the left-hand needle.

Types of Knitting

3. Knit the two stitches on the cable needle to produce a twist to the **left.**

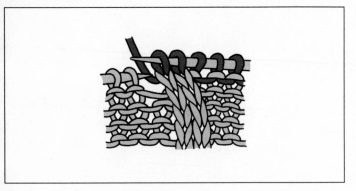

These two techniques are sometimes referred to as 'T3R' (Twist 3 Right) or 'T3L' (Twist 3 Left). The actual name of any cable can be different in various patterns, but working details are always given either in the abbreviations or where the technique first occurs in the instructions.

Cables Without Cable Needles

A cable needle is not required for the simple action of transposing two stitches. The technique of crossing or twisting two stitches can be used to create a 'mock cable' in a vertical panel, or to work a diagonal line of one raised stitch in stocking stitch on a stocking stitch or reverse stocking stitch background.

Crossing Two Stitches

Two stitches in stocking stitch can be crossed on every right side row, either to the right or left. Working this into a 'mock cable' rib makes a very decorative pattern.

C2R (Cross 2 Right)

1. On a right side row, work to the position of the two-stitch cross. Miss the first stitch on the left-hand needle and knit the second stitch, working through the front of the loop only.

2. Do not slip the worked stitch off the needle, but twist the needle back and knit the missed stitch through the front of the loop. Then slip both stitches off the needle together.

By purling these two stitches on the following row and repeating these 2 rows a small mock cable twisting to the right is produced.

C2L (Cross 2 Left)

Work as given for C2R, but knit the second stitch on the left-hand needle through the **back** of the loop working behind the first stitch. This produces a mock cable that twists to the left.

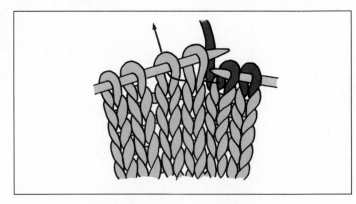

Twisting Two Stitches

The following techniques are used to make a diagonal line or 'travelling stitch' of one stitch in stocking stitch on a reverse stocking stitch background.

T2R (Twist 2 Right)

1. On a right side row, work to one stitch before the knit stitch. Miss the first stitch, then knit the second stitch through the front of the loop.

2. Without slipping the worked stitch off the needle, purl the missed stitch through the front of the loop, then slip both stitches off the needle at the same time.

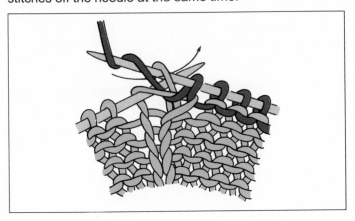

This reverses the position of the two stitches and produces a diagonal twist to the right.

T2L (Twist 2 Left)

1. On a right side row, work to the knit stitch. Miss the knit stitch and purl the following stitch through the **back** of the loop working behind the first stitch.

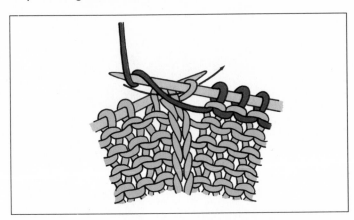

2. Without slipping the purled stitch off the needle bring the needle to the front of the work and knit the missed stitch then slip both stitches off the needle at the same time.

This produces a diagonal twist towards the left. As this is rather awkward to work, you may find it easier to use a cable needle to hold the knit stitch at the front of the work.

When shaping your knitting, if there are insufficient stitches to complete a cable, work the odd stitches in stocking stitch keeping the cable correct for as long as possible. Do not work a cable right on the edge of the fabric as this makes the seams untidy and does not make a neat edge for picking up stitches for borders.

Keep the pattern symmetrical when shaping a V neck, for instance, by stopping the cable at the same place on either side of the neck.

It is preferable, where possible, to fully fashion a V-neck on a cabled garment by keeping the cable running up the neck edge as follows:

V-Neck Sweater

If there is a single rope cable at the centre front, divide the stitches for the V-neck immediately after the cable has been crossed, then keep each half of the cable in stocking stitch, decreasing inside these stocking stitch stitches. For example, a 6 stitch cable is divided so that there are 3 stitches in stocking stitch on either side of the neck. For these stitches to be distinct, they should be bordered by a purl stitch. Therefore, on the right side of work, the decrease rows on the left front neck shaping would be worked as 'work to last 5 sts, p2tog, k3', and on the right front would be 'k3, p2tog, work to end'. On the other rows the 3 knit stitches and the purl stitch would be worked as established.

V-Neck Cardigan

A V-Neck Cardigan can be fully fashioned if there is a cable running up the front edge. When the start of the neck shaping is reached, the decreases are worked inside the cable panel, that is **before** the panel on the left front and **after** the panel on the right front. This ensures that the cable continues along the entire length of the front edge.

Types of Knitting

Bobbles

Bobbles are an important feature of textured knitting where they can be used either as an all-over fabric or individually - frequently as an accent in an Aran design.

The bobbles range in size from the smallest 'tuft' (or 'popcorn') to a large bobble that stands away from the background fabric.

Methods vary slightly, but the basic principle is always the same - a bobble is produced by creating extra stitches out of one original stitch or between 2 stitches. These stitches are then decreased immediately or on subsequent rows, or extra rows are worked on these stitches only before decreasing back to the original one stitch. Exact details of how to work a bobble are always given within pattern instructions but the following example shows a frequently used method.

☆ TIP SHEET ☆
BOBBLES

Allow plenty of extra yarn if you are adding bobbles to a plain fabric. If the bobbles are worked in a contrasting colour, use a separate length of the contrasting yarn for each bobble. When the bobble is completed knot the two ends together and run them into the back of the bobble or along the wrong side of the work (see securing ends page 25).

Large Bobbles

Individual bobbles are produced by making three or more stitches out of the original one and then working extra rows over these stitches only. For an eye-catching effect these bobbles can be worked in a contrasting colour, or in decorative clusters.

Bobbles can be worked in stocking stitch, reverse stocking stitch or garter stitch and usually consist of three, four or five stitches. The number of rows worked over the bobble stitches varies according to the size of bobble required.

The following instructions are for a large bobble worked in stocking stitch against a stocking stitch background and involve making five stitches out of one.

1. On a right side row, knit to the position of the bobble. Knit into the front, back, front, back and front again of the next stitch and slip the stitch off the left-hand needle so that five new stitches are on the right-hand needle instead of one.

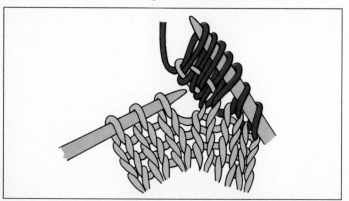

2. Turn the work so that the wrong side is facing and purl the five bobble stitches then turn again and knit them. Repeat the last two rows once more thus making four rows in stocking stitch over the bobble stitches.

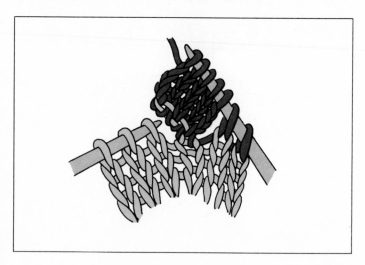

3. With the right side facing use the left-hand needle point to lift the second, third, fourth and fifth bobble stitches, in order, over the first one on the needle.

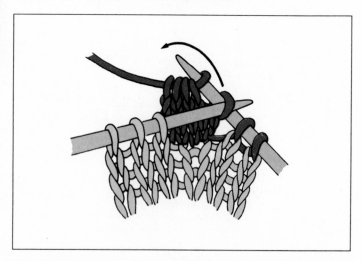

4. One stitch remains and you can continue to work the remainder of the row as required. Any small gap in the fabric when you continue knitting is hidden by the bobble.

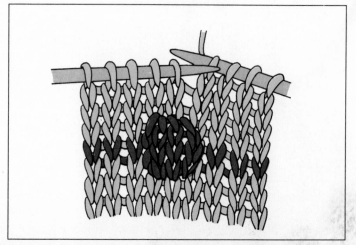

All-Over Patterns

The smallest bobbles do not have as much individual definition as the larger bobbles and are often incorporated into an all-over pattern. The following patterns all use the technique of creating extra stitches out of one stitch to produce very different fabrics. See page 6 for abbreviations.

1. Bramble Stitch

Also known as blackberry, trinity or popcorn stitch, this is popular either as an all-over pattern or as a background or panel in an Aran garment.

Cast on a multiple of four stitches plus two extra.

1st row (right side): Purl.

2nd row: K1, *work [k1, p1, k1] all into next st, p3tog; rep from * to last st, k1.

3rd row: Purl.

4th row: K1, *p3tog, work [k1, p1, k1] into next st; rep from * to last st, k1.

These 4 rows form the pattern.

By working [k1, p1, k1] all into the same stitch, a multiple increase is achieved which makes three stitches out of the original one. The extra two stitches are immediately compensated for when the following three stitches are purled together, therefore the number of stitches at the end of the row remains the same.

2. Cobnut Stitch

The 'cobnuts' in this pattern are worked in stocking stitch on a reverse stocking stitch background. The extra stitches of the cob nut are not decreased on the same row as they are made, but are decreased three rows further on. It is therefore important during shaping only to count the stitches after they have been decreased, either on the 4th, 5th, 6th, 10th, 11th or 12th rows. If stitches are counted on any of the other rows, remember that the three stitches of the cobnut count as only one stitch.

Cast on a multiple of four stitches plus three extra.

1st row (right side): P3, *work (k1, yf, k1) all into next st, p3; rep from * to end.

2nd row: K3, *p3, k3; rep from * to end.

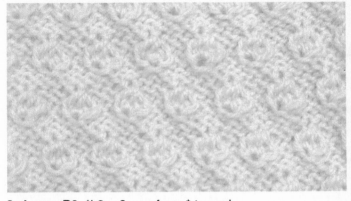

3rd row: P3, *k3, p3; rep from * to end.

4th row: K3, *p3tog, k3; rep from * to end.

5th row: Purl.

6th row: Knit.

7th row: P1, *work [k1, yf, k1] all into next st, p3; rep from * to last 2 sts, work [k1, yf, k1] into next st, p1.

8th row: K1, *p3, k3; rep from * to last 4 sts, p3, k1.

9th row: P1, *k3, p3; rep from * to last 4 sts, k3, p1.

10th row: K1, *p3tog, k3; rep from * to last 4 sts, p3tog, k1.

11th row: Purl.

12th row: Knit.

These 12 rows form the pattern.

3. Mini Bobble Stitch

This makes a highly textured stitch where the bobble stitches are made and decreased immediately on the same row. This stitch is effective worked in two or more colours, working two rows in each colour. Note that although the bobbles are made on the wrong side rows, they are raised on the right side of the fabric.

Cast on an odd number of stitches.

1st row (right side): Knit.

2nd row: K1, *work [p1, k1, p1, k1] all into next st, using the left-hand needle lift the 2nd, 3rd and 4th stitches over the first st on the right-hand needle, k1; rep from * to end.

3rd row: Knit.

4th row: K2, *work [p1, k1, p1, k1] into next st, lift 2nd, 3rd and 4th sts over first st, k1; rep from * to last st, k1.

These 4 rows form the pattern.

Types of Knitting

Aran Pattern Panels

The following 2 pattern panels can be produced by using the cable and bobble techniques described on pages 35-40. There are of course many other variations and combinations of stitches, but the following two are good examples of traditional Aran panels. To work these panels, cast on a few extra sts to be worked in reverse stocking stitch at either side. See page 6 for abbreviations.

1. Triple Criss Cross Cable

Worked over 26 sts on a background of reversed stocking stitch.

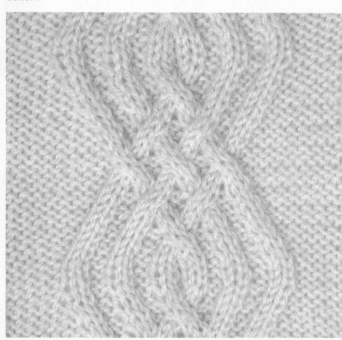

1st row (right side): P5, [C4F, p2] twice, C4F, p5.

2nd row: K5, [p4, k2] twice, p4, k5.

3rd row: P4, [T3B, T3F] 3 times, p4.

4th row: K4, p2, [k2, p4] twice, k2, p2, k4.

5th row: P3, T3B, [p2, C4B] twice, p2, T3F, p3.

6th row: K3, p2, k3, p4, k2, p4, k3, p2, k3.

7th row: P2, T3B, p2, [T3B, T3F] twice, p2, T3F, p2.

8th row: K2, p2, k3, p2, k2, p4, k2, p2, k3, p2, k2.

9th row: P1, [T3B, p2] twice, C4F, [p2, T3F] twice, p1.

10th row: K1, [p2, k3] twice, p4, [k3, p2] twice, k1.

11th row: [T3B, p2] twice, T3B, [T3F, p2] twice, T3F.

12th row: [P2, k3] twice, p2, k2, [p2, k3] twice, p2.

13th row: [K2, p3] twice, k2, p2, [k2, p3] twice, k2.

14th row: As 12th row.

15th row: [T3F, p2] twice, T3F, [T3B, p2] twice, T3B.

16th row: As 10th row.

17th row: P1, [T3F, p2] twice, C4F, [p2, T3B] twice, p1.

18th row: As 8th row.

19th row: [P2, T3F] twice, T3B, T3F, [T3B, p2] twice.

20th row: As 6th row.

21st row: P3, T3F, [p2, C4B] twice, p2, T3B, p3.

22nd row: As 4th row.

23rd row: P4, [T3F, T3B] 3 times, p4.

24th row: As 2nd row.

These 24 rows form the pattern.

2. Trellis with Bobbles

Worked over 23 sts on a background of reversed stocking stitch.

1st row (wrong side): P2, k7, p2, k1, p2, k7, p2.

2nd row: K2, p3, Make Bobble as follows: work [k1, p1, k1, p1, k1] all into next st, [turn and p5, turn and k5] twice, then pass 2nd, 3rd, 4th and 5th sts over first st on right-hand needle (called MB), p3, slip next 3 sts onto cable needle and hold at back of work, k2 from left-hand needle, then p1, k2 from cable needle (called T5B), p3, MB, p3, k2.

3rd row: As 1st row.

4th row: T3F, p5, T3B, p1, T3F, p5, T3B.

5th row: K1, p2, k5, p2, k3, p2, k5, p2, k1.

6th row: P1, T3F, p3, T3B, p3, T3F, p3, T3B, p1.

7th row: K2, p2, k3, p2, k5, p2, k3, p2, k2.

8th row: P2, T3F, p1, T3B, p5, T3F, p1, T3B, p2.

9th row: K3, p2, k1, p2, k7, p2, k1, p2, k3.

10th row: P3, slip next 2 sts onto cable needle and hold at front of work, p1, k2 from left-hand needle, then k2 from cable needle (called T5F), p3, MB, p3, T5F, p3.

11th row: As 9th row.

12th row: P2, T3B, p1, T3F, p5, T3B, p1, T3F, p2.

13th row: As 7th row.

14th row: P1, T3B, p3, T3F, p3, T3B, p3, T3F, p1.

15th row: As 5th row.

16th row: T3B, p5, T3F, p1, T3B, p5, T3F.

These 16 rows form the pattern.

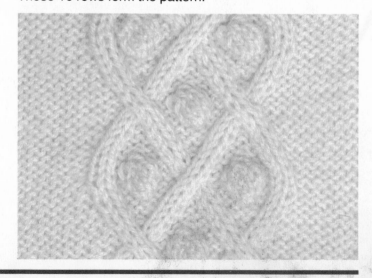

Smocking

There are two basic methods of working smocking on a knitted piece - either using a cable needle and smocking the stitches while the work is in progress, or using a sewing needle and smocking the work once the knitting is complete. Smocking is usually worked on a ribbed fabric, drawing together the knit stitches on the right side.

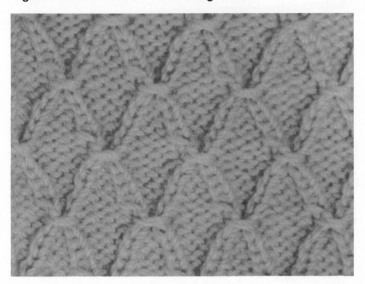

Cable Needle Method

This method is far quicker than the embroidered method and involves slipping the stitches to be smocked onto a cable needle or double pointed needle and winding the yarn around these stitches. The tension of the smocked fabric depends on the tightness of the yarn wound around the stitches and also the number of rows worked between rows of smocking.

For smocking worked on a k1, p3 rib pattern, work as follows:

Cast on a multiple of 8 sts, plus 7 extra.

1st row (right side): P1, k1, *p3, k1; rep from * to last st, p1.

2nd row: K1, p1, *k3, p1; rep from * to last st, k1.

3rd row (smocking row): P1, slip next 5 sts onto cable needle and hold at front of work, wind yarn twice around sts on cable needle in an anti-clockwise direction then work the stitches from the cable needle as follows: k1, p3, k1 (this will now be called 'smock 5'), *p3, 'smock 5'; rep from * to last st, p1.

Rep 2nd row, then 1st and 2nd rows twice more.

9th row: P1, k1, p3, *'smock 5', p3; rep from * to last 2 sts, k1, p1.

10th row: As 2nd row.

11th and 12th rows: As 1st and 2nd rows.

Repeat these 12 rows.

This method creates a small gap in the work at either side of the smocked stitches. The technique can be adapted to any rib pattern, providing the stitches on the cable needle

begin and end with a knit stitch. The number of rows between the smocked stitches can also be varied as required.

Embroidery Method

In this method the ribbed fabric is worked first and the smocking is applied to the completed fabric. The smocking can either be worked in the same yarn as the main fabric, or in a contrasting yarn for more emphasis. The tension is dependent upon how tightly the embroidery is worked, and how many rows there are between the smocked stitches. Use a blunt-ended sewing needle to pass easily between the stitches and work two oversewn stitches through the work to draw the knit stitches together (see diagram). Count the number of rows between the smocking rows to make sure the smocking is worked evenly. Fasten off each smocked stitch to avoid long floats at the back of the work. This type of smocking can be applied to any ribbed fabric - the greater the distance between the knit stitches the more pronounced the smocking will be.

Types of Knitting

Fairisle Knitting

Fairisle is a general term used for multi-coloured stocking stitch patterns, where two or more colours are used across a single row of knitting. Traditional Fairisle knitting originates from the Shetland Isles, although similar patterns can also be found in traditional Scandinavian garments. The patterns are built up from small basic motifs which are repeated, often in a striped formation, to give complex looking designs. Authentic Fairisles are very colourful, but there are rarely more than two colours used in a single row. The term 'jacquard' is sometimes used instead of 'Fairisle'. This is not strictly correct as the origin of the word 'jacquard' is in industrial machine knitting.

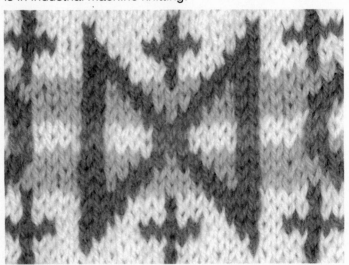

There are two basic methods of working Fairisle patterns, either carrying or 'stranding' the unused yarn across the wrong side of the work, or 'weaving' the two yarns together on the wrong side to avoid long strands of yarn at the back of the work. If you are adding a fairisle pattern to a stocking stitch garment, bear in mind that the tension will probably not be the same. Generally the stitches tend to be 'squarer' than stocking stitch - in other words the number of stitches to 10 cm (4 inches) is often the same as the number of rows to the same measurement. Always work a tension piece beforehand as tensions can vary enormously between different fairisle patterns.

Stranding Colours

For this method the colour not in use is carried **loosely** across the wrong side of the work so as not to distort the shape of the stitches being knitted.

If the strands have to be carried over more than six stitches, there is a danger that they could be pulled when the garment is put on or taken off. To avoid this it is necessary to twist together the yarn being used with the yarn not in use every 3rd or 4th stitch to avoid long floats at the back of the work.

As well as mastering the technique of working with two colours, it is vital to watch out for problems with the tension. The yarn must be stranded very loosely, loosely enough to maintain the elasticity of the fabric; this is difficult to achieve until you have practised the techniques involved and feel relaxed with the work. If you pull the strands even slightly you will buckle the work giving the finished fabric a puckered uneven appearance and making the material too small.

1. On a knit row, hold the first colour in your right hand and the second colour in your left hand. Work as normal with the first colour, carrying the second loosely across the wrong side of the work.

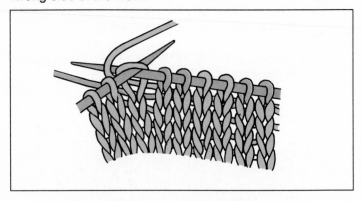

2. When the second colour is required, insert the right-hand needle into the next stitch and draw a loop through from the yarn held in the left hand, carrying the yarn in the right hand loosely across the wrong side until next required.

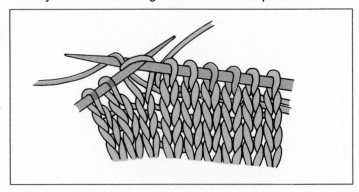

3. On a purl row, work as usual with the first colour held in the right hand, holding the second colour in the left hand.

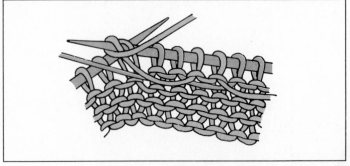

4. To purl a stitch in the second colour insert the right-hand needle into the next stitch purlwise and draw a loop through from the yarn held in the left hand.

If there are more than 6 stitches worked in one colour, cross the yarns over each other on every third or fourth stitch to avoid long, loose strands or 'floats'. Simply lay the colour not in use across the yarn being used before working the next stitch.

Stranded knitting should look as neat on the wrong side as it does on the right. Keeping the colours in order in the same hand each time and taking both of them to the end of the rows (twisting together once at the end of the row to keep in place) helps to give the fabric a professional appearance.

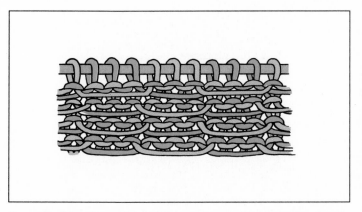

If you find it awkward to hold the yarns in both hands, simply work as usual, dropping the yarn not in use and picking it up again when required, making sure that it is not pulled across the wrong side. Always carry the same colour across the top throughout the row for a neat appearance on the wrong side, and to avoid the yarns becoming twisted.

Weaving

Weaving is a method of looping the colour not in use around the yarn being used on every stitch to create a woven effect on the wrong side of the work. The back of a woven fabric looks extremely neat, but it distorts the shape of the stitches and alters the tension. Unless the pattern specifically states that this method should be used DO NOT weave the yarn in but follow the stranding method. This method also tends to create a solid, less elastic fabric than the weaving method.

The following diagrams illustrate the way in which the yarns are twisted together to produce the woven effect from the right and wrong side of the work.

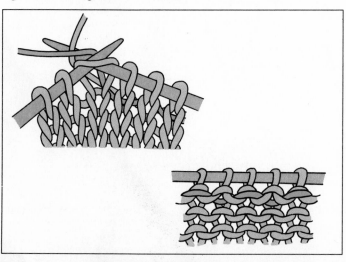

Working from a Chart

Knitting instructions for a Fairisle pattern are usually given in chart form. This gives a visual impression of how the design will look when knitted. A single pattern repeat of the complete design (which must be worked across the width and depth of the fabric) is shown as a chart on a squared grid. The colours in the pattern are either represented by symbols that are identified in an adjacent key, or the squares are shaded in the relevant colour.

Reading a chart is easier if you visualise it as a piece of knitting working from the lower edge to the top. Horizontally across the grid each square represents a stitch and vertically up the grid each square represents a row of knitting.

The details of how to follow a chart are usually given with the pattern but generally the following rules apply.

Rows For stocking stitch, work across a line of squares from right to left for the knit rows, then follow the line immediately above from left to right for the purl rows. Odd numbers - 1, 3, 5, etc - at the right-hand edge usually indicate the knit rows, while even numbers - 2, 4, 6, etc - at the left-hand edge denote the purl rows. For a completely symmetrical pattern, every row may be read from right to left. To make following a chart easier, use a row counter (see page 10) or place a ruler under the row being worked and move the ruler up as each row is completed.

Stitches Usually only one repeat of the pattern is given in the chart and this has to be repeated across the width of the material. This section is usually contained within bold vertical lines with a bracketed indication that it is to be repeated across the row. There may be extra stitches at either end which are edge stitches worked at the beginning and end of rows to complete the pattern so that the rows are symmetrical or 'balanced'.

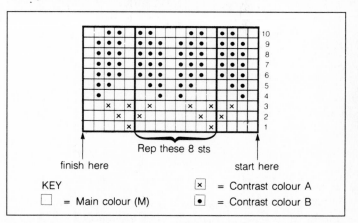

Rep these 8 sts

finish here   start here

KEY

☐ = Main colour (M)

☒ = Contrast colour A

⊡ = Contrast colour B

Types of Knitting

Fisherman's Rib and Half Fisherman's Rib

There are various methods of working fisherman's rib or half fisherman's rib. The most common way is to use the 'knit 1 below' technique, where you knit into the next stitch on the row below. The other methods achieve the same result by taking the yarn over the work on one row and knitting this thread together with the stitch on the following row. Whichever method you use, the finished fabric will appear the same, although the tension and 'feel' may vary. Remember when measuring tension that only one row may be visible on the right side for every **two rows** worked, depending on the method used.

Knit one Below (K1B)

To knit one below insert the right-hand needle through the centre of the stitch below the next stitch on the left-hand needle. Knit this in the usual way, drawing the loop through, then drop the stitch above off the needle.

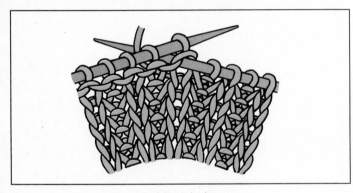

See page 6 for general abbreviations.

Fisherman's Rib

This fabric has the same appearance on either side, and can therefore be used for reversible items such as scarves. The slipped stitch at the beginning of every row gives the fabric a firmer edge. K1B should never be worked into the first or last stitch of a row.

Method 1

Cast on an odd number of stitches.

Foundation row: Knit (Note: this row is not repeated).

2nd row (right side): Sl 1, *K1B (see description above), p1; rep from * to end.

3rd row: Sl 1, *p1, K1B; rep from * to last 2 sts, p1, k1.

Repeat the 2nd and 3rd rows for pattern.

Method 2

Cast on an odd number of stitches.

Foundation row: Knit (Note: this row is not repeated).

2nd row (right side): Sl 1, *K1B (see description opposite), k1; rep from * to end.

3rd row: Sl 1, *k1, K1B; rep from * to last 2 sts, k2.

Repeat the 2nd and 3rd rows for pattern.

Method 3

This method creates the same structure as the ones above without working K1B. Cast on a multiple of three stitches plus 1 extra.

1st row (right side): K1, *k2tog, yf, sl 1 purlwise; rep from * to last 3 sts, k2tog, yf, k1.

2nd row: *K2tog (the yf and sl 1 of the previous row), yf, sl 1 purlwise; rep from * to last st, k1.

Repeat these two rows for pattern.

Half Fisherman's Rib

Half Fisherman's Rib has a different appearance on each side of the fabric, either of which may be used as the right side. Both methods given here use the 'knit one below' technique. The slipped stitch at the beginning of the row gives the fabric a firmer edge. K1B should never be worked in the first or last stitch of the row.

Method 1

Cast on an odd number of stitches.

1st row (right side): Sl 1, knit to end.

2nd row: Sl 1, *K1B (see description opposite), p1; rep from * to end.

Repeat these two rows for pattern.

Method 2

Cast on an odd number of stitches.

1st row (right side): Sl 1, *p1, k1; rep from * to end.

2nd row: Sl 1, *K1B (see description opposite), p1; rep from * to end.

Repeat these two rows for pattern.

Slip Markers

It is sometimes necessary to insert a marker within a knitted piece, for example to separate a panel or motif from the background fabric, to mark a certain number of stitches for measuring tension or for marking the beginning/end of a round in circular knitting. To do this, make a slip knot in a short length of contrasting yarn or use a commercially bought marker (see photograph on page4) and place on the left-hand needle where indicated or where required. Slip the marker onto the right-hand needle on every row as it is reached until the pattern is established or the motif is completed and the marker is no longer required. For circular knitting, leave the marker in place throughout.

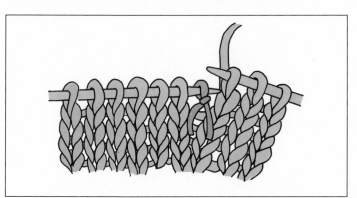

Correcting Mistakes

Even the most experienced knitter makes the occasional mistake, but there are very few mistakes which cannot subsequently be put right.

There are a few ways of avoiding making mistakes, or seeing the error before you have worked too many rows above it. Firstly, try out the stitch pattern in a spare yarn before working the garment. In this way you will become familiar with the pattern and will be less likely to make a mistake. While working the garment check back after every pattern row to make sure the pattern has been worked correctly. It is far easier and less frustrating to unravel one row than several. When working a lace pattern check that the number of stitches is correct at the end of the row. If there are too few, you will probably find that a 'yarn forward' has been missed - check back along the row to see where the mistake has been made. Check that cables have been crossed in the right direction and on the correct row.

If, despite these precautions you still find you have made a mistake don't despair, most mistakes can be remedied with a little patience.

Dropped Stitches

This is the most common mistake made by knitters. A stitch dropped a few rows below the work on the needles can be picked up and re-created on each row as long as the work

has not progressed too far. If the stitch has dropped down and formed a ladder it is easy to pick it up and re-work it. However, if you have continued knitting, the stitches above the dropped stitch will be drawn too tightly across the back of the work to leave enough spare yarn to re-create the lost stitch. In this case it is recommended that you unravel the work to the point where the stitch was dropped and re-knit the unravelled rows.

On the row below, picking up a knit stitch

1. Working from front to back, pick up the stitch and the horizontal strand above it with the right-hand needle (the strand should be **behind** the stitch).

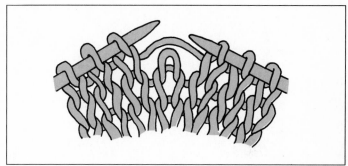

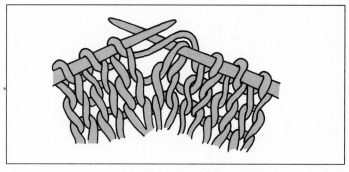

2. Insert the left-hand needle through the stitch and lift it over the strand and off the needle as though casting it off.

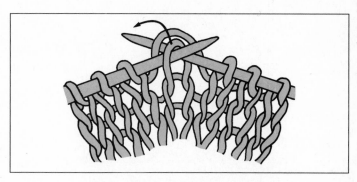

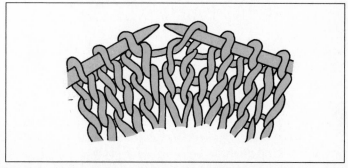

Correcting Mistakes

On the row below, correcting a purl stitch

1. Working from back to front, pick up the stitch and the horizontal strand above it with the right-hand needle (the strand should be **in front of** the stitch).

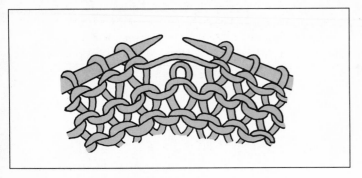

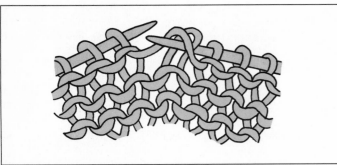

2. Insert the left-hand needle through the stitch, lift it over the strand and off the needle, using the right-hand needle to draw the strand through the stitch so forming a stitch on the right-hand needle. Replace the stitch on the left-hand needle to continue.

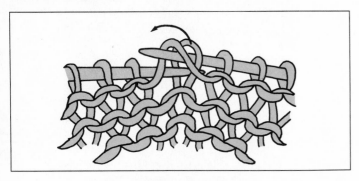

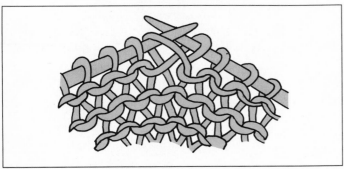

Several rows below

If a dropped stitch is not noticed immediately it can easily form a ladder running down a number of rows. In this case the stitch must be reformed all the way up the ladder using

a crochet hook. Always work from the front - or knit side - of the fabric. Insert the hook into the free stitch from the front. With the hook pointing upwards, catch the first strand of the ladder from above and draw it through the stitch. Continue in this way up the ladder until all the strands have been worked, then replace the stitch on the left-hand needle taking care not to twist it. If more than one stitch has dropped, secure the others with a safety pin until you are ready to pick them up.

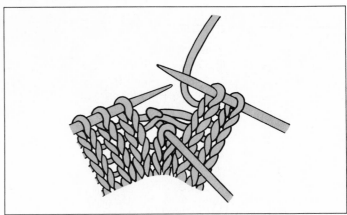

Unravelling

A single row This is best done stitch by stitch. Keeping the needles and yarn in the normal working position, insert the left-hand needle from front to back through the centre of the first stitch **below** the stitch on the right-hand needle. Drop the stitch above from the right-hand needle and pull the yarn free. Continue in this way until you reach the stitch to be corrected or picked up.

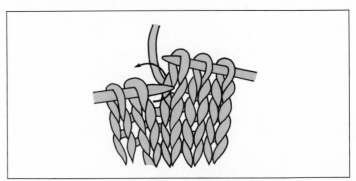

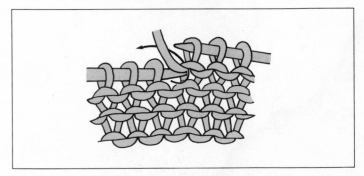

Several rows To go back stitch by stitch here would be too tedious. The quick way of doing this is to take the work off the needles and pull the yarn. Firstly, though, mark the row below the mistake and use a spare needle of a smaller size to pick up the stitches along this row so preventing more dropped stitches as you try to get them back on to the needle. Unwind the yarn gently - do not tug on difficult stitches or they will become tighter. Waggle the yarn so that the stitches ease themselves apart. You will need extra patience with textured or fluffy yarns. Use small nail scissors to cut away excess fibres forming a knot around the yarn, taking care not to cut the yarn itself.

Yarn that has recently been knitted for the first time can be wound into a ball while it is still attached to the knitting and re-used straight away. If the yarn has been knitted up for some time it might be too crinkly for re-use - instead you will have to use a new ball of yarn.

A complete piece of knitting This drastic form of unravelling is sometimes necessary if you notice a mistake only when you have finished a complete section of the garment. It is worthwhile re-knitting the piece if the mistake is very noticeable. You will notice that the work must be pulled out in the opposite direction to the knitting, (from the cast-off edge downwards).

Re-Crossing Cables

A common mistake which occurs in the working of Cable or Aran patterns is that you find you have crossed a cable in the wrong direction several rows below. This is easily put right and gives you the opportunity of practising a technique that can be useful in many other ways. If you have crossed a cable of 6 stitches (3 over 3) in the wrong direction, work as follows:

1. Carefully cut the centre stitch of the top 3 stitches of the row at the point where the cable crosses over. Undo these three top stitches leaving the ends of yarn loose on either side.

2. Lift up the underneath 3 sts which in fact now become the top ones and graft the original 3 sts back in position underneath (see page 29), from wrong side following diagram below, thus correcting the slope of the cable.

Correcting Texture Patterns

On a texture pattern you may find that you have worked a knit stitch instead of a purl stitch or vice versa several rows below. To correct the mistake, work to the stitch above the stitch to be corrected and drop the stitch off the needle. Unravel the stitch down to the row where the mistake was made, then re-create the stitch using a crochet hook as given for dropped stitches, turning the work as required so that the knit side of the stitch is always facing you (if the stitch should be purled on the right side, turn the work so that you are working from the wrong side).

Knitting Left on the Needles

If a piece of knitting is left on the needles for a long period of time, the row on the needles will stretch, leaving a visible line across the work. To avoid this undo the row on the needles plus one more row below, discard this worked yarn and continue knitting using new yarn.

Broken or Pulled Stitches

A stitch which has been pulled leaving a long loop can be worked back across the row. Firstly, give the knitting a sharp tug across the area containing the pulled stitch, thus drawing back some of the excess yarn. Then pull the yarn stitch by stitch through the stitches at either side of the pulled stitch until all the excess yarn has been worked back into the row. However, if the yarn is broken but the stitch has not come undone, draw up some extra yarn from the stitches at either side so that the yarn ends are long enough to darn in at the back of the work, then using a sharp needle secure the ends on the wrong side by running them in and around the stitches (see page 25).

☆ TIP SHEET ☆
CORRECTING MISTAKES

Emergency equipment for coping with dropped stitches include a safety-pin and crochet hook. A dropped stitch is stopped in its tracks if it is slipped onto a safety-pin.

Knit and Purl Patterns

Stocking Stitch Triangles

Multiple of 5
1st row (right side): Knit.
2nd row: *K1, p4; rep from * to end.
3rd row: *K3, p2; rep from * to end.
4th row: *K3, p2; rep from * to end.
5th row: *K1, p4; rep from * to end.
6th row: Knit.
Rep these 6 rows.

Dot Stitch

Multiple of 4+3
1st row (right side): K1, *p1, k3; rep from * to last 2 sts, p1, k1.
2nd row: Purl.
3rd row: *K3, p1; rep from * to last 3 sts, k3.
4th row: Purl.
Rep these 4 rows.

Box Stitch

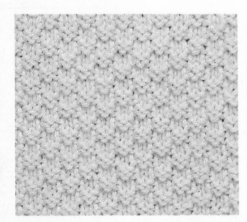

Multiple of 4+2
1st row: K2, *p2, k2; rep from * to end.
2nd row: P2, *k2, p2; rep from * to end.
3rd row: As 2nd row.
4th row: As 1st row.
Rep these 4 rows.

Double Moss Stitch

Multiple of 2+1
1st row: K1, *p1, k1; rep from * to end.
2nd row: P1, *k1, p1; rep from * to end.
3rd row: As 2nd row.
4th row: As 1st row.
Rep these 4 rows.

Moss Stitch I

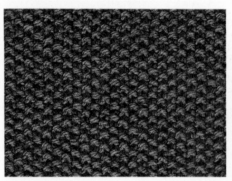

Multiple of 2+1
1st row: K1, *p1, k1; rep from * to end.
Rep this row.

Moss Stitch II

Worked as Moss Stitch I.
2 rows in colour A, 2 rows in B, 2 rows in A and 2 rows in C throughout.

Diagonal Garter Ribs

Multiple of 5+2
1st and every alt row (right side): Knit.
2nd row: *P2, k3; rep from * to last 2 sts, p2.
4th row: K1, *p2, k3; rep from * to last st, p1.
6th row: K2, *p2, k3; rep from * to end.
8th row: *K3, p2; rep from * to last 2 sts, k2.
10th row: P1, *k3, p2; rep from * to last st, k1.
Rep these 10 rows.

Garter Ribs

Panels of alternate knit and purl garter st are effective with any number of sts in each panel. Here we show a 2 st and a 4 st version.

2-Stitch Ribs I

Multiple of 4+2
1st row: K2, *p2, k2; rep from * to end.
Rep this row.

2-Stitch Ribs II

Worked as 2-Stitch Ribs I.
Worked in 1 row each in colours A, B and C throughout.

4-Stitch Ribs

Multiple of 8+4
1st row: K4, *p4, k4; rep from * to end.
Rep this row.

Fleck Stitch

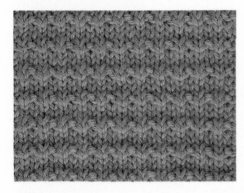

Multiple of 2+1
1st row (right side): Knit.
2nd row: Purl.
3rd row: K1, *p1, k1; rep from * to end.
4th row: Purl.
Rep these 4 rows.

Double Fleck Stitch

Multiple of 6+4
1st and 3rd rows (right side): Knit.
2nd row P4, *k2, p4; rep from * to end.
4th row: P1, *k2, p4; rep from * to last 3 sts, k2, p1.
Rep these 4 rows.

Check Stitch

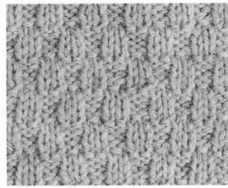

Multiple of 4+2
1st row: K2, *p2, k2; rep from * to end.
2nd row: P2, *k2, p2; rep from * to end.
Rep these last 2 rows once more.
5th row: As 2nd row.
6th row: As 1st row.
Rep these last 2 rows once more.
Rep these 8 rows.

Double Basket Weave

Multiple of 4+3
1st and every alt row (right side): Knit.
2nd row: *K3, p1; rep from * to last 3 sts, k3.
4th row: As 2nd row.
6th row: K1, *p1, k3; rep from * to last 2 sts, p1, k1.
8th row: As 6th row.
Rep these 8 rows.

Reverse Stocking Stitch Chevrons

Multiple of 6+5
1st row (right side): K5, *p1, k5; rep from * to end.
2nd row: K1, *p3, k3; rep from * to last 4 sts, p3, k1.
3rd row: P2, *k1, p2; rep from * to end.
4th row: P1, *k3, p3; rep from * to last 4 sts, k3, p1.
5th row: K2, *p1, k5; rep from * to last 3 sts, p1, k2.
6th row: Purl.
Rep these 6 rows.

Ladder Stitch

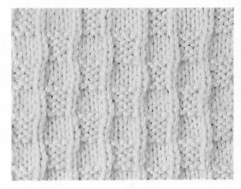

Multiple of 8+5
1st row (right side): K5, *p3, k5; rep from * to end.
2nd row: P5, *k3, p5; rep from * to end.
Rep the last 2 rows once more.
5th row: K1, *p3, k5; rep from * to last 4 sts, p3, k1.
6th row: P1, *k3, p5; rep from * to last 4 sts, k3, p1.
Rep these last 2 rows once more.
Rep these 8 rows.

Dotted Ladder Stitch

Multiple of 8+5
1st row (right side): K2, p1, k2, *p3, k2, p1, k2; rep from * to end.
2nd row: [P1, k1] twice, p1, *k3, [p1, k1] twice, p1; rep from * to end.
Rep the last 2 rows once more.
5th row: K1, *p3, k2, p1, k2; rep from * to last 4 sts, p3, k1.
6th row: P1, k3, p1, *[k1, p1] twice, k3, p1; rep from * to end.
Rep the last 2 rows once more.
Rep these 8 rows.

Knit and Purl Patterns

Interrupted Rib

Multiple of 2 + 1
1st row (right side): P1, *k1, p1; rep from * to end.
2nd row: K1, *p1, k1; rep from * to end.
3rd row: Purl.
4th row: Knit.
Rep these 4 rows.

Basket Weave

Multiple of 4 + 3
1st and 3rd rows (right side): Knit.
2nd row: *K3, p1; rep from * to last 3 sts, k3.
4th row: K1, *p1, k3; rep from * to last 2 sts, p1, k1.
Rep these 4 rows.

Ridged Rib

Multiple of 2 + 1
1st and 2nd rows: Knit.
3rd row (right side): P1, *k1, p1; rep from * to end.
4th row: K1, *p1, k1; rep from * to end.
Rep these 4 rows.

Double Ridged Rib

Multiple of 2 + 1
1st and 2nd rows: Knit.
3rd row (right side): P1, *k1, p1; rep from * to end.
4th row: K1, *p1, k1; rep from * to end.
5th and 6th rows: Knit.
7th row: As 4th row.
8th row: P1, *k1, p1; rep from * to end.
Rep these 8 rows.

Lattice Stitch

Multiple of 6 + 1
1st row (right side): K3, *p1, k5; rep from * to last 4 sts, p1, k3.
2nd row: P2, *k1, p1, k1, p3; rep from * to last 5 sts, k1, p1, k1, p2.
3rd row: K1, *p1, k3, p1, k1; rep from * to end.
4th row: K1, *p5, k1; rep from * to end.
5th row: As 3rd row.
6th row: As 2nd row.
Rep these 6 rows.

Alternating Triangles

Multiple of 5
1st row (right side): *P1, k4; rep from * to end.
2nd and 3rd rows: *P3, k2; rep from * to end.
4th row: *P1, k4; rep from * to end.
5th row: *K4, p1; rep from * to end.
6th and 7th rows: *K2, p3; rep from * to end.
8th row: As 5th row.
Rep these 8 rows.

Steps

Multiple of 8 + 2
1st row (right side): *K4, p4; rep from * to last 2 sts, k2.
2nd row: P2, *k4, p4, rep from * to end.
Rep the last 2 rows once more.
5th row: K2, *p4, k4; rep from * to end.
6th row: *P4, k4; rep from * to last 2 sts, p2.
7th row: As 5th row.
8th row: As 6th row.
9th row: *P4, k4; rep from * to last 2 sts, p2.
10th row: K2, *p4, k4; rep from * to end.
Rep the last 2 rows once more.
13th row: As 2nd row.
14th row: *K4, p4; rep from * to last 2 sts, k2.
Rep the last 2 rows once more.
Rep these 16 rows.

Diagonal Checks

Multiple of 5 sts.
1st row (right side): *P1, k4; rep from * to end.
2nd row: *P3, k2; rep from * to end.
3rd row: As 2nd row.
4th row: *P1, k4; rep from * to end.
5th row: *K1, p4; rep from * to end.
6th row: *K3, p2; rep from * to end.
7th row: As 6th row.
8th row: As 5th row.
Rep these 8 rows.

Garter Stitch Steps

Multiple of 8

1st and every alt row (right side): Knit.
2nd and 4th rows: *K4, p4; rep from * to end.
6th and 8th rows: K2, *p4, k4; rep from * to last 6 sts, p4, k2.
10th and 12th rows: *P4, k4; rep from * to end.
14th and 16th rows: P2, *k4, p4; rep from * to last 6 sts, k4, p2.
Rep these 16 rows.

Purled Ladder Stitch

Multiple of 4 + 2

1st and 2nd rows: Knit.
3rd row (right side): P2, *k2, p2; rep from * to end.
4th row: K2, *p2, k2; rep from * to end.
5th and 6th rows: Knit.
7th row: As 4th row.
8th row: P2, *k2, p2; rep from * to end.
Rep these 8 rows.

Tile Stitch

Moss Diamonds

Multiple of 6 + 4

1st row (right side): K4, *p2, k4; rep from * to end.
2nd row: P4, *k2, p4; rep from * to end.
Rep the last 2 rows twice more.
7th row: As 2nd row.
8th row: K4, *p2, k4; rep from * to end.
Rep these 8 rows.

Multiple of 10 + 7

1st row (right side): *[K3, p1] twice, k1, p1; rep from * to last 7 sts, k3, p1, k3.
2nd row: *[P3, k1] twice, p1, k1; rep from * to last 7 sts, p3, k1, p3.
3rd row: K2, p1, k1, p1, *[k3, p1] twice, k1, p1; rep from * to last 2 sts, k2.
4th row: P2, k1, p1, k1, *[p3, k1] twice, p1, k1; rep from * to last 2 sts, p2.
5th row: [K1, p1] 3 times, *[k2, p1] twice, [k1, p1] twice; rep from * to last st, k1.
6th row: [P1, k1] 3 times, *[p2, k1] twice, [p1, k1] twice; rep from * to last st, p1.
7th row: As 3rd row.
8th row: As 4th row.
9th row: As 1st row.
10th row: As 2nd row.
11th row: K3, p1, *k2 [p1, k1] twice, p1, k2, p1; rep from * to last 3 sts, k3.
12th row: P3, k1, *p2, [k1, p1] twice, k1, p2, k1; rep from * to last 3 sts, p3.
Rep these 12 rows.

Moss Panels

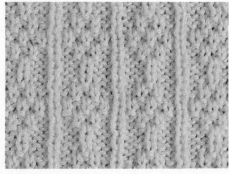

Multiple of 8 + 7

1st row (wrong side): K3, *p1, k3; rep from

---

* to end.
2nd row: P3, *k1, p3; rep from * to end.
3rd row: K2, p1, k1, *[p1, k2] twice, p1, k1; rep from * to last 3 sts, p1, k2.
4th row: P2, k1, p1, *[k1, p2] twice, k1, p1; rep from * to last 3 sts, k1, p2.
5th row: K1, *p1, k1; rep from * to end.
6th row: P1, *k1, p1; rep from * to end.
7th row: As 3rd row.
8th row: As 4th row.
9th row: As 1st row.
10th row: As 2nd row.
Rep these 10 rows.

Woven Stitch

Multiple of 4 + 2

1st row (right side): Knit.
2nd row: Purl.
3rd row: K2, *p2, k2; rep from * to end.
4th row: P2, *k2, p2; rep from * to end.
5th row: Knit.
6th row: Purl.
7th row: As 4th row.
8th row: As 3rd row.
Rep these 8 rows.

Diagonal Rib

Multiple of 4

1st and 2nd rows: *K2, p2; rep from * to end.
3rd row (right side): K1, *p2, k2; rep from * to last 3 sts, p2, k1.
4th row: P1, *k2, p2; rep from * to last 3 sts, k2, p1.
5th and 6th rows: *P2, k2; rep from * to end.
7th row: As 4th row.
8th row: As 3rd row.
Rep these 8 rows.

Knit and Purl Patterns

Unusual Check Pattern

Multiple of 8 sts.
1st row (right side): Knit.
2nd row: *K4, p4; rep from * to end.
3rd row: P1, *k4, p4; rep from * to last 7 sts, k4, p3.
4th row: K2, *p4, k4; rep from * to last 6 sts, p4, k2.
5th row: P3, *k4, p4; rep from * to last 5 sts, k4, p1.
6th row: *P4, k4; rep from * to end.
7th row: Knit.
8th row: *K4, p4; rep from * to end.
Rep the last row 3 times more.
12th row: Purl.
13th row: As 6th row.
14th row: K1, *p4, k4; rep from * to last 7 sts, p4, k3.
15th row: P2, *k4, p4; rep from * to last 6 sts, k4, p2.
16th row: K3, *p4, k4; rep from * to last 5 sts, p4, k1.
17th row: As 2nd row.
18th row: Purl.
19th row: *P4, k4; rep from * to end.
Rep the last row 3 times more.
Rep these last 22 rows.

Horizontal Dash Stitch

Multiple of 10 + 6
1st row (right side): P6, *k4, p6; rep from * to end.
2nd and every alt row: Purl.
3rd row: Knit.
5th row: P1, *k4, p6; rep from * to last 5 sts, k4, p1.
7th row: Knit.
8th row: Purl.
Rep these 8 rows.

Diamond Panels

Multiple of 8 + 1
1st row (right side): Knit.
2nd row: K1, *p7, k1; rep from * to end.
3rd row: K4, *p1, k7; rep from * to last 5 sts, p1, k4.
4th row: K1, *p2, k1, p1, k1, p2, k1; rep from * to end.
5th row: K2, *[p1, k1] twice, p1, k3; rep from * to last 7 sts, [p1, k1] twice, p1, k2.
6th row: As 4th row.
7th row: As 3rd row.
8th row: As 2nd row.
Rep these 8 rows.

Enlarged Basket Stitch

Multiple of 18 + 10
1st row (right side): K11, *p2, k2, p2, k12; rep from * to last 17sts, p2, k2, p2, k11.
2nd row: P1, *k8, [p2, k2] twice, p2; rep from * to last 9 sts, k8, p1.
3rd row: K1, *p8, [k2, p2] twice, k2; rep from * to last 9 sts, p8, k1.
4th row: P11, *k2, p2, k2, p12; rep from * to last 17 sts, k2, p2, k2, p11.
Rep the last 4 rows once more.
9th row: Knit.
10th row: [P2, k2] twice, p12, *k2, p2, k2, p12; rep from * to last 8 sts, [k2, p2] twice.
11th row: [K2, p2] twice, k2, *p8, [k2, p2] twice, k2; rep from * to end.
12th row: [P2, k2] twice, p2, *k8, [p2, k2] twice, p2; rep from * to end.
13th row: [K2, p2] twice, k12, *p2, k2, p2, k12; rep from * to last 8 sts, [p2, k2] twice.
Rep the last 4 rows once more
18th row: Purl.
Rep these 18 rows.

Chevron

Multiple of 8 + 1
1st row (right side): K1, *p7, k1; rep from * to end.
2nd row: P1, *k7, p1; rep from * to end.
3rd row: K2, *p5, k3; rep from * to last 7 sts, p5, k2.
4th row: P2, *k5, p3; rep from * to last 7 sts, k5, p2.
5th row: K3, *p3, k5; rep from * to last 6 sts, p3, k3.
6th row: P3, *k3, p5; rep from * to last 6 sts, k3, p3.
7th row: K4, *p1, k7; rep from * to last 5 sts, p1, k4.
8th row: P4, *k1, p7; rep from * to last 5 sts, k1, p4.
9th row: As 2nd row.
10th row: As 1st row.
11th row: As 4th row.
12th row: As 3rd row.
13th row: As 6th row.
14th row: As 5th row.
15th row: As 8th row.
16th row: As 7th row.
Rep these 16 rows.

Large Basket Weave

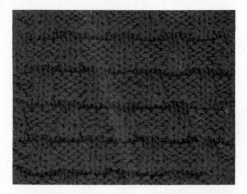

Multiple of 6 + 2
1st row (right side): Knit.
2nd row: Purl.
3rd row: K2, *p4, k2; rep from * to end.
4th row: P2, *k4, p2; rep from * to end.
Rep the last 2 rows once more.
7th row: Knit.
8th row: Purl.
9th row: P3, *k2, p4; rep from * to last 5 sts, k2, p3.

10th row: K3, *p2, k4; rep from * to last 5 sts, p2, k3.
Rep the last 2 rows once more.
Rep these 12 rows.

Tweed Pattern

Multiple of 6+3
1st row (right side): K3, *p3, k3; rep from * to end.
Rep the last row twice more.
4th row: Knit.
5th row: Purl.
6th row: Knit.
7th row: K3, *p3, k3; rep from * to end.
Rep the last row twice more.
10th row: Purl.
11th row: Knit.
12th row: Purl.
Rep these 12 rows.

Pyramids

Multiple of 8+1
1st row (wrong side): P1, *k1, p1; rep from * to end.
2nd row: K1, *p1, k1; rep from * to end.
Rep these 2 rows once more.
5th row: P2, *[k1, p1] twice, k1, p3; rep from * to last 7 sts, [k1, p1] twice, k1, p2.
6th row: K2, *[p1, k1] twice, p1, k3; rep from * to last 7 sts, [p1, k1] twice, p1, k2.
Rep the last 2 rows once more.
9th row: P3, *k1, p1, k1, p5; rep from *

to last 6 sts, k1, p1, k1, p3.
10th row: K3, *p1, k1, p1, k5; rep from * to last 6 sts, p1, k1, p1, k3.
Rep the last 2 rows once more.
13th row: P4, *k1, p7; rep from * to last 5 sts, k1, p4.
14th row: K4, *p1, k7; rep from * to last 5 sts, p1, k4.
Rep the last 2 rows once more.
Rep these 16 rows.

Spaced Checks

Multiple of 10+1
1st row (wrong side): Purl.
2nd row: K4, *p3, k7; rep from * to last 7 sts, p3, k4.
3rd row: P4, *k3, k7; rep from * to last 7 sts, k3, p4.
4th row: As 2nd row.
5th row: Purl.
6th row: Knit.
7th row: K2, *p7, k3; rep from * to last 9 sts, p7, k2.
8th row: P2, *k7, p3; rep from * to last 9 sts, k7, p2.
9th row: As 7th row.
10th row: Knit.
Rep these 10 rows.

Close Checks

Multiple of 6+3
1st row (right side): K3, *p3, k3; rep from * to end.
2nd row: P3, *k3, p3; rep from * to end.
Rep the last 2 rows once more.
5th row: As 2nd row.
6th row: As 1st row.
Rep the last 2 rows once more.
Rep these 8 rows.

Squares

Multiple of 10+2
1st row (right side): Knit.
2nd row: Purl.
3rd row: K2, *p8, k2; rep from * to end.
4th row: P2, *k8, p2; rep from * to end.
5th row: K2, *p2, k4, p2, k2; rep from * to end.
6th row: P2, *k2, p4, k2, p2; rep from * to end.
Rep the last 2 rows twice more.
11th row: As 3rd row.
12th row: As 4th row.
Rep these 12 rows.

Elongated Chevron

Multiple of 18+1
1st row (right side): P1, *[k2, p2] twice, k1, [p2, k2] twice, p1; rep from * to end.
2nd row: K1, *[p2, k2] twice, p1, [k2, p2] twice, k1; rep from * to end.
Rep the last 2 rows once more.
5th row: [P2, k2] twice, *p3, k2, p2, k2; rep from * to last 2 sts, p2.
6th row: [K2, p2] twice, *k3, p2, k2, p2; rep from * to last 2 sts, k2.
Rep the last 2 rows once more.
9th row: As 2nd row.
10th row: As 1st row.
11th row: As 2nd row.
12th row: As 1st row.
13th row: As 6th row.
14th row: As 5th row.
15th row: As 6th row.
16th row: As 5th row.
Rep these 16 rows.

Knit and Purl Patterns

Chequerboard

Multiple of 8+4
1st row: K4, *p4, k4; rep from * to end.
2nd row: P4, *k4, p4; rep from * to end.
Rep the last 2 rows once more.
5th row: As 2nd row.
6th row: As 1st row.
Rep the last 2 rows once more.
Rep these 8 rows.

Top Hat Pattern

Multiple of 6+4
1st row (right side): K4, *p2, k4; rep from * to end.
2nd row: P4, *k2, p4; rep from * to end.
Rep the last 2 rows once more.
5th row: P1, k2, *p4, k2; rep from * to last st, p1.
6th row: K1, p2, *k4, p2; rep from * to last st, k1.
Rep the last 2 rows once more.
9th row: Purl.
10th row: Knit.
Rep these 10 rows.

King Charles Brocade

Multiple of 12+1
1st row (right side): K1, *p1, k9, p1, k1; rep from * to end.
2nd row: K1, p1, k1, *p7, [k1, p1] twice, k1; rep from * to last 10 sts, p7, k1, p1, k1.
3rd row: [K1, p1] twice, *k5, [p1, k1] 3 times, p1; rep from * to last 9 sts, k5, [p1, k1] twice.
4th row: P2, *k1, p1, k1, p3; rep from * to last 5 sts, k1, p1, k1, p2.
5th row: K3, *[p1, k1] 3 times, p1, k5; rep from * to last 10 sts, [p1, k1] 3 times, p1, k3.
6th row: P4, *[k1, p1] twice, k1, p7; rep from * to last 9 sts, [k1, p1] twice, k1, p4.
7th row: K5, *p1, k1, p1, k9; rep from * to last 8 sts, p1, k1, p1, k5.
8th row: As 6th row.
9th row: As 5th row.
10th row: As 4th row.
11th row: As 3rd row.
12th row: As 2nd row.
Rep these 12 rows.

Fancy Chevron

Multiple of 22+1
1st row (right side): K1, *p3, [k1,p1] twice, k1, p5, k1, [p1, k1] twice, p3, k1; rep from * to end.
2nd row: P2, *k3, [p1, k1] twice, p1, k3, p1, [k1, p1] twice, k3, p3; rep from * to last 21 sts, k3, [p1, k1] twice, p1, k3, p1, [k1, p1] twice, k3, p2.
3rd row: K3, *p3, [k1, p1] 5 times, k1, p3, k5; rep from * to last 20 sts, p3, [k1, p1] 5 times, k1, p3, k3.
4th row: K1, *p3, k3, [p1, k1] 4 times, p1, k3, p3, k1; rep from * to end.
5th row: P2, *k3, p3, [k1, p1] 3 times, k1, p3, k3, p3; rep from * to last 21 sts, k3, p3, [k1, p1] 3 times, k1, p3, k3, p2.
6th row: K3, *p3, k3, [p1, k1] twice, p1, k3, p3, k5; rep from * to last 20 sts, p3, k3, [p1, k1] twice, p1, k3, p3, k3.
7th row: K1, *p3, k3, p3, k1, p1, k1, p3, k3, p3, k1; rep from * to end.
8th row: K1, *[p1, k3, p3, k3] twice, p1, k1; rep from * to end.
9th row: K1, *p1, k1, p3, k3, p5, k3, p3, k1, p1, k1; rep from * to end.
10th row: K1, *p1, k1, p1, [k3, p3] twice, k3, [p1, k1] twice; rep from * to end.
11th row: K1, [p1, k1] twice, p3, k3, p1, k3, p3, *[k1, p1] 4 times, k1, p3, k3, p1, k3, p3; rep from * to last 5 sts, [k1, p1] twice, k1.
12th row: K1, [p1, k1] twice, p1, k3, p5, k3, *[p1, k1] 5 times, p1, k3, p5, k3; rep from * to last 6 sts, [p1, k1] 3 times.

13th row: P2, *[k1, p1] twice, k1, p3, k3, p3, [k1, p1] twice, k1, p3; rep from * to last 21 sts, [k1, p1] twice, k1, p3, k3, p3, [k1, p1] twice, k1, p2.
14th row: K3, *[p1, k1] twice, [p1, k3] twice, [p1, k1] twice, p1, k5; rep from * to last 20 sts, [p1, k1] twice, [p1, k3] twice, [p1, k1] twice, p1, k3.
Rep these 14 rows.

Dotted Chevron

Multiple of 18 sts.
1st row (right side): K8, *p2, k16; rep from * to last 10 sts, p2, k8.
2nd row: P7, *k4, p14; rep from * to last 11 sts, k4, p7.
3rd row: P1, *k5, p2, k2, p2, k5, p2; rep from * to last 17 sts, k5, p2, k2, p2, k5, p1.
4th row: K2, *p3, k2, p4, k2, p3, k4; rep from * to last 16 sts, p3, k2, p4, k2, p3, k2.
5th row: P1, *k3, p2, k6, p2, k3, p2; rep from * to last 17 sts, k3, p2, k6, p2, k3, p1.
6th row: P3, *k2 [p3, k2] twice, p6; rep from * to last 15 sts, k2, [p3, k2] twice, p3.
7th row: K2, *p2, k3, p4, k3, p2, k4; rep from * to last 16 sts, p2, k3, p4, k3, p2, k2.
8th row: P1, *k2, [p5, k2] twice, p2; rep from * to last 17 sts, k2, [p5, k2] twice, p1.
9th row: P2, *k14, p4; rep from * to last 16 sts, k14, p2.
10th row: K1, *p16, k2; rep from * to last 17 sts, p16, k1.
Rep these 10 rows.

Zigzag Stitch

Multiple of 6 sts.

1st row (right side): *K3, p3; rep from * to end.

2nd and every alt row: Purl.

3rd row: P1, *k3, p3; rep from * to last 5 sts, k3, p2.

5th row: P2, *k3, p3; rep from * to last 4 sts, k3, p1.

7th row: *P3, k3; rep from * to end.

9th row: As 5th row.

11th row: As 3rd row.

12th row: Purl.

Rep these 12 rows.

Fancy Diamond Pattern

Multiple of 15 sts.

1st row (right side): K1, *p13, k2; rep from * to last 14 sts, p13, k1.

2nd row: P2, *k11, p4; rep from * to last 13 sts, k11, p2.

3rd row: K3, *p9, k6; rep from * to last 12 sts, p9, k3.

4th row: P4, *k7, p8; rep from * to last 11 sts, k7, p4.

5th row: K5, *p5, k10; rep from * to last 10 sts, p5, k5.

6th row: K1, *p5, k3, p5, k2; rep from * to last 14 sts, p5, k3, p5, k1.

7th row: P2, *k5, p1, k5, p4; rep from * to last 13 sts, k5, p1, k5, p2.

8th row: As 3rd row.

9th row: As 7th row.

10th row: As 6th row.

11th row: As 5th row.

12th row: As 4th row.

13th row: As 3rd row.

14th row: As 2nd row.

Rep these 14 rows.

Repeating Diamonds

Multiple of 22 + 1

1st row (right side): K2, *p2, k2, p1, k3, p1, k1, p1, k3, p1, k2, p2, k3; rep from * to last 21 sts, p2, k2, p1, k3, p1, k1, p1, k3, p1, k2, p2, k2.

2nd row: P2, *k2, p2, k5, p1, k5, p2, k2, p3; rep from * to last 21 sts, k2, p2, k5, p1, k5, p2, k2, p2.

Rep the last 2 rows once more.

5th row: K1, *p2, k2, [p1, k3] 3 times, p1, k2, p2, k1; rep from * to end.

6th row: P1, *k2, p2, k5, p3, k5, p2, k2, p1; rep from * to end.

Rep the last 2 rows once more.

9th row: P2, *k2, p1, k3, [p1, k2] twice, p1, k3, p1, k2, p3; rep from * to last 21 sts, k2, p1, k3, [p1, k2] twice, p1, k3, p1, k2, p2.

10th row: K2, *p2, k5, p2, k1, p2, k5, p2, k3; rep from * to last 21 sts, p2, k5, p2, k1, p2, k5, p2, k2.

Rep the last 2 rows once more.

13th row: P1, *k2, p1, k3, p1, k2, p3, k2, p1, k3, p1, k2, p1; rep from * to end.

14th row: K1, *p2, k5, p2, k3, p2, k5, p2, k1; rep from * to end.

Rep the last 2 rows once more.

17th row: K2, *p1, k3, p1, k2, p2, k1, p2, k2, p1, k3, p1, k3; rep from * to last 21 sts, p1, k3, p1, k2, p2, k1, p2, k2, p1, k3, p1, k2.

18th row: P2, *k5, p2, k2, p1, k2, p2, k5, p3; rep from * to last 21 sts, k5, p2, k2, p1, k2, p2, k5, p2.

Rep the last 2 rows once more.

21st row: K1, *p1, k3, p1, k2, p2, k3, p2, k2, p1, k3, p1, k1; rep from * to end.

22nd row: P1, *k5, p2, k2, p3, k2, p2, k5, p1; rep from * to end.

Rep the last 2 rows once more.

25th to 28th rows: Work 17th and 18th rows twice.

29th to 32nd rows: Work 13th and 14th rows twice.

33rd to 36th rows: Work 9th and 10th rows twice.

37th to 40th rows: Work 5th and 6th rows twice.

Rep these 40 rows.

Parallelogram Check

Multiple of 10 sts.

1st row (right side): *K5, p5; rep from * to end.

2nd row: K4, *p5, k5; rep from * to last 6 sts, p5, k1.

3rd row: P2, *k5, p5; rep from * to last 8 sts, k5, p3.

4th row: K2, *p5, k5; rep from * to last 8 sts, p5, k3.

5th row: P4, *k5, p5; rep from * to last 6 sts, k5, p1.

6th row: *P5, k5; rep from * to end.

Rep these 6 rows.

Wavy Rib

Multiple of 6 + 2

1st row (right side): P2, *k4, p2; rep from * to end.

2nd row: K2, *p4, k2; rep from * to end.

Rep the last 2 rows once more.

5th row: K3, p2, *k4, p2; rep from * to last 3 sts, k3.

6th row: P3, k2, *p4, k2; rep from * to last 3 sts, p3.

Rep the last 2 rows once more.

Rep these 8 rows.

Diamond Brocade

Multiple of 8 + 1

1st row (right side): K4, *p1, k7; rep from * to last 5 sts, p1, k4.

2nd row: P3, *k1, p1, k1, p5; rep from * to last 6 sts, k1, p1, k1, p3.

3rd row: K2, *p1, k3; rep from * to last 3 sts, p1, k2.

4th row: P1, *k1, p5, k1, p1; rep from * to end.

5th row: *P1, k7; rep from * to last st, p1.

6th row: As 4th row.

7th row: As 3rd row.

8th row: As 2nd row.

Rep these 8 rows.

Knit and Purl Patterns

Textured Stripe

Multiple of 3 sts.
1st row (right side): Knit.
2nd row: Purl.
Rep the last 2 rows once more.
5th row: K1, *p1, k2; rep from * to last 2 sts, p1, k1.
6th row: P1, *k1, p2; rep from * to last 2 sts, k1, p1.
Rep the last 2 rows once more.
9th row: *P2, k1; rep from * to end.
10th row: *P1, k2; rep from * to end.
Rep the last 2 rows once more.
Rep these 12 rows.

Check Pattern

Multiple of 3 + 1
1st row (right side): Knit.
2nd row: Purl.
3rd row: K1, *p2, k1; rep from * to end.
4th row: Purl.
Rep these 4 rows.

Banded Basket Stitch

Multiple of 9 + 6
1st row (right side): P6, *k3, p6; rep from * to end.
2nd row: K6, *p3, k6; rep from * to end.
Rep the last 2 rows twice more.
7th row: As 2nd row.
8th row: P6, *k3, p6; rep from * to end.
Rep the last 2 rows once more.
Rep these 10 rows.

Chevron Rib

Multiple of 12 + 1
1st row (right side): P2, k2, p2, k1, p2, k2, *p3, k2, p2, k1, p2, k2; rep from * to last 2 sts, p2.
2nd row: K2, p2, k2, p1, k2, p2, *k3, p2, k2, p1, k2, p2; rep from * to last 2 sts, k2.
3rd row: P1, *k2, p2, k3, p2, k2, p1; rep from * to end.
4th row: K1, *p2, k2, p3, k2, p2, k1; rep from * to end.
5th row: As 2nd row.
6th row: P2, k2, p2, k1, p2, k2, *p3, k2, p2, k1, p2, k2; rep from * to last 2 sts, p2.
7th row: As 4th row.
8th row: As 3rd row.
Rep these 8 rows.

Broken Diagonal Check

Multiple of 8
1st row (right side): *K6, p2; rep from * to end.
2nd row: P1, * k2, p6; rep from * last 7 sts, k2, p5.
3rd row: K4, * p2, k6; rep from * to last 4 sts, p2, k2.
4th row: P3, *k2, p6; rep from * to last 5 sts, k2, p3.
5th row: K2, *p2, k6; rep from * to last 6 sts, p2, k4.
6th row: P5, *k2, p6; rep from * to last 3 sts, k2, p1. **7th row**: Purl.
8th row: K1, *p6, k2; rep from * to last 7 sts, p6, k1.

9th row: As 3rd row.
10th row: As 4th row.
11th row: As 5th row.
12th row: As 6th row.
13th row: *P2, k6; rep from * to end.
14th row: Knit.
Rep these 14 rows.

Pennant Stitch

Multiple of 5
1st row (right side): Knit.
2nd row: *K1, p4; rep from * to end.
3rd row: *K3, p2; rep from * to end.
4th row: As 3rd row.
5th row: As 2nd row.
Knit 2 rows.
8th row: *P4, k1; rep from * to end.
9th row: *P2, k3; rep from * to end.
10th row: As 9th row.
11th row: As 8th row.
12th row: Knit.
Rep these 12 rows.

Diagonal Seed Stitch

Multiple of 6
1st row (right side): *K5, p1; rep from * to end.
2nd row: P1, *k1, p5; rep from * to last 5 sts, k1, p4.
3rd row: K3, *p1, k5; rep from * to last 3 sts, p1, k2.
4th row: P3, *k1, p5; rep from * to last 3 sts, k1, p2.
5th row: K1, *p1, k5; rep from * to last 5 sts, p1, k4.
6th row: *P5, k1; rep from * to end.
Rep these 6 rows.

Piqué Triangles

Multiple of 5
1st row (right side): *P1, k4; rep from * to end.
2nd row: *P3, k2; rep from * to end.
3rd row: As 2nd row.
4th row: *P1, k4; rep from * to end.
Rep these 4 rows.

Mosaic Stitch

Multiple of 10 + 7
1st row (right side): P3, *k1, p3, k1, p1, k1, p3; rep from * to last 4 sts, k1, p3.
2nd row: K3, *p1, k3, p1, k1, p1, k3; rep from * to last 4 sts, p1, k3.
Rep the last 2 rows once more.
5th row: P2, *k1, p1, k1, p3, k1, p3; rep from * to last 5 sts, k1, p1, k1, p2.
6th row: K2, *p1, k1, p1, k3, p1, k3; rep from * to last 5 sts, p1, k1, p1, k2.
Rep the last 2 rows once more.
Rep these 8 rows.

Embossed Diamonds

Multiple of 10 + 3
1st row (right side): P1, k1, p1, *[k3, p1] twice, k1, p1; rep from * to end.
2nd row: P1, k1, *p3, k1, p1, k1, p3, k1; rep from * to last st, p1.
3rd row: K4, *[p1, k1] twice, p1, k5; rep from * to last 9 sts, [p1, k1] twice, p1, k4.
4th row: P3, *[k1, p1] 3 times, k1, p3; rep from * to end
5th row: As 3rd row.
6th row: As 2nd row.
7th row: As 1st row.
8th row: P1, k1, p1, *k1, p5, [k1, p1] twice; rep from * to end.
9th row: [P1, k1] twice, *p1, k3, [p1, k1] 3 times; rep from * to last 9 sts, p1, k3, [p1, k1] twice, p1.
10th row: As 8th row.
Rep these 10 rows.

Moss Stitch Parallelograms

Multiple of 10
1st row (right side): *K5, [p1, k1] twice, p1; rep from * to end.
2nd row: [P1, k1] 3 times, *p5, [k1, p1] twice, k1; rep from * to last 4 sts, p4.
3rd row: K3, *[p1, k1] twice, p1, k5; rep from * to last 7 sts, [p1, k1] twice, p1, k2.
4th row: P3, *[k1, p1] twice, k1, p5; rep from * to last 7 sts, [k1, p1] twice, k1, p2.
5th row: [K1, p1] 3 times, *k5, [p1, k1] twice, p1; rep from * to last 4 sts, k4.
6th row: Purl.
Rep these 6 rows.

Plain Diamonds

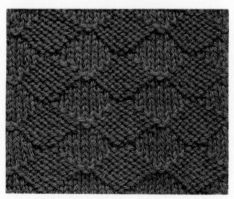

Multiple of 9
1st row (right side): K4, *p1, k8; rep from * to last 5 sts, p1, k4.

2nd row: P3, *k3, p6; rep from * to last 6 sts, k3, p3.
3rd row: K2, *p5, k4; rep from * to last 7 sts, p5, k2.
4th row: P1, *k7, p2; rep from * to last 8 sts, k7, p1.
5th row: Purl.
6th row: As 4th row.
7th row: As 3rd row.
8th row: As 2nd row.
Rep these 8 rows.

Triangle Ribs

Multiple of 8
1st row (right side): *P2, k6; rep from * to end.
2nd row: *P6, k2; rep from * to end.
3rd row: *P3, k5; rep from * to end.
4th row: *P4, k4; rep from * to end.
5th row: *P5, k3; rep from * to end.
6th row: *P2, k6; rep from * to end.
7th row: *P7, k1; rep from * to end.
8th row: *P2, k6; rep from * to end.
9th row: As 5th row.
10th row: As 4th row.
11th row: As 3rd row.
12th row: As 2nd row.
Rep these 12 rows.

Garter Stitch Ridges

Any number of stitches
1st row (right side): Knit.
2nd row: Purl.
Rep the last 2 rows once more.
Purl 6 rows.
Rep these 10 rows.

Knit and Purl Patterns

Moss Stitch Zigzag

Multiple of 9

1st row (right side): *[K1, p1] twice, k4, p1; rep from * to end.

2nd row: *P4, [k1, p1] twice, k1; rep from * to end.

3rd row: [K1, p1] 3 times, *k4, [p1, k1] twice, p1; rep from * to last 3 sts, k3.

4th row: P2,*[k1, p1] twice, k1, p4; rep from * to last 7 sts, [k1, p1] twice, k1, p2.

5th row: K3, *[p1, k1] twice, p1, k4; rep from * to last 6 sts, [p1, k1] 3 times.

6th row: *[K1, p1] twice, k1, p4; rep from * to end.

7th row: As 5th row.

8th row: As 4th row.

9th row: As 3rd row.

10th row: As 2nd row.

Rep these 10 rows.

Moss Stitch Triangles

Multiple of 8

1st row (right side): *P1, k7; rep from * to end.

2nd row: P6, *k1, p7; rep from * to last 2 sts, k1, p1.

3rd row: *P1, k1, p1, k5; rep from * to end

4th row: P4, *k1, p1, k1, p5; rep from * to last 4 sts, [k1, p1] twice.

5th row: *[P1, k1] twice, p1, k3; rep from * to end.

6th row: P2, *[k1, p1] twice, k1, p3; rep from * to last 6 sts, [k1, p1] 3 times.

7th row: *P1, k1; rep from * to end.

8th row: As 6th row.

9th row: As 5th row.

10th row: As 4th row.

11th row: As 3rd row.

12th row: As 2nd row.

Rep these 12 rows.

Hexagon Stitch

Multiple of 10 + 1

1st row (right side): Knit.

2nd row: Purl.

3rd row: K4, *p1, k1, p1, k7; rep from * to last 7 sts, p1, k1, p1, k4.

4th row: P3, *[k1, p1] twice, k1, p5; rep from * to last 8 sts, [k1, p1] twice, k1, p3.

5th row: K2, *[p1, k1] 3 times, p1, k3; rep from * to last 9 sts, [p1, k1] 3 times, p1, k2.

Rep the last 2 rows once more.

8th row: As 4th row.

9th row: As 3rd row.

10th row: Purl.

11th row: Knit.

12th row: Purl.

13th row: K1, p1, *k7, p1, k1, p1; rep from * to last 9 sts, k7, p1, k1.

14th row: K1, p1, k1, *p5, [k1, p1] twice, k1; rep from * to last 8 sts, p5, k1, p1, k1.

15th row: [K1, p1] twice, *k3, [p1, k1] 3 times, p1; rep from * to last 7 sts, k3, [p1, k1] twice.

Rep the last 2 rows once more.

18th row: As 14th row.

19th row: As 13th row.

20th row: Purl.

Rep these 20 rows.

Chevron Stripes

Multiple of 18 + 9

1st row (right side): P4, k1, p4, *k4, p1, k4, p4, k1, p4; rep from * to end.

2nd row: K3, *p3, k3; rep from * to end.

3rd row: P2, k5, p2, *k2, p5, k2, p2, k5, p2; rep from * to end.

4th row: K1, p7, k1, *p1, k7, p1, k1, p7, k1; rep from * to end.

5th row: K4, p1, k4, *p4, k1, p4, k4, p1, k4; rep from * to end.

6th row: P3, *k3, p3; rep from * to end.

7th row: K2, p5, k2, *p2, k5, p2, k2, p5, k2; rep from * to end.

8th row: P1, k7, p1, *k1, p7, k1, p1, k7, p1; rep from * to end.

Rep these 8 rows.

Moss Stitch Squares

Multiple of 12 + 3

1st row (right side): Knit.

2nd row: Purl.

3rd row: K4, *[p1, k1] 3 times, p1, k5; rep from * to last 11 sts, [p1, k1] 3 times, p1, k4.

4th row: P3, *[k1, p1] 4 times, k1, p3; rep from * to end.

5th row: K4, *p1, k5; rep from * to last 5 sts, p1, k4.

6th row: P3, *k1, p7, k1, p3; rep from * to end.

Rep the last 2 rows twice more, then the 5th row again.

12th row: As 4th row.

13th row: As 3rd row.

14th row: Purl.

Rep these 14 rows.

Moss Stitch Panes

Multiple of 10 + 3

1st row (right side): P1, *k1, p1; rep from * to end.

2nd row: P1, *k1, p1; rep from * to end.

3rd row: P1, k1, p1, *k7, p1, k1, p1; rep from * to end.

4th row: P1, k1, p9, *k1, p9; rep from * to last 2 sts, k1, p1.

Rep the last 2 rows 3 times more.

Rep these 10 rows.

Moss Stitch Diagonal

Multiple of 8 + 3

1st row (right side): K4, *p1, k1, p1, k5; rep from * to last 7 sts, p1, k1, p1, k4.

2nd row: P3, *[k1, p1] twice, k1, p3; rep from * to end.

3rd row: K2, *p1, k1, p1, k5; rep from * to last st, p1.

4th row: P1, k1, *p3, [k1, p1] twice, k1; rep from * to last st, p1.

5th row: *P1, k1, p1, k5; rep from * to last 3 sts, p1, k1, p1.

6th row: *[P1, k1] twice, p3, k1; rep from * to last 3 sts, p1, k1, p1.

7th row: P1, *k5, p1, k1, p1; rep from * to last 2 sts, k2.

8th row: [P1, k1] 3 times, *p3, [k1, p1] twice, k1; rep from * to last 5 sts, p3, k1, p1.

Rep these 8 rows.

Garter Stitch Triangles

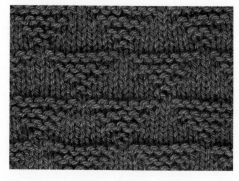

Multiple of 8 + 1

1st row (right side): P1, *k7, p1; rep from * to end.

2nd row and every alt row: Purl.

3rd row: P2, *k5, p3; rep from * to last 7 sts, k5, p2.

5th row: P3, *k3, p5; rep from * to last 6 sts, k3, p3.

7th row: P4, *k1, p7; rep from * to last 5 sts, k1, p4.

9th row: K4, *p1, k7; rep from * to last 5 sts, p1, k4.

11th row: K3, *p3, k5; rep from * to last 6 sts, p3, k3.

13th row: K2, *p5, k3; rep from * to last 7 sts, p5, k2.

15th row: K1, *p7, k1; rep from * to end.

16th row: Purl.

Rep these 16 rows.

Seed Stitch Checks

Multiple of 10 + 5

1st row (right side): K5, *[p1, k1] twice, p1, k5; rep from * to end.

2nd row: P6, *k1, p1, k1, p7; rep from * to last 9 sts, k1, p1, k1, p6.

Rep the last 2 rows once more then the 1st row again.

6th row: *[K1, p1] twice, k1, p5; rep from * to last 5 sts, [k1, p1] twice, k1.

7th row: [K1, p1] twice, *k7, p1, k1, p1; rep from * to last st, k1.

Rep the last 2 rows once more then the 6th row again.

Rep these 10 rows.

Purl Triangles

Multiple of 8 + 1

1st row (right side): K1, *p7, k1; rep from * to end.

2nd row: P1, *k7, p1; rep from * to end.

3rd row: K2, *p5, k3; rep from * to last 7 sts, p5, k2.

4th row: P2, *k5, p3; rep from * to last 7 sts, k5, p2.

5th row: K3, *p3, k5; rep from * to last 6 sts, p3, k3.

6th row: P3, *k3, p5; rep from * to last 6 sts, k3, p3.

7th row: K4, *p1, k7; rep from * to last 5 sts, p1, k4.

8th row: P4, *k1, p7; rep from * to last 5 sts, k1, p4.

9th row: As 8th row.

10th row: As 7th row.

11th row: As 6th row.

12th row: As 5th row.

13th row: As 4th row.

14th row: As 3rd row.

15th row: As 2nd row.

16th row: K1, *p7, k1; rep from * to end.

Rep these 16 rows.

Double Parallelogram Stitch

Multiple of 10

1st row (right side): *P5, k5; rep from * to end.

2nd row: K1, *p5, k5; rep from * to last 9 sts, p5, k4.

3rd row: P3, *k5, p5; rep from * to last 7 sts, k5, p2.

4th row: K3, *p5, k5; rep from * to last 7 sts, p5, k2.

5th row: P1, *k5, p5; rep from * to last 9 sts, k5, p4.

6th row: P4, *k5, p5; rep from * to last 6 sts, k5, p1.

7th row: K2, *p5, k5; rep from * to last 8 sts, p5, k3.

8th row: P2, *k5, p5; rep from * to last 8 sts, k5, p3.

9th row: K4, *p5, k5; rep from * to last 6 sts, p5, k1.

10th row: *K5, p5; rep from * to end.

Rep these 10 rows.

Moss Stitch Diamonds

Multiple of 10 + 9

1st row (right side): K4, *p1, k9; rep from * to last 5 sts, p1, k4.

2nd row: P3, *k1, p1, k1, p7; rep from * to last 6 sts, k1, p1, k1, p3.

3rd row: K2, *[p1, k1] twice, p1, k5; rep from * to last 7 sts, [p1, k1] twice, p1, k2.

4th row: [P1, k1] 4 times, *p3, [k1, p1] 3 times, k1; rep from * to last st, p1.

5th row: P1, *k1, p1; rep from * to end.

6th row: As 4th row.

7th row: As 3rd row.

8th row: As 2nd row.

9th row: As 1st row.

10th row: Purl.

Rep these 10 rows.

Knit and Purl Patterns

Seed Stitch I

Multiple of 4 sts + 3.
1st row (right side): P1, k1, *p3, k1; rep from * to last st, p1.
2nd row: K3, *p1, k3; rep from * to end.
Rep these 2 rows.

Seed Stitch II

Worked as Seed Stitch I, using reverse side as right side.

Banded Rib

Multiple of 2 sts + 1.
1st row (right side): K1, *p1, k1; rep from * to end.
2nd row: P1, *k1, p1; rep from * to end.
Rep the last 2 rows twice more.
7th row: P1, *k1, p1; rep from * to end.
8th row: K1, *p1, k1; rep from * to end.
Rep the last 2 rows twice more.
Rep these 12 rows.

Waffle Stitch

Multiple of 3 sts + 1.
1st row (right side): P1, *k2, p1; rep from * to end.
2nd row: K1, *p2, k1; rep from * to end.
3rd row: As 1st row.
4th row: Knit.
Rep these 4 rows.

Seeded Texture

Multiple of 5 sts + 2.
1st row (right side): K2, *p3, k2; rep from * to end.
2nd row: Purl.
3rd row: *P3, k2; rep from * to last 2 sts, p2.
4th row: Purl.
Rep these 4 rows.

Space Invaders

Multiple of 6 sts + 3.

1st row (right side): K1, p1, k1, *p3, k1, p1, k1; rep from * to end.
2nd row: P3, *k3, p3; rep from * to end.
3rd row: P1, k1, *p5, k1; rep from * to last st, p1.
4th row: K1, p1, *k5, p1; rep from * to last st, k1.
5th row: P3, *k1, p1, k1, p3; rep from * to end.
6th row: K3, *p1, k1, p1, k3; rep from * to end.
7th row: P3, *k3, p3; rep from * to end.
8th row: K4, p1, *k5, p1; rep from * to last 4 sts, k4.
9th row: P4, k1, *p5, k1; rep from * to last 4 sts, p4.
10th row: P1, k1, p1, *k3, p1, k1, p1; rep from * to end.
Rep these 10 rows.

Box and Stripe Pattern

Multiple of 6 sts + 3.
Work 5 rows in garter stitch (1st row is right side).
6th row: K3, *p3, k3; rep from * to end.
7th row: Knit.
8th row: As 6th row.
Work 5 rows in garter stitch.
14th row: P3, *k3, p3; rep from * to end.
15th row: Knit.
16th row: As 14th row.
Rep these 16 rows.

Little Arrows

Mutliple of 8 sts + 1.

1st row (right side): K2, p2, k1, p2, *k3, p2, k1, p2; rep from * to last 2 sts, k2.

2nd row: P3, k1, p1, k1, *p5, k1, p1, k1; rep from * to last 3 sts, p3.

3rd row: K1, *p1, k5, p1, k1; rep from * to end.

4th row: P1, *k2, p3, k2, p1; rep from * to end.

Rep these 4 rows.

Oblong Texture

Multiple of 10 sts + 1.

1st row (right side): K3, p5, *k5, p5; rep from * to last 3 sts, k3.

2nd row: P3, k5, *p5, k5; rep from * to last 3 sts, p3.

3rd row: As 2nd row.

4th row: As 1st row.

Rep these 4 rows.

Basketweave Stitch I

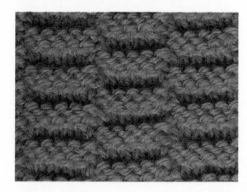

Multiple of 8 sts + 3.

1st row (right side): Knit.

2nd row: K4, p3, *k5, p3; rep from * to last 4 sts, k4.

3rd row: P4, k3, *p5, k3; rep from * to last 4 sts, p4.

4th row: As 2nd row.

5th row: Knit.

6th row: P3, *k5, p3; rep from * to end.

7th row: K3, *p5, k3; rep from * to end.

8th row: As 6th row.

Rep these 8 rows.

Basketweave Stitch II

Worked as Basketweave Stitch I, using reverse side as right side.

Fancy Box Stitch

Multiple of 8 sts + 6.

1st row (right side): K2, *p2, k2; rep from * to end.

2nd row: P2, *k2, p2; rep from * to end.

3rd row: As 1st row.

4th row: K1, p4, *k4, p4; rep from * to last st, k1.

5th row: P1, k4, *p4, k4; rep from * to last st, p1.

6th row: As 4th row.

Rep these 6 rows.

Diagonal Texture

Multiple of 8 sts.

1st row (right side): *K1, p1, k1, p5; rep from * to end.

2nd row: *K5, p1, k1, p1; rep from * to end.

3rd row: *K1, p1, k5, p1; rep from * to end.

4th row: *K1, p5, k1, p1; rep from * to end.

5th row: As 4th row.

6th row: As 3rd row.

7th row: As 2nd row.

8th row: *K1, p1, k1, p5; rep from * to end.

9th row: P4, *k1, p1, k1, p5; rep from * to last 4 sts, [k1, p1] twice.

10th row: [K1, p1] twice, *k5, p1, k1, p1; rep from * to last 4 sts, k4.

11th row: K3, p1, k1, p1, *k5, p1, k1, p1; rep from * to last 2 sts, k2.

12th row: P2, k1, p1, k1, *p5, k1, p1, k1; rep from * to last 3 sts, p3.

13th row: As 12th row.

14th row: As 11th row.

15th row: As 10th row.

16th row: As 9th row.

Rep these 16 rows.

Diamond Web

Multiple of 6 sts + 1.

1st row (right side): P3, *k1, p5; rep from * to last 4 sts, k1, p3.

2nd row: K3, *p1, k5; rep from * to last 4 sts, p1, k3.

Rep these 2 rows once more.

5th row: P2, *k1, p1, k1, p3; rep from * to last 5 sts, k1, p1, k1, p2.

6th row: K2, *p1, k1, p1, k3; rep from * to last 5 sts, p1, k1, p1, k2.

Rep the last 2 rows once more.

9th row: P1, *k1, p3, k1, p1; rep from * to end.

10th row: K1, *p1, k3, p1, k1; rep from * to end.

Rep the last 2 rows once more.

13th row: K1, *p5, k1; rep from * to end.

14th row: P1, *k5, p1; rep from * to end.

Rep the last 2 rows once more.

17th row: As 9th row.

18th row: As 10th row.

Rep the last 2 rows once more.

21st row: As 5th row.

22nd row: As 6th row.

Rep the last 2 rows once more.

Rep these 24 rows.

Knit and Purl Patterns

Knife Pleats

Multiple of 13 sts.
1st row (right side): *K4, [p1, k1] 3 times, p3; rep from * to end.
2nd row: *K3, [p1, k1] 3 times, p4; rep from * to end.
Rep these 2 rows.

Multiple of 6 sts + 1.
1st row (right side): K1, *p2, k1; rep from * to end.
2nd row: P1, *k2, p1; rep from * to end.
Rep the last 2 rows once more.
5th row: K1, *p5, k1; rep from * to end.
6th row: P1, *k5, p1; rep from * to end.
Rep the last 2 rows once more.
9th and 11th rows: As 1st row.
10th and 12th rows: As 2nd row.
13th row: P3, *k1, p3; rep from * to end.
14th row: K3, *p1, k3; rep from * to end.
Rep the last 2 rows once more.
Rep these 16 rows.

2nd row: P1, k2, *p2, k2; rep from * to last st, p1.
3rd row: *P4, k2; rep from * to end.
4th row: *P2, k4; rep from * to end.
5th row: As 2nd row.
6th row: K1, p2, *k2, p2; rep from * to last st, k1.
7th row: *K2, p6, k2, p2; rep from * to end.
8th row: *K2, p2, k6, p2; rep from * to end.
Rep 1st to 6th rows once more.
15th row: [P2, k2] twice, *p6, k2, p2, k2; rep from * to last 4 sts, p4.
16th row: K4, p2, k2, p2, *k6, p2, k2, p2; rep from * to last 2 sts, k2.
Rep these 16 rows.

Vertical Dash Stitch

Multiple of 6 sts + 1.
1st row (right side): P3, k1, *p5, k1; rep from * to last 3 sts, p3.
2nd row: K3, p1, *k5, p1; rep from * to last 3 sts, k3.
Rep the last 2 rows once more.
5th row: K1, *p5, k1; rep from * to end.
6th row: P1, *k5, p1; rep from * to end.
Rep the last 2 rows once more.
Rep these 8 rows.

Fancy Track Pattern

Multiple of 12 sts + 1.
1st row (right side): K3, p3, k1, p3, *k5, p3, k1, p3; rep from * to last 3 sts, k3.
2nd row: K6, p1, *k11, p1; rep from * to last 6 sts, k6.
Rep the last 2 rows once more.
5th row: K3, p2, k1, p1, k1, p2, *k5, p2, k1, p1, k1, p2; rep from * to last 3 sts, k3.
6th row: K5, p1, k1, p1, *k9, p1, k1, p1; rep from * to last 5 sts, k5.
Rep the last 2 rows once more.
Rep these 8 rows.

Random Dash Pattern

Broken Chevron

Multiple of 12 sts.
1st row (right side): K1, p2, *k2, p2; rep from * to last st, k1.

Seed Pearl Grid

Multiple of 8 sts + 1.
1st and every alt row (wrong side): Purl.
2nd row: P1, *k1, p1; rep from * to end.
4th row: Knit.
6th row: P1, *k7, p1; rep from * to end.
8th row: Knit.
10th row: As 6th row.
12th row: Knit.
Rep these 12 rows.

Simple Seed Stitch

Multiple of 4 sts + 1.
1st row (right side): P1, *k3, p1; rep from * to end.
2nd and every alt row: Purl.
3rd row: Knit.
5th row: K2, p1, *k3, p1; rep from * to last 2 sts, k2.
7th row: Knit.

8th row: Purl.
Rep these 8 rows.

Ripple Pattern

Multiple of 8 sts + 6.

1st row (right side): K6, *p2, k6; rep from * to end.

2nd row: K1, *p4, k4; rep from * to last 5 sts, p4, k1.

3rd row: P2, *k2, p2; rep from * to end.

4th row: P1, *k4, p4; rep from * to last 5 sts, k4, p1.

5th row: K2, *p2, k6; rep from * to last 4 sts, p2, k2.

6th row: P6, *k2, p6; rep from * to end.

7th row: As 4th row.

8th row: K2, *p2, k2; rep from * to end.

9th row: As 2nd row.

10th row: P2, *k2, p6; rep from * to last 4 sts, k2, p2.

Rep these 10 rows.

Zigzag Moss Stitch

Multiple of 6 sts + 1.

1st row (right side): Knit.

2nd row: Purl.

3rd row: P1, *k5, p1; rep from * to end.

4th row: P1, *k1, p3, k1, p1; rep from * to end.

5th row: P1, *k1, p1; rep from * to end.

6th row: As 5th row.

7th row: K2, p1, k1, p1, *k3, p1, k1, p1; rep from * to last 2 sts, k2.

8th row: P3, k1, *p5, k1; rep from * to last 3 sts, p3.

9th row: Knit.

10th row: Purl.

11th row: K3, p1, *k5, p1; rep from * to last 3 sts, k3.

12th row: P2, k1, p1, k1, *p3, k1, p1, k1; rep from * to last 2 sts, p2.

13th row: K1, *p1, k1; rep from * to end.

14th row: As 13th row.

15th row: K1, *p1, k3, p1, k1; rep from * to end.

16th row: K1, *p5, k1; rep from * to end.
Rep these 16 rows.

Vertical Zigzag Moss Stitch

Multiple of 7 sts.

1st row (right side): *P1, k1, p1, k4; rep from * to end.

2nd row: *P4, k1, p1, k1; rep from * to end.

3rd row: *[k1, p1] twice, k3; rep from * to end.

4th row: *P3, [k1, p1] twice; rep from * to end.

5th row: K2, p1, k1, p1, *k4, p1, k1, p1; rep from * to last 2 sts, k2.

6th row: P2, k1, p1, k1, *p4, k1, p1, k1; rep from * to last 2 sts, p2.

7th row: K3, p1, k1, p1, *k4, p1, k1, p1; rep from * to last st, k1.

8th row: [P1, k1] twice, *p4, k1, p1, k1; rep from * to last 3 sts, p3.

9th row: *K4, p1, k1, p1; rep from * to end.

10th row: *K1, p1, k1, p4; rep from * to end.

11th and 12th rows: As 7th and 8th rows.

13th and 14th rows: As 5th and 6th rows.

15th and 16th rows: As 3rd and 4th rows.
Rep these 16 rows.

Caterpillar Stitch

Diagonals I

Multiple of 8 sts + 6.

1st row (right side): K4, p2, *k6, p2; rep from * to end.

2nd row: P1, k2, *p6, k2; rep from * to last 3 sts, p3.

3rd row: K2, p2, *k6, p2; rep from * to last 2 sts, k2.

4th row: P3, k2, *p6, k2; rep from * to last st, p1.

5th row: P2, *k6, p2; rep from * to last 4 sts, k4.

6th row: Purl.
Rep these 6 rows.

Multiple of 8 sts + 6.

1st row (right side): P3, *k5, p3; rep from * to last 3 sts, k3.

2nd row: P4, *k3, p5; rep from * to last 2 sts, k2.

3rd row: P1, k5, *p3, k5; rep from * to end.

4th row: K1, p5, *k3, p5; rep from * to end.

5th row: K4, *p3, k5; rep from * to last 2 sts, p2.

6th row: K3, *p5, k3; rep from * to last 3 sts, p3.

7th row: K2, p3, *k5, p3; rep from * to last st, k1.

8th row: P2, k3, *p5, k3; rep from * to last st, p1.
Rep these 8 rows.

Diagonals II

Worked as Diagonals I, using reverse side as right side.

Knit and Purl Patterns

Diamond Pattern

Multiple of 8 sts + 1.

1st row (right side): P1, *k7, p1; rep from * to end.

2nd row: K2, p5, *k3, p5; rep from * to last 2 sts, k2.

3rd row: K1, *p2, k3, p2, k1; rep from * to end.

4th row: P2, k2, p1, k2, *p3, k2, p1, k2; rep from * to last 2 sts, p2.

5th row: K3, p3, *k5, p3; rep from * to last 3 sts, k3.

6th row: P4, k1, *p7, k1; rep from * to last 4 sts, p4.

7th row: As 5th row.

8th row: As 4th row.

9th row: As 3rd row.

10th row: As 2nd row.

Rep these 10 rows.

Slanting Diamonds

Multiple of 10 sts.

1st row (right side): *K9, p1; rep from * to end.

2nd row: *K2, p8; rep from * to end.

3rd row: *K7, p3; rep from * to end.

4th row: *K4, p6; rep from * to end.

5th and 6th rows: *K5, p5; rep from * to end.

7th row: K5, p4, *k6, p4; rep from * to last st, k1.

8th row: P2, k3, *p7, k3; rep from * to last 5 sts, p5.

9th row: K5, p2, *k8, p2; rep from * to last 3 sts, k3.

10th row: P4, k1, *p9, k1; rep from * to last 5 sts, p5.

11th row: K4, p1, *k9, p1; rep from * to last 5 sts, k5.

12th row: P5, k2, *p8, k2; rep from * to last 3 sts, p3.

13th row: K2, p3, *k7, p3; rep from * to last 5 sts, k5.

14th row: P5, k4, *p6, k4; rep from * to last st, p1.

15th and 16th rows: *P5, k5; rep from * to end.

17th row: *P4, k6; rep from * to end.

18th row: *P7, k3; rep from * to end.

19th row: *P2, k8; rep from * to end.

20th row: *P9, k1; rep from * to end.

Rep these 20 rows.

Polperro Laughing Boy

Multiple of 6 sts.

1st row (right side): Knit.

2nd row: P2, k2, *p4, k2; rep from * to last 2 sts, p2.

Rep these 2 rows once more.

Work 4 rows in st st, starting knit.

Rep these 8 rows.

Cross Motif Pattern I

Multiple of 12 sts.

1st row (right side): P1, k10, *p2, k10; rep from * to last st, p1.

2nd row: K1, p10, *k2, p10; rep from * to last st, k1.

Rep the last 2 rows once more.

5th row: P3, k6, *p6, k6; rep from * to last 3 sts, p3.

6th row: K3, p6, *k6, p6; rep from * to last 3 sts, k3.

7th row: As 1st row.

8th row: As 2nd row.

Rep the last 2 rows once more.

11th row: Knit.

12th row: Purl.

13th row: K5, p2, *k10, p2; rep from * to last 5 sts, k5.

14th row: P5, k2, *p10, k2; rep from * to last 5 sts, p5.

Rep the last 2 rows once more.

17th row: K3, p6, *k6, p6; rep from * to last 3 sts, k3.

18th row: P3, k6, *p6, k6; rep from * to last 3 sts, p3.

19th row: K5, p2, *k10, p2; rep from * to last 5 sts, k5.

20th row: P5, k2, *p10, k2; rep from * to last 5 sts, p5.

Rep the last 2 rows once more.

23rd row: Knit.

24th row: Purl.

Rep these 24 rows.

Cross Motif Pattern II

Worked as Cross Motif Pattern I, using reverse side as right side.

Lizard Lattice

Multiple of 6 sts + 3.
Work 4 rows in st st, starting knit (1st row is right side).
5th row: P3, *k3, p3; rep from * to end.
6th row: Purl.
Rep the last 2 rows once more, then 5th row again.
Work 4 rows in st st, starting purl.
14th row: P3, *k3, p3; rep from * to end.
15th row: Knit.
Rep the last 2 rows once more, then 14th row again.
Rep these 18 rows.

Looe Eddystone

Multiple of 11 sts.
1st and every alt row (right side): Knit.
2nd row: P2, k7, *p4, k7; rep from * to last 2 sts, p2.
4th row: P3, k5, *p6, k5; rep from * to last 3 sts, p3.
6th row: P4, k3, *p8, k3; rep from * to last 4 sts, p4.
8th and 10th rows: P5, k1, *p10, k1; rep from * to last 5 sts, p5.
Work 4 rows in st st.
Rep these 14 rows.

Alans Pattern I

Multiple of 8 sts + 4.
1st row (right side) Knit.
2nd row: K4, *p4, k4; rep from * to end.
3rd row: P4, *k4, p4; rep from * to end.
4th row: Knit.
5th row: As 3rd row.

6th row: As 2nd row.
7th row: Knit.
Rep last 3 rows once more.
11th row: As 2nd row.
12th row: As 3rd row.
Rep these 12 rows.

Alans Pattern II

Worked as Alans Pattern I, using reverse side as right side.

Polperro Horizontal Diamonds

Multiple of 12 sts + 1.
Work 3 rows in garter st (1st row is right side).
Work 3 rows in st st, starting purl.
7th row: K6, p1, *k11, p1; rep from * to last 6 sts, k6.
8th row: P5, k1, p1, k1, *p9, k1, p1, k1; rep from * to last 5 sts, p5.
9th row: K4, p1, k3, p1, *k7, p1, k3, p1; rep from * to last 4 sts, k4.
10th row: P3, k1, *p5, k1; rep from * to last 3 sts, p3.
11th row: K2, p1, k7, p1, *k3, p1, k7, p1; rep from * to last 2 sts, k2.
12th row: P1, *k1, p9, k1, p1; rep from * to end.
13th row: P1, *k11, p1; rep from * to end.
14th row: As 12th row.
15th row: As 11th row.
16th row: As 10th row.
17th row: As 9th row.
18th row: As 8th row.

19th row: As 7th row.
Work 3 rows in st st, starting purl.
Rep these 22 rows.

Polperro Musician

Multiple of 23 sts.
1st row (wrong side): K1, p2, k1, [p7, k1] twice, p2, *k2, p2, k1, [p7, k1] twice, p2; rep from * to last st, k1.
2nd row: K10, p1, k1, p1, *k20, p1, k1, p1; rep from * to last 10 sts, k10.
3rd row: P1, k2, p6, k1, p3, k1, p6, k2, *p2, k2, p6, k1, p3, k1, p6, k2; rep from * to last st, p1.
4th row: K8, p1, k5, p1, *k16, p1, k5, p1; rep from * to last 8 sts, k8.
5th row: K1, p6, k1, p7, k1, p6, *k2, p6, k1, p7, k1, p6; rep from * to last st, k1.
6th row: K6, p1, k9, p1, *k12, p1, k9, p1; rep from * to last 6 sts, k6.
7th row: P1, k2, p2, k1, p11, k1, p2, k2, *p2, k2, p2, k1, p11, k1, p2, k2; rep from * to last st, p1.
8th row: K4, p1, k13, p1, *k8, p1, k13, p1; rep from * to last 4 sts, k4.
Rep these 8 rows.

Polperro Northcott

Multiple of 4 sts + 2.
Work 3 rows in garter st (1st row is right side).
4th row: K2, *p2, k2; rep from * to end.
5th row: Knit.
Rep the last 2 rows 10 times more.
Work 2 rows in garter st.
28th row: Purl.
Rep these 28 rows.

Knit and Purl Patterns

Maze Pattern

Multiple of 13 sts.
1st row (right side): Knit.
2nd row: Purl.
3rd row: Knit.
4th row: P1, k11, *p2, k11; rep from * to last st, p1.
5th row: K1, p11, *k2, p11; rep from * to last st, k1.
6th row: As 4th row.
7th row: K1, p2, k7, p2, *k2, p2, k7, p2; rep from * to last st, k1.
8th row: P1, k2, p7, k2, *p2, k2, p7, k2; rep from * to last st, p1.
9th row: As 7th row.
10th row: P1, k2, p2, k3, *[p2, k2] twice, p2, k3; rep from * to last 5 sts, p2, k2, p1.
11th row: K1, p2, k2, p3, *[k2, p2] twice, k2, p3; rep from * to last 5 sts, k2, p2, k1.
Rep the last 2 rows once more.
14th row: As 8th row.
15th row: As 7th row.
16th row: As 8th row.
17th row: As 5th row.
18th row: As 4th row.
19th row: As 5th row.
20th row: As 2nd row.
Rep these 20 rows.

Stripes in Relief

Multiple of 14 sts + 6.
1st row (wrong side): K6, *p3, k2, p3, k6; rep from * to end.
2nd row: P6, *k3, p2, k3, p6; rep from * to end.

3rd row: P9, k2, *p12, k2; rep from * to last 9 sts, p9.
4th row: K9, p2, *k12, p2; rep from * to last 9 sts, k9.
5th row: P2, k2, *p12, k2; rep from * to last 2 sts, p2.
6th row: K2, p2, *k12, p2; rep from * to last 2 sts, k2.
7th row: P2, k2, *p3, k6, p3, k2; rep from * to last 2 sts, p2.
8th row: K2, p2, *k3, p6, k3, p2; rep from * to last 2 sts, k2.
9th row: As 5th row.
10th row: As 6th row.
11th row: As 3rd row.
12th row: As 4th row.
Rep these 12 rows.

Diamond and Lozenge Pattern I

Multiple of 12 sts.
1st row (right side): *K6, p6; rep from * to end.
2nd row: *K6, p6; rep from * to end.
3rd and 4th rows: *P1, k5, p5, k1; rep from * to end.
5th and 6th rows: K1, p1, k4, p4, *[k1, p1] twice, k4, p4; rep from * to last 2 sts, k1, p1.
7th and 8th rows: P1, k1, p1, k3, p3, *[k1, p1] 3 times, k3, p3; rep from * to last 3 sts, k1, p1, k1.
9th and 10th rows: [K1, p1] twice, k2, p2, *[k1, p1] 4 times, k2, p2; rep from * to last 4 sts, [k1, p1] twice.
11th and 12th rows: *P1, k1; rep from * to end.
13th and 14th rows: *K1, p1; rep from * to end.
15th and 16th rows: [P1, k1] twice, p2, k2, *[p1, k1] 4 times, p2, k2; rep from * to last 4 sts, [p1, k1] twice.
17th and 18th rows: K1, p1, k1, p3, k3, *[p1, k1] 3 times, p3, k3; rep from * to last 3 sts, p1, k1, p1.
19th and 20th rows: P1, k1, p4, k4, *[p1, k1] twice, p4, k4; rep from * to last 2 sts, p1, k1.
21st and 22nd rows: *K1, p5, k5, p1; rep from * to end.
23rd and 24th rows: *P6, k6; rep from * to end.

25th and 26th rows: *P5, k1, p1, k5; rep from * to end.
27th and 28th rows: *P4, [k1, p1] twice, k4; rep from * to end.
29th and 30th rows: *P3, [k1, p1] 3 times, k3; rep from * to end.
31st and 32nd rows: *P2, [k1, p1] 4 times, k2; rep from * to end.
33rd and 34th rows: As 11th and 12th rows.
35th and 36th rows: As 13th and 14th rows.
37th and 38th rows: *K2, [p1, k1] 4 times, p2; rep from * to end.
39th and 40th rows: *K3, [p1, k1] 3 times, p3; rep from * to end.
41st and 42nd rows: *K4, [p1, k1] twice, p4; rep from * to end.
43rd and 44th rows: *K5, p1, k1, p5; rep from * to end.
Rep these 44 rows.

Diamond and Lozenge Pattern II

Multiple of 12 sts.
Rep rows 1 to 24 of Diamond and Lozenge Pattern I.

Diamond and Block

Multiple of 14 sts + 5.
1st row (right side): P5, *k4, p1, k4, p5; rep from * to end.

2nd row: K5, *p3, k3, p3, k5; rep from * to end.
3rd row: K7, p5, *k9, p5; rep from * to last 7 sts, k7.
4th row: P6, k7, *p7, k7; rep from * to last 6 sts, p6.
5th row: K5, *p9, k5; rep from * to end.
6th row: As 4th row.
7th row: As 3rd row.
8th row: As 2nd row.
Rep these 8 rows.

Divided Boxes

Multiple of 5 sts.
1st row (right side): Knit.
2nd row: *K1, p4; rep from * to end.
3rd row: *K3, p2; rep from * to end.
4th row: As 3rd row.
5th row: As 2nd row.
6th row: Knit.
Rep these 6 rows.

Staircase Pattern I

Multiple of 16 sts.
1st and 3rd rows (right side): *K5, p11; rep from * to end.
2nd row: *K11, p5; rep from * to end.
4th and 6th rows: Purl.
5th row: Knit.
7th and 9th rows: P4, *k5, p11; rep from

* to last 12 sts, k5, p7.
8th row: K7, *p5, k11; rep from * to last 9 sts, p5, k4.
10th and 12th rows: Purl.
11th row: Knit.
13th and 15th rows: P8, *k5, p11; rep from * to last 8 sts, k5, p3.
14th row: K3, *p5, k11; rep from * to last 13 sts, p5, k8.
16th and 18th rows: Purl.
17th row: Knit.
19th and 21st rows: K1, p11, *k5, p11; rep from * to last 4 sts, k4.
20th row: P4, *k11, p5; rep from * to last 12 sts, k11, p1.
22nd row: Purl.
23rd row: Knit.
24th row: Purl.
Rep these 24 rows.

Staircase Pattern II

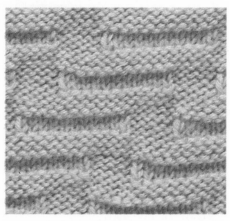

Worked as Staircase Pattern I, using reverse side as right side.

Textured Triangle Stack

Multiple of 10 sts + 1.
1st row (right side): P5, *k1, p9; rep from * to last 6 sts, k1, p5.
2nd row: K5, *p1, k9; rep from * to last 6 sts, p1, k5.
3rd row: P4, *k3, p7; rep from * to last 7 sts, p3, k4.
4th row: K4, *p3, k7; rep from * to last 7 sts, k3, p4.
5th row: P3, *k5, p5; rep from * to last 8 sts, k5, p3.
6th row: K3, *p5, k5; rep from * to last 8 sts, p5, k3.
7th row: P2, *k7, p3; rep from * to last 9 sts, k7, p2.
8th row: K2, *p7, k3; rep from * to last 9 sts, p7, k2.
9th row: P1, *k9, p1; rep from * to end.
10th row: K1, *p9, k1; rep from * to end.
Rep these 10 rows.

Windmill Pattern

Multiple of 20 sts.
1st row (right side): *P1, k9, p9, k1; rep from * to end.
2nd row: *P2, k8, p8, k2; rep from * to end.
3rd row: *P3, k7, p7, k3: rep from * to end.
4th row: *P4, k6, p6, k4; rep from * to end.
5th row: *P5, k5; rep from * to end.
6th row: *P6, k4, p4, k6; rep from * to end.
7th row: *P7, k3, p3, k7; rep from * to end.
8th row: *P8, k2, p2, k8; rep from * to end.
9th row: *P9, k1, p1, k9; rep from * to end.
10th row: *P10, k10; rep from * to end.
11th row: *K10, p10; rep from * to end.
12th row: *K9, p1, k1, p9; rep from * to end.
13th row: *K8, p2, k2, p8; rep from * to end.
14th row: *K7, p3, k3, p7; rep from * to end.
15th row: *K6, p4, k4, p6; rep from * to end.
16th row: *K5, p5; rep from * to end.
17th row: *K4, p6, k6, p4; rep from * to end.
18th row: *K3, p7, k7, p3; rep from * to end.
19th row: *K2, p8, k8, p2; rep from * to end.
20th row: *K1, p9, k9, p1; rep from * to end.
21st row: As 10th row.
22nd row: As 11th row.
Rep these 22 rows.

Knit and Purl Patterns

Flag Pattern I

Multiple of 11 sts.
1st row (right side): *P1, k10; rep from * to end.
2nd row: *P9, k2; rep from * to end.
3rd row: *P3, k8; rep from * to end.
4th row: *P7, k4; rep from * to end.
5th row: *P5, k6; rep from * to end.
6th row: As 5th row.
7th row: As 5th row.
8th row: As 4th row.
9th row: As 3rd row.
10th row: As 2nd row.
11th row: As 1st row.
12th row: *K1, p10; rep from * to end.
13th row: *K9, p2; rep from * to end.
14th row: *K3, p8; rep from * to end.
15th row: *K7, p4; rep from * to end.
16th row: *K5, p6; rep from * to end.
17th row: As 16th row.
18th row: As 16th row.
19th row: As 15th row.
20th row: As 14th row.
21st row: As 13th row.
22nd row: As 12th row.
Rep these 22 rows.

Flag Pattern II

Worked as Flag Pattern I, using reverse side as right side.

Divided Triangles

Multiple of 14 sts + 1.
1st row (wrong side): Knit.
2nd row: Knit.
3rd row: K1, *p13, k1; rep from * to end.
4th row: K1, *p1, k11, p1, k1; rep from * to end.
5th row: P1, *k2, p9, k2, p1; rep from * to end.
6th row: K1, *p3, k7, p3, k1; rep from * to end.
7th row: P1, *k4, p5, k4, p1; rep from * to end.
8th row: K1, *p5, k3, p5, k1; rep from * to end.
9th row: P1, *[k6, p1] twice; rep from * to end.
10th and 11th rows: Purl.
12th row: K7, p1, *k13, p1; rep from * to last 7 sts, k7.
13th row: P6, k1, p1, k1, *p11, k1, p1, k1; rep from * to last 6 sts, p6.
14th row: K5, p2, k1, p2, *k9, p2, k1, p2; rep from * to last 5 sts, k5.
15th row: P4, k3, p1, k3, *p7, k3, p1, k3; rep from * to last 4 sts, p4.
16th row: K3, p4, k1, p4, *k5, p4, k1, p4; rep from * to last 3 sts, k3.
17th row: P2, k5, p1, k5, *p3, k5, p1, k5; rep from * to last 2 sts, p2.
18th row: K1, *p6, k1; rep from * to end.
Rep these 18 rows.

Compass Check Pattern

Multiple of 14 sts + 7.
1st row (wrong side):[P1,KB1] twice,*k10, [p1, KB1] twice; rep from * to last 3 sts, k3.
2nd row: K3, [PB1, k1] twice, *p7, k3, [PB1, k1] twice; rep from * to end.
Rep the last 2 rows once more.
5th row: Knit.
6th row: [K1, PB1] twice, *p10, [k1, PB1] twice; rep from * to last 3 sts, p3.
7th row: P3, [KB1, p1] twice, *k7, p3, [KB1, p1] twice; rep from * to end.
Rep the last 2 rows once more.
10th row: P7, *[k1, PB1] twice, p10; rep from * to end.
11th row: K7, *p3, [KB1, p1] twice, k7; rep from * to end.
Rep the last 2 rows once more.
14th row: Purl.
15th row: K7, *[p1, KB1] twice, k10; rep from * to end.
16th row: P7, *k3, [PB1, k1] twice, p7; rep from * to end.
Rep the last 2 rows once more.
Rep these 18 rows.

Rib and Arrow Pattern I

Multiple of 14 sts + 2.
1st row (right side): K2, *p4, k4, p4, k2; rep from * to end.
2nd row: P2, *k4, p4, k4, p2; rep from * to end.
3rd row: K2, *p3, k6, p3, k2; rep from * to end.
4th row: P2, *k3, p6, k3, p2; rep from * to end.
5th row: K2, p2, k2, [p1, k2] twice, *[p2, k2] twice, [p1, k2] twice; rep from * to last 4 sts, p2, k2.
6th row: P2, k2, p2, [k1, p2] twice, *[k2, p2] twice, [k1, p2] twice; rep from * to last 4 sts, k2, p2.
7th row: K2, *p1, k2, [p2, k2] twice, p1, k2; rep from * to end.
8th row: P2, *k1, p2, [k2, p2] twice, k1, p2; rep from * to end.
9th row: K4, p3, k2, p3, *k6, p3, k2, p3; rep from * to last 4 sts, k4.
10th row: P4, k3, p2, k3, *p6, k3, p2, k3; rep from * to last 4 sts, p4.
11th row: K3, p4, k2, p4, *k4, p4, k2, p4;

rep from * to last 3 sts, k3.
12th row: P3, k4, p2, k4, *p4, k4, p2, k4; rep from * to last 3 sts, p3.
13th row: K2, *p5, k2; rep from * to end.
14th row: P2, *k5, p2; rep from * to end.
Rep these 14 rows.

Rib and Arrow Pattern II

Worked as Rib and Arrow Pattern I, using reverse side as right side.

Ridge and Diamond Stripes

Multiple of 8 sts + 7.
1st row (right side): P7, *k1, p7; rep from * to end.
2nd row: K3, p1, *k2, p3, k2, p1; rep from * to last 3 sts, k3.
3rd row: P2, k3, *p2, k1, p2, k3; rep from * to last 2 sts, p2.
4th row: K1, p5, *k3, p5; rep from * to last st, k1.
5th row: K7, *p1, k7; rep from * to end.
6th row: As 4th row.
7th row: As 3rd row.
8th row: As 2nd row.
9th row: As 1st row.

10th, 11th and 12th rows: Purl.
Rep these 12 rows.

Spiral Pattern

Multiple of 7 sts.
1st row (right side): P2, k4, *p3, k4; rep from * to last st, p1.
2nd row: K1, p3, *k4, p3; rep from * to last 3 sts, k3.
3rd row: P1, k1, p2, *k2, p2, k1, p2; rep from * to last 3 sts, k2, p1.
4th row: K1, p1, k2, p2, *k2, p1, k2, p2; rep from * to last st, k1.
5th row: P1, k3, *p4, k3; rep from * to last 3 sts, p3.
6th row: K2, p4, *k3, p4; rep from * to last st, k1.
7th row: P1, k5, *p2, k5; rep from * to last st, p1.
8th row: K1, p5, *k2, p5; rep from * to last st, k1.
Rep these 8 rows.

Zigzag and Stripe Columns

Multiple of 10 sts.
1st row (right side): P1, k1, p2, k5, *p2, k1, p2, k5; rep from * to last st, p1.
2nd row: K1, p4, k2, p2, *k2, p4, k2, p2; rep from * to last st, k1.

3rd row: P1, k3, *p2, k3; rep from * to last st, p1.
4th row: K1, p2, k2, p4, *k2, p2, k2, p4; rep from * to last st, k1.
5th row: Purl.
6th row: Knit.
7th row: P1, k4, p2, k2, *p2, k4, p2, k2; rep from * to last st, p1.
8th row: K1, p3, *k2, p3; rep from * to last st, k1.
9th row: P1, k2, p2, k4, *p2, k2, p2, k4; rep from * to last st, p1.
10th row: K1, p5, k2, p1, *k2, p5, k2, p1; rep from * to last st, k1.
Rep these 10 rows.

Valentine Hearts

Multiple of 12 sts + 9.
1st row (right side): P4, k1, *p11, k1; rep from * to last 4 sts, p4.
2nd row: K3, p3, *k9, p3; rep from * to last 3 sts, k3.
3rd row: P3, k3, *p9, k3; rep from * to last 3 sts, p3.
4th row: K2, p5, *k7, p5; rep from * to last 2 sts, k2.
5th row: P1, k7, *p5, k7; rep from * to last st, p1.
6th row: P9, *k3, p9; rep from * to end.
7th row: K9, *p3, k9; rep from * to end.
8th row: As 6th row.
9th row: K4, p1, *k4, p3, k4, p1; rep from * to last 4 sts, k4.
10th row: K1, p2, k3, p2, *k2, p1, k2, p2, k3, p2; rep from * to last st, k1.
11th row: P10, *k1, p11; rep from * to last 11 sts, k1, p10.
12th row: As 7th row.
13th row: As 6th row.
14th row: As 5th row.
15th row: As 4th row.
16th row: As 3rd row.
17th row: As 2nd row.
18th row: As 3rd row.
19th row: K3, p3, *k4, p1, k4, p3; rep from * to last 3 sts, k3.
20th row: P2, k2, p1, k2, *p2, k3, p2, k2, p1, k2; rep from * to last 2 sts, p2.
Rep these 20 rows.

Knit and Purl Panels

Ridge and Furrow

Worked over 23 sts on a background of st st.
1st row (right side): P4, k7, p1, k7, p4.
2nd row: K1, p2, k1, p5, [k1, p1] twice, k1, p5, k1, p2, k1.
3rd row: P4, k4, [p1, k2] twice, p1, k4, p4.
4th row: K1, p2, [k1, p3] 4 times, k1, p2, k1.
5th row: P4, k2, [p1, k4] twice, p1, k2, p4.
6th row: K1, p2, k1, p1, [k1, p5] twice, k1, p1, k1, p2, k1.
Rep these 6 rows.

Tree of Life

Worked over 23 sts on a background of st st.
1st row (right side): P4, k7, p1, k7, p4.
2nd row: K1, p2, k1, p6, k1, p1, k1, p6, k1, p2, k1.
3rd row: P4, k5, p1, k3, p1, k5, p4.
4th row: K1, p2, k1, p4, [k1, p2] twice, k1, p4, k1, p2, k1.
5th row: P4, k3, p1, k2, p1, k1, p1, k2, p1, k3, p4.
6th row: [K1, p2] 3 times, k1, p3, [k1, p2] 3 times, k1.
7th row: P4, k1, [p1, k2] 4 times, p1, k1, p4.
8th row: K1, p2, k1, p3, k1, p2, k1, p1, k1, p2, k1, p3, k1, p2, k1.
9th row: P4, [k2, p1] twice, k3, [p1, k2] twice, p4.
10th row: As 4th row.
11th row: As 5th row.

12th row: K1, p2, k1, p5, k1, p3, k1, p5, k1, p2, k1.
13th row: P4, k4, [p1, k2] twice, p1, k4, p4.
14th row: As 2nd row.
15th row: As 3rd row.
16th row: K1, p2, k1, [p7, k1] twice, p2, k1.
17th row: P4, k6, p1, k1, p1, k6, p4.
18th row: K1, p2, k1, p15, k1, p2, k1.
19th row: As 1st row.
20th row: As 18th row.
Rep these 20 rows.

Triple Wave

Worked over 14 sts on a background of st st.
1st row (right side): P3, k8, p3.
2nd row: [K1, p1] twice, k2, p2, k2, [p1, k1] twice.
3rd row: P3, k3, p2, k3, p3.
4th row: K1, p1, k1, p8, k1, p1, k1.
5th row: P3, k1, p2, k2, p2, k1, p3.
6th row: K1, p1, k1, p3, k2, p3, k1, p1, k1.
Rep these 6 rows.

Anchor

Worked over 17 sts on a background of st st.
1st row (right side): P3, k11, p3.

2nd row: K1, p1, [k1, p5] twice, k1, p1, k1.
3rd row: P3, k4, p1, k1, p1, k4, p3.
4th row: K1, p1, k1, p3, [k1, p1] twice, k1, p3, k1, p1, k1.
5th row: P3, k2, p1, k5, p1, k2, p3.
6th row: [K1, p1] twice, [k1, p3] twice, [k1, p1] twice, k1.
7th row: P3, k1, p1, k7, p1, k1, p3.
8th row: K1, p1, [k1, p5] twice, k1, p1, k1.
9th row: As 1st row.
Rep the last 2 rows once more.
12th row: K1, p1, k1, p3, k5, p3, k1, p1, k1.
13th row: P3, k3, p5, k3, p3.
14th row: As 12th row.
15th row: As 1st row.
16th row: As 8th row.
Rep the last 2 rows once more.
19th row: As 3rd row.
20th row: K1, p1, [k1, p3] 3 times, k1, p1, k1.
21st row: As 3rd row.
22nd row: As 2nd row.
23rd row: As 1st row.
24th row: K1, p1, k1, p11, k1, p1, k1.
Rep these 24 rows.

Diamond Net Mask

Worked over 19 sts on a background of st st.
1st row (right side): P3, k6, p1, k6, p3.
2nd row: K1, p1, k1, [p6, k1] twice, p1, k1.
3rd row: P3, k5, p1, k1, p1, k5, p3.
4th row: K1, p1, k1, [p5, k1, p1, k1] twice.
5th row: P3, k4, [p1, k1] twice, p1, k4, p3.
6th row: K1, p1, k1, p4, [k1, p1] twice, k1, p4, k1, p1, k1.
7th row: P3, k3, [p1, k1] 3 times, p1, k3, p3.
8th row: K1, p1, k1, p3, [k1, p1] 3 times, k1, p3, k1, p1, k1.
9th row: P3, k2, p1, k1, p1, k3, p1, k1, p1, k2, p3.
10th row: K1, p1, k1, p2, k1, p1, k1, p3, k1, p1, k1, p2, k1, p1, k1.
11th row: P3, [k1, p1] twice, k5, [p1, k1] twice, p3.
12th row: [K1, p1] 3 times, k1, p5, [k1, p1] 3 times, k1.
13th row: As 9th row.
14th row: As 10th row.
15th row: As 7th row.

16th row: As 8th row.
17th row: As 5th row.
18th row: As 6th row.
19th row: As 3rd row.
20th row: As 4th row.
Rep these 20 rows.

Ladder

Worked over 11 sts on a background of st st.
1st row (right side): P2, k7, p2.
2nd row: K2, p7, k2.
Rep the last 2 rows once more.
5th row: Purl.
6th row: As 2nd row.
7th row: As 1st row.
Rep the last 2 rows once more.
10th row: Knit.
Rep these 10 rows.

Marriage Lines

Worked over 17 sts on a background of st st.
1st row (right side): P3, k6, p1, k2, p1, k1, p3.
2nd row: K1, p1, [k1, p2] twice, k1, p5, k1, p1, k1.
3rd row: P3, k4, p1, k2, p1, k3, p3.
4th row: K1, p1, k1, p4, k1, p2, k1, p3, k1, p1, k1.

5th row: P3, [k2, p1] twice, k5, p3.
6th row: K1, p1, k1, p6, k1, p2, [k1, p1] twice, k1.
7th row: As 5th row.
8th row: As 4th row.
9th row: As 3rd row.
10th row: As 2nd row.
Rep these 10 rows.

Thin Star

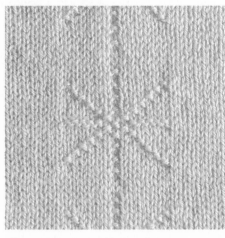

Worked over 13 sts on a background of st st.
1st row (wrong side): Purl.
2nd row: Knit.
3rd row: P6, k1, p6.
4th row: Knit.
5th row: K1, [p5, k1] twice.
6th row: K1, p1, k9, p1, k1.
7th row: P2, [k1, p3] twice, k1, p2.
8th row: K3, p1, k5, p1, k3.
9th row: P4, [k1, p1] twice, k1, p4.
10th row: K5, p1, k1, p1, k5.
Rep the last row twice more.
Work in reverse order from 9th to 2nd row inclusive.
Rep these 20 rows.

Latin Star

Worked over 19 sts on a background of st st.
1st row (wrong side): Purl.
2nd row: Knit.
3rd row: P9, k1, p9.
4th row: K8, p1, k1, p1, k8.
5th row: P1, k1, [p7, k1] twice, p1.
6th row: K2, p1, k5, p1, k1, p1, k5, p1, k2.
7th row: [P1, k1] twice, p5, k1, p5, [k1, p1] twice.
8th row: K2, [p1, k1, p1, k3] twice, p1, k1, p1, k2.
9th row: P3, k1, p1, [k1, p3] twice, k1, p1, k1, p3.
10th row: K4, [p1, k1] 5 times, p1, k4.
11th row: P5, [k1, p1] 4 times, k1, p5.
12th row: K6, p1, k5, p1, k6.
13th row: [P1, k1] 3 times, p2, k1, p1, k1, p2, [k1, p1] 3 times.
14th row: [P1, k1] 3 times, p1, [k2, p1] twice, [k1, p1] 3 times.
Work in reverse order from 13th row to 2nd row inclusive.
Rep these 26 rows.

Flying Wedge

Worked over 18 sts on a background of st st.
1st row (wrong side): Purl.
2nd row: K11, p1, k6.
3rd row: P7, k1, p10.
4th row: K9, p1, k1, p1, k6.
5th row: P7, k1, p1, k1, p8.
6th row: K7, [p1, k1] twice, p1, k6.
7th row: P7, [k1, p1] 5 times, k1.
8th row: [K1, p1] 6 times, k6.
9th row: P5, [k1, p1] 5 times, k1, p2.
10th row: K3, [p1, k1] 5 times, p1, k4.
11th row: P3, [k1, p1] 5 times, k1, þ4.
12th row: K5, [p1, k1] 5 times, p1, k2.
13th row: [P1, k1] 6 times, p6.
14th row: K7, [p1, k1] 5 times, p1.
15th row: P7, [k1, p1] twice, k1, p6.
16th row: K7, p1, k1, p1, k8.
17th row: P9, k1, p1, k1, p6.
18th row: K7, p1, k10.
19th row: P11, k1, p6.
20th row: Knit.
Rep these 20 rows.

Rib Patterns

Brioche Rib

Multiple of 2 sts.
Foundation row: Knit.
Commence Pattern
1st row: *K1, K1B; rep from * to last 2 sts, k2.
Rep 1st row throughout.

Staggered Brioche Rib

Multiple of 2 sts + 1.
Foundation row (wrong side): Knit.
Commence Pattern
1st row: K1, *K1B, k1; rep from * to end.
Rep the 1st row 3 times more.
5th row: K2, k1B, *k1, K1B; rep from * to last 2 sts, k2.
Rep the 5th row 3 times more.
Rep the last 8 rows.

Hunters Stitch

Multiple of 11 sts + 4.

1st row (right side): P4, *[KB1, p1] 3 times, KB1, p4; rep from * to end.
2nd row: K4, *p1, [KB1, p1] 3 times, k4; rep from * to end.
Rep these 2 rows.

Rib Stitch

Multiple of 2 sts + 1.
1st row (right side): K1, *yf, sl 1 purlwise, yb, k1; rep from * to end.
2nd row: P1, *k1, p1; rep from * to end.
Rep these 2 rows.

Shadow Rib

Multiple of 3 sts + 2.
1st row (right side): Knit.
2nd row: P2, *KB1, p2; rep from * to end.
Rep these 2 rows.

Blanket Rib

Multiple of 2 sts + 1.
1st row (right side): Knit into front and back of each st (thus doubling the number of sts).
2nd row: K2tog, *p2tog, k2tog; rep from * to end (original number of sts restored).
Rep these 2 rows.

Puff Ribbing Pattern I

Multiple of 6 sts + 3.

Special Abbreviation
K3W = knit 3 sts wrapping yarn twice around needle for each st.

1st row (wrong side): P3, *K3W, p3; rep from * to end.
2nd row: K3, *p3 (dropping extra loops), k3; rep from * to end.
Rep these 2 rows.

Puff Ribbing Pattern II

Multiple of 8 sts + 5.

Special Abbreviation
K3W = knit 3 sts wrapping yarn twice around needle for each st.

1st row (right side): P5, *K3W, p5; rep from * to end.
2nd row: K5, *p3 (dropping extra loops), k5; rep from * to end.
Rep these 2 rows.

Little Bobble Rib

Multiple of 8 sts + 3.

1st row (right side): K3, *p2, [p1, k1] twice into next st then slip 2nd, 3rd and 4th sts of this group over first st (bobble completed), p2, k3; rep from * to end.

2nd row: P3, *k5, p3; rep from * to end.

3rd row: K3, *p5, k3; rep from * to end.

4th row: As 2nd row.

Rep these 4 rows.

Large Bobble Rib

Multiple of 7 sts + 2.

1st row (right side): K2, *p2, k1, p2, k2; rep from * to end.

2nd row: P2, *k2, p1, k2, p2; rep from * to end.

3rd row: K2, *p2, MB, p2, k2; rep from * to end.

4th row: As 2nd row.

Rep these 4 rows.

Chunky Rib Pattern I

Multiple of 8 sts + 6.

1st row (right side): P6, *k2, p6; rep from * to end.

2nd row: K6, *p2, k6; rep from * to end.

Rep the last 2 rows twice more.

7th row: P2, *k2, p2; rep from * to end.

8th row: K2, *p2, k2; rep from * to end.

Rep the last 2 rows twice more.

13th row: P2, k2, *p6, k2; rep from * to last 2 sts, p2.

14th row: K2, p2, *k6, p2; rep from * to last 2 sts, k2.

Rep the last 2 rows twice more.

19th row: As 7th row.

20th row: As 8th row.

Rep the last 2 rows twice more.

Rep these 24 rows.

Chunky Rib Pattern II

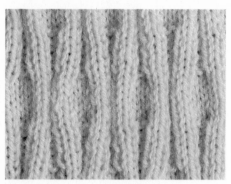

Worked as Chunky Rib Pattern I, using reverse side as right side.

Harris Tweed Ribbing

Multiple of 4 sts + 2.

1st row (right side): K2, *p2, k2; rep from * to end.

2nd row: P2, *k2, p2; rep from * to end.

3rd row: Knit.

4th row: Purl.

5th row: As 1st row.

6th row: As 2nd row.

7th row: Purl.

8th row: Knit.

Rep these 8 rows.

Thick and Thin Ribbing

Multiple of 4 sts + 1.

1st row (right side): K1, *p1, k1; rep from * to end.

2nd row: P1, *k1, p1; rep from * to end.

Rep the last 2 rows 3 times more.

9th row: K1, *p3, k1; rep from * to end.

10th row: P1, *k3, p1; rep from * to end.

Rep the last 2 rows 3 times more.

Rep these 16 rows.

Slipped Stitch Ribbing

Multiple of 8 sts + 3.

Note: Slip all sts purlwise.

1st row (right side): P3, *k1 wrapping yarn twice around needle, p3, k1, p3; rep from * to end.

2nd row: K3, *p1, k3, yf, sl 1 dropping extra loop, yb, k3; rep from * to end.

3rd row: P3, *yb, sl 1, yf, p3, k1, p3; rep from * to end.

4th row: K3, *p1, k3, yf, sl 1, yb, k3; rep from * to end.

Rep these 4 rows.

Rib Patterns

Seeded Rib

Multiple of 4 sts + 1.
1st row (right side): P1, *k3, p1; rep from
* to end.
2nd row: K2, p1, *k3, p1; rep from * to last
2 sts, k2.
Rep these 2 rows.

Cluster Rib

Multiple of 3 sts + 1.
1st row (right side): P1, *k2, p1; rep from
* to end.
2nd row: K1, *yf, k2, slip the yf over the 2
knit sts, k1; rep from * to end.
Rep these 2 rows.

Textured Ribbing

Multiple of 6 sts + 3.
1st row (right side): P3, *k3, p3; rep from
* to end.
2nd row: K3, *p1, yb, sl 1 knitwise, yf, p1,
k3; rep from * to end.
Rep these 2 rows twice more.
7th row: Knit.

8th row: P4, *yb, sl 1 knitwise, yf, p5; rep
from * to last 5 sts, yb, sl 1 knitwise, yf, p4.
Rep these 8 rows.

Sailors Rib

Multiple of 5 sts + 1.
1st row (right side): KB1, *p1, k2, p1, KB1;
rep from * to end.
2nd row: P1, *k1, p2, k1, p1; rep from *
to end.
3rd row: KB1, *p4, KB1; rep from * to end.
4th row: P1, *k4, p1; rep from * to end.
Rep these 4 rows.

Feather Rib

Multiple of 5 sts + 2.
1st row (right side): P2, *yon, k2tog tbl, k1,
p2; rep from * to end.
2nd row: K2, *yf, k2tog tbl, p1, k2; rep from
* to end.
Rep these 2 rows.

Rib with Eyelets

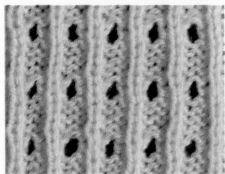

Mutliple of 4 sts + 1.
1st row (right side): K1, *p3, k1; rep from
* to end.
2nd row: P1, *k3, p1; rep from * to end.
Rep the last 2 rows once more.
5th row: K1, *p2tog, yrn, p1, k1; rep from
* to end.
6th row: As 2nd row.
Rep these 6 rows.

Perforated Ribbing

Multiple of 6 sts + 3.
1st row (right side): P1, k1, p1, *yrn, p3tog,
yrn, p1, k1, p1; rep from * to end.
2nd row: K1, p1, k1, *p3, k1, p1, k1; rep
from * to end.
3rd row: P1, k1, p1, *k3, p1, k1, p1; rep
from * to end.
4th row: As 2nd row.
Rep these 4 rows.

Eyelet and Slip Stitch Rib

Multiple of 11 sts + 7.
1st row (right side): P3, yb, sl 1 knitwise, yf,
p3, *k1, yf, k2tog, k1, p3, yb, sl 1 knitwise,
yf, p3; rep from * to end.
2nd row: K3, p1, k3, *p4, k3, p1, k3; rep
from * to end.
3rd row: P3, yb, sl 1 knitwise, yf, p3, *k1,
sl 1, k1, psso, yf, k1, p3, yb, sl 1 knitwise,
yf, p3; rep from * to end.
4th row: As 2nd row.
Rep these 4 rows.

Double Twisted Rib

Multiple of 6 sts + 2.

1st row (right side): P2, *C2B, C2F, p2; rep from * to end.

2nd row: K2, *p4, k2; rep from * to end.

Rep these 2 rows.

Bobble Twists

Multiple of 8 sts + 6.

1st row (right side): P2, *C2B, p2; rep from * to end.

2nd and every alt row: K2, *p2, k2; rep from * to end.

3rd row: P2, k1, MB (make bobble) as follows: [k1, yf, k1, yf, k1] into next st, turn, p5, turn k5, turn p2tog, p1, p2tog, turn, sl 1, k2tog, psso (bobble completed), p2, *C2B, p2, k1, MB, p2; rep from * to end.

5th row: As 1st row.

7th row: P2, C2B, p2, *k1, MB, p2, C2B, p2; rep from * to end.

8th row: As 2nd row.

Rep these 8 rows.

Tracery Rib

Multiple of 8 sts + 2.

1st row (right side): P2, *k6, p2; rep from * to end.

2nd row: K2, *p6, k2; rep from * to end.

3rd row: P2, *C3R, C3L, p2; rep from * to end.

4th row: K2, *yf, sl 1 purlwise, p4, sl 1 purlwise, yb, k2; rep from * to end.

5th row: P2, *yb, sl 1, k1, psso, yf, C2F, yf, k2tog, p2; rep from * to end.

6th row: As 4th row.

7th row: As 5th row.

8th row: As 2nd row.

9th row: P2, *C3L, C3R, p2; rep from * to end.

10th row: As 2nd row.

Rep these 10 rows.

Cable and Eyelet Rib I

Multiple of 7 sts + 3.

1st row (right side): P3, *k4, p3; rep from * to end.

2nd row: K1, yf, k2tog, *p4, k1, yf, k2tog; rep from * to end.

3rd row: P3, *C4B, p3; rep from * to end.

4th row: As 2nd row.

5th row: As 1st row.

6th row: As 2nd row.

Rep the last 6 rows.

Cable and Eyelet Rib II

Multiple of 10 sts + 4.

1st row (right side): P1, k2tog, yfrn, *p2, k4, p2, k2tog, yfrn; rep from * to last st, p1.

2nd and every alt row: K1, p2, *k2, p4, k2, p2; rep from * to last st, k1.

3rd row: P1, yon, sl 1, k1, psso, *p2, C4F, p2, yon, sl 1, k1, psso; rep from * to last st, p1.

5th row: As 1st row.

7th row: P1, yon, sl 1, k1, psso, *p2, k4, p2, yon, sl 1, k1, psso; rep from * to last st, p1.

8th row: As 2nd row.

Rep these 8 rows.

Turkish Rib I

(Slanting to the Left)

Multiple of 2 sts.

Special Abbreviation

PR (Purl Reverse) = purl 1 st, return it to left-hand needle, insert right-hand needle through the st beyond and lift this st over the purled st and off the needle. Return st to right-hand needle.

Foundation row (right side): Knit.

1st row: P1, *yrn, PR; rep from * to last st, p1.

2nd row: K1, *sl 1, k1, psso, yf; rep from * to last st, k1.

Rep the last 2 rows.

Turkish Rib II

(Slanting to the Right)

Multiple of 2 sts.

Foundation row (right side): Knit.

1st row: P1, *p2tog, yrn; rep from * to last st, p1.

2nd row: K1, *yf, k2tog; rep from * to last st, k1.

Rep the last 2 rows.

Rib Patterns

3-Stitch Twisted Rib

Multiple of 5+2
1st row (wrong side): K2, *p3, k2; rep from * to end.
2nd row: P2, *C3, p2; rep from * to end.
Rep these 2 rows.

Broken Rib

Multiple of of 2+1
1st row (right side): Knit.
2nd row: P1, *k1, p1; rep from * to end.
Rep these 2 rows.

Embossed Rib

Multiple of 6+2
1st row (right side): P2, *KB1, k1, p1, KB1, p2; rep from * to end.
2nd row: K2, *PB1, k1, p1, PB1, k2; rep from * to end.
3rd row: P2, *KB1, p1, k1, KB1, p2; rep from * to end.
4th row: K2, *PB1, p1, k1, PB1, k2; rep from * to end.
Rep these 4 rows.

Corded Rib

Multiple of 4+2
1st row: K1, *k2tog tbl, pick up horizontal strand of yarn lying between stitch just worked and next st and knit into back of it, p2; rep from * to last st, k1.
Rep this row.

Moss Rib

Multiple of 4+1
1st row: K2, *p1, k3; rep from * to last 3 sts, p1, k2.
2nd row: P1, *k3, p1; rep from * to end.
Rep these 2 rows.

Diagonal Rib

Multiple of 4
1st row (right side): *K2, p2; rep from * to end.
2nd row: As 1st row.
3rd row: K1, *p2, k2; rep from * to last 3 sts, p2, k1.
4th row: P1, *k2, p2; rep from * to last 3 sts, k2, p1.
5th row: *P2, k2; rep from * to end.
6th row: As 5th row.

7th row: As 4th row.
8th row: As 3rd row.
Rep these 8 rows.

Open Twisted Rib

Multiple of 5+3
Note: Sts should not be counted after the 2nd or 3rd rows of this pattern.
1st row (wrong side): K1, PB1, k1, *p2, k1, PB1, k1; rep from * to end.
2nd row: P1, KB1, p1, *k1, yf, k1, p1, KB1, p1; rep from * to end.
3rd row: K1, PB1, k1, *p3, k1, PB1, k1; rep from * to end.
4th row: P1, KB1, p1, *k3, pass 3rd st on right-hand needle over first 2 sts, p1, KB1, p1; rep from * to end.
Rep these 4 rows.

Broken Rib Diagonal

Multiple of 6
1st row (right side): *K4, p2; rep from * to end.
2nd row: *K2, p4; rep from * to end.
3rd row: As 1st row.
4th row: As 2nd row.
5th row: K2, *p2, k4; rep from * to last 4 sts, p2, k2.
6th row: P2, *k2, p4; rep from * to last 4 sts, k2, p2.
7th row: As 5th row.
8th row: As 6th row.
9th row: *P2, k4; rep from * to end.
10th row: *P4, k2; rep from * to end.
11th row: As 9th row.
12th row: As 10th row.
Rep these 12 rows.

Piqué Rib

Multiple of 10 + 3
1st row (right side): K3, *p3, k1, p3, k3; rep from * to end.
2nd row: P3, *k3, p1, k3, p3; rep from * to end.
3rd row: As 1st row.
4th row: Knit.
Rep these 4 rows.

Bobble Rib

Multiple of 8 + 3
1st row (right side): K3, *p2, [p1, k1] twice into next st, pass the first 3 of these sts, one at a time, over the 4th st (bobble made), p2, k3; rep from * to end.
2nd row: P3, *k2, p1, k2, p3; rep from * to end.
3rd row: K3, *p2, k1, p2, k3; rep from * to end.
4th row: As 2nd row.
Rep these 4 rows.

Granite Rib

Basket Weave Rib

Multiple of 8 + 2
1st row (right side): K2, *[C2F]3 times, k2; rep from * to end.
2nd row: Purl.
3rd row: K2, *[knit 3rd st from left-hand needle, then 2nd st, then 1st stitch, slipping all 3 sts off needle together] twice, k2; rep from * to end.
4th row: Purl.
Rep these 4 rows.

Multiple of 15 + 8
1st row (right side): *P3, k2, p3, k1, [C2F] 3 times; rep from * to last 8 sts, p3, k2, p3.
2nd row: *K3, purl into 2nd st on needle, then purl first st slipping both sts off needle together (called C2P), k3, p1, [C2P] 3 times; rep from * to last 8 sts, k3, C2P, k3.
Rep these 2 rows.

Spiral Rib

Multiple of 6 + 3
1st row (right side): K3, *p3, k3; rep from * to end.
2nd row: P3, *k3, p3; rep from * to end.
3rd row: As 1st row.
4th row: K1, *p3, k3; rep from * to last 2 sts, p2.
5th row: K2, *p3, k3; rep from * to last st, p1.
6th row: As 4th row.
7th row: As 4th row.
8th row: As 5th row.
9th row: As 4th row.
10th row: K3, *p3, k3; rep from * to end.
11th row: As 2nd row.

12th row: As 10th row.
13th row: P2, *k3, p3; rep from * to last st, k1.
14th row: P1, *k3, p3; rep from * to last 2 sts, k2.
15th row: As 13th row.
16th row: As 13th row.
17th row: As 14th row.
18th row: As 13th row.
Rep these 18 rows.

Chain Stitch Rib

Multiple of 3 + 2
1st row (wrong side): K2, *p1, k2; rep from * to end.
2nd row: P2, *k1, p2; rep from * to end.
3rd row: As 1st row.
4th row: P2, *yb, insert needle through centre of st 3 rows below next st on needle and knit this in the usual way, slipping st above off needle at the same time, p2; rep from * to end.
Rep these 4 rows.

Mock Cable Rib

Multiple of 7 + 2
1st row (right side): P2, *C2B, k3, p2; rep from * to end.
2nd and every alt row: K2, *p5, k2; rep from * to end.
3rd row: P2, *k1, C2B, k2, p2; rep from * to end.
5th row: P2, *k2, C2B, k1, p2; rep from * to end.
7th row: P2, *k3, C2B, p2; rep from * to end.
8th row: K2, *p5, k2; rep from * to end.
Rep these 8 rows.

Rib Patterns

Wavy Rib

Multiple of 3+1
1st row (wrong side): K1, *p2, k1; rep from * to end.
2nd row: P1, *C2F, p1; rep from * to end.
3rd row: As 1st row.
4th row: P1, *C2B, p1; rep from * to end.
Rep these 4 rows.

Square Rib

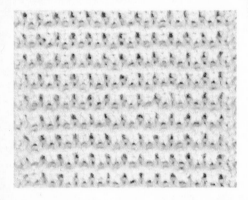

Multiple of 2+1
1st row (right side): K2, p1, *k1, p1; rep from * to last 2 sts, k2.
2nd row: K1, *p1, k1; rep from * to end.
3rd row: As 1st row.
4th row: K1, p1, *yb, insert needle through centre of st 2 rows below next st on needle and knit this in the usual way slipping st above off needle at the same time, p1; rep from * to last st, k1.
Rep these 4 rows.

Single Eyelet Rib

Multiple of 5+2
1st row (right side): P2, *k3, p2; rep from * to end.
2nd and every alt row: K2, *p3, k2; rep from * to end.
3rd row: P2, *k2tog, yf, k1, p2; rep from * to end.
5th row: As 1st row.
7th row: P2, *k1, yf, sl 1, k1, psso, p2; rep from * to end.
8th row: As 2nd row.
Rep these 8 rows.

Double Eyelet Rib

Multiple of 7+2
1st row (right side): P2, *k5, p2; rep from * to end.
2nd row: K2, *p5, k2; rep from * to end.
3rd row: P2, *k2tog, yf, k1, yf, sl 1, k1, psso, p2; rep from * to end.
4th row: As 2nd row.
Rep these 4 rows.

Little Hour Glass Ribbing

Multiple of 4+2
Note: Sts should not be counted after 3rd row.
1st row (wrong side): K2, *p2, k2; rep from * to end.
2nd row: P2, *k2tog tbl, then knit same 2 sts tog through front loops, p2; rep from * to end.
3rd row: K2, *p1, yrn, p1, k2; rep from * to end.
4th row: P2, *yb, sl 1, k1, psso, k1, p2; rep from * to end.
Rep these 4 rows.

Fisherman's Rib

Note: Each set of instructions gives the same appearance but a different 'feel'. For example (C) is a firmer fabric than (A).

(A) Multiple of 2+1
Foundation row: Knit.
1st row (right side): Sl 1, *K1B, p1; rep from * to end.
2nd row: Sl 1, *p1, K1B; rep from * to last 2 sts, p1, k1.
Rep the last 2 rows only.

(B) Multiple of 2+1
Foundation row: Knit.
1st row (right side): Sl 1, *K1B, k1; rep from * to end.
2nd row: Sl 1, *k1, K1B; rep from * to last 2 sts, k2.
Rep the last 2 rows only.

(C) Multiple of 3+1
1st row (right side): Sl 1, *k2tog, yfon, sl1 purlwise; rep from * to last 3 sts, k2tog, k1.
2nd row: Sl 1, *yfon, sl 1 purlwise, k2tog (the yfon and sl 1 of previous row); rep from * to last 2 sts, yfon, sl 1 purlwise, k1.
Rep the last 2 rows.

Half Fisherman's Rib

Note: Both sets of instructions give the same appearance but a different 'feel'. (B) is a firmer fabric than (A).
(A) Multiple of 2+1
1st row (right side): Sl 1, knit to end.
2nd row: Sl 1, *K1B, p1; rep from * to end.
Rep these 2 rows.

(B) Multiple of 2+1
1st row (right side): Sl 1, *p1, k1; rep from * to end.
2nd row: Sl 1, *K1B, p1; rep from * to end.
Rep these 2 rows.

'Faggotted' Rib

Multiple of 4 + 2
1st row: K3, *yf, sl 1, k1, psso, k2; rep from * to last 3 sts, yf, sl 1, k1, psso, k1.
2nd row: P3, *yrn, p2tog, p2; rep from * to last 3 sts, yrn, p2tog, p1.
Rep these 2 rows.

Slipped Rib

Multiple of 2 + 1
1st row (right side): K1, *yf, sl 1 purlwise, yb, k1; rep from * to end.
2nd row: Purl.
Rep these 2 rows.

Contrary Fisherman's Rib

Multiple of 2 + 1
Foundation row: Knit.
1st row (right side): Sl 1, *K1B, k1; rep from * to end.
2nd row: Sl 1, *k1, K1B; rep from * to last 2 sts, k2.

3rd row: As 1st row.
4th row: As 2nd row.
5th row: As 1st row.
6th row: Sl 1,*K1B, k1; rep from * to end.
7th row: As 2nd row.
8th row: As 6th row.
9th row: As 2nd row.
10th row: As 6th row.
Rep the last 10 rows only.

Mock Wavy Cable Rib

Multiple of 4 + 2
1st row (right side): P2, *k2, p2; rep from * to end.
2nd and every alt row: K2, *p2, k2; rep from * to end.
3rd row: P2, *C2B, p2; rep from * to end.
5th row: As 1st row.
7th row: P2, *k2tog but do not slip off needle, then insert right-hand needle between these 2 sts and knit the 1st st again, slipping both sts off needle tog, p2; rep from * to end.
8th row: As 2nd row.
Rep these 8 rows.

Mock Cable — Right

Multiple of 4 + 2
1st row (right side): P2, *k2, p2; rep from * to end.
2nd row: K2, *p2, k2; rep from * to end.
3rd row: P2, *C2F, p2; rep from * to end.
4th row: As 2nd row.
Rep these 4 rows.

Mock Cable — Left

Multiple of 4 + 2
1st row (right side): P2, *k2, p2; rep from * to end.
2nd row: K2, *p2, k2; rep from * to end.
3rd row: P2, *C2B, p2; rep from * to end.
4th row: As 2nd row.
Rep these 4 rows.

Fancy Slip Stitch Rib

Multiple of 5 + 2
1st row (right side): P2, *k1, sl 1 purlwise, k1, p2; rep from * to end.
2nd row: K2, *p3, k2; rep from * to end.
Rep these 2 rows.

Supple Rib

Multiple of 3 + 1
1st row (right side): K1, *knit the next st but do not slip it off the left-hand needle, then purl the same st and the next st tog, k1; rep from * to end.
2nd row: Purl.
Rep these 2 rows.

Rib Patterns

Farrow Rib

Multiple of 3 + 1
1st row (right side): *K2, p1; rep from * to last st, k1.
2nd row: P1, *k2, p1; rep from * to end.
Rep these 2 rows.

Oblique Rib

Multiple of 4
1st row (right side): *K2, p2; rep from * to end.
2nd row: K1, *p2, k2; rep from * to last 3 sts, p2, k1.
3rd row: *P2, k2; rep from * to end.
4th row: P1, *k2, p2; rep from * to last 3 sts, k2, p1.
Rep these 4 rows.

Open Chain Ribbing

Multiple of 6 + 2
1st row (wrong side): K2, *p4, k2; rep from * to end.
2nd row: P2, *k2tog, [yf] twice,.sl 1, k1, psso, p2; rep from * to end.
3rd row: K2, *p1, purl into front of first yf, purl into back of 2nd yf, p1, k2; rep from * to end.
4th row: P2, *yon, sl 1, k1, psso, k2tog, yfrn, p2; rep from * to end.
Rep these 4 rows.

Beaded Rib

Multiple of 5 + 2
1st row (right side): P2, *k1, p1, k1, p2; rep from * to end.
2nd row: K2, *p3, k2; rep from * to end.
Rep these 2 rows.

Eyelet Mock Cable Ribbing

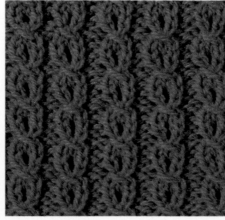

Multiple of 5 + 2
1st row (right side): P2, *sl 1, k2, psso, p2; rep from * to end.
2nd row: K2, *p1, yrn, p1, k2; rep from * to end.
3rd row: P2, *k3, p2; rep from * to end.
4th row: K2, *p3, k2; rep from * to end.
Rep these 4 rows.

Rib Checks

Multiple of 10 + 5
1st row (right side): P5, *[KB1, p1] twice, KB1, p5; rep from * to end.
2nd row: K5, *[PB1, k1] twice, PB1, k5; rep from * to end.
Rep the last 2 rows once more then the 1st row again.
6th row: [PB1, k1] twice, PB1, *k5, [PB1, k1] twice, PB1; rep from * to end.
7th row: [KB1, p1] twice, KB1, *p5, [KB1, p1] twice, KB1; rep from * to end.
Rep the last 2 rows once more then the 6th row again.
Rep these 10 rows.

Large Eyelet Rib

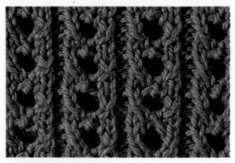

Multiple of 6 + 2
1st row (right side): *P2, k2tog, [yf] twice, sl 1, k1, psso; rep from * to last 2 sts, p2.
2nd row: K2, *p1, knit into first yf, purl into 2nd yf, p1, k2; rep from * to end.
3rd row: *P2, k4; rep from * to last 2 sts, p2.
4th row: K2, *p4, k2; rep from * to end.
Rep these 4 rows.

Woven Rib

Multiple of 6 + 3

1st row (right side): P3, *sl 1 purlwise, yb, k1, yf, sl 1 purlwise, p3; rep from * to end.

2nd row: K3, *p3, k3; rep from * to end.

3rd row: *P3, k1, yf, sl 1 purlwise, yb, k1; rep from * to last 3 sts, p3.

4th row: As 2nd row.

Rep these 4 rows.

Medallion Rib

Multiple of 8 + 4

1st row (right side): P4, *yb, sl 2 purlwise, C2B, p4; rep from * to end.

2nd row: K4, *yf, sl 2 purlwise, purl the 2nd st on left-hand needle, then the 1st st, slipping both sts from needle tog, k4; rep from * to end.

3rd row: Knit.

4th row: Purl.

Rep these 4 rows.

Twisted Cable Rib

Multiple of 4 + 2

1st row (right side): P2, *k2, p2; rep from * to end.

2nd row: K2, *p2, k2; rep from * to end.

3rd row: P2, *k2tog but do not slip off needle, then insert right-hand needle between these 2 sts and knit the 1st st again, slipping both sts off needle tog, p2; rep from * to end.

4th row: As 2nd row.

Rep these 4 rows.

Uneven Rib

Multiple of 4 + 3

1st row: *K2, p2; rep from * to last 3 sts, k2, p1.

Rep this row.

Puffed Rib

Multiple of 3 + 2

Note: Stitches should only be counted after the 4th row.

1st row (right side): P2, *yon, k1, yfrn, p2; rep from * to end.

2nd row: K2, *p3, k2; rep from * to end.

3rd row: P2, *k3, p2; rep from * to end.

4th row: K2, *p3tog, k2; rep from * to end.

Rep these 4 rows.

Linked Ribs

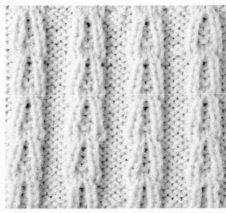

Multiple of 8 + 4

1st row (right side): P4, *k1, p2, k1, p4; rep from * to end.

2nd row: K4, *p1, k2, p1, k4; rep from * to end.

Rep the last 2 rows once more.

5th row: P4, *C2L, C2R, p4; rep from * to end.

6th row: K4, *p4, k4; rep from * to end.

Rep these 6 rows.

Chevron Rib

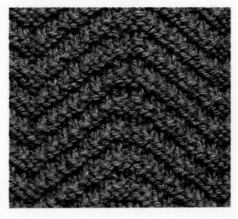

Multiple of 18 + 1

1st row (right side): P1, *k1, p2, k2, p2, k1, p1; rep from * to end.

2nd row: *K3, p2, k2, p2, k1, [p2, k2] twice; rep from * to last st, k1.

3rd row: *[P2, k2] twice, p3, k2, p2, k2, p1; rep from * to last st, p1.

4th row: *K1, p2, k2, p2, k5, p2, k2, p2; rep from * to last st, k1.

Rep these 4 rows.

Little Chevron Rib

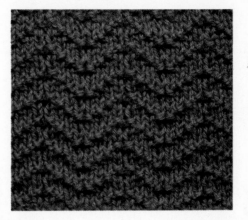

Multiple of 10 + 1

1st row (right side): P1, *k1, p1, [k2, p1] twice, k1, p1; rep from * to end.

2nd row: K1, *p2, [k1, p1] twice, k1, p2, k1; rep from * to end.

3rd row: P1, *k3, p3, k3, p1; rep from * to end.

4th row: K2, *p3, k1, p3, k3; rep from * to last 9 sts, p3, k1, p3, k2.

Rep these 4 rows.

Cable Panels

9-Stitch Plait

Down   Up

Downwards Plait
1st row (right side): Knit.
2nd and every alt row: Purl.
3rd row: C6F, k3.
5th row: Knit.
7th row: K3, C6B.
8th row: Purl.
Rep these 8 rows.

Upwards Plait
1st row (right side): Knit.
2nd and every alt row: Purl.
3rd row: C6B, k3.
5th row: Knit.
7th row: K3, C6F.
8th row: Purl.
Rep these 8 rows.

6-Stitch Plait

Down   Up

Downwards Plait
1st row (right side): C4F, k2.
2nd row: Purl.
3rd row: K2, C4B.
4th row: Purl.
Rep these 4 rows.

Upwards Plait
1st row (right side): C4B, k2.
2nd row: Purl.
3rd row: K2, C4F.
4th row: Purl.
Rep these 4 rows.

4-Stitch Cable I

1st row (right side): Knit.
2nd row: Purl.
3rd row: C4B.
4th row: Purl.
Rep these 4 rows.
The cable as given above twists to the right. To work the 4 st cable twisted to the left work C4F instead of C4B in the 3rd row.

4-Stitch Cable II

1st row (right side): Knit.
2nd row: Purl.
Rep the last 2 rows once more.
5th row: C4B.
6th row: Purl.
Rep these 6 rows.
The cable as given above twists to the right. To work the 4 st cable twisted to the left, work C4F instead of C4B in the 5th row.

6-Stitch Cable

4-Stitch Cable I (continued)

1st row (right side): Knit.
2nd row: Purl.
3rd row: C6B.
4th row: Purl.
Rep these 4 rows.
The cable as given above twists to the right. To work the 6 st cable twisted to the left work C6F instead of C6B in the 3rd row.

8-Stitch Cable

1st row (right side): Knit.
2nd row: Purl.
Rep the last 2 rows once more.
5th row: C8B.
6th row: Purl.
Rep 1st and 2nd rows twice more.
Rep these 10 rows.
The cable as given above twists to the right. To work the 8 st cable twisted to the left, work C8F instead of C8B in the 5th row.

Claw Pattern I

Down   Up

Worked over 8 sts.
Downwards Claw
1st row (right side): Knit.
2nd row: Purl.
3rd row: C4F, C4B.
4th row: Purl.
Rep these 4 rows.

Upwards Claw
1st row (right side): Knit.
2nd row: Purl.
3rd row: C4B, C4F.
4th row: Purl.
Rep these 4 rows.

Claw Pattern II

Down   Up

Worked over 9 sts.

Downwards Claw
1st row (right side): Knit.
2nd row: Purl.
3rd row: C4L, k1, C4R.
4th row: Purl.
Rep these 4 rows.

Upwards Claw
1st row (right side): Knit.
2nd row: Purl.
3rd row: C4R, k1, C4L.
4th row: Purl.
Rep these 4 rows.

Double Cable

Down   Up

Worked over 12 sts.

Downwards Cable
1st row (right side): Knit.
2nd row: Purl.
3rd row: C6F, C6B.
4th row: Purl.
Rep 1st and 2nd rows twice more.
Rep these 8 rows.

Upwards Cable
1st row (right side): Knit.
2nd row: Purl.
3rd row: C6B, C6F.
4th row: Purl.
Rep 1st and 2nd rows twice more.
Rep these 8 rows.

Small Double Cable

Down   Up

Worked over 8 sts

Downwards Cable
1st row (right side): Knit.
2nd row: Purl.
Rep the last 2 rows once more.
5th row: C4F, C4B.
6th row: Purl.
Rep these 6 rows.

Upwards Cable
1st row (right side): Knit.
2nd row: Purl.
Rep the last 2 rows once more.
5th row: C4B, C4F.
6th row: Purl.
Rep these 6 rows.

Braid Cable

Worked over 9 sts on a background of reversed st st.
1st row (right side): T2L, p2, T2R, T2L, p1.
2nd row: K1, [PB1, k2] twice, PB1, k1.
3rd row: P1, T2L, T2R, p2, T2L.
4th row: PB1, k4, [PB1] twice, k2.
5th row: P2, slip next st onto cable needle and hold at back of work, KB1 from left hand needle, then KB1 from cable needle, p4, KB1.
6th row: As 4th row.
7th row: P1, T2R, T2L, p2, T2R.
8th row: As 2nd row.
9th row: T2R, p2, T2L, T2R, p1.
10th row: K2, [PB1] twice, k4, PB1.
11th row: KB1, p4, slip next st onto cable needle and hold at front of work, KB1 from left-hand needle, then KB1 from cable needle, p2.
12th row: As 10th row.
Rep these 12 rows.

Round Cable

Worked over 8 sts.
1st row (right side): P2, k4, p2.
2nd row: K2, p4, k2.
Rep the last 2 rows once more.
5th row: T4B, T4F.
6th row: P2, k4, p2.
7th row: As 2nd row.
Rep the last 2 rows once more then the 6th row again.
11th row: T4F, T4B.
12th row: As 2nd row.
Rep these 12 rows.

Triple Rib Cable

Worked over 5 sts.

Cable to the Right
1st row (right side): KB1, [p1, KB1] twice.
2nd row: PB1, [k1, PB1] twice.
Rep these 2 rows twice more.
7th row: Slip first 2 sts onto a cable needle and hold at back of work, work [KB1, p1, KB1] from left-hand needle, then work [p1, KB1] from cable needle.
8th row: As 2nd row.
Rep 1st and 2nd rows 3 times more.
Rep these 14 rows.

Cable to the Left
1st row (right side): KB1, [p1, KB1] twice.
2nd row: PB1, [k1, PB1] twice.
Rep these 2 rows twice more.
7th row: Slip first 3 sts onto a cable needle and hold at front of work, work [KB1, p1] from left-hand needle, then work [KB1, p1, KB1] from cable needle.
8th row: As 2nd row.
Rep 1st and 2nd rows 3 times more.
Rep these 14 rows.

Cable Panels

Claw Pattern With Bobbles

Worked over 9 sts.

Downwards Claw

1st row (right side): C4L, k1, C4R.

2nd row: Purl.

3rd row: K4, k into front, back and front of next st, [turn, k3] twice, slip 2nd and 3rd sts of this group over first st, k4.

4th row: Purl.

Rep these 4 rows.

Bobbles may be added to the Upwards Claw in the same way.

9-Stitch Cable

1st row (right side): Knit.

2nd row: Purl.

Rep the last 2 rows once more.

5th row: C9B.

6th row: Purl.

Rep 1st and 2nd rows 3 times more.

Rep these 12 rows.

The cable as given above twists to the right. To work the 9 st cable twisted to the left, work C9F instead of C9B in the 5th row.

13-Stitch Claw Pattern

Down   Up

Downwards Claw

1st row (right side): Knit.

2nd row: Purl.

3rd row: C6F, k1, C6B.

4th row: Purl.

Rep these 4 rows.

Upwards Claw

1st row (right side): Knit.

2nd row: Purl.

3rd row: C6B, k1, C6F.

4th row: Purl.

Rep these 4 rows.

Folded Cable

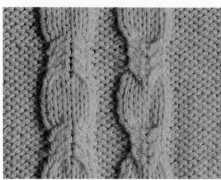

Down   Up

Worked over 6 sts.

Downwards Cable

1st row (right side): Knit.

2nd row: Purl.

Rep the last 2 rows once more.

5th row: C3L, C3R.

6th row: Purl.

Rep the last 2 rows twice more, then work 1st and 2nd rows once more.

Rep these 12 rows.

Upwards Cable

1st row (right side): Knit.

2nd row: Purl.

Rep the last 2 rows once more.

5th row: C3R, C3L.

6th row: Purl.

Rep the last 2 rows twice more, then work 1st and 2nd rows once more.

Rep these 12 rows.

Open Cable With Bobbles

Worked over 5 sts on a background of reversed st st.

Special Abbreviations

T5R (Twist 5 Right) = slip next 4 sts onto cable needle and hold at back of work, k1 from left-hand needle, then p3, k1 from cable needle.

T5L (Twist 5 Left) = slip next st onto cable needle and hold at front of work, k1, p3 from left-hand needle, then knit st from cable needle.

1st row (right side): T5R.

2nd row: P1, k3, p1.

3rd row: K1, p3, k1.

Rep 2nd and 3rd rows once more then 2nd row again.

7th row: K1, p1, MB, p1, k1.

Rep 2nd and 3rd rows twice more, then 2nd row again.

Rep these 12 rows.

The cable as given above twists to the right. To work the cable twisted to the left, work T5L instead of T5R in the 1st row.

Little Pearl Cable

Worked over 4 sts.

1st row (right side): C2F, C2B.

2nd row: Purl.

3rd row: C2B, C2F.

4th row: Purl.

Rep these 4 rows.

4-Stitch Snakey Cable

1st row (right side): Knit.

2nd row: Purl.

3rd row: C4B.

4th row: Purl.

Rep 1st and 2nd rows once more.

7th row: C4F.

8th row: Purl.

Rep these 8 rows.

Double Snakey Cable

Worked over 8 sts.
1st row (right side): Knit.
2nd row: Purl.
3rd row: C4B, C4F.
4th row: Purl.
Rep 1st and 2nd rows once more.
7th row: C4F, C4B.
8th row: Purl.
Rep these 8 rows.

Giant Cable

Worked over 12 sts.
1st row (right side): Knit.
2nd row: Purl.
Rep the last 2 rows once more.
5th row: C12B.
6th row: Purl.
Rep the 1st and 2nd rows once more.
Rep these 8 rows.
The cable as given above twists to the right. To work the 12 st cable twisted to the left, work C12F instead of C12B in the 5th row.

Wave Cable

Worked over 6 sts.
1st row (right side): Knit.
2nd row: Purl.
3rd row: C6B.
4th row: Purl.
Now work 1st and 2nd rows twice more.
9th row: C6F.
10th row: Purl.
Now work 1st and 2nd rows once more.
Rep these 12 rows.

Striped Medallion Cable

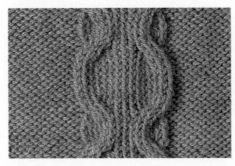

Worked over 15 sts on a background of reversed st st.
1st row (right side): Knit into the back of every st.
2nd row: Purl into the back of every st.
3rd row: C6F but working into back of sts, [KB1] 3 times, C6B working into the back of sts.
4th row: Purl into the back of every st.
Now work 1st and 2nd rows twice more.
9th row: C6B as before, [KB1] 3 times, C6F as before.
10th row: As 2nd row.
Now work 1st and 2nd rows 3 times more.
Rep these 16 rows.

Oxo Cable

Worked over 8 sts on a background of reversed st st.
1st row (right side): Knit.
2nd row and every alt row: Purl.
3rd row: C4F, C4B.
5th row: Knit.
7th row: C4B, C4F.
9th row: Knit.
11th row: C4B, C4F.
13th row: Knit.
15th row: C4F, C4B.
16th row: Purl.
Rep these 16 rows.

Honeycomb Cable

Worked over 12 sts on a background of reversed st st.
1st row (right side): K4, C2F, C2B, k4.
2nd and every alt row: Purl.
3rd row: K2, [C2F, C2B] twice, k2.
5th row: [C2F, C2B] 3 times.
7th row: [C2B, C2F] 3 times.
9th row: K2, [C2B, C2F] twice, k2.
11th row: K4, C2B, C2F, k4.
12th row: Purl.
Rep these 12 rows.

Chain Cable

Worked over 9 sts.
1st row (right side): P2, T5R, p2.
2nd row: K2, p2, k1, p2, k2.
3rd row: P1, T3B, p1, T3F, p1.
4th row: K1, p2, k3, p2, k1.
5th row: T3B, p3, T3F.
6th row: P2, k5, p2.
7th row: K2, p5, k2.
8th row: As 6th row.
9th row: T3F, p3, T3B.
10th row: As 4th row.
11th row: P1, T3F, p1, T3B, p1.
12th row: As 2nd row.
Rep these 12 rows.
The cable as given above twists to the right. To work the cable twisted to the left, work T5L instead of T5R in the 1st row.

Cable Panels

Rib Twist Cable

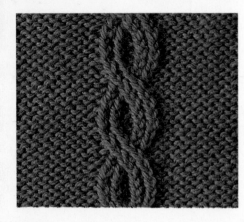

Worked over 9 sts.
Special Abbreviations
T4BR (Twist 4 Back Right) = slip next st onto cable needle and hold at back of work, KB1, p1, KB1 from left-hand needle, then purl st from cable needle.
T4FL (Twist 4 Front Left) = slip next 3 sts onto cable needle and hold at front of work, p1 from left-hand needle, then KB1, p1, KB1 from cable needle.
T7L (Twist 7 Left) = slip next 3 sts onto cable needle and hold at front of work, [KB1, p1] twice from left-hand needle, then KB1, p1, KB1 from cable needle.
T7R (Twist 7 Right) = slip next 4 sts onto cable needle and hold at back of work, KB1, p1, KB1 from left-hand needle, then [p1, KB1] twice from cable needle.
1st row (right side): T4BR, p1, T4FL.
2nd row: PB1, k1, PB1, k3, PB1, k1, PB1.
3rd row: KB1, p1, KB1, p3, KB1, p1, KB1.
4th row: As 2nd row.
5th row: T4FL, p1, T4BR.
6th row: [K1, PB1] 4 times, k1.
7th row: P1, T7L, p1.
8th row: As 6th row.
Rep these 8 rows.
The cable as given above twists to the left. To work the cable twisted to the right, work T7R instead of T7L in the 7th row..

Medallion Cable

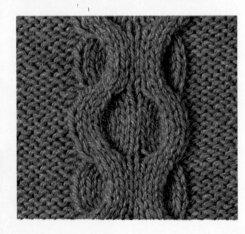

Worked over 13 sts.
1st row (right side): Knit.

2nd row: Purl.
Rep the last 2 rows once more.
5th row: C6F, k1, C6B.
6th row: As 2nd row.
7th row: As 1st row.
Rep the last 2 rows twice more.
12th row: As 2nd row.
13th row: C6B, k1, C6F.
14th row: As 2nd row.
15th row: As 1st row.
16th row: As 2nd row.
Rep these 16 rows.

Staghorn Cable I

Worked over 16 sts.
Foundation row: Purl.
1st row (right side): K4, C4B, C4F, k4.
2nd and 4th rows: Purl.
3rd row: K2, C4B, k4, C4F, k2.
5th row: C4B, k8, C4F.
6th row: Purl.
Rep these 6 rows.

Staghorn Cable II

Worked over 16 sts.
Foundation row: Purl.
1st row (right side): C4F, k8, C4B.
2nd and 4th rows: Purl.
3rd row: K2, C4F, k4, C4B, k2.
5th row: K4, C4F, C4B, k4.
6th row: Purl.
Rep these 6 rows.

Figure-Of-Eight Cable

Worked over 8 sts.
1st row (right side): P3, k2, p3.
2nd row: K3, p2, k3.
3rd row: P2, k4, p2.
4th row: K2, p4, k2.
5th row: P1, T3B, T3F, p1.
6th row: K1, p2, k2, p2, k1.
7th row: T3B, p2, T3F.
8th row: As 3rd row.
9th row: T3F, p2, T3B.
10th row: As 6th row.
11th row: P1, T3F, T3B, p1.
12th row: As 4th row.
13th row: P2, C4B, p2.
14th row: As 4th row.
Rep 5th-12th rows once more.
23rd row: P3, k2, p3.
24th row: K3, p2, k3.
Rep the last 2 rows twice more.
Rep these 28 rows.
The cable as given above twists to the right. To work the figure of 8 cable twisted to the left, work C4F instead of C4B in the 13th row.

Braided Cable

Worked over 9 sts on a background of reversed st st.
1st row: T3F, T3B, T3F.
2nd row: P2, k2, p4, k1.
3rd row: P1, C4B, p2, k2.
4th row: As 2nd row.
5th row: T3B, T3F, T3B.

6th row: K1, p4, k2, p2.
7th row: K2, p2, C4F, p1.
8th row: As 6th row.
Rep these 8 rows.

Giant Oxo Cable

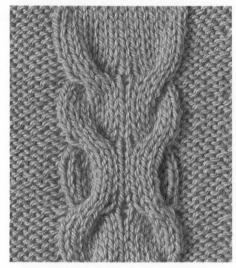

Worked over 13 sts.
1st Foundation row (right side): Knit.
2nd Foundation row: Purl.
Rep the last 2 rows once more.
1st row: C6B, k1, C6F.
2nd row: Purl.
3rd row: Knit.
Rep the last 2 rows twice more.
8th row: As 2nd row.
Rep the last 8 rows once more.
17th row: C6F, k1, C6B.
18th row: As 2nd row.
19th row: As 3rd row.
Rep the last 2 rows twice more.
24th row: As 2nd row.
Rep the last 8 rows once more.
Rep these 32 rows.

Cable With Bobbles

Worked over 9 sts.
1st row (right side): P2, T5R, p2.
2nd row: K2, p2, k1, p2, k2.
3rd row: P1, T3B, p1, T3F, p1.
4th row: K1, p2, k3, p2, k1.
5th row: T3B, p3, T3F.
6th row: P2, k5, p2.

7th row: K2, p2, MB, p2, k2.
8th row: As 6th row.
9th row: T3F, p3, T3B.
10th row: As 4th row.
11th row: P1, T3F, p1, T3B, p1.
12th row: As 2nd row.
Rep these 12 rows.
Bobbles may also be added to this cable twisted to the left.

Oxo Ripple

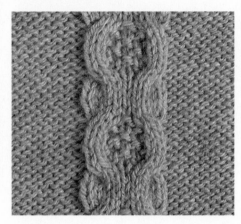

Worked over 9 sts.
1st row (right side): C4B, k1, C4F.
2nd row: P2, [k1, p1] twice, k1, p2.
3rd row: K3, p1, k1, p1, k3.
Rep the 2nd and 3rd rows once more then the 2nd row again.
7th row: C4F, k1, C4B.
8th row: Purl.
9th row: Knit.
Rep 8th and 9th rows once more.
12th row: Purl.
Rep these 12 rows.

8-Stitch Snakey Cable

1st row (right side): Knit.
2nd row: Purl.
3rd row: C8B.
4th row: Purl.
Rep 1st and 2nd rows twice more.
9th row: C8F.
10th row: Purl.
Rep 1st and 2nd rows once.
Rep these 12 rows.

Slipped 5-Stitch Cable Plait

Down   Up

Downwards Plait
1st row (right side): Sl 1 purlwise, k4.
2nd row: P4, sl 1 purlwise.
3rd row: C3L, k2.
4th row: Purl.
5th row: K4, sl 1 purlwise.
6th row: Sl 1 purlwise, p4.
7th row: K2, C3R.
8th row: Purl.
Rep these 8 rows.

Upwards Plait
1st row (right side): K2, sl 1 purlwise, k2.
2nd row: P2, sl 1 purlwise, p2.
3rd row: K2, C3L.
4th row: Purl.
Rep 1st and 2nd rows once.
7th row: C3R, k2.
8th row: Purl.
Rep these 8 rows.

Slipped Wavy Cable

Worked over 3 sts.
1st row (right side): Sl 1 purlwise, k2.
2nd row: P2, sl 1 purlwise.
3rd row: C3L.
4th row: Purl.
5th row: K2, sl 1 purlwise.
6th row: Sl 1 purlwise, p2.
7th row: C3R.
8th row: Purl.
Rep these 8 rows.

Cable Panels

6-Stitch Slipped Double Cable

Down   Up

Downwards Cable

1st row (right side): Sl 1 purlwise, k4, sl 1 purlwise.
2nd row: Sl 1 purlwise, p4, sl 1 purlwise.
Rep the last 2 rows once more.
5th row: C3L, C3R.
6th row: Purl.
Rep these 6 rows.

Upwards Cable

1st row (right side): K2, [sl 1 purlwise] twice, k2.
2nd row: P2, [sl 1 purlwise] twice, p2.
Rep the last 2 rows once more.
5th row: C3R, C3L.
6th row: Purl.
Rep these 6 rows.

Slipped 3-Stitch Cable

Slipped to the Left

1st row (right side): Sl 1 purlwise, k2.
2nd row: P2, sl 1 purlwise.
3rd row: C3L.
4th row: Purl.
Rep these 4 rows.

Slipped to the Right

1st row (right side): K2, sl 1 purlwise.
2nd row: Sl 1 purlwise, p2.
3rd row: C3R.
4th row: Purl.
Rep these 4 rows.

Slipped Double Chain

Worked over 7 sts.

1st row (right side): Sl 1 purlwise, k5, sl 1 purlwise.
2nd row: Sl 1 purlwise, p5, sl 1 purlwise.
3rd row: C3L, k1, C3R.
4th row: Purl.
5th row: K2, sl 1 purlwise, k1, sl 1 purlwise, k2.
6th row: P2, sl 1 purlwise, p1, sl 1 purlwise, p2.
7th row: C3R, k1, C3L.
8th row: Purl.
Rep these 8 rows.

12-Stitch Plait

Down   Up

Downwards Plait

1st row (right side): Knit.
2nd and every alt row: Purl.
3rd row: C8F, k4.
5th and 7th rows: Knit.
9th row: K4, C8B.
11th row: Knit.
12th row: Purl.
Rep these 12 rows.

Upwards Plait

1st row (right side): Knit.
2nd row and every alt row: Purl.
3rd row: C8B, k4.
5th and 7th rows: Knit.
9th row: K4, C8F.
11th row: Knit.
12th row: Purl.
Rep these 12 rows.

Medallion Moss Cable

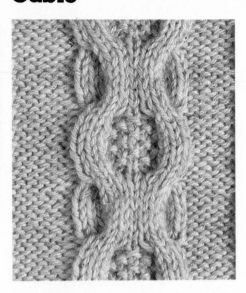

Worked over 13 sts.

1st row (right side): K4, [p1, k1] 3 times, k3.
2nd row: P3, [k1, p1] 4 times, p2.
Rep the last 2 rows once more.
5th row: C6F, k1, C6B.
6th row: Purl.
7th row: Knit.
Rep the last 2 rows twice more.
12th row: Purl.
13th row: C6B, k1, C6F.
14th row: As 2nd row.
15th row: As 1st row.
16th row: As 2nd row.
Rep these 16 rows.

6-Stitch Spiral Cable

1st row (right side): [C2F] 3 times.
2nd row: Purl.
3rd row: K1, [C2F] twice, k1.
4th row: Purl.
Rep these 4 rows.

Alternated Cable

Worked over 10 sts on a background of reversed st st.

1st row (right side): P1, k8, p1.
2nd row: K1, p8, k1.
3rd row: P1, C4B, C4F, p1.
4th row: K1, p2, k4, p2, k1.
5th row: T3B,p4, T3F.
6th row: P2, k6, p2.
7th row: K2, p6, k2.
Work the 6th and 7th rows once more, then 6th row again.
11th row: T3F, p4, T3B.
12th row: As 4th row.
13th row: P1, C4F, C4B, p1.
14th row: K1, p8, k1.
15th row: P1, C4B, C4F, p1.
16th row: K1, p8, k1.
17th row: P1, k8, p1.
Work the 14th, 15th and 16th rows once more.
Rep these 20 rows.

Trellis With Bobbles

Worked over 23 sts on a background of reversed st st.

1st row (wrong side): P2, k7, p2, k1, p2, k7, p2.
2nd row: K2, p3, make bobble as follows: — knit into front, back, front, back and front of next st, [turn and p5, turn and k5] twice, then pass 2nd, 3rd, 4th and 5th sts over the first st (bobble completed), p3, C5B, p3, make bobble as before, p3, k2.
3rd row: As 1st row.
4th row: T3F, p5, T3B, p1, T3F, p5, T3B.
5th row: K1, p2, k5, p2, k3, p2, k5, p2, k1.
6th row: P1, T3F, p3, T3B, p3, T3F, p3, T3B, p1.
7th row: K2, p2, k3, p2, k5, p2, k3, p2, k2.
8th row: P2, T3F, p1, T3B, p5, T3F, p1, T3B, p2.
9th row: K3, p2, k1, p2, k7, p2, k1, p2, k3
10th row: P3, C5F, p3, make bobble as before, p3, C5F, p3.
11th row: As 9th row.
12th row: P2, T3B, p1, T3F, p5, T3B, p1, T3F, p2.
13th row: As 7th row.
14th row: P1, T3B, p3, T3F, p3, T3B, p3, T3F, p1.
15th row: As 5th row.
16th row: T3B, p5, T3F, p1, T3B, p5, T3F.
Rep these 16 rows.

Framed Basket Weave

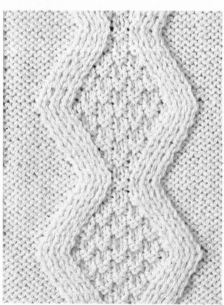

Worked over 24 sts on a background of reversed st st.

1st row (right side): P5, [T2B] 3 times, k2, [T2F] 3 times, p5.
2nd row: K5, [p1, k1] twice, p2, k2, p2, [k1, p1] twice, k5.
3rd row: P4, [T2B] 3 times, k1, p2, k1, [T2F] 3 times, p4.
4th row: K4, [p1, k1] twice, p1, k2, p2, k2, [p1, k1] twice, p1, k4.

5th row: P3, [T2B] 3 times, p2, k2, p2, [T2F] 3 times, p3.
6th row: K3, [p1, k1] 3 times, p2, k2, p2, [k1, p1] 3 times, k3.
7th row: P2, [T2B] 3 times, p1, k2, p2, k2, p1, [T2F] 3 times, p2.
8th row: K2, [p1, k1] twice, p3, k2, p2, k2, p3, [k1, p1] twice, k2.
9th row: P1, [T2B] 3 times, [k2, p2] twice, k2, [T2F] 3 times, p1.
10th row: K1, [p1, k1] twice, [p2, k2] 3 times, p2, [k1, p1] twice, k1.
11th row: [T2B] 3 times, k1, [p2, k2] twice, p2, k1, [T2F] 3 times.
12th row: [P1, k1] twice, p1, [k2, p2] 3 times, k2, [p1, k1] twice, p1.
13th row: [T2F] 3 times, p1, [k2, p2] twice, k2, p1, [T2B] 3 times.
14th row: As 10th row.
15th row: P1, [T2F] 3 times, [p2, k2] twice, p2, [T2B] 3 times, p1.
16th row: As 8th row.
17th row: P2, [T2F] 3 times, k1, p2, k2, p2, k1, [T2B] 3 times, p2.
18th row: As 6th row.
19th row: P3, [T2F] 3 times, k2, p2, k2, [T2B] 3 times, p3.
20th row: As 4th row.
21st row: P4, [T2F] 3 times, p1, k2, p1, [T2B] 3 times, p4.
22nd row: As 2nd row.
23rd row: P5, [T2F] 3 times, p2, [T2B] 3 times, p5.
24th row: K6, [p1, k1] twice, p4, [k1, p1] twice, k6.
Rep these 24 rows.

Honeycomb Pattern

Worked over a multiple of 8 sts. The example shown is worked over 24 sts.

1st row (right side): *C4B, C4F; rep from * to end of panel.
2nd row: Purl.
3rd row: Knit.
4th row: Purl.
5th row: *C4F, C4B; rep from * to end of panel.
6th row: Purl.
7th row: Knit.
8th row: Purl.
Rep these 8 rows.

Cable Panels

Celtic Plait

Worked over a multiple of 10 + 5 (minimum 25). The example shown is worked over 25 stitches.

1st Foundation row (right side): K3, *p4, k6, rep from * to last 2 sts, p2.

2nd Foundation row: K2, *p6, k4; rep from * to last 3 sts, p3.

1st row: K3, *p4, C6F; rep from * to last 2 sts, p2.

2nd row: K2, *p6, k4; rep from * to last 3 sts, p3.

3rd row: *T5F, T5B; rep from * to last 5 sts, T5F.

4th row: P3, *k4, p6; rep from * to last 2 sts, k2.

5th row: P2, *C6B, p4, rep from * to last 3 sts, k3.

6th row: As 4th row.

7th row: *T5B, T5F, rep from * to last 5 sts, T5B.

8th row: As 2nd row.
Rep these 8 rows.

Lattice Pattern

Worked over a multiple of 16 + 1 (minimum 33) on a background of reversed st st. The example shown is worked over 33 sts.

1st row (right side): K1, *yf, k2, sl 1, k1, psso, p7, k2tog, k2, yf, k1; rep from * to end.

2nd row: P5, *k7, p9; rep from * to last 12 sts, k7, p5.

3rd row: K2, *yf, k2, sl 1, k1, psso, p5, k2tog, k2, yf, k2tog, yf, k1; rep from * to last 15 sts, yf, k2, sl 1, k1, psso, p5, k2tog, k2, yf, k2.

4th row: P6, *k5, p11; rep from * to last 11 sts, k5, p6.

5th row: *K2tog, yf, k1, yf, k2, sl 1, k1, psso, p3, k2tog, k2, yf, k2tog, yf; rep from * to last st, k1.

6th row: P7, *k3, p13; rep from * to last 10 sts, k3, p7.

7th row: K1, *k2tog, yf, k1, yf, k2, sl 1, k1, psso, p1, k2tog, k2, yf, [k2tog, yf] twice; rep from * to last 16 sts, k2tog, yf, k1, yf, k2, sl 1, k1, psso, p1, k2tog, k2, yf, k2tog, yf, k2.

8th row: P8, *k1, p15; rep from * to last 9 sts, k1, p8.

9th row: P5, *C7B, p9; rep from * to last 12 sts, C7B, p5.

10th row: K5, *p3, k1, p3, k9; rep from * to last 12 sts, p3, k1, p3, k5.

11th row: P4, *k2tog, k2, yf, k1, yf, k2, sl 1, k1, psso, p7; rep from * to last 13 sts, k2tog, k2, yf, k1, yf, k2, sl 1, k1, psso, p4.

12th row: K4, *p9, k7; rep from * to last 13 sts, p9, k4.

13th row: P3, *k2tog, k2, yf, k2tog, yf, k1, yf, k2, sl 1, k1, psso, p5; rep from * to last 14 sts, k2tog, k2, yf, k2tog, yf, k1, yf, k2, sl 1, k1, psso, p3.

14th row: K3, *p11, k5; rep from * to last 14 sts, p11, k3.

15th row: P2, *k2tog, k2, yf, [k2tog, yf] twice, k1, yf, k2, sl 1, k1, psso, p3; rep from * to last 15 sts, k2tog, k2, yf, [k2tog, yf] twice, k1, yf, k2, sl 1, k1, psso, p2.

16th row: K2, *p13, k3; rep from * to last 15 sts, p13, k2.

17th row: P1, *k2tog, k2, yf, [k2tog, yf] 3 times, k1, yf, k2, sl 1, k1, psso, p1; rep from * to end.

18th row: K1, *p15, k1; rep from * to end.

19th row: P1, k3, *p9, C7F; rep from * to last 13 sts, p9, k3, p1.

20th row: K1, p3, *k9, p3, k1, p3; rep from * to last 13 sts, k9, p3, k1.
Rep these 20 rows.

Hourglass

Worked over a multiple of 14 + 2 sts on a background of reversed st st. The example shown is worked over 30 sts.

1st row (wrong side): K1, p1, *k2, p1, k6, p1, k2, p2; rep from * to last 14 sts, k2, p1,
k6, p1, k2, p1, k1.

2nd row: P1, *T2F, p1, T2F, p4, T2B, p1, T2B; rep from * to last st, p1.

3rd row: [K2, p1] twice, *k4, [p1, k2] 3 times, p1; rep from * to last 10 sts, k4, [p1, k2] twice.

4th row: P2, *T2F, p1, T2F, p2, T2B, p1, T2B, p2; rep from * to end.

5th row: K3,*[p1, k2] 3 times, p1, k4; rep from * to last 13 sts, [p1, k2] 3 times, p1, k3.

6th row: P3, *T2F, p1, T2F, T2B, p1, T2B, p4; rep from * to last 13 sts, T2F, p1, T2F, T2B, p1, T2B, p3.

7th row: K4, *p1, k2, p2, k2, p1, k6; rep from * to last 12 sts, p1, k2, p2, k2, p1, k4.

8th row: P4, *k1, p2, k2, p2, k1 p6; rep from * to last 12 sts, k1, p2, k2, p2, k1, p4.

9th row: As 7th row.

10th row: P3, *T2B, p1, T2B, T2F, p1, T2F, p4; rep from * to last 13 sts, T2B, p1, T2B, T2F, p1, T2F, p3.

11th row: As 5th row.

12th row: P2, *T2B, p1, T2B, p2, T2F, p1, T2F, p2; rep from * to end.

13th row: As 3rd row.

14th row: P1, *T2B, p1, T2B, p4, T2F, p1, T2F; rep from * to last st, p1.

15th row: As 1st row.

16th row: P1, k1, *p2, k1, p6, k1, p2, k2; rep from * to last 14sts, p2, k1, p6, k1, p2, k1, p1.
Rep these 16 rows.

Four Dot Cable

Worked over 25 sts on a background of reversed st st.

1st row (right side): P6, T4F, p2, MB (make bobble) as follows: knit into front, back and front of next st, [turn, k3] 3 times, turn, sl 1, k2tog, psso (bobble completed), p2, T4B, p6.

2nd row: K8, p2, k5, p2, k8.
3rd row: P8, T4F, p1, T4B, p8.
4th row: K10, p2, k1, p2, k10.
5th row: P8, T4B, p1, T4F, p8.
6th row: K6, MB, k1, p2, k5, p2, k1, MB, k6.
7th row: P8, k2, p5, k2, p8.
8th row: As 2nd row.
9th row: As 3rd row.
10th row: As 4th row.
11th row: P8, T4B, MB, T4F, p8.
12th row: As 2nd row.
13th row: P6, T4B, p5, T4F, p6.
14th row: K6, p2, k9, p2, k6.
15th row: P4, T4B, p9, T4F, p4.
16th row: K4, p2, k13, p2, k4.
17th row: P2, T4B, p13, T4F, p2.
18th row: K2, p2, k17, p2, k2.
19th row: T4B, p17, T4F.
20th row: P2, k21, p2.
21st row: K2, p21, k2.
Rep the last 2 rows twice more, then the 20th row again.
27th row: T4F, p17, T4B.
28th row: As 18th row.
29th row: P2, T4F, p13, T4B, p2.
30th row: As 16th row.
31st row: P4, T4F, p9, T4B, p4.
32nd row: As 14th row.
Rep these 32 rows.

Vine And Twist

Worked over 17 sts on a background of reversed st st.
1st row (right side): P6, C5, p6.
2nd row: K6, p5, k6.

3rd row: P5, T3B, k1, T3F, p5.
4th row: K5, p2, k1, p1, k1, p2, k5.
5th row: P4, T3B, p1, k1, p1, T3F, p4.
6th row: K4, p2, k2, p1, k2, p2, k4.
7th row: P3, k2tog, k1, p2, yon, k1, yfrn, p2, k1, sl 1, k1, psso, p3.
8th row: K3, p2, k2, p3, k2, p2, k3.
9th row: P2, k2tog, k1, p2, [k1, yf] twice, k1, p2, k1, sl 1, k1, psso, p2.
10th row: K2, p2, k2, p5, k2, p2, k2.
11th row: P1, k2tog, k1, p2, k2, yf, k1, yf, k2, p2, k1, sl 1, k1, psso, p1.
12th row: K1, p2, k2, p7, k2, p2, k1.
13th row: Purl into front and back of next st (called inc 1), k2, p2, k2, insert needle into next 2 sts on left-hand needle as if to k2tog, then slip both sts onto right-hand needle without knitting them (called sl 2tog knitwise), k1, pass 2 slipped sts over (called p2sso), k2, p2, k2, inc 1.
14th row: As 10th row.
15th row: P1, inc 1, k2, p2, k1, sl 2tog knitwise, k1, p2sso, k1, p2, k2, inc 1, p1.
16th row: As 8th row.
17th row: P2, inc 1, k2, p2, sl 2tog knitwise, k1, p2sso, p2, k2, inc 1, p2.
18th row: As 6th row.
19th row: P4, T3F, p1, k1, p1, T3B, p4.
20th row: As 4th row.
21st row: P5, T3F, k1, T3B, p5.
22nd row: As 2nd row.
23rd row: As 1st row.
24th row: As 2nd row.
25th row: P6, k5, p6.
26th row: As 2nd row.
Rep these 26 rows.

Twisted Ladder Cable

Work over 12 sts on a background of reversed st st.
1st row (right side): T3F, p2, T3B, T3F, p1.

2nd row: K1, [yfrn, p2, pass yfrn over the 2 purled sts, k2] twice, yfrn, p2, pass yfrn over 2 purled sts, k1.
3rd row: P1, T3F, T3B, p2, T3F.
4th row: *Yfrn, p2, pass yfrn over the 2 purled sts*, k4; rep from * to * once more, yrn, p2, pass yrn over 2 purled sts, k2.
5th row: P2, C4B, p4, k2.
6th row: As 4th row.
7th row: P1, T3B, T3F, p2, T3B.
8th row: As 2nd row.
9th row: T3B, p2, T3F, T3B, p1.
10th row: K2, *yfrn, p2, pass yfrn over 2 purled sts*, yrn, p2, pass yrn over 2 purled sts, k4, rep from * to * once more.
11th row: K2, p4, C4F, p2.
12th row: As 10th row.
Rep these 12 rows.

Two And Three Cross

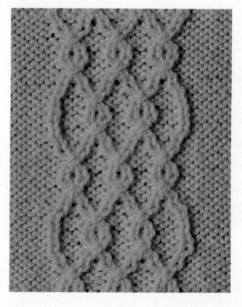

Worked over 18 sts on a background of reversed st st.
1st row (right side): P1, [T2B, T2F, p2] twice, T2B, T2F, p1.
2nd row: K1, [p1, k2] 5 times, p1, k1.
3rd row: P1, [T2F, T2B, p2] twice, T2F, T2B, p1.
4th row: K2, [C2P, k4] twice, C2P, k2.
5th row: As 1st row.
6th row: As 2nd row.
7th row: [T2B, p2, T2F] 3 times.
8th row: P1, [k4, C2P] twice, k4, p1.
9th row: K1, p3, T2B, T2F, p2, T2B, T2F, p3, k1.
10th row: P1, k3, [p1, k2] 3 times, p1, k3, p1.
11th row: K1, p3, T2F, T2B, p2, T2F, T2B, p3, k1.
12th row: As 8th row.
13th row: [T2F, p2, T2B] 3 times.
14th row: As 2nd row.
15th row: As 3rd row.
16th row: As 4th row.
Rep these 16 rows.

Cable Panels

Lattice Cross

Worked over 32 sts on a background of reversed st st.

1st row (right side): *[T2L] twice, p2, T2R, T2L, p2, [T2R] twice; rep from * once more.

2nd row: [K1,PB1] twice, [k2, PB1] 3 times, [k1, PB1, k2, PB1] twice, [k2, PB1] twice, k1, PB1, k1.

3rd row: P1, *[T2L] twice, T2R, p2, T2L, [T2R] twice*, p2 ; rep from * to * once more, p1.

4th row: K2, *PB1, k1, [PB1] twice, k4, [PB1] twice, k1, PB1*, k4, rep from * to * once more, k2.

5th row: P2, [T2L] twice, p4, [T2R] twice, p4, [T2L] twice, p4, [T2R] twice, p2.

6th row: K3, PB1, k1, PB1, k4, PB1, k1, [PB1] twice, k4, [PB1] twice, k1, PB1, k4, PB1, k1, PB1, k3.

7th row: P3, [T2L] twice, p2, [T2R] twice, T2L, p2, T2R, [T2L] twice, p2, [T2R] twice, p3.

8th row: K4, [PB1, k1, PB1, k2] twice, PB1, k2,PB1[k2, PB1, k1, PB1] twice, k4.

9th row: P4, [T2L] twice, [T2R] twice, p2, T2L, T2R, p2, [T2L] twice, [T2R] twice, p4.

10th row: K5, *PB1, k1, T2, k1, PB1*, k4, T2, k4;rep from * to * once more, k5.

11th row: P4, [T2R] twice, [T2L] twice, p2, T2R, T2L, p2, [T2R] twice, [T2L] twice, p4.

12th row: As 8th row.

13th row: P3, [T2R] twice, p2, [T2L] twice, T2R, p2, T2L, [T2R] twice, p2, [T2L] twice, p3.

14th row: As 6th row.

15th row: P2, [T2R] twice, p4, [T2L] twice, p4, [T2R] twice, p4, [T2L] twice, p2.

16th row: As 4th row.

17th row: P1, *[T2R] twice, T2L, p2, T2R, [T2L] twice*, p2; rep from * to * once more, p1.

18th row: As 2nd row.

19th row: *[T2R] twice, p2, T2L, T2R, p2, [T2L] twice; rep from * once more.

20th row: PB1, k1, PB1, k4, T2, k4, PB1, k1, T2, k1, PB1, k4, T2, k4, PB1, k1, PB1.
Rep these 20 rows.

Bobble Tree

Worked over 12 sts.

1st row (wrong side): K5, p2, k5.

2nd row: P4, C2B, C2F, p4.

3rd row: K3, T2F, p2, T2B, k3.

4th row: P2, T2B, C2B, C2F, T2F, p2.

5th row: K1, T2F, k1, p4, k1, T2B, k1.

6th row: T2B, p1, T2B, k2, T2F, p1, T2F.

7th row: P1, k2, p1, k1, p2, k1, p1, k2, p1.

8th row: MB, p1, T2B, p1, k2, p1, T2F, p1, MB.

9th row: K2, p1, k2, p2, k2, p1, k2.

10th row: P2, MB, p2, k2, p2, MB, p2.
Rep these 10 rows.

Triple Criss Cross Cable

Worked over 26 sts on a background of reversed st st.

1st row (right side): P5, [C4F, p2] twice, C4F, p5.

2nd row: K5, [p4, k2] twice, p4, k5.

3rd row: P4, [T3B, T3F] 3 times, p4.

4th row: K4, p2, [k2, p4] twice, k2, p2, k4.

5th row: P3, T3B, [p2, C4B] twice, p2, T3F, p3.

6th row: K3, p2, k3, p4, k2, p4, k3, p2, k3.

7th row: P2, T3B, p2, [T3B, T3F] twice, p2, T3F, p2.

8th row: K2, p2, k3, p2, k2, p4, k2, p2, k3, p2, k2.

9th row: P1, [T3B, p2] twice, C4F, [p2, T3F] twice, p1.

10th row: K1, [p2, k3] twice, p4, [k3, p2] twice, k1.

11th row: [T3B, p2] twice, T3B, [T3F, p2] twice, T3F.

12th row: [P2, k3] twice, p2, k2, [p2, k3] twice, p2.

13th row: [K2, p3] twice, k2, p2, [k2, p3] twice, k2.

14th row: As 12th row.

15th row: [T3F, p2] twice, T3F, [T3B, p2] twice, T3B.

16th row: As 10th row.

17th row: P1, [T3F, p2] twice, C4F, [p2, T3B] twice, p1.

18th row: As 8th row.

19th row: [P2, T3F] twice, T3B, T3F, [T3B, p2] twice.

20th row: As 6th row.

21st row: P3, T3F, [p2, C4B] twice, p2, T3B, p3.

22nd row: As 4th row.

23rd row: P4, [T3F, T3B] 3 times, p4.

24th row: As 2nd row.
Rep these 24 rows.

Double Cross

Worked over 24 sts on a background of reversed st st.

1st row (right side): K4, p4, k8, p4, k4.

2nd row: P4, k4, p8, k4, p4.
3rd row: K4, p4, C8B, p4, k4.
4th row: As 2nd row.
5th row: C5L, p2, C5R, C5L, p2, C5R.
6th row: K1, p4, [k2, p4] 3 times, k1.
7th row: P1, C5L, C5R, p2, C5L, C5R, p1.
8th row: K2, p8, k4, p8, k2.
9th row: P2, C8B, p4, C8B, p2.
10th row: As 8th row.
11th row: P2, k8, p4, k8, p2.
12th row: As 8th row.
13th row: As 9th row.
14th row: As 8th row.
15th row: P1, C5R, C5L, p2, C5R, C5L, p1.
16th row: As 6th row.
17th row: C5R, p2, C5L, C5R, p2, C5L.
18th row: As 2nd row.
19th row: As 3rd row.
20th row: As 2nd row.
21st row: As 1st row.
22nd row: As 2nd row.
Rep these 22 rows.

Interrupted Weave

Worked over 24 sts on a background of reversed st st.
1st row (right side): K1, p2, k3, p2, k2, p2, k9, p2, k1.
2nd row: [P1, k2] twice, p2, k2, p11, k2, p1.
Rep the last 2 rows once more.
5th row: K1, p2, k3, p2, k2, p2, C8F, k1, p2, k1.
6th row: As 2nd row.
Now work 1st and 2nd rows twice more.
11th row: K1, p2, k9, p2, k2, p2, k3, p2, k1.
12th row: P1, k2, p11, k2, p2, [k2, p1] twice.
Rep the last 2 rows once more.
15th row: K1, p2, k1, C8F, p2, k2, p2, k3, p2, k1.

16th row: As 12th row.
Now work 11th and 12th rows twice more.
Rep these 20 rows.

Narrow Cross And Twist

Worked over 12 sts on a background of reversed st st.
1st row (right side): C4F, p4, C4B.
2nd row: P4, k4, p4.
3rd row: K2, T3F, p2, T3B, k2.
4th row: P2, k1, p2, k2, p2, k1, p2.
5th row: K2, p1, T3F, T3B, p1, k2.
6th row: P2, k2, p4, k2, p2.
7th row: K2, p2, C4B, p2, k2.
8th row: As 6th row.
9th row: K2, p1, T3B, T3F, p1, k2.
10th row: As 4th row.
11th row: K2, T3B, p2, T3F, k2.
12th row: As 2nd row.
Rep these 12 rows.

Wide Cross And Twist

Worked over 18 sts on a background of reversed st st.
Special Abbreviations
T4BP (Twist 4 Back Purl) = slip next st onto cable needle and hold at back of work, knit next 3 sts from left-hand needle, then purl st from cable needle.
T4FK (Twist 4 Front Knit) = slip next 3 sts onto cable needle and hold at front of work, purl next st from left-hand needle, then knit sts from cable needle.
1st row (right side): C6F, p6, C6B.
2nd row: P6, k6, p6.
3rd row: K3, T4FK, p4, T4BP, k3.
4th row: P3, k1, p3, k4, p3, k1, p3.
5th row: K3, p1, T4FK, p2, T4BP, p1, k3.
6th row: P3, [k2, p3] 3 times.
7th row: K3, p2, T4FK, T4BP, p2, k3.
8th row: P3, k3, p6, k3, p3.
9th row: K3, p3, C6B, p3, k3.
10th row: P3, k3, p6, k3, p3.
11th row: K3, p2, T4BP, T4FK, p2, k3.
12th row: As 6th row.
13th row: K3, p1, T4BP, p2, T4FK, p1, k3.
14th row: P3, k1, p3, k4, p3, k1, p3.
15th row: K3, T4BP, p4, T4FK, k3.
16th row: As 2nd row.
Rep these 16 rows.

Ladder Cross

Worked over 8 sts on a background of reversed st st.
1st row (right side): C2L, p4, C2R.
2nd row: P2, k4, p2.
3rd row: K1, T2F, p2, T2B, k1.
4th row: P1, k1, p1, k2, p1, k1, p1.
5th row: K1, p1, T2F, T2B, p1, k1.
6th row: P1, k2, p2, k2, p1.
7th row: K1, p2, C2B, p2, k1.
8th row: As 6th row.
9th row: K1, p1, T2B, T2F, p1, k1.
10th row: As 4th row.
11th row: K1, T2B, p2, T2F, k1.
12th row: As 2nd row.
Rep these 12 rows.

Cable Panels

Serpent Panel

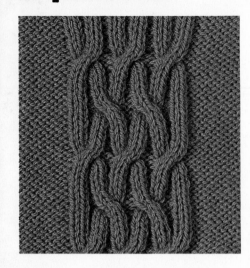

Worked over a multiple of 8 + 6 sts on a background of reversed st st. The example shown is worked over 22 sts.

Special Abbreviation

Twist 6 Back (or Front) = slip next 4 sts onto cable needle and hold at back (or front) of work, knit next 2 sts from left-hand needle, slip the 2 purl sts from cable needle back to left-hand needle and purl them, then k2 sts from cable needle.

1st row (right side): K2, *p2, k2; rep from * to end.
2nd row: P2, *k2, p2; rep from * to end.
3rd row: *Twist 6 Back (see Special Abbreviation), p2; rep from * to last 6 sts, Twist 6 Back.
4th row: As 2nd row.
5th row: As 1st row.
Rep the last 2 rows twice more, then the first of these rows again.
11th row: K2, *p2, Twist 6 Front; rep from * to last 4 sts, p2, k2.
12th row: As 2nd row.
13th row: As 1st row.
Rep the last 2 rows once more, then the first of these rows again.

Rep these 16 rows.

Twisted Tree

Worked over 9 sts.
1st row (right side): P3, [KB1] 3 times, p3.
2nd row: K3, [PB1] 3 times, k3.
3rd row: P2, T2R, KB1, T2L, p2.
4th row: K2, [PB1, k1] twice, PB1, k2.
5th row: P1, T2R, p1, KB1, p1, T2L, p1.
6th row: K1, [PB1, k2] twice, PB1, k1.
7th row: T2R, p1, [KB1] 3 times, p1, T2L.
8th row: PB1, k2, [PB1] 3 times, k2, PB1.
Rep these 8 rows.

Branched Cable I

Worked over 10 sts on a background of reversed st st.
1st row (right side): P3, C4F, p3.
2nd row: K3, p4, k3.
3rd row: P2, C3B, C3F, p2.
4th row: K2, p6, k2.
5th row: P1, C3B, k2, C3F, p1.
6th row: K1, p8, k1.
7th row: C3B, k4, C3F.
8th row: Purl.
Rep these 8 rows.

The cable as given above crosses to the left. To work the cable crossed to the right, work C4B instead of C4F in the 1st row.

Branched Cable II

Worked over 10 sts on a background of reversed st st.
1st row (right side): P3, C4B, p3.
2nd row: K3, p4, k3.
3rd row: P2, T3B, T3F, p2.
4th row: [K2, p2] twice, k2.
5th row: P1, T3B, p2, T3F, p1.
6th row: K1, p2, k4, p2, k1.
7th row: T3B, p4, T3F.
8th row: P2, k6, p2.
Rep these 8 rows.

The cable as given above crosses to the right. To work the cable crossed to the left, work C4F instead of C4B in the 1st row.

Interlocking Twist

Worked over 27 sts.
1st row (right side): K5, p1, k6, p3, k6, p1, k5.
2nd row: P5, k1, p6, k3, p6, k1, p5.
3rd row: K5, p1, C6B, p3, C6F, p1, k5.
4th row: As 2nd row.
Rep the last 4 rows once more, then 1st and 2nd rows again.
11th row: C12F, p3, C12B.
12th row: P6, k1, p5, k3, p5, k1, p6.
13th row: K6, p1, k5, p3, k5, p1, k6.
14th row: As 12th row.
15th row: C6F, p1, k5, p3, k5, p1, C6B.
16th row: As 12th row.
Rep the last 4 rows 3 times more, then 13th and 14th rows again.
31st row: C12B, p3, C12F.
32nd row: As 2nd row.
33rd-36th rows: As 1st-4th rows inclusive.
Rep these 4 rows once more.
Rep these 40 rows.

Knot Cable

Worked over 6 sts on a background of reverse st st.

Special Abbreviation

C6LR (Cross 6 Left and Right) = slip next 2 sts onto cable needle and hold at back of work, slip next 2 sts onto 2nd cable needle and hold at front of work, knit next 2 sts from left-hand needle then knit the 2 sts from 2nd cable needle, then knit the 2 sts from 1st cable needle.

1st row (right side): Knit.
2nd row: Purl.
3rd row: C6LR.
4th row: Purl.
5th row: Knit.
Rep the last 2 rows once more.
8th row: Purl.
Rep these 8 rows.

9-Stitch Cable with Bobbles

Worked over 9 sts on a background of reverse st st.

1st row (right side): Knit.
2nd row: Purl.
Rep the last 2 rows once more.
5th row: C9F.
6th row: Purl.
7th row: K4, [k1, yf, k1, yf, k1] into next st, turn and k5, turn and p5, turn and sl 1, k1,

psso, k1, k2tog, turn and p3tog (1 bobble completed), k4.
8th row: Purl.
Rep 1st and 2nd rows twice more.
Rep these 12 rows.

5-Stitch Cable with Bobbles

Worked over 5 sts on a background of reverse st st.

Special Abbreviation

MK (Make Knot) = [K1, p1, k1, p1, k1] into next st, then pass 2nd, 3rd, 4th and 5th sts over 1st (knot completed).

1st row (right side): C5.
2nd and every alt row: Purl.
3rd row: Knit.
5th row: K2, MK, k2.
7th row: Knit.
8th row: Purl.
Rep these 8 rows.

Sloping Cable

Worked over 10 sts on a background of reverse st st.

Note: Increases should be made by knitting into front and back of next st.

1st row (wrong side): K1, p8, k1.
2nd row: P1, yb, sl 1, k1, psso, k4, inc in next st, k1, p1.
Rep the last 2 rows 3 times more then the first row again.
10th row: P1, C8F, p1.

11th row: As 1st row.
12th row: P1, inc in next st, k5, k2tog, p1.
Rep the last 2 rows 3 times more then the first row again.
20th row: P1, C8B, p1.
Rep these 20 rows.

Double Twisted Cable

Worked over 8 sts on a background of reverse st st.

1st row: Knit.
2nd and every alt row: Purl.
3rd row: [C4B] twice.
5th row: Knit.
7th row: As 3rd row.
9th row: Knit.
11th row: As 3rd row.
12th row: Purl.
Rep 1st and 2nd rows 5 times more.
Rep these 22 rows.

8-Stitch Plait

Worked over 8 sts on a background of reverse st st.

1st and every alt row (wrong side): Purl.
2nd row: K2, C4B, k2.
4th row: C4B, k4.
6th row: K2, C4F, k2.
8th row: K4, C4F.
Rep these 8 rows.

Cable Panels

Alternating Plait

Worked over 8 sts on a background of reverse st st.

1st and every alt row (wrong side): Purl.
2nd row: K4, C4F.
4th row: Knit.
6th row: As 2nd row.
8th row: C4B, k4.
10th row: Knit.
12th row: As 8th row.
Rep these 12 rows.

Wandering Cable

Worked over 12 sts on a background of reverse st st.

Note: Increases to be made by purling into front and back of next st.

1st row (wrong side): K2, p4, k6.
2nd row: P6, k4, p2.
3rd row: As 1st row.

4th row: P6, C4F, p2.
5th row: As 1st row.
6th row: P4, p2tog, k4, inc in next st, p1.
7th row: K3, p4, k5.
8th row: P5, C4F, p3.
9th row: As 7th row.
10th row: P3, p2tog, k4, inc in next st, p2.
11th row: K4, p4, k4.
12th row: P4, C4F, p4.
13th row: As 11th row.
14th row: P2, p2tog, k4, inc in next st, p3.
15th row: K5, p4, k3.
16th row: P3, C4F, p5.
17th row: As 15th row.
18th row: P1, p2tog, k4, inc in next st, p4.
19th row: K6, p4, k2.
20th row: P2, C4F, p6.
21st row: As 19th row.
22nd row: P2, k4, p6.
23rd row: As 19th row.
24th row: P2, C4B, p6.
25th row: As 19th row.
26th row: P1, inc in next st, k4, p2tog, p4.
27th row: As 15th row.
28th row: P3, C4B, p5.
29th row: As 15th row.
30th row: P2, inc in next st, k4, p2tog, p3.
31st row: As 11th row.
32nd row: P4, C4B, p4.
33rd row: As 11th row.
34th row: P3, inc in next st, k4, p2tog, p2.
35th row: As 7th row.
36th row: P5, C4B, p3.
37th row: As 7th row.
38th row: P4, inc in next st, k4, p2tog, p1.
39th row: As 1st row.
40th row: P6, C4B, p2.
Rep these 40 rows.

Small Moss Stitch Cable

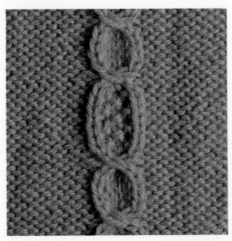

Worked over 5 sts on a background of reverse st st.
1st row (wrong side): [P1, k1] twice, p1.
2nd row: K2, p1, k2.
Rep the last 2 rows once more then the 1st row again.

6th row: Slip next st onto cable needle and hold at front of work, slip next 3 sts onto 2nd cable needle and hold at back of work, knit next st from left-hand needle, knit the 3 sts from 2nd cable needle, then knit st from 1st cable needle.
Work 5 rows in st st, starting purl.
12th row: As 6th row.
Work 1st and 2nd rows twice more.
Rep these 16 rows.

Twisted Eyelet Cable

Worked over 8 sts on a background of reverse st st.

1st row (right side): Knit.
2nd and every alt row: Purl.
3rd row: K2, yf, slip next 2 sts onto cable needle and hold at front of work, k2tog from left-hand needle, then k2tog from cable needle, yf, k2.
5th row: Knit.
7th row: C3F, k2, C3B.
9th row: K1, C3F, C3B, k1.
10th row: Purl.
Rep these 10 rows.

12-Stitch Braid Cable

Worked over 12 sts on a background of reverse st st.

1st row (right side): C4F, k4, C4B.
2nd row: Purl.
3rd row: K2, C4F, C4B, k2.
4th row: Purl.
5th row: K4, C4B, k4.
6th row: Purl.
Rep these 6 rows.

Tight Braid Cable

Worked over 10 sts on a background of reverse st st.
1st row (wrong side): Purl.
2nd row: K2, [C4F] twice.
3rd row: Purl.
4th row: [C4B] twice, k2.
Rep these 4 rows.

Noughts and Crosses Cable

Worked over 12 sts on a background of reverse st st.

Work 4 rows in st st, starting knit.
5th row: C6B, C6F.
6th row: Purl.
Rep these 6 rows once more.
Work 4 rows in st st, starting knit.
17th row: C6F, C6B.
18th row: Purl.
Rep the last 6 rows once more.
Rep these 24 rows.

Lace Cable Pattern I

Worked over 8 sts on a background of reversed st st.
1st row (right side): K2, yf, sl 1, k1, psso, k4.
2nd and every alt row: Purl.
3rd row: K3, yf, sl 1, k1, psso, k3.
5th row: K4, yf, sl 1, k1, psso, k2.
7th row: K5, yf, sl 1, k1, psso, k1.
9th row: C6B, yf, sl 1, k1, psso.
10th row: Purl.
Rep these 10 rows.

Lace Cable Pattern II

Worked over 8 sts on a background of reverse st st.
1st and every alt row (wrong side): K1, p6, k1.
2nd row: P1, k6, p1.
4th row: P1, C6B, p1.
6th row: As 2nd row.
8th row: P1, k1, yf, k2tog, k3, p1.
10th row: P1, sl 1, k1, psso, yf, k4, p1.
12th row: As 8th row.
14th row: As 2nd row.
16th row: As 4th row.
18th row: As 2nd row.
20th row: P1, k3, sl 1, k1, psso, yf, k1, p1.
22nd row: P1, k4, yf, k2tog, p1.
24th row: As 20th row.
Rep these 24 rows.

Old Scottish Stitch

Worked over 12 sts on a background of reverse st st.
1st row (right side): Knit.
2nd and every alt row to 14th row: Purl.
3rd row: C8B, k4.
5th row: Knit.
7th row: K4, C8F.
9th row: Knit.
11th row: As 3rd row.
13th row: Knit.
15th row: K3, yf, sl 1, k1, psso, k4, yf, sl 1, k1, psso, k1.
16th row: P3, yrn, p2tog, p4, yrn, p2tog, p1.
Rep the last 2 rows 3 times more then 15th row again.
24th row: Purl.
Rep these 24 rows.

Cable Panels

Braid Twist

Worked over 6 sts on a background of reverse st st.

1st row (wrong side): K1, p5.
2nd row: K3, C2F, p1.
3rd row: As 1st row.
4th row: C2B, C2F, C2B.
5th row: P5, k1.
6th row: P1, C2B, k3.
7th row: As 5th row.
8th row: C2F, C2B, C2F.
Rep these 8 rows.

Cross and Diamond Twist

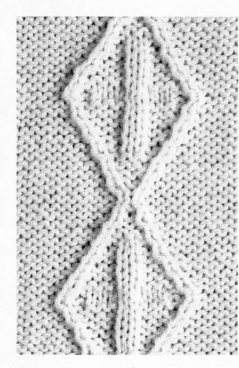

Worked over 14 sts on a background of reversed st st.

1st row (wrong side): K6, p2, k6.
2nd row: P5, T2B, T2F, p5.
3rd row: K5, p1, k2, p1, k5.
4th row: P4, T2B, p2, T2F, p4.
5th row: K4, [p1, k4] twice.
6th row: P3, T2B, p1, k2, p1, T2F, p3.
7th row: K3, p1, k2, p2, k2, p1, k3.
8th row: P2, T2B, p2, k2, p2, T2F, p2.

9th row: K2, p1, k3, p2, k3, p1, k2.
10th row: P1, T2B, p3, k2, p3, T2F, p1.
11th row: K1, p1, k4, p2, k4, p1, k1.
12th row: T2B, p1, k8, p1, T2F.
13th row: P1, k2, p8, k2, p1.
14th row: T2F, p4, k2, p4, T2B.
15th row: As 11th row.
16th row: P1, T2F, p3, k2, p3, T2B, p1.
17th row: As 9th row.
18th row: P2, T2F, p2, k2, p2, T2B, p2.
19th row: As 7th row.
20th row: P3, T2F, p4, T2B, p3.
21st row: As 5th row.
22nd row: P4, T2F, p2, T2B, p4.
23rd row: As 3rd row.
24th row: P5, T2F, T2B, p5.
Rep these 24 rows.

Triangular Twists

Worked over 10 sts on a background of st st.
1st row (right side): Knit.
2nd row: Purl.
3rd row: T2F, k6, T2B.
4th row: K1, p8, k1.
5th row: P1, T2F, k4, T2B, p1.
6th row: K2, p6, k2.
7th row: P2, T2F, k2, T2B, p2.
8th row: K3, p4, k3.
9th row: P3, T2F, T2B, p3.
10th row: K4, p2, k4.
Rep these 10 rows.

Tree Twist

Worked over 12 sts on a background of reverse st st.

1st row (wrong side): K5, p2, k5.
2nd row: P5, k2, p5.
Rep these 2 rows once more then the 1st row again.
6th row: P4, C2R, C2L, p4.
7th row: K3, p1, k1, p2, k1, p1, k3.
8th row: P2, T2B, C2R, C2L, T2F, p2.
9th row: K1, p1, k2, p4, k2, p1, k1.
10th row: T2B, p1, T2B, k2, T2F, p1, T2F.
11th row: P1, k2, p1, k1, p2, k1, p1, k2, p1.
12th row: P3, k1, p1, k2, p1, k1, p3.
13th row: As 7th row.
14th row: As 2nd row.
Rep these 14 rows.

Honeycomb Diamond Twist

Worked over 12 sts on a background of st st.
1st and every alt row (wrong side): Purl.
2nd row: K4, C2F, C2B, k4.
4th row: K2, [C2F, C2B] twice, k2.
6th row: [C2F, C2B] 3 times.
8th row: [C2B, C2F] 3 times.
10th row: K2, [C2B, C2F] twice, k2.
12th row: K4, C2B, C2F, k4.
Rep these 12 rows.

Long Lozenge Twists

Worked over 16 sts on a background of reverse st st.

Special Abbreviation
T4 (Twist 4) = slip next 3 sts onto cable needle and hold at back of work, knit next st from left-hand needle, then slip the 2 purl sts from cable needle back to left-hand needle, bring remaining st on cable needle to front of work, purl next 2 sts from left-hand needle, then knit st from cable needle.

1st row (right side): K1, [p2, k1] 5 times.
2nd row: P1, [k2, p1] 5 times.
3rd row: [K1, p2] twice, T4, [p2, k1] twice.
4th row: As 2nd row.
5th row: As 1st row.
6th row: As 2nd row.
Rep the last 4 rows 3 times more.
19th row: T4, p2, [k1, p2] twice, T4.
20th row: As 2nd row.
21st row: As 1st row.
22nd row: As 2nd row.
Rep the last 4 rows twice more.
31st row: As 19th row.
32nd row: As 2nd row.
Rep these 32 rows.

Diamond Twists

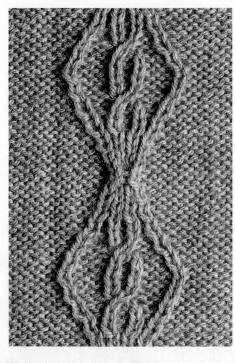

Worked over 14 sts on a background of reverse st st.

Special Abbreviation
T3BR (Twist 3 Back Right) = slip next 3 sts onto cable needle and hold at back of work, knit next st from left-hand needle, then slip the 2 purl sts from cable needle back onto left-hand needle and purl them, then knit remaining st on cable needle.

1st row (right side): P5, C2R, C2L, p5.

2nd row: K5, p4, k5.
3rd row: P4, T2B, k2, T2F, p4.
4th row: K4, p1, k1, p2, k1, p1, k4.
5th row: P3, [T2B] twice, [T2F] twice, p3.
6th row: K3, p1, k1, p1, k2, p1, k1, p1, k3.
7th row: P2, T2B, p1, k1, p2, k1, p1, T2F, p2.
8th row: K2, [p1, k2] 4 times.
9th row: P1, T2B, p2, T3BR, p2, T2F, p1.
10th row: K1, p1, k3, p1, k2, p1, k3, p1, k1.
11th row: T2B, p3, k1, p2, k1, p3, T2F.
12th row: P1, k4, p1, k2, p1, k4, p1.
13th row: T2F, p3, k1, p2, k1, p3, T2B.
14th row: As 10th row.
15th row: P1, T2F, p2, T3BR, p2, T2B, p1.
16th row: As 8th row.
17th row: P2, T2F, p1, k1, p2, k1, p1, T2B, p2.
18th row: As 6th row.
19th row: P3, [T2F] twice, [T2B] twice, p3.
20th row: As 4th row.
21st row: P4, T2F, k2, T2B, p4.
22nd row: As 2nd row.
23rd row: P5, T2F, T2B, p5.
24th row: K6, p2, k6.
Rep these 24 rows.

Big Arrow Twist

Worked over 14 sts on a background of reverse st st.

1st row (right side): T2F, k1, p1, C2L, k2, C2R, p1, k1, T2B.
2nd row: K1, p2, k1, p6, k1, p2, k1.
3rd row: P1, T2F, p1, k1, T2F, T2B, k1, p1, T2B, p1.
4th row: K2, [p1, k1] twice, p2, [k1, p1] twice, k2.
5th row: P2, T2F, k1, p1, C2L, p1, k1, T2B, p2.
6th row: K3, p2, [k1, p2] twice, k3.
7th row: P3, T2F, p1, k2, p1, T2B, p3.
8th row: K4, p1, k1, p2, k1, p1, k4.
9th row: P4, T2F, k2, T2B, p4.
10th row: K5, p4, k5.
11th row: P5, T2F, T2B, p5.
12th row: K6, p2, k6.
13th row: C2L, p4, C2L, p4, C2R.
14th row: P2, [k4, p2] twice.

15th row: K1, T2F, p3, k2, p3, T2B, k1.
16th row: P1, k1, p1, k3, p2, k3, p1, k1, p1.
17th row: K1, p1, C2L, p2, C2L, p2, C2R, p1, k1.
18th row: P1, k1, [p2, k2] twice, p2, k1, p1.
19th row: K1, p1, k1, T2F, p1, k2, p1, T2B, k1, p1, k1.
20th row: [P1, k1] 3 times, p2, [k1, p1] 3 times.
Rep these 20 rows.

Ripple Twist

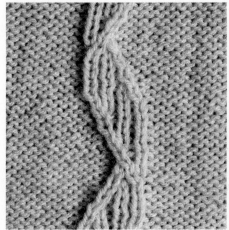

Worked over 9 sts on a background of reverse st st.
1st row (right side): P5, T2B, k1, p1.
2nd row: [K1, p1] twice, k5.
3rd row: P4, C2R, p1, k1, p1.
4th row: K1, p1, k1, p2, k4.
5th row: P3, T2B, [k1, p1] twice.
6th row: [K1, p1] 3 times, k3.
7th row: P2, C2R, [p1, k1] twice, p1.
8th row: [K1, p1] twice, k1, p2, k2.
9th row: P1, T2B, k1, p1, k1, T2B, p1.
10th row: K2, p2, [k1, p1] twice, k1.
11th row: [P1, k1] twice, p1, T2B, p2.
12th row: K3, [p1, k1] 3 times.
13th row: [P1, k1] twice, T2B, p3.
14th row: K4, p2, k1, p1, k1.
15th row: P1, C2L, T2B, p4.
16th row: K5, p3, k1.
17th row: P1, k1, T2F, p5.
18th row: K5, [p1, k1] twice.
19th row: P1, k1, p1, C2L, p4.
20th row: As 14th row.
21st row: [P1, k1] twice, T2F, p3.
22nd row: As 12th row.
23rd row: [P1, k1] twice, p1, C2L, p2.
24th row: As 10th row.
25th row: P1, T2F, k1, p1, k1, T2F, p1.
26th row: As 8th row.
27th row: P2, T2F, [p1, k1] twice, p1.
28th row: As 6th row.
29th row: P3, T2F, [k1, p1] twice.
30th row: As 4th row.
31st row: P4, T2F, C2R, p1.
32nd row: K1, p3, k5.
Rep these 32 rows.

Cable Panels

Climbing Vine

Worked over 14 sts on a background of reverse st st.

Special Abbreviations
C2BP or C2FP (Cross 2 Back or Cross 2 Front Purlwise) = slip next st onto cable needle and hold a back (or front) of work, purl next st from left-hand needle, then purl st from cable needle.

1st row (wrong side): P3, k3, p4, C2BP, k2.
2nd row: P1, C2F, k1, T2B, k2, p3, T2F, k1.
3rd row: P2, k4, p2, k1, p3, C2BP.
4th row: K3, T2B, p1, k1, C2B, p3, T2F.
5th row: K4, C2FP, p2, k2, p4.
6th row: K2, T2B, p2, k1, [C2B] twice, p3.
7th row: K2, C2FP, p4, k3, p3.
8th row: K1, T2B, p3, k2, T2F, k1, C2B, p1.
9th row: C2FP, p3, k1, p2, k4, p2.
10th row: T2B, p3, C2F, k1, p1, T2F, k3.
11th row: P4, k2, p2, C2BP, k4.
12th row: P3, [C2F] twice, k1, p2, T2F, k2.
Rep these 12 rows.

Arch Twists

Worked over 8 sts on a background of reverse st st.
Work 6 rows in st st, starting knit (right side).
7th row: T2F, k4, T2B.

8th row: K1, p6, k1.
9th row: P1, T2F, k2, T2B, p1.
10th row: K2, p4, k2.
11th row: P2, T2F, T2B, p2.
12th row: K3, p2, k3.
Rep these 12 rows.

Corn Panel

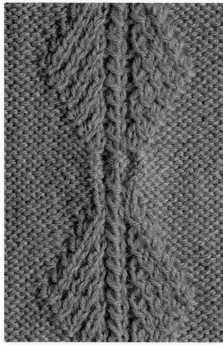

Worked over 18 sts on a background of reverse st st.

1st row (right side): P5, C2B, p1, C2B, p1, C2F, p5.
2nd row: K5, p2, [k1, p2] twice, k5.
3rd row: P4, C2B, k1, p1, C2B, p1, k1, C2F, p4.
4th row: K4, p3, k1, p2, k1, p3, k4.
5th row: P3, [C2B] twice, p1, C2B, p1, [C2F] twice, p3.
6th row: K3, p4, k1, p2, k1, p4, k3.
7th row: P2, [C2B] twice, k1, p1, C2B, p1, k1, [C2F] twice, p2.
8th row: K2, p5, k1, p2, k1, p5, k2.
9th row: P1, [C2B] 3 times, p1, C2B, p1, [C2F] 3 times, p1.
10th row: K1, p6, k1, p2, k1, p6, k1.
11th row: [C2B] 3 times, k1, p1, C2B, p1, k1, [C2F] 3 times.
12th row: P7, k1, p2, k1, p7.
13th row: As 9th row.
14th row: As 10th row.
15th row: As 7th row.
16th row: As 8th row.
17th row: As 5th row.
18th row: As 6th row.
19th row: As 3rd row.
20th row: As 4th row.
21st row: As 1st row.
22nd row: As 2nd row.
23rd row: P6, k1, p1, C2B, p1, k1, p6.
24th row: K6, p1, k1, p2, k1, p1, k6.

25th row: P8, C2B, p8.
26th row: K8, p2, k8.
27th row: Purl.
28th row: Knit.
Rep these 28 rows.

Branched Grapevine Panel

Worked over 13 sts on a background of reverse st st.

1st and every alt row (wrong side): Purl.
2nd row: K2, C2B, k2, C2F, k5.
4th row: K3, C2B, C2F, k6.
6th row: K4, C2B, k4, MB (make bobble) as follows: [k1, yf, k1, yf, k1] into next st, turn and k5, turn and p5, turn and k1, sl 1, k2tog, psso, k1, turn and p3tog (bobble completed), k2.
8th row: K5, C2B, k2, C2F, k2.
10th row: K6, C2B, C2F, k3.
12th row: K2, MB, k4, C2F, k4.
Rep these 12 rows.

Diamond and Bobble Twist

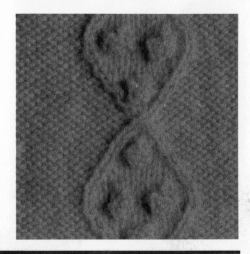

Work over 13 sts on a background of reverse st st.

1st row (right side): P5, C3R, p5.
2nd row: K5, p3, k5.
3rd row: P4, C2R, k1, C2L, p4.
4th row: K4, p5, k4.
5th row: P3, C2R, k1, MB, k1, C2L, p3.
6th row: K3, p7, k3.
7th row: P2, C2R, k5, C2L, p2.
8th row: K2, p9, k2.
9th row: P1, C2R, k7, C2L, p1.
10th row: K1, p11, k1.
11th row: P1, k3, MB, k3, MB, k3, p1.
12th row: As 10th row.
13th row: P1, T2F, k7, T2B, p1.
14th row: As 8th row.
15th row: P2, T2F, k5, T2B, p2.
16th row: As 6th row.
17th row: P3, T2F, k1, MB, k1, T2B, p3.
18th row: As 4th row.
19th row: P4, T2F, k1, T2B, p4.
20th row: As 2nd row.
Rep these 20 rows.

Arrow and Bobble

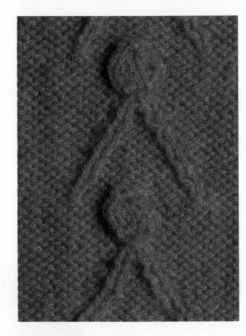

Worked over 14 sts on a background of reverse st st.

1st row (right side): P1, k1, p10, k1, p1.
2nd row: K1, p1, k10, p1, k1.
3rd row: P1, T2F, p8, T2B, p1.
4th row: K2, p1, k8, p1, k2.
5th row: P2, T2F, p6, T2B, p2.
6th row: K3, p1, k6, p1, k3.
7th row: P3, T2F, p4, T2B, p3.
8th row: [K4, p1] twice, k4.
9th row: P4, T2F, p2, T2B, p4.
10th row: K5, p1, k2, p1, k5.
11th row: P5, T2F, T2B, p5.
12th row: K6, p2, k6.
13th row: P6, C2L, p6.
14th row: As 12th row.

15th row: P6, made bobble thus: k1, p1, k1, into each of next 2 sts, turn, p6, turn, k6, turn, p6, turn, [k3tog] twice, p6.
16th row: Knit.
Rep these 16 rows.

Raised Diamonds

Worked over 18 sts on a background of st st.
1st row (right side): K7, T2B, T2F, k7.
2nd row: P8, k2, p8.
3rd row: K6, T2B, p2, T2F, k6.
4th row: P7, k4, p7.
5th row: K5, [T2B] twice, [T2F] twice, k5.
6th row: P6, k1, p1, k2, p1, k1, p6.
7th row: K4, [T2B] twice, p2, [T2F] twice, k4.
8th row: P5, k1, p1, k4, p1, k1, p5.
9th row: K3, [T2B] 3 times, [T2F] 3 times, k3.
10th row: P4, [k1, p1] twice, k2, [p1, k1] twice, p4.
11th row: K2, [T2B] 3 times, p2, [T2F] 3 times, k2.
12th row: P3, [k1, p1] twice, k4, [p1, k1] twice, p3.
13th row: K1, [T2B] 4 times, [T2F] 4 times, k1.
14th row: P2, [k1, p1] 3 times, k2, [p1, k1] 3 times, p2.
15th row: [T2B] 4 times, p2, [T2F] 4 times.
16th row: [P1, k1] 3 times, p1, k4, [p1, k1] 3 times, p1.
17th row: C2L, [T2F] 3 times, p2, [T2B] 3 times, C2R.
18th row: As 14th row.
19th row: K1, C2L, [T2F] 3 times, [T2B] 3 times, C2R, k1.
20th row: As 12th row.
21st row: K2, C2L, [T2F] twice, p2, [T2B] twice, C2R, k2.
22nd row: As 10th row.
23rd row: K3, C2L, [T2F] twice, [T2B] twice, C2R, k3.
24th row: As 8th row.

25th row: K4, C2L, T2F, p2, T2B, C2R, k4.
26th row: As 6th row.
27th row: K5, C2L, T2F, T2B, C2R, k5.
28th row: As 4th row.
29th row: K6, C2L, p2, C2R, k6.
30th row: As 2nd row.
31st row: K7, C2L, C2R, k7.
32nd row: Purl.
Rep these 32 rows.

Twist and Wave

Worked over 18 sts on a background of reversed st st.
1st row (right side): P5, k8, p5.
2nd row: K5, p8, k5.
3rd row: As 1st row.
4th row: K5, [p2, k1] twice, p2, k5.
5th row: P4, T3B, C2R, C2L, T3F, p4.
6th row: K4, p2, k1, p4, k1, p2, k4.
7th row: P3, T3B, p1, T2F, T2B, p1, T3F, p3.
8th row: [K3, p2] 3 times, k3.
9th row: P2, T3B, p2, C2R, C2L, p2, T3F, p2.
10th row: K2, p2, k3, p4, k3, p2, k2.
11th row: P1, T3B, p3, T2F, T2B, p3, T3F, p1.
12th row: K1, [p2, k5] twice, p2, k1.
13th row: T3B, p4, C2R, C2L, p4, T3F.
14th row: P2, k5, p4, k5, p2.
15th row: T3F, p4, T2F, T2B, p4, T3B.
16th row: As 12th row.
17th row: P1, T3F, p3, C2R, C2L, p3, T3B, p1.
18th row: As 10th row.
19th row: P2, T3F, p2, T2F, T2B, p2, T3B, p2.
20th row: As 8th row.
21st row: P3, T3F, p1, C2R, C2L, p1, T3B, p3.
22nd row: As 6th row.
23rd row: P4, T3F, T2F, T2B, T3B, p4.
24th row: As 2nd row.
Rep these 24 rows.

Cable Panels

Twist and Cable

Worked over 16 sts on a background of reverse st st.

1st row (wrong side): K4, p8, k4.
2nd row: P3, T2B, k6, T2F, p3.
3rd row: K3, p1, k1, p6, k1, p1, k3.
4th row: P2, T2B, p1, k6, p1, T2F, p2.
5th row: K2, p1, k2, p6, k2, p1, k2.
6th row: P1, T2B, p2, C6B, p2, T2F, p1.
7th row: K1, p1, k3, p6, k3, p1, k1.
8th row: T2B, p3, k6, p3, T2F.
9th row: P1, k4, p6, k4, p1.
10th row: T2F, p3, k6, p3, T2B.
11th row: As 7th row.
12th row: P1, T2F, p2, C6B, p2, T2B, p1.
13th row: As 5th row.
14th row: P2, T2F, p1, k6, p1, T2B, p2.
15th row: As 3rd row.
16th row: P3, T2F, k6, T2B, p3.
Rep these 16 rows.

Cable and Twist Ripple

Worked over 9 sts on a background of reverse st st.

1st row (right side): T2F, T3B, p1, T3B.
2nd row: K1, p2, k2, p3, k1.
3rd row: P1, T3B, p1, C3B, p1.
4th row: K1, p3, k2, p2, k1.
5th row: T3B, p1, T3B, T2F.
6th row: P1, [k2, p2] twice.

7th row: [K2, p2] twice, k1.
8th row: As 6th row.
9th row: T3F, p1, T3F, T2B.
10th row: As 4th row.
11th row: P1, C3F, p1, T3F, p1.
12th row: As 2nd row.
13th row: T2B, T3F, p1, T3F.
14th row: [P2, k2] twice, p1.
15th row: K1, [p2, k2] twice.
16th row: As 14th row.
Rep these 16 rows.

Cable Gate

Worked over 16 sts on a background of reverse st st.

Note: Increases should be made by purling into front and back of next st.

Special Abbreviations
T4BR (Twist 4 Back Right) = slip next st onto cable needle and hold at back of work, knit next 3 sts from left-hand needle, then purl st from cable needle.
C4BR (Cross 4 Back Right) = slip next st onto cable needle and hold at back of work, knit next 3 sts from left-hand needle, then knit st from cable needle.
C5RI (Cross 5 Right Increase) = slip next st onto cable needle and hold at back of work, knit next 4 sts from left-hand needle, then knit into front and back of st on cable needle.

1st row (right side): P2, [k5, p2] twice.
2nd row: K2, [p5, k2] twice.
3rd row: P1, inc in next st, k4, sl 1, k1, psso, k2tog, k4, inc in next st, p1.
4th row: K3, p10, k3.
5th row: P2, inc in next st, k2, sl 1, k1, psso, C5R, T2F, p2.
6th row: K2, p1, k2, p7, k4.

7th row: P3, inc in next st, k2, sl 1, k1, psso, T3B, p2, T2F, p1.
8th row: K1, p1, k4, p5, k5.
9th row: P5, T4BR, T2F, p3, T2F.
10th row: P1, k4, p1, k2, p3, k5.
11th row: P4, T4BR, p2, T2F, p2, T2B.
12th row: K1, p1, k2, p1, k4, p3, k4.
13th row: P3, T3B, T2F, p3, T2F, T2B, p1.
14th row: K2, p2, k4, p1, k2, p2, k3.
15th row: P2, T3B, p2, T2F, p2, T3B, p2.
16th row: K3, p2, k2, p1, k4, p2, k2.
17th row: P1, T2B, T2F, p3, T2F, T3B, p3.
18th row: K4, p3, k4, p1, k2, p1, k1.
19th row: T2B, p2, T2F, p2, T4BR, p4.
20th row: K5, p3, k2, p1, k4, p1.
21st row: T2F, p3, T2F, T4BR, p5.
22nd row: K6, p4, k4, p1, k1.
23rd row: P1, T2F, p2, C5RI, k1, p2tog, p3.
24th row: K4, p7, k2, p1, k2.
25th row: P2, T2F, C5RI, k3, p2tog, p2.
26th row: K3, p10, k3.
27th row: P1, p2tog, k5, purl into front and back of loop lying between stitch just worked and next stitch, k5, p2tog, p1.
28th row: As 2nd row.
Rep these 28 rows.

Diamond Lattice Panel

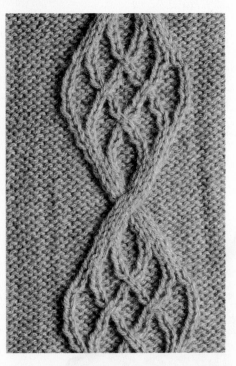

Worked over 18 sts on a background of reverse st st.

Special Abbreviations
T4BR (Twist 4 Back Right) = slip next st onto cable needle and hold at back of work, knit next 3 sts from left-hand needle, then purl st from cable needle.
T4FL (Twist 4 Front Left) = slip next 3 sts onto cable needle and hold at front of work, purl next st from left-hand needle, then knit sts from cable needle.

C2FP or C2BP (Cross 2 Front Purlwise or Cross 2 Back Purlwise) = slip next st onto cable needle and hold at front (or back) of work, purl next st from left-hand needle then purl st from cable needle.

1st row (wrong side): K6, p6, k6.
2nd row: P6, C6B, p6.
3rd row: As 1st row.
4th row: P5, T4BR, T4FL, p5.
5th row: K5, p3, k2, p3, k5.
6th row: P4, T4BR, p2, T4FL, p4.
7th row: [K4, p3] twice, k4.
8th row: P3, T3B, k1, p4, k1, T3F, p3.
9th row: K3, p2, k1, p1, k4, p1, k1, p2, k3.
10th row: P2, T3B, p1, T2F, p2, T2B, p1, T3F, p2.
11th row: K2, p2, k3, p1, k2, p1, k3, p2, k2.
12th row: P1, T2B, k1, p3, T2F, T2B, p3, k1, T2F, p1.
13th row: [K1, p1] twice, k4, C2FP, k4, [p1, k1] twice.
14th row: T2B, p1, T2F, p2, T2B, T2F, p2, T2B, p1, T2F.
15th row: P1, k3, [p1, k2] 3 times, p1, k3, p1.
16th row: K1, p3, T2F, T2B, p2, T2F, T2B, p3, k1.
17th row: P1, [k4, C2BP] twice, k4, p1.
18th row: K1, p3, T2B, T2F, p2, T2B, T2F, p3, k1.
19th row: As 15th row.
20th row: T2F, p1, T2B, p2, T2F, T2B, p2, T2F, p1, T2B.
21st row: As 13th row.
22nd row: P1, T2F, k1, p3, T2B, T2F, p3, k1, T2B, p1.
23rd row: As 11th row.
24th row: P2, T3F, p1, T2B, p2, T2F, p1, T3B, p2.
25th row: As 9th row.
26th row: P3, T3F, k1, p4, k1, T3B, p3.
27th row: As 7th row.
28th row: P4, T4F, p2, T4B, p4.
29th row: As 5th row.
30th row: P5, T4F, T4B, p5.
Rep these 30 rows.

Chalice Cable

Worked over 16 sts on a background of reverse st st.
1st row (right side): K1, [p2, k2] 3 times, p2, k1.
2nd row: P1, k2, [p2, k2] 3 times, p1.

Rep the last 2 rows twice more.
7th row: Slip next 4 sts onto cable needle and hold at back of work, k1, p2, k1 from left-hand needle, then k1, p2, k1 from cable needle, slip next 4 sts onto cable needle and hold at front of work, k1, p2, k1 from left-hand needle, then k1, p2, k1 from cable needle.
8th row: As 2nd row.
9th row: As 1st row.
10th row: As 2nd row.
Rep these 10 rows.

Candle Cable

Worked over 18 sts on a background of reverse st st.
1st row (wrong side): [K1, p1] twice, k3, p4, k3, [p1, k1] twice.
2nd row: P1, T2F, k1, p3, C4F, p3, k1, T2B, p1.
3rd row: K7, p4, k7.
4th row: P6, T3B, T3F, p6.
5th row: K6, p2, k2, p2, k6.
6th row: P5, T3B, p2, T3F, p5.
7th row: K5, p8, k5.
8th row: P4, C3B, C2R, C2L, C3F, p4.
9th row: K4, p10, k4.
10th row: P3, C3B, C2R, k2, C2L, C3F, p3.
11th row: K3, p12, k3.
12th row: P2, C3B, C2R, k4, C2L, C3F, p2.
13th row: K2, p14, k2.
14th row: P1, T2B, k1, T3F, k4, T3B, k1, T2F, p1.
15th row: K1, [p1, k1] twice, p8, [k1, p1] twice, k1.
16th row: T2B, p1, k1, p1, T3F, k2, T3B, p1, k1, p1, T2F.
17th row: [P1, k2] twice, p6, [k2, p1] twice.
18th row: T2F, p1, k1, p2, T3F, T3B, p2, k1, p1, T2B.
Rep these 18 rows.

Banjo Cable

Worked over 8 sts on a background of reverse st st.
1st row (wrong side): K2, p4, k2.
2nd row: P2, k4, p2.
3rd row: K2, p1, sl 2 purlwise, p1, k2.
4th row: Slip next 3 sts onto cable needle and hold at back of work, knit next st from left-hand needle, then p1, k1, p1 from cable needle, slip next st onto cable needle and hold at front of work, k1, p1, k1 from left-hand needle, then k1 from cable needle.
5th row: [P1, k1] 3 times, p2.
6th row: [K1, p1] 3 times, k2.
Rep the last 2 rows twice more.
11th row: Yf, sl 1 purlwise, yb, [k1, p1] 3 times, sl 1 purlwise, yb.
12th row: Slip next st onto cable needle and hold at front of work, p2, k1 from left-hand needle, then k1 from cable needle, slip next 3 sts onto cable needle and hold at back of work, knit next st from left-hand needle then k1, p2 from cable needle.
13th row: As 1st row.
14th row: As 2nd row.
Rep the last 2 rows once more.
Rep these 16 rows.

Cable Arrows

Worked over 8 sts on a background of reverse st st.
1st row (right side): Knit.
2nd row: Purl.
3rd row: P1, T3B, T3F, p1.
4th row: K1, p2, k2, p2, k1.
5th row: T3B, p2, T3F.
6th row: P2, k4, p2.
Rep these 6 rows.

Cable Panels

Cable and Box Panel

Worked over 8 sts on a background of reverse st st.
1st row (right side): Knit.
2nd row: Purl.
3rd row: C8F.
Work 4 rows in st st, starting purl.
8th row: P2, k4, p2.
9th row: K2, p4, k2.
Rep the last 2 rows twice more.
Work 3 rows in st st, starting purl.
Rep these 16 rows.

Garter and Stocking Stitch Cable

Worked over 8 sts on a background of reverse st st.
1st row (right side): Knit.
2nd row: P4, k4.

Rep the last 2 rows twice more.
7th row: C8B.
8th row: K4, p4.
9th row: Knit.
Rep the last 2 rows 4 times more, then the 8th row again.
19th row: C8B.
20th row: As 2nd row.
21st row: Knit.
Rep the last 2 rows once more then the 20th row again.
Rep these 24 rows.

Cable with Moss Stitch and Rib

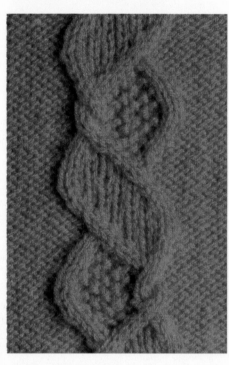

Worked over 15 sts on a background of reverse st st.

Special Abbreviations
T4BR (Twist 4 Back Right) = slip next 2 sts onto cable needle and hold at back of work, k2 from left-hand needle, then k1, p1 from cable needle.

T4FL (Twist 4 Front Left) = slip next 2 sts onto cable needle and hold at front of work, p1, k1 from left-hand needle, then knit sts from cable needle.

1st row (right side): K3, p1, [k1, p1] twice, k5, p2.
2nd row: K2, p4, k1, [p1, k1] 3 times, p2.
3rd row: T3F, [p1, k1] 3 times, C4F, p2.
4th row: K2, p4, k1, [p1, k1] twice, p3, k1.
5th row: P1, T3F, k1, p1, k1, T4BR, C3F, p1.
6th row: [K1, p3] twice, k1, p1, k1, p2, k2.
7th row: P2, T3F, T4BR, k1, p1, k1, T3F.
8th row: P2, k1, [p1, k1] twice, p5, k3.
9th row: P3, T4BR, [k1, p1] 3 times, k2.
10th row: P2, k1, [p1, k1] 3 times, p3, k3.

11th row: P1, T4BR, k1, [p1, k1] 3 times, T3B.
12th row: K1, p3, k1, [p1, k1] 3 times, p3, k1.
13th row: T3B, k1, [p1, k1] 3 times, T4B, p1.
14th row: K3, p3, k1, [p1, k1] 3 times, p2.
15th row: K2, [p1, k1] 3 times, C4B, p3.
16th row: K3, p5, k1, [p1, k1] twice, p2.
17th row: T3F, k1, p1, k1, T4BR, C3F, p2.
18th row: K2, p2, k1, p1, k1, [p3, k1] twice.
19th row: P1, T3F, T4BR, k1, p1, k1, T3F, p1.
20th row: K1, p3, k1, [p1, k1] twice, p4, k2.
21st row: P2, C4B, [k1, p1] 3 times, C3F.
22nd row: P2, k1, [p1, k1] 3 times, p4, k2.
23rd row: P2, k5, p1, [k1, p1] twice, k3.
24th row: As 22nd row.
25th row: P2, C4B, [k1, p1] 3 times, T3B.
26th row: As 20th row.
27th row: P1, C3B, T4FL, k1, p1, k1, T3B, p1.
28th row: As 18th row.
29th row: T3B, k1, p1, k1, T4FL, T3B, p2.
30th row: As 16th row.
31st row: K2, [p1, k1] 3 times, T4FL, p3.
32nd row: As 14th row.
33rd row: T3F, k1, [p1, k1] 3 times, T4FL, p1.
34th row: As 12th row.
35th row: P1, T4F, k1, [p1, k1] 3 times, T3F.
36th row: As 10th row.
37th row: P3, T4F, [k1, p1] 3 times, k2.
38th row: As 8th row.
39th row: P2, C3B, T4FL, k1, p1, k1, T3B.
40th row: As 6th row.
41st row: P1, T3B, k1, p1, k1, T4FL, T3B, p1.
42nd row: As 4th row.
43rd row: T3B, [p1, k1] 3 times, C4F, p2.
44th row: As 2nd row.
Rep these 44 rows.

Cable Circles

Worked over 12 sts on a background of reverse st st.
1st row (right side): Purl.
2nd row: Knit.

3rd row: P3, k6, p3.
4th row: K3, p6, k3.
5th row: C6B, C6F.
Work 5 rows in st st, starting purl.
11th row: T6F, T6B.
12th row: K3, p6, k3.
Rep these 12 rows.

Knotted Cable

Worked over 6 sts on a background of reverse st st.
1st row (right side): K2, p2, k2.
2nd and every alt row: P2, k2, p2.
3rd row: C6.
5th, 7th and 9th rows: K2, p2, k2.
10th row: As 2nd row.
Rep these 10 rows.

Double Chain

Worked over 18 sts on a background of reverse st st.

1st row (right side): P3, k3, [p1, k1] twice, p1, k4, p3.
2nd row: K3, p3, [k1, p1] twice, k1, p4, k3.
Rep the last 2 rows once more.
5th row: P3, slip next 3 sts onto cable needle and hold at back of work, k1, p1, k1 from left-hand needle, then k3 from cable needle, slip next 3 sts onto cable needle and hold at front of work, knit the next 3 sts from left-hand needle, then p1, k1, p1 from cable needle, p3.
6th row: K3, p1, k1, p7, k1, p1, k4.
7th row: P3, k1, p1, k7, p1, k1, p4.
Rep the last 2 rows 3 times more then work 6th row again.
15th row: P3, slip next 3 sts onto cable needle and leave at front of work, knit next 3 sts from left-hand needle, then p1, k1, p1 from cable needle, slip next 3 sts onto cable needle and leave at back of work, k1, p1, k1 from left-hand needle, then k3 from cable needle, p3.
16th row: As 2nd row.
17th row: As 1st row.
Rep the last 2 rows 3 times more then work 16th row again.
Rep these 24 rows.

Cable Rope

Worked over 8 sts on a background of reverse st st.

Special Abbreviations
T4BR (Twist 4 Back) = slip next st onto cable needle and hold back of work, knit next 3 sts from left-hand needle, then purl st from cable needle.
T4FL (Twist 4 Front) = slip next 3 sts onto cable needle and hold at front of work, purl next st from left-hand needle then knit sts from cable needle.

1st row (wrong side): K1, p6, k1.
2nd row: P1, k6, p1.
3rd row: As 1st row.
4th row: P1, C6B, p1.
5th row: As 1st row.
6th row: T4BR, T4FL.
7th row: P3, k2, p3.
8th row: K3, p2, k3.
Rep the last 2 rows 5 times more then the 7th row again.
20th row: T4FL, T4BR.
Rep the first 4 rows once more, then 1st and 2nd rows again.
Rep these 26 rows.

Triple Cable Rope

Worked over 14 sts on a background of reverse st st.
1st row (right side): P2, [k2, p2] 3 times.
2nd row: K2, [p2, k2] 3 times.
Rep these 2 rows twice more.
7th row: P2, T3F, p1, k2, p1, T3B, p2.
8th row: K3, p2, [k1, p2] twice, k3.
9th row: P3, T3F, k2, T3B, p3.
10th row: K4, p6, k4.
11th row: P4, T3F, T3B, p4.
12th row: K5, p4, k5.
13th row: P5, C4F, p5.
14th row: As 12th row.
15th row: P4, C3B, C3F, p4.
16th row: As 10th row.
17th row: P3, T3B, k2, T3F, p3.
18th row: As 8th row.
19th row: P2, T3B, p1, k2, p1, T3F, p2.
20th row: As 2nd row.
Rep 1st and 2nd rows twice more.
Rep these 24 rows.

Cable Panels

Cabled Arrows

Worked over 14 sts on a background of reverse st st.

1st row (right side): K4, p2, k2, p2, k4.
2nd row: P4, k2, p2, k2, p4.
Rep these 2 rows 3 times more.
9th row: C4F, p2, k2, p2, C4B.
10th row: As 2nd row.
11th row: K2, C4F, k2, C4B, k2.
12th row: Purl.
13th row: K4, p1, T2F, T2B, p1, k4.
14th row: As 2nd row.
15th row: As 1st row.
16th row: As 2nd row.
Rep these 16 rows.

Ribbed Cable Rope

Worked over 8 sts on a background of reverse st st.

Special Abbreviations
T6L (Twist 6 Left) = slip next 3 sts onto cable needle and hold at front of work, k1, p1, k1 from left-hand needle, then k1, p1, k1 from cable needle.
T4BR (Twist 4 Back Right) = slip 1 st onto cable needle and hold at back of work, k1, p1, k1 from left-hand needle, then p1 from cable needle.
T4FL (Twist 4 Front Left) = slip next 3 sts onto cable needle and hold at front of work, p1 from left-hand needle, then k1, p1, k1 from cable needle.

1st row (right side): P1, T6L, p1.
2nd row: K1, p1, k1, p2, k1, p1, k1.
3rd row: P1, k1, p1, k2, p1, k1, p1.
4th row: As 2nd row.
5th row: As 1st row.
6th row: As 2nd row.
7th row: T4BR, T4FL.
8th row: As 3rd row.
9th row: As 2nd row.
Rep the last 2 rows 3 times more, then the 3rd row again.
17th row: T4FL, T4BR.
18th row: As 2nd row.
Rep these 18 rows.

Big Wavy Cable Pattern

Worked over 16 sts on a background of reverse st st.

1st row (right side): P2, k4, p4, k4, p2.
2nd row: K2, p4, k4, p4, k2.
3rd row: P2, C4F, p4, C4B, p2.
4th row: As 2nd row.

Rep the last 4 rows once more.
9th row: [T4B, T4F] twice.
10th row: P2, k4, p4, k4, p2.
11th row: K2, p4, k4, p4, k2.
12th row: As 10th row.
13th row: [T4F, T4B] twice.
14th row: As 2nd row.
15th row: P2, C4B, p4, C4F, p2.
16th row: As 2nd row.
17th row: As 1st row.
18th row: As 2nd row.
Rep the last 4 rows once more, then first 2 rows again.
25th row: As 9th row.
26th row: As 10th row.
27th row: As 11th row.
28th row: As 10th row.
29th row: As 13th row.
30th row: As 2nd row.
31st row: As 3rd row.
32nd row: As 2nd row.
Rep these 32 rows.

Ornamental Lantern Cable

Worked over 22 sts on a background of reverse st st.

1st row (wrong side): K9, p4, k9.
2nd row: P9, k4, p9.
3rd row: As 1st row.
4th row: P7, C4B, C4F, p7.
5th row: K7, p8, k7.
6th row: P5, T4B, C4F, T4F, p5.
7th row: K5, p2, k2, p4, k2, p2, k5.
8th row: P3, T4B, p2, k4, p2, T4F, p3.
9th row: K3, p2, k4, p4, k4, p2, k3.
10th row: P2, T3B, p4, C4F, p4, T3F, p2.
11th row: K2, p2, k5, p4, k5, p2, k2.

12th row: P1, T3B, p3, C4B, C4F, p3, T3F, p1.
13th row: K1, p2, k4, p8, k4, p2, k1.
14th row: T3B, p2, T4B, k4, T4F, p2, T3F.
15th row: P2, k3, p2, k2, p4, k2, p2, k3, p2.
16th row: K2, p1, T4B, p2, C4B, p2, T4F, p1, k2.
17th row: P2, k1, p2, k4, p4, k4, p2, k1, p2.
18th row: K2, p1, k2, p4, k4, p4, k2, p1, k2.
19th row: As 17th row.
20th row: K2, p1, T4F, p2, C4B, p2, T4B, p1, k2.
21st row: As 15th row.
22nd row: T3F, p2, T4F, k4, T4B, p2, T3B.
23rd row: As 13th row.
24th row: P1, T3F, p3, T4F, T4B, p3, T3B, p1.
25th row: As 11th row.
26th row: P2, T3F, p4, C4F, p4, T3B, p2.
27th row: As 9th row.
28th row: P3, T4F, p2, k4, p2, T4B, p3.
29th row: As 7th row.
30th row: P5, T4F, C4F, T4B, p5.
31st row: As 5th row.
32nd row: P7, T4F, T4B, p7.
Rep these 32 rows.

Wavy Cable Pattern

Worked over 14 sts on a background of reverse st st.
1st row (wrong side): K5, p4, k5.
2nd row: P5, C4B, p5.
3rd row: As 1st row.
4th row: P4, T3B, T3F, p4.
5th row: K4, p2, k2, p2, k4.
6th row: P2, T4B, p2, T4F, p2.
7th row: K2, p2, k6, p2, k2.

8th row: P2, T4F, p2, T4B, p2.
9th row: As 5th row.
10th row: P4, T3F, T3B, p4.
11th and 13th rows: As 1st row.
12th row: As 2nd row.
14th row: P5, k4, p5.
15th row: As 1st row.
16th row: As 2nd row.
17th row: As 1st row.
18th row: As 14th row.
Rep these 18 rows.

Moss and Bobble Cable

Worked over 13 sts on a background of reverse st st.
1st row (wrong side): K4, p2, k1, p2, k4.
2nd row: P3, T3B, k1, T3F, p3.
3rd row: K3, p2, k1, p1, k1, p2, k3.
4th row: P2, T3B, k1, p1, k1, T3F, p2.
5th row: K2, p2, [k1, p1] twice, k1, p2, k2.
6th row: P1, T3B, [k1, p1] twice, k1, T3F, p1.
7th row: K1, p2, [k1, p1] 3 times, k1, p2, k1.
8th row: T3B, [k1, p1] 3 times, k1, T3F.
9th row: P2, [k1, p1] 4 times, k1, p2.
10th row: T3F, [p1, k1] 3 times, p1, T3B.
11th row: K1, p2, [k1, p1] 3 times, k1, p2, k1.
12th row: P1, T3F, [p1, k1] twice, p1, T3B, p1.
13th row: As 5th row.
14th row: P2, T3F, p1, k1, p1, T3B, p2.
15th row: As 3rd row.
16th row: P3, T3F, p1, T3B, p3.
17th row: As 1st row.
18th row: P4, C5B, p4.
19th row: As 1st row.
20th row: P3, T3B, p1, T3F, p3.

21st row: [K3, p2] twice, k3.
22nd row: P2, T3B, p3, T3F, p2.
23rd row: K2, p2, k5, p2, k2.
24th row: P2, k2, p2, make bobble (MB) as follows: [k1, yf, k1, yf, k1] into next st, turn, p5, turn, k5, turn, p2tog, p1, p2tog, turn, sl 1, k2tog, psso (bobble completed), p2, k2, p2.
25th row: As 23rd row.
26th row: P2, T3F, p3, T3B, p2.
27th row: As 21st row.
28th row: P3, T3F, p1, T3B, p3.
29th row: As 1st row.
30th row: As 18th row.
Rep these 30 rows.

Elongated Cable Plait

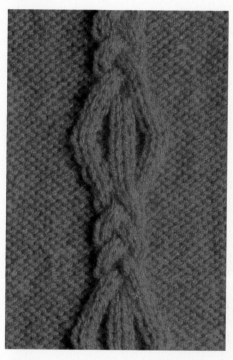

Worked over 12 sts on a background of reverse st st.
1st row (wrong side): K3, p6, k3.
2nd row: P3, k2, C4B, p3.
3rd row: As 1st row.
4th row: P3, C4F, k2, p3.
Rep the last 4 rows once more, then the 1st row again.
10th row: P2, T3B, k2, T3F, p2.
11th row: K2, p2, [k1, p2] twice, k2.
12th row: P1, T3B, p1, k2, p1, T3F, p1.
13th row: K1, [p2, k2] twice, p2, k1.
14th row: T3B, p2, k2, p2, T3F.
15th row: [P2, k3] twice, p2.
16th row: T3F, p2, k2, p2, T3B.
17th row: As 13th row.
18th row: P1, T3F, p1, k2, p1, T3B, p1.
19th row: As 15th row.
20th row: P2, T3F, k2, T3B, p2.
Rep first 4 rows once more.
Rep these 24 rows.

Cable Panels

Broken Cross Panel

Worked over 18 sts on a background of reverse st st.

1st row (right side): K6, p2, k2, p2, k6.
2nd row: P6, k2, p2, k2, p6.
Rep the last 2 rows once more.
5th row: C6F, p2, k2, p2, C6F.
6th row: As 2nd row.
7th row: As 1st row.
8th row: As 2nd row.
9th row: P2, k2, p2, k6, p2, k2, p2.
10th row: K2, p2, k2, p6, k2, p2, k2.
Rep the last 2 rows once more.
13th row: P2, k2, p2, C6F, p2, k2, p2.
14th row: As 10th row.
15th row: As 9th row.
16th row: As 10th row.
Rep these 16 rows.

Enclosed Cables

Worked over 14 sts on a background of reverse st st.

1st row (right side): P1, k2, p2, C4F, p2, k2, p1.
2nd row: K1, p2, k2, p4, k2, p2, k1.
3rd row: P1, k2, p2, k4, p2, k2, p1.
4th row: As 2nd row.
Rep the last 4 rows once more, then the 1st and 2nd rows again.
11th row: P1, [T3F, T3B] twice, p1.
12th row: K2, [p4, k2] twice.
13th row: P2, [C4F, p2] twice.
14th row: As 12th row.
15th row: P1, [T3B, T3F] twice, p1.
16th row: As 2nd row.
17th row: As 1st row.
18th row: As 2nd row.
19th row: As 3rd row.
20th row: As 2nd row.
Rep these 20 rows.

Plaited Lattice Panel

Worked over 23 sts on a background of reverse st st.

1st row (right side): K3, [p1, k3] 5 times.
2nd row: P3, [k1, p3] 5 times.
Rep the last 2 rows twice more.
7th row: [K3, p1] twice, C7B, [p1, k3] twice.
8th and every alt row: As 2nd row.
9th row: As 1st row.
11th row: K3, p1, [C7F, p1] twice, k3.
13th row: As 1st row.
15th row: [C7B, p1] twice, C7B.
17th row: As 1st row.
19th row: As 11th row.
21st row: As 1st row.
23rd row: As 7th row.
25th row: As 1st row.

27th row: As 1st row.
28th row: As 2nd row.
Rep these 28 rows.

Bunched Cable

Worked over 16 sts on a background of reverse st st.

1st row (right side): K4, p3, k2, p3, k4.
2nd row: P4, k3, p2, k3, p4.
Rep the last 2 rows 4 times more.
11th row: C8F, C8B.
12th row: Purl.
Rep these 12 rows.

Fancy Cross and Cable Panel

Worked over 24 sts on a background of reverse st st.

1st row (wrong side): [K2, p2] 3 times, [p2, k2] 3 times.
2nd row: P2, C2R, p2, T4F, C4F, T4B, p2, C2R, p2.

3rd row: K2, p2, k4, p8, k4, p2, k2.
4th row: P2, k2, p4, [C4B] twice, p4, k2, p2.
5th row: As 3rd row.
6th row: P2, C2R, p2, T4B, C4F, T4F, p2, C2R, p2.
7th row: [K2, p2] twice, k2, p4, [k2, p2] twice, k2.
8th row: P2, [k2, p2] twice, k4, p2, [k2, p2] twice.
9th row: K2, [p4, k4] twice, p4, k2.
10th row: P2, [k4, p4] twice, k4, p2.
11th row: As 9th row.
12th row: P2, k4, p4, C4F, p4, k4, p2.
13th row: As 9th row.
14th row: As 10th row.
15th row: As 9th row.
16th row: P2, k2, T4F, p2, k4, p2, T4B, k2, p2.
Rep these 16 rows.

Twisted Rope Panel

Worked over 22 sts on a background of reverse st st.
1st row (right side): K2, p2, [k6, p2] twice, k2.
2nd row: P2, k2, [p6, k2] twice, p2.
3rd row: K2, p2, C6F, p2, C6B, p2, k2.
4th row: As 2nd row.
5th row: As 1st row.
6th row: As 2nd row.
Rep these 6 rows twice more.
19th row: K6, [p2, k2] twice, p2, k6.
20th row: P6, [k2, p2] twice, k2, p6.
21st row: C6B, [p2, k2] twice, p2, C6F.
22nd row: As 20th row.
23rd row: As 19th row.
24th row: As 20th row.
Rep the last 6 rows twice more.
Rep these 36 rows.

Lattice Cable

Worked across 24 sts on a background of reverse st st.
1st row (right side): K2, p8, C4B, p8, k2.
2nd row: P2, k8, p4, k8, p2.
3rd row: T4F, p4, T4B, T4F, p4, T4B.
4th row: K2, [p2, k4] 3 times, p2, k2.
5th row: P2, T4F, T4B, p4, T4F, T4B, p2.
6th row: K4, p4, k8, p4, k4.
7th row: P4, C4B, p8, C4F, p4.
8th row: As 6th row.
9th row: P2, T4B, T4F, p4, T4B, T4F, p2.
10th row: As 4th row.
11th row: T4B, p4, T4F, T4B, p4, T4F.
12th row: As 2nd row.
Rep these 12 rows.

Criss-Cross Cable Panel

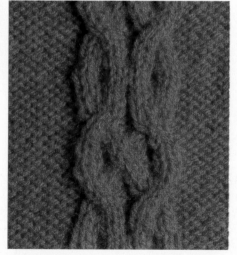

Worked over 12 sts on a background of reverse st st.
1st row (wrong side): K1, p4, k2, p4, k1.
2nd row: [T3B, T3F] twice.
3rd row: P2, k2, p4, k2, p2.
4th row: [T3F, T3B] twice.

Criss-Cross Cable with Twists

5th row: As 1st row.
6th row: P1, k4, p2, k4, p1.
7th row: As 1st row.
8th row: P1, C4B, p2, C4F, p1.
9th row: As 1st row.
10th row: As 2nd row.
11th row: As 3rd row.
12th row: K2, p2, C4F, p2, k2.
13th row: As 3rd row.
14th row: As 4th row.
15th row: As 1st row.
16th row: P1, C4F, p2, C4B, p1.
17th row: As 1st row.
18th row: As 6th row.
Rep these 18 rows.

Worked over 16 sts on a background of reverse st st.
1st row (right side): P2, C4F, p4, C4F, p2.
2nd row: K2, p4, k4, p4, k2.
3rd row: P2, k4, p4, k4, p2.
4th row: As 2nd row.
5th row: As 1st row.
6th row: As 2nd row.
7th row: [T4B, T4F] twice.
8th row: As 3rd row.
9th row: K2, p4, C4F, p4, k2.
10th row: As 3rd row.
11th row: As 2nd row.
12th row: As 3rd row.
13th row: As 9th row.
Rep the last 4 rows twice more.
22nd row: As 3rd row.
23rd row: [T4F, T4B] twice.
24th row: As 2nd row.
Rep these 24 rows.

Cable Patterns

Eyelet Cable

Multiple of 8 sts + 1.
Special Abbreviation
C3tog (Cross 3 together) = slip next 2 sts onto cable needle and hold at back of work, knit next st from left-hand needle, then k2tog from cable needle.
1st row (right side): P1, *C3tog, p1, k3, p1; rep from * to end.
2nd row: K1, *p3, k1, p1, yrn, p1, k1; rep from * to end.
3rd row: P1, *k3, p1, C3tog, p1; rep from * to end.
4th row: K1, *p1, yrn, p1, k1, p3, k1; rep from * to end.
Rep these 4 rows.

Medallion Pattern

Multiple of 10 sts + 2.
Note: Sts should only be counted after the 1st, 6th, 7th or 12th rows.
Foundation row (right side): K1, p3, k4, *p6, k4; rep from * to last 4 sts, p3, k1.
Commence Pattern
1st row: K4, p4, *k6, p4; rep from * to last 4 sts, k4.
2nd row: K1, p1, T4B, pick up horizontal thread lying between st just worked and next st and [k1, p1] into it (called M2), T4F, *p2, T4B, M2, T4F; rep from * to last 2 sts, p1, k1.
3rd row: K2, *p2, k2; rep from * to end.
4th row: K1, p1, *k2, p2; rep from * to last 4 sts, k2, p1, k1.
5th row: As 3rd row.
6th row: K2, *sl 1, k1, psso, p6, k2tog, k2; rep from * to end.
7th row: K1, p2, k6, *p4, k6; rep from * to last 3 sts, p2, k1.
8th row: K1, M1, T4F, p2, T4B, *M2, T4F, p2, T4B; rep from * to last st, M1, k1.
9th row: K1, p1, k2, *p2, k2; rep from * to

last 2 sts, p1, k1.
10th row: As 3rd row.
11th row: As 9th row.
12th row: K1, p3, k2tog, k2, sl 1, k1, psso, *p6, k2tog, k2, sl 1, k1, psso; rep from * to last 4 sts, p3, k1.
Rep these 12 rows.

Textured Diagonals

Multiple of 12 sts.
1st row (right side): Knit.
2nd row: P4, k6, *p6, k6; rep from * to last 2 sts, p2.
3rd row: Knit.
4th row: *P6, k6; rep from * to end.
5th row: *K6, C6F; rep from * to end.
6th row: K2, p6, *k6, p6; rep from * to last 4 sts, k4.
7th row: Knit.
8th row: K4, p6, *k6, p6; rep from * to last 2 sts, k2.
9th row: Knit.
10th row: *K6, p6; rep from * to end.
11th row: *C6F, k6; rep from * to end.
12th row: P2, k6, *p6, k6; rep from * to last 4 sts, p4.
Rep these 12 rows.

Loose Woven Cables

Multiple of 6 sts + 2.
1st row (right side): Knit.
2nd row: K1, knit to last st wrapping yarn twice around needle for each st, k1.
3rd row: K1, *C6B (dropping extra loops); rep from * to last st, k1.
Work 2 rows in garter st.

6th row: K4, *knit to last 4 sts, wrapping yarn twice around needle for each st, k4.
7th row: K4, *C6F (dropping extra loops); rep from * to last 4 sts, k4.
8th row: Knit.
Rep these 8 rows.

Zigzag Twists

Multiple of 7 sts + 1.
Special Abbreviations
C6BP or C6FP (Cable 6 Back or Cable 6 Front Purlwise) = slip next 3 sts onto cable needle and hold at back (or front) of work, purl next 3 sts from left-hand needle, then purl sts from cable needle.
1st row (right side): Knit.
2nd row: Purl.
3rd row: K1, *knit next 6 sts wrapping yarn twice round needle for each st, k1; rep from * to end.
4th row: P1, *C6BP dropping extra loops, p1; rep from * to end.
5th row: Knit.
6th row: Purl.
7th row: As 3rd row.
8th row: P1, *C6FP dropping extra loops, p1; rep from * to end.
Rep these 8 rows.

Slip Stitch Twists with Bobbles

Multiple of 9 sts + 1.
Note: Sts should only be counted after the 11th and 12th rows.
Special Abbreviation
MB (Make Bobble) = [k1, yf, k1, yf, k1] into next st, turn and k5, turn and p5, turn and

k1, sl 1, k2tog, psso, k1, turn and p3tog (bobble completed).

1st row (wrong side): K4, p1, yrn, p1, *k7, p1, yrn, p1; rep from * to last 4 sts, k4.

2nd row: P4, k3, *p7, k3; rep from * to last 4 sts, p4.

3rd row: K4, p3, *k7, p3; rep from * to last 4 sts, k4.

Rep the last 2 rows 3 times more then the 2nd row again.

11th row: K4, p1, slip next st off left-hand needle and allow it to drop down 10 rows to the made loop, p1, *k7, p1, slip next st off needle, p1; rep from * to last 4 sts, k4.

12th row: P4, C2F, *p3, MB, p3, C2F; rep from * to last 4 sts, p4.

Rep these 12 rows.

Forked Cable

Multiple of 8 sts + 2.

1st row (wrong side): Purl.

2nd row: P3, k4, *p4, k4; rep from * to last 3 sts, p3.

Rep the last 2 rows twice more then the 1st row again.

8th row: K3, p4, *k4, p4; rep from * to last 3 sts, k3.

9th row: Purl.

10th row: K1 *C4F, C4B; rep from * to last st, k1.

Rep these 10 rows.

Turtle Check

Multiple of 12 sts + 2.

Special Abbreviations

T4LF (Twist 4 Left) = slip next st onto cable needle and hold at front of work, purl 3 sts from left-hand needle, then knit st from cable needle.

T4RB (Twist 4 Right) = slip next 3 sts onto cable needle and hold at back of work, knit next st from left-hand needle, then purl sts from cable needle.

1st row (right side): K4, p6, *k6, p6; rep from * to last 4 sts, k4.

2nd row: P4, k6, *p6, k6; rep from * to last 4 sts, p4.

3rd row: K3, T4LF, T4RB, *k4, T4LF, T4RB; rep from * to last 3 sts, k3.

4th row: P3, k3, p2, k3, *p4, k3, p2, k3; rep from * to last 3 sts, p3.

5th row: K2, *T4LF, k2, T4RB, k2; rep from * to end.

6th row: P2, *k3, p4, k3, p2; rep from * to end.

7th row: K1, *T4LF, k4, T4RB; rep from * to last st, k1.

8th row: K4, p6, *k6, p6; rep from * to last 4 sts, k4.

9th row: As 2nd row.

Rep the last 2 rows once more then the 8th row again.

13th row: K1, *T4RB, k4, T4LF; rep from * to last st, k1.

14th row: As 6th row.

15th row: K2, *T4RB, k2, T4LF, k2; rep from * to end.

16th row: As 4th row.

17th row: K3, T4RB, T4LF, *k4, T4RB, T4LF; rep from * to last 3 sts, k3.

18th row: As 2nd row.

19th row: As 1st row.

20th row: As 2nd row.

Rep these 20 rows.

Twisted Pyramids

Multiple of 6 sts + 2.

1st row (wrong side): Purl.

2nd row: P1, *T2F, k2, T2B; rep from * to last st, p1.

3rd row: K2, *p4, k2; rep from * to end.

4th row: P2, *k4, p2; rep from * to end.

5th row: As 3rd row.

6th row: P2, *T2F, T2B, p2; rep from * to end.

7th row: K3, p2, *k4, p2; rep from * to last 3 sts, k3.

8th row: K3, C2L, *k4, C2L; rep from * to last 3 sts, k3.

9th row: Purl.

10th row: K2, *T2B, T2F, k2; rep from * to end.

11th row: P3, k2, *p4, k2; rep from * to last 3 sts, p3.

12th row: K3, p2, *k4, p2; rep from * to last 3 sts, k3.

13th row: As 11th row.

14th row: K1, *T2B, p2, T2F; rep from * to last st, k1.

15th row: P2, *k4, p2; rep from * to end.

16th row: C2L, *k4, C2L; rep from * to end.

Rep these 16 rows.

Twisted Arches

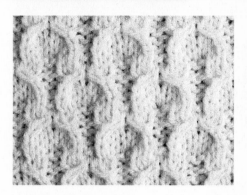

Multiple of 8 sts + 2.

1st row (right side): P2, *k6, p2; rep from * to end.

2nd row: K2, *p6, k2; rep from * to end.

Rep the last 2 rows once more.

5th row: P2, *C3L, C3R, p2; rep from * to end.

6th row: As 2nd row.

7th row: K4, p2, *k6, p2; rep from * to last 4 sts, k4.

8th row: P4, k2, *p6, k2; rep from * to last 4 sts, p4.

Rep the last 2 rows once more.

11th row: K1, *C3R, p2, C3L; rep from * to last st, k1.

12th row: As 8th row.

Rep these 12 rows.

Small Twist Pattern

Multiple of 8 sts + 6.

1st row (right side): Knit.

2nd and every alt row: Purl.

3rd row: K1, C4F, *k4, C4F; rep from * to last st, k1.

5th row: Knit.

7th row: K5, C4F, *k4, C4F; rep from * to last 5 sts, k5.

8th row: Purl.

Rep these 8 rows.

Cable Patterns

Doughnut Pattern

Multiple of 16 sts + 10.
Work 3 rows in st st, starting purl (1st row is wrong side).
4th row: K9, C4F, C4B, *k8, C4F, C4B; rep from * to last 9 sts, k9.
Work 3 rows in st st, starting purl.
8th row: K1, C4B, C4F, *k8, C4B, C4F; rep from * to last st, k1.
Work 3 rows in st st, starting purl.
12th row: K1, C4F, C4B, *k8, C4F, C4B; rep from * to last st, k1.
Work 3 rows in st st, starting purl.
16th row: K9, C4B, C4F, *k8, C4B, C4F; rep from * to last 9 sts, k9.
Rep these 16 rows.

Large Lattice Diamonds

Multiple of 12 sts.
1st row (right side): K2, p8, *C4F, p8; rep from * to last 2 sts, k2.
2nd row: P2, k8, *p4, k8; rep from * to last 2 sts, p2.
3rd row: K2, p8, *k4, p8; rep from * to last 2 sts, k2.

4th row: As 2nd row.
5th row: As 1st row.
6th row: As 2nd row.
7th row: *T3F, p6, T3B; rep from * to end.
8th row: K1, p2, k6, p2, *k2, p2, k6, p2; rep from * to last st, k1.
9th row: P1, T3F, p4, T3B, *p2, T3F, p4, T3B; rep from * to last st, p1.
10th row: K2, p2, *k4, p2; rep from * to last 2 sts, k2.
11th row: P2, T3F, p2, T3B, *p4, T3F, p2, T3B; rep from * to last 2 sts, p2.
12th row: K3, p2, k2, p2, *k6, p2, k2, p2; rep from * to last 3 sts, k3.
13th row: P3, T3F, T3B, *p6, T3F, T3B; rep from * to last 3 sts, p3.
14th row: K4, p4, *k8, p4; rep from * to last 4 sts, k4.
15th row: P4, C4F, *p8, C4F; rep from * to last 4 sts, p4.
16th row: As 14th row.
17th row: P4, k4, *p8, k4; rep from * to last 4 sts, p4.
18th row: As 14th row.
19th row: As 15th row.
20th row: As 14th row.
21st row: P3, T3B, T3F, *p6, T3B, T3F; rep from * to last 3 sts, p3.
22nd row: As 12th row.
23rd row: P2, T3B, p2, T3F, *p4, T3B, p2, T3F; rep from * to last 2 sts, p2.
24th row: As 10th row.
25th row: P1, T3B, p4, T3F, *p2, T3B, p4, T3F; rep from * to last st, p1.
26th row: As 8th row.
27th row: *T3B, p6, T3F; rep from * to end.
28th row: As 2nd row.
Rep these 28 rows.

Woven Lattice Pattern

Multiple of 6 sts + 2.
1st row (wrong side): K3, p4, *k2, p4; rep from * to last st, k1.
2nd row: P1, C4F, *p2, C4F; rep from * to last 3 sts, p3.
3rd row: As 1st row.
4th row: P3, *k2, T4B; rep from * to last 5 sts, k4, p1.
5th row: K1, p4, *k2, p4; rep from * to last 3 sts, k3.
6th row: P3, C4B, *p2, C4B; rep from * to last st, p1.

7th row: As 5th row.
8th row: P1, k4, *T4F, k2; rep from * to last 3 sts, p3.
Rep these 8 rows.

All-Over Lattice Stitch

Multiple of 12 sts + 2.
Work 3 rows in st st, starting purl (1st row is wrong side).
4th row: K1, *C4B, k4, C4F; rep from * to last st, k1.
Work 3 rows in st st, starting purl.
8th row: K3, C4F, C4B, *k4, C4F, C4B; rep from * to last 3 sts, k3.
Rep these 8 rows.

Woven Cables in Relief

Multiple of 15 sts + 2.
1st row (right side): Knit.
2nd row: Purl.
3rd row: K1, C10F, *k5, C10F; rep from * to last 6 sts, k6.
Work 5 rows in st st, starting purl.
9th row: K6, C10B, *k5, C10B; rep from * to last st, k1.
Work 3 rows in st st, starting purl.
Rep these 12 rows.

Large Honeycomb

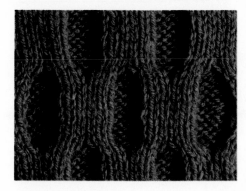

Multiple of 12 sts + 2.

1st row (right side): K4, p6, *k6, p6; rep from * to last 4 sts, k4.

2nd row: P4, k6, *p6, k6; rep from * to last 4 sts, p4.

Rep the last 2 rows 3 times more.

9th row: K1, *T6F, T6B; rep from * to last st, k1.

10th row: As 1st row.

11th row: As 2nd row.

Rep the last 2 rows 3 times more, then the 10th row again.

19th row: K1, *T6B, T6F; rep from * to last st, k1.

20th row: As 2nd row.

Rep these 20 rows.

Hourglass Pattern I

Multiple of 10 sts + 6.

Special Abbreviation

C4FP (Cable 4 Front Purlwise) = slip next 2 sts onto a cable needle and hold at front of work, purl next 2 sts from left-hand needle, then purl sts on cable needle.

1st row (right side): K6, *p4, k6; rep from * to end.

2nd row: P6, *k4, p6; rep from * to end.

Rep the last 2 rows once more.

5th row: K6, *C4FP, k6; rep from * to end.

6th row: As 2nd row.

Rep the last 2 rows once more.

9th row: As 1st row.

10th row: As 2nd row.

11th row: K1, p4, *k6, p4; rep from * to last st, k1.

12th row: P1, k4, *p6, k4; rep from * to last st, p1.

Rep the last 2 rows once more.

15th row: K1, C4FP, *k6, C4FP; rep from * to last st, k1.

16th row: As 12th row.

Rep the last 2 rows once more.

19th row: As 11th row.

20th row: As 12th row.

Rep these 20 rows.

Hourglass Pattern II

Worked as Hourglass Pattern I, using reverse side as right side.

Ridge and Cable Stripes

Multiple of 10 sts + 8.

Work 5 rows in st st, starting purl (1st row is wrong side).

6th row: K7, C4B, *k6, C4B; rep from * to last 7 sts, k7.

7th row: K7, p4, *k6, p4; rep from * to last 7 sts, k7.

8th row: P7, k4, *p6, k4; rep from * to last 7 sts, p7.

9th row: As 7th row.

10th row: P7, C4B, *p6, C4B; rep from * to last 7 sts, p7.

11th row: As 7th row.

12th row: As 8th row.

13th row: As 7th row.

14th row: As 6th row.

Work 5 rows in st st, starting purl.

20th row: K2, C4F, *k6, C4F; rep from *

to last 2 sts, k2.

21st row: K2, p4, *k6, p4; rep from * to last 2 sts, k2.

22nd row: P2, k4, *p6, k4; rep from * to last 2 sts, p2.

23rd row: As 21st row.

24th row: P2, C4F, *p6, C4F; rep from * to last 2 sts, p2.

25th row: As 21st row.

26th row: As 22nd row.

27th row: As 21st row.

28th row: As 20th row.

Rep these 28 rows.

Little Cable Check

Multiple of 20 sts + 2.

Note: Sts should not be counted after 1st, 5th, 9th and 13th rows.

Special Abbreviation

C3tog (Cross 3tog) = slip next 2 sts onto cable needle and hold at back of work, knit next st from left-hand needle then k2tog tbl from cable needle.

1st row (right side): P2, C3tog, p2, [C3R, p2] twice, *[C3tog, p2] twice, [C3R, p2] twice; rep from * to last 5 sts, C3tog, p2.

2nd row: K2, p1, yrn, p1, k2, [p3, k2] twice, *[p1, yrn, p1, k2] twice, [p3, k2] twice; rep from * to last 4 sts, p1, yrn, p1, k2.

3rd row: P2, *k3, p2; rep from * to end.

4th row: K2, *p3, k2; rep from * to end.

5th row: P2, C3tog, p2, [k3, p2] twice, *[C3tog, p2] twice, [k3, p2] twice; rep from * to last 5 sts, C3tog, p2.

6th row: As 2nd row.

7th row: As 3rd row.

8th row: As 4th row.

9th row: P2, C3R, p2, [C3tog, p2] twice, *[C3R, p2] twice, [C3tog, p2] twice; rep from * to last 5 sts, C3R, p2.

10th row: K2, p3, k2, [p1, yrn, p1, k2] twice, *[p3, k2] twice, [p1, yrn, p1, k2] twice; rep from * to last 5 sts, p3, k2.

11th row: As 3rd row.

12th row: As 4th row.

13th row: P2, k3, p2, [C3tog, p2] twice, *[k3, p2] twice, [C3tog, p2] twice; rep from * to last 5 sts, k3, p2.

14th row: As 10th row.

15th row: As 3rd row.

16th row: As 4th row.

Rep these 16 rows.

Cable Patterns

Crosses and Stripes

Multiple of 12 sts + 2.

Work 6 rows in garter st (1st row is right side).

7th row: K2, *p2, k2; rep from * to end.

8th row: P2, *k2, p2; rep from * to end.

Rep the last 2 rows once more.

11th row: K2, *p2, slip next 4 sts onto cable needle and hold at back of work, knit next 2 sts from left-hand needle then slip the 2 purl sts from cable needle back to left-hand needle, purl these 2 sts (keeping cable needle at back of work), then knit 2 sts from cable needle, p2, k2; rep from * to end.

12th row: As 8th row.

13th row: As 7th row.

14th row: As 8th row.

Rep these 14 rows.

Criss Cross Pattern Stitch

Multiple of 12 sts + 6.

1st row (right side): K6, *p2, k2, p2, k6; rep from * to end.

2nd row: P6, *k2, p2, k2, p6; rep from * to end.

Rep the last 2 rows once more.

5th row: C6F, *p2, k2, p2, C6F; rep from * to end.

6th row: As 2nd row.

7th row: As 1st row.

8th row: As 2nd row.

9th row: P2, k2, p2, *k6, p2, k2, p2; rep from * to end.

10th row: K2, p2, k2, *p6, k2, p2, k2; rep from * to end.

Rep the last 2 rows once more.

13th row: P2, k2, p2, *C6F, p2, k2, p2; rep from * to end.

14th row: As 10th row.

15th row: As 9th row.

Squares and Twists

16th row: As 10th row.

Rep these 16 rows.

Multiple of 10 sts + 4.

1st row (wrong side): P4, *k2, p2, k2, p4; rep from * to end.

2nd row: K4, *p2, C2F, p2, k4; rep from * to end.

Rep the last 2 rows once more.

5th row: K1, p2, *k2, p4, k2, p2; rep from * to last st, k1.

6th row: P1, C2F, *p2, k4, p2, C2F; rep from * to last st, p1.

Rep the last 2 rows once more.

Rep these 8 rows.

Honeycomb Trellis

Multiple of 6 sts + 2.

Special Abbreviations

T3FL = slip next st onto cable needle and hold at front of work, p2, then k1 from cable needle.

T3BR = slip next 2 sts onto cable needle and hold at back of work, k1, then p2 from cable needle.

1st row (right side): K2, *p4, k2; rep from * to end.

2nd row: P2, *k4, p2; rep from * to end.

3rd row: K1, *T3FL, T3BR; rep from * to last st, k1.

4th row: K3, p2, *k4, p2; rep from * to last 3 sts, k3.

5th row: P3, k2, *p4, k2; rep from * to last 3 sts, p3.

6th row: As 4th row.

7th row: K1, *T3BR, T3FL; rep from * to last st, k1.

8th row: As 2nd row.

Rep these 8 rows.

Twist Motif

Multiple of 16 sts + 2.

Work 4 rows in st st, starting knit (1st row is right side).

5th row: K7, C2F, C2B, *k12, C2F, C2B; rep from * to last 7 sts, k7.

6th row: Purl.

7th row: K7, C2B, C2F, *k12, C2B, C2F; rep from * to last 7 sts, k7.

Work 7 rows in st st, starting purl.

15th row: K1, *C2B, k12, C2F; rep from * to last st, k1.

16th row: Purl.

17th row: K1, *C2F, k12, C2B; rep from * to last st, k1.

Work 3 rows in st st, starting purl.

Rep these 20 rows.

Diagonal Twists

Multiple of 6 sts.

1st row (wrong side): *K5, p1; rep from * to end.

2nd row: *T2F, p4; rep from * to end.

3rd row: K4, p1, *k5, p1; rep from * to last st, k1.

4th row: P1, T2F, *p4, T2F; rep from * to last 3 sts, p3.

5th row: K3, p1, *k5, p1; rep from * to last 2 sts, k2.

6th row: P2, T2F, *p4, T2F; rep from * to last 2 sts, p2.

7th row: K2, p1, *k5, p1; rep from * to last 3 sts, k3.

8th row: P3, T2F, *p4, T2F; rep from * to last st, p1.

9th row: K1, p1, *k5, p1; rep from * to last 4 sts, k4.

10th row: *P4, T2F; rep from * to end.

11th row: *P1, k5; rep from * to end.

12th row: P5, T2F, *p4, T2F; rep from * to last 5 sts, p5.
Rep these 12 rows.

Twisted Diagonals

Multiple of 6 sts.
1st and every alt row (wrong side): Purl.
2nd row: *K4, C2F; rep from * to end.
4th row: K3, C2F, *k4, C2F; rep from * to last st, k1.
6th row: K2, C2F, *k4, C2F; rep from * to last 2 sts, k2.
8th row: K1, C2F, *k4, C2F; rep from * to last 3 sts, k3.
10th row: *C2F, k4; rep from * to end.
12th row: K5, C2F, *k4, C2F; rep from * to last 5 sts, k5.
Rep these 12 rows.

Arrowheads

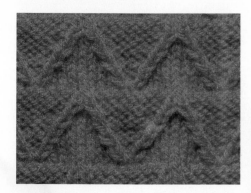

Multiple of 10 sts.
1st row (right side): Knit.
2nd row: Purl.
3rd row: *T2F, k6, T2B; rep from * to end.
4th row: K1, p8, *k2, p8; rep from * to last st, k1.
5th row: P1, T2F, k4, T2B, *p2, T2F, k4, T2B; rep from * to last st, p1.
6th row: K2, p6, *k4, p6; rep from * to last 2 sts, k2.
7th row: P2, T2F, k2, T2B, *p4, T2F, k2, T2B; rep from * to last 2 sts, p2.
8th row: K3, p4, *k6, p4; rep from * to last 3 sts, k3.
9th row: P3, T2F, T2B, *p6, T2F, T2B; rep from * to last 3 sts, p3.
10th row: K4, p2, *k8, p2; rep from * to last 4 sts, k4.
Rep these 10 rows.

Lozenge Pattern

Multiple of 12 sts + 8.
Special Abbreviation
T4 (Twist 4) = slip next 3 sts onto cable needle and hold at back of work, knit next st from left-hand needle, slip the 2 purl sts from cable needle back to left-hand needle, bring remaining st on cable needle to front of work, purl next 2 sts from left-hand needle, then knit st from cable needle.

1st row (right side): P2, *k1, p2; rep from * to end.
2nd row: K2, *p1, k2; rep from * to end.
3rd row: P2, [k1, p2] twice, *T4, p2, [k1, p2] twice; rep from * to end.
4th row: As 2nd row.
Rep the last 4 rows 3 times more, then first 2 rows again.
19th row: P2, T4, p2, *[k1, p2] twice, T4, p2; rep from * to end.
20th row: As 2nd row.
21st row: As 1st row.
22nd row: As 2nd row.
Rep the last 4 rows twice more, then 19th and 20th rows again.
Rep these 32 rows.

Wheat Pattern

Multiple of 10 sts + 1.
1st row (wrong side): P1, *k2, p5, k2, p1; rep from * to end.
2nd row: KB1, *p2, C2B, k1, C2F, p2, KB1; rep from * to end.
Rep the last 2 rows 4 times more.
11th row: P3, k2, p1, k2, *p5, k2, p1, k2; rep from * to last 3 sts, p3.
12th row: K1, *C2F, p2, KB1, p2, C2B, k1; rep from * to end.
Rep the last 2 rows 4 times more.
Rep these 20 rows.

Little Wave

Multiple of 7 sts + 4.
1st row (right side): Knit.
2nd row: P4, *k2, p5; rep from * to end.
3rd row: K4, *C2B, k5; rep from * to end.
4th row: P4, *k1, p1, k1, p4; rep from * to end.
5th row: *K5, C2B; rep from * to last 4 sts, k4.
6th row: *P5, k2; rep from * to last 4 sts, p4.
7th row: Knit.
8th row: As 6th row.
9th row: *K5, C2F; rep from * to last 4 sts, k4.
10th row: As 4th row.
11th row: K4, *C2F, k5; rep from * to end.
12th row: As 2nd row.
Rep these 12 rows.

Openwork and Twist Pattern

Multiple of 15 sts + 12.
Special Abbreviation
T4LR (Twist 4 Left and Right) = slip next 3 sts onto cable needle and hold at back of work, knit next st from left-hand needle then slip the first st on cable needle back to left-hand needle, p2 from cable needle then k1 from left-hand needle.

1st row (right side): P1, T4LR, p2, T4LR, p1, *k1, yf, sl 1, k1, psso, p1, T4LR, p2, T4LR, p1; rep from * to end.
2nd row: K1, p1, [k2, p1] 3 times, k1, *p3, k1, p1, [k2, p1] 3 times, k1; rep from * to end.
3rd row: P1, k1, p2, T4LR, p2, k1, p1, *k2tog, yf, k1, p1, k1, p2, T4LR, p2, k1, p1; rep from * to end.
4th row: As 2nd row.
Rep these 4 rows.

Cable Patterns

Textured Lozenge Stitch

Multiple of 6 sts + 2.

1st row (wrong side): Purl.
2nd row: P1, *T2F, k2, T2B; rep from * to last st, p1.
3rd row: K2, *p4, k2; rep from * to end.
4th row: P2, *T2F, T2B, p2; rep from * to end.
5th row: K3, p2, *k4, p2; rep from * to last 3 sts, k3.
6th row: K3, C2L, *k4, C2L; rep from * to last 3 sts, k3.
7th row: Purl.
8th row: K2, *T2B, T2F, k2; rep from * to end.
9th row: P3, k2, *p4, k2; rep from * to last 3 sts, p3.
10th row: K1, *T2B, p2, T2F; rep from * to last st, k1.
11th row: P2, *k4, p2; rep from * to end.
12th row: C2L, *k4, C2L; rep from * to end.
Rep these 12 rows.

Stocking Stitch Hearts

Multiple of 14 sts + 4.

1st row (wrong side): Knit.
2nd row: Purl.
3rd row: K8, p2, *k12, p2; rep from * to last 8 sts, k8.
4th row: P7, C2F, C2B, *p10, C2F, C2B; rep from * to last 7 sts, p7.
5th row: K7, p4, *k10, p4; rep from * to last 7 sts, k7.
6th row: P6, C2F, k2, C2B, *p8, C2F, k2, C2B; rep from * to last 6 sts, p6.
7th row: K6, p6, *k8, p6; rep from * to last 6 sts, k6.
8th row: P5, C2F, k4, C2B, *p6, C2F, k4, C2B; rep from * to last 5 sts, p5.
9th row: K5, p8, *k6, p8; rep from * to last 5 sts, k5.
10th row: P4, *C2F, k6, C2B, p4; rep from * to end.
11th row: K4, *p10, k4; rep from * to end.
12th row: P4, *k3, T2B, T2F, k3, p4; rep from * to end.
13th row: K4, *p4, k2, p4, k4; rep from * to end.
14th row: P4, *T2F, T2B, p2, T2F, T2B, p4; rep from * to end.
15th row: K5, p2, k4, p2, *k6, p2, k4, p2; rep from * to last 5 sts, k5.
16th row: P5, M1, k2tog tbl, p4, k2tog, M1, *p6, M1, k2tog tbl, p4, k2tog, M1; rep from * to last 5 sts, p5.
17th row: Knit.
18th row: Purl.
Rep these 18 rows.

Rosebud Garden

Multiple of 14 sts + 5.

Note: Count each M5 and sts resulting from M5 on following rows as 1 st.

1st row (wrong side): K7, [p1, k1] twice, p1, *k9, [p1, k1] twice, p1; rep from * to last 7 sts, k7.

2nd row: P7, [k1, p1] twice, k1, *p9, [k1, p1] twice, k1; rep from * to last 7 sts, p7.
Rep the last 2 rows once more then the 1st row again.
6th row: P6, T2B, p1, k1, p1, T2F, *p7, T2B, p1, k1, p1, T2F; rep from * to last 6 sts, p6.
7th row: K6, [p1, k2] twice, p1, *k7, [p1, k2] twice, p1; rep from * to last 6 sts, k6.
8th row: P5, *T2B, p2, k1, p2, T2F, p5; rep from * to end.
9th row: K5, *[p1, k3] twice, p1, k5; rep from * to end.
10th row: P5, *M5 as follows: [k1, yf, k1, yf, k1] into next st, p3, k1, p3, M5, p5; rep from * to end.
11th row: K5, *p5, k3, p1, k3, p5, k5; rep from * to end.
12th row: P5, *k5, p3, k1, p3, k5, p5; rep from * to end.
13th row: As 11th row.
14th row: P5, *k5, p3, M5, p3, k5, p5; rep from * to end.
15th row: K5, *[p5, k3] twice, p5, k5; rep from * to end.
16th row: P5, *D5 as follows: k2tog tbl, k3tog, pass k2tog st over k3tog st, p3, k5, p3, D5, p5; rep from * to end.
17th row: K9, p5, *k13, p5; rep from * to last 9 sts, k9.
18th row: P9, k5, *p13, k5; rep from * to last 9 sts, p9.
19th row: As 17th row.
20th row: P9, D5, *p13, D5; rep from * to last 9 sts, p9.
21st row: K2, p1, k1, p1, k9, *[p1, k1] twice, p1, k9; rep from * to last 5 sts, p1, k1, p1, k2.
22nd row: P2, k1, p1, k1, p9, *[k1, p1] twice, k1, p9; rep from * to last 5 sts, k1, p1, k1, p2.

Rep the last 2 rows once more then the 21st row again.

26th row: P2, k1, *p1, T2F, p7, T2B, p1, k1; rep from * to last 2 sts, p2.
27th row: [K2, p1] twice, k7, *[p1, k2] twice, p1, k7; rep from * to last 6 sts, [p1, k2] twice.
28th row: P2, k1, *p2, T2F, p5, T2B, p2, k1; rep from * to last 2 sts, p2.
29th row: K2, p1, k3, p1, k5, *[p1, k3] twice, p1, k5; rep from * to last 7 sts, p1, k3, p1, k2.
30th row: P2, k1, *p3, M5, p5, M5, p3, k1; rep from * to last 2 sts, p2.
31st row: K2, p1, *k3, p5, k5, p5, k3, p1; rep from * to last 2 sts, k2.
32nd row: P2, k1, *p3, k5, p5, k5, p3, k1; rep from * to last 2 sts, p2.
33rd row: As 31st row.
34th row: P2, M5, *p3, k5, p5, k5, p3, M5; rep from * to last 2 sts, p2.
35th row: K2, p5, *k3, p5, k5, p5, k3, p5; rep from * to last 2 sts, k2.
36th row: P2, k5, *p3, D5, p5, D5, p3, k5; rep from * to last 2 sts, p2.
37th row: K2, p5, *k13, p5; rep from * to last 2 sts, k2.
38th row: P2, k5, *p13, k5; rep from * to last 2 sts, p2.
39th row: As 37th row.
40th row: P2, D5, *p13, D5; rep from * to last 2 sts, p2.
Rep these 40 rows.

Eyelets

Multiple of 3 + 2
Work 2 rows in st st, starting knit.
3rd row (right side): K2, *yf, k2tog, k1; rep from * to end.
4th row: Purl.
Rep these 4 rows.

Braided Openwork

Multiple of 2
1st row (wrong side): Purl.
2nd row (right side): K1, *sl 1, k1, psso, M1; rep from * to last st, k1.
3rd row: Purl.
4th row: K1, *M1, k2tog; rep from * to last st, k1.
Rep these 4 rows.

Butterfly Lace

Multiple of 8 + 7
1st row (right side): K1, *k2tog, yf, k1, yf, sl 1, k1, psso, k3; rep from * to last 6

sts, k2tog, yf, k1, yf, sl 1, k1, psso, k1.
2nd row: P3, *sl 1 purlwise, p7; rep from * to last 4 sts, sl 1 purlwise, p3.
Rep the last 2 rows once more.
5th row: K5, *k2tog, yf, k1, yf, sl 1, k1, psso, k3; rep from * to last 2 sts, k2.
6th row: P7, *sl 1 purlwise, p7; rep from * to end.
Rep the last 2 rows once more.
Rep these 8 rows.

Knotted Openwork

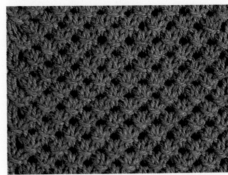

Multiple of 3
1st row (wrong side): Purl.
2nd row: K2, *yf, k3, with left-hand needle lift first of the 3 sts just knitted over the last 2; rep from * to last st, k1.
3rd row: Purl.
4th row: K1, *k3, with left-hand needle lift first of the 3 sts just knitted over the last 2, yf; rep from * to last 2 sts, k2.
Rep these 4 rows.

Eyelet Panes

Multiple of 6 + 3
Note: Stitches should *not* be counted after the 3rd, 4th, 9th or 10th rows of this pattern.
1st row (right side): K2, *yf, sl 1, k1, psso, k1, k2tog, yf, k1; rep from * to last st, k1.
2nd and every alt row: Purl.
3rd row: K3, *yf, k3; rep from * to end.
5th row: K1, k2tog, *yf, sl 1, k1, psso, k1, k2tog, yf, sl 1, k2tog, psso; rep from * to last 8 sts, yf, sl 1, k1, psso, k1, k2tog, yf, sl 1, k1, psso, k1.
7th row: K2, *k2tog, yf, k1, yf, sl 1, k1, psso, k1; rep from * to last st, k1.
9th row: As 3rd row.

11th row: K2, *k2tog, yf, sl 1, k2tog, psso, yf, sl 1, k1, psso, k1; rep from * to last st, k1.
12th row: Purl.
Rep these 12 rows.

Tunnel Lace

Multiple of 3 + 2
Note: Stitches should only be counted after the 4th row of this pattern.
1st row (right side): P2, *yon, k1, yfrn, p2; rep from * to end.
2nd row: K2, *p3, k2; rep from * to end.
3rd row: P2, *k3, p2; rep from * to end.
4th row: K2, *p3tog, k2; rep from * to end.
Rep these 4 rows.

Diamond Lace

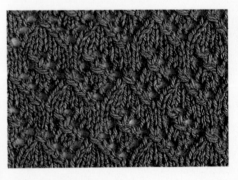

Multiple of 6 + 3
1st row (right side): *K4, yf, sl 1, k1, psso; rep from * to last 3 sts, k3.
2nd and every alt row: Purl.
3rd row: K2, *k2tog, yf, k1, yf, sl 1, k1, psso, k1; rep from * to last st, k1.
5th row: K1, k2tog, yf, *k3, yf, sl 1, k2tog, psso, yf; rep from * to last 6 sts, k3, yf, sl 1, k1, psso, k1.
7th row: K3, *yf, sl 1, k2tog, psso, yf, k3; rep from * to end.
9th row: As 1st row.
11th row: K1, *yf, sl 1, k1, psso, k4; rep from * to last 2 sts, yf, sl 1, k1, psso.
13th row: K2, *yf, sl 1, k1, psso, k1, k2tog, yf, k1; rep from * to last st, k1.
15th row: As 7th row.
17th row: As 5th row.
19th row: As 11th row.
20th row: Purl.
Rep these 20 rows.

All-over Lace Patterns

Falling Leaves

Multiple of 10 + 3

1st row (right side): K1, k2tog, k3, *yf, k1, yf, k3, sl 1, k2tog, psso, k3; rep from * to last 7 sts, yf, k1, yf, k3, sl 1, k1, psso, k1.

2nd and every alt row: Purl.

3rd row: K1, k2tog, k2, *yf, k3, yf, k2, sl 1, k2tog, psso, k2; rep from * to last 8 sts, yf, k3, yf, k2, sl 1, k1, psso, k1.

5th row: K1, k2tog, k1, *yf, k5, yf, k1, sl 1, k2tog, psso, k1; rep from * to last 9 sts, yf, k5, yf, k1, sl 1, k1, psso, k1.

7th row: K1, k2tog, yf, k7, *yf, sl 1, k2tog, psso, yf, k7; rep from * to last 3 sts, sl 1, k1, psso, k1.

9th row: K2, yf, k3, *sl 1, k2tog, psso, k3, yf, k1, yf, k3; rep from * to last 8 sts, sl 1, k2tog, psso, k3, yf, k2.

11th row: K3, yf, k2, *sl 1, k2tog, psso, k2, yf, k3, yf, k2; rep from * to last 8 sts, sl 1, k2tog, psso, k2, yf, k3.

13th row: K4, yf, k1, *sl 1, k2tog, psso, k1, yf, k5, yf, k1; rep from * to last 8 sts, sl 1, k2tog, psso, k1, yf, k4.

15th row: K5, *yf, sl 1, k2tog, psso, yf, k7; rep from * to last 8 sts, yf, sl 1, k2tog, psso, yf, k5.

16th row: Purl.
Rep these 16 rows.

Herringbone Lace Rib

Multiple of 7 + 1

1st row (right side): K1, *p1, k1, yfrn, p2tog, k1, p1, k1; rep from * to end.

2nd row: P1, *k2, yfrn, p2tog, k2, p1; rep from * to end.
Rep these 2 rows.

Garter Stitch Lacy Diamonds

Multiple of 10 + 1

1st and every alt row (right side): Knit.

2nd row: K3, *k2tog, yf, k1, yf, k2tog, k5; rep from * to last 8 sts, k2tog, yf, k1, yf, k2tog, k3.

4th row: K2, *k2tog, yf, k3, yf, k2tog, k3; rep from * to last 9 sts, k2tog, yf, k3, yf, k2tog, k2.

6th row: K1, *k2tog, yf, k5, yf, k2tog, k1; rep from * to end.

8th row: K1, *yf, k2tog, k5, k2tog, yf, k1; rep from * to end.

10th row: K2, *yf, k2tog, k3, k2tog, yf, k3; rep from * to last 9 sts, yf, k2tog, k3, k2tog, yf, k2.

12th row: K3, *yf, k2tog, k1, k2tog, yf, k5; rep from * to last 8 sts, yf, k2tog, k1, k2tog, yf, k3.
Rep these 12 rows.

Diamond Lace

Multiple of 8 + 7

1st row (right side): Knit.

2nd row: and every alt row: Purl.

3rd row: K3, *yf, sl 1, k1, psso, k6; rep from * to last 4 sts, yf, sl 1, k1, psso, k2.

5th row: K2, *yf, sl 1, k2tog, psso, yf, k5; rep from * to last 5 sts, yf, sl 1, k2tog, psso, yf, k2.

7th row: As 3rd row.

9th row: Knit.

11th row: K7, *yf, sl 1, k1, psso, k6; rep from * to end.

13th row: K6, *yf, sl 1, k2tog, psso, yf, k5; rep from * to last st, k1.

15th row: As 11th row.

16th row: Purl.
Rep these 16 rows.

Open Diamonds with Bobbles

Multiple of 10 + 1

1st row (right side): P1, *yon, sl 1, k1, psso, p5, k2tog, yfrn, p1; rep from * to end.

2nd row: K2, *p1, k5, p1, k3; rep from * to last 9 sts, p1, k5, p1, k2.

3rd row: P2, *yon, sl 1, k1, psso, p3, k2tog, yfrn, p3; rep from * to last 9 sts, yon, sl 1, k1, psso, p3, k2tog, yfrn, p2.

4th row: K3, *p1, k3, p1, k5; rep from * to last 8 sts, p1, k3, p1, k3.

5th row: P3, *yon, sl 1, k1, psso, p1, k2tog, yfrn, p5; rep from * to last 8 sts, yon, sl 1, k1, psso, p1, k2tog, yfrn, p3.

6th row: K4, *p1, k1, p1, k7; rep from * to last 7 sts, p1, k1, p1, k4.

7th row: P4, *yon, sl 1, k2tog, psso, yfrn, p3, make bobble (MB) as follows: [k1, p1, k1, p1, k1] into next st, turn and k5, turn and p5, turn and sl 1, k1, psso, k1, k2tog, turn and p3tog, (bobble completed), p3; rep from * to last 7 sts, yon, sl 1, k2tog, psso, yfrn, p4.

8th row: K4, *p3, k3, PB1, k3; rep from * to last 7 sts, p3, k4.

9th row: P3, *k2tog, yfrn, p1, yon, sl 1, k1, psso, p5; rep from * to last 8 sts, k2tog, yfrn, p1, yon, sl 1, k1, psso, p3.

10th row: K3, *p1, k3, p1, k5; rep from * to last 8 sts, p1, k3, p1, k3.

11th row: P2, *k2tog, yfrn, p3, yon, sl 1, k1, psso, p3; rep from * to last 9 sts, k2tog, yfrn, p3, yon, sl 1, k1, psso, p2.

12th row: K2, *p1, k5, p1, k3; rep from * to last 9 sts, p1, k5, p1, k2.

13th row: P1, *k2tog, yfrn, p5, yon, sl 1, k1, psso, p1; rep from * to end.

14th row: K1, *p1, k7, p1, k1; rep from * to end.

15th row: K2tog, *yfrn, p3, MB, p3, yon, sl 1, k2tog, psso; rep from * to last 9 sts, yfrn, p3, MB, p3, yon, sl 1, k1, psso.

16th row: P2; *k3, PB1, k3, p3; rep from * to last 9 sts, k3, PB1, k3, p2.
Rep these 16 rows.

Fishtail Lace

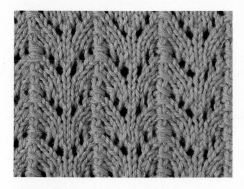

Multiple of 8 + 1

1st row (right side): K1, *yf, k2, sl 1, k2tog, psso, k2, yf, k1; rep from * to end.

2nd row: Purl.

3rd row: K2, *yf, k1, sl 1, k2tog, psso, k1, yf, k3; rep from * to last 7 sts, yf, k1, sl 1, k2tog, psso, k1, yf, k2.

4th row: Purl.

5th row: K3, *yf, sl 1, k2tog, psso, yf, k5; rep from * to last 6 sts, yf, sl 1, k2tog, psso, yf, k3.

6th row: Purl.

Rep these 6 rows.

Ridged Lace Pattern

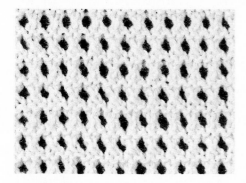

Multiple of 2 + 1

Purl 3 rows.

4th row (right side): K1, *yf, sl 1, k1, psso; rep from * to end.

Purl 3 rows.

8th row: K1, *yf, k2tog; rep from * to end.

Rep these 8 rows.

Feather Lace

Multiple of 6 + 1

1st row (right side): K1, *yf, k2tog tbl, k1, k2tog, yf, k1; rep from * to end.

2nd and every alt row: Purl.

3rd row: K1, *yf, k1, sl 1, k2tog, psso, k1, yf, k1; rep from * to end.

5th row: K1, *k2tog, yf, k1, yf, k2tog tbl, k1; rep from * to end.

7th row: K2tog, *[k1, yf] twice, k1, sl 1, k2tog, psso; rep from * to last 5 sts, [k1, yf] twice, k1, k2tog tbl.

8th row: Purl.

Rep these 8 rows.

Trellis Lace

Multiple of 6 + 5

1st row (right side): K4, *yf, sl 1, k2tog, psso, yf, k3; rep from * to last st, k1.

2nd row: Purl.

3rd row: K1, *yf, sl 1, k2tog, psso, yf, k3; rep from * to last 4 sts, yf, sl 1, k2tog, psso, yf, k1.

4th row: Purl.

Rep these 4 rows.

Diamond And Eyelet Pattern

Multiple of 6 + 3

1st row (wrong side): Knit.

2nd row: P1, *yrn, p2tog; rep from * to end.

3rd and 4th rows: Knit.

5th row and every wrong side row to 15th row: Purl.

6th row: *K4, yf, sl 1, k1, psso; rep from * to last 3 sts, k3.

8th row: K2, *k2tog, yf, k1, yf, sl 1, k1, psso, k1; rep from * to last st, k1.

10th row: K1, k2tog, yf, *k3, yf, sl 1, k2tog, psso, yf; rep from * to last 6 sts, k3, yf, sl 1, k1, psso, k1.

12th row: K3, *yf, sl 1, k2tog, psso, yf, k3; rep from * to end.

14th row: As 6th row.

16th row: Knit.

Rep these 16 rows.

Lattice Lace

Multiple of 7 + 2

1st row (right side): K3, *k2tog, yf, k5; rep from * to last 6 sts, k2tog, yf, k4.

2nd row: P2, *p2tog tbl, yrn, p1, yrn, p2tog, p2; rep from * to end.

3rd row: K1, *k2tog, yf, k3, yf, sl 1, k1, psso; rep from * to last st, k1.

4th row: Purl.

5th row: K1, *yf, sl 1, k1, psso, k5; rep from * to last st, k1.

6th row: *P1, yrn, p2tog, p2, p2tog tbl, yrn; rep from * to last 2 sts, p2.

7th row: *K3, yf, sl 1, k1, psso, k2tog, yf; rep from * to last 2 sts, k2.

8th row: Purl.

Rep these 8 rows.

Lacy Checks

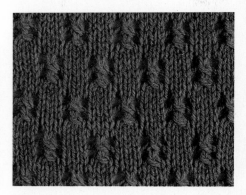

Multiple of 6 + 5

1st row (right side): K1, *yf, sl 1, k2tog, psso, yf, k3; rep from * to last 4 sts, yf, sl 1, k2tog, psso, yf, k1.

2nd and every alt row: Purl.

3rd row: As 1st row.

5th row: Knit.

7th row: K4, *yf, sl 1, k2tog, psso, yf, k3; rep from * to last st, k1.

9th row: As 7th row.

11th row: Knit.

12th row: Purl.

Rep these 12 rows.

All-over Lace Patterns

Ridged Lace

Multiple of 2
1st row (right side): K1, *yf, k2tog tbl; rep from * to last st, k1.
2nd row: P1, *yrn, p2tog; rep from * to last st, p1.
Rep these 2 rows.

Double Lace Rib

Multiple of.6 + 2
1st row (right side): K2, *p1, yon, k2tog tb1,p1, k2; rep from * to end.
2nd row: P2, *k1, p2; rep from * to end.
3rd row: K2, *p1, k2tog, yfrn, p1, k2; rep from * to end.
4th row: As 2nd row.
Rep these 4 rows.

Trellis Pattern

Multiple of 4 + 2
1st row (right side): K1, yf, *sl 1, k1, psso, k2tog, [yfon] twice (2 sts made); rep from * to last 5 sts, sl 1, k1, psso, k2tog, yf, k1.
2nd row: K2, p2, *k into front of first loop

of double yfon, then k into back of 2nd loop, p2; rep from * to last 2 sts, k2.
3rd row: K1, p1, *C2B, p2; rep from * to last 4 sts, C2B, p1, k1.
4th row: K2, *p2, k2; rep from * to end.
5th row: K1, k2tog, *[yfon] twice, sl 1, k1, psso, k2tog; rep from * to last 3 sts, [yfon] twice, sl 1, k1, psso, k1.
6th row: K1, p1, k into front of first loop of double yfon, then k into back of 2nd loop, *p2, work into double yfon as before; rep from * to last 2 sts, p1, k1.
7th row: K2, *p2, C2B; rep from * to last 4 sts, p2, k2.
8th row: K1, p1, k2, *p2, k2; rep from * to last 2 sts, p1, k1.
Rep these 8 rows.

Chequerboard Lace

Multiple of 12 + 8
1st row (right side): K7, *[yf, k2tog] 3 times, k6; rep from * to last st, k1.
2nd and every alt row: Purl.
3rd row: K7, *[k2tog, yf] 3 times, k6; rep from * to last st, k1.
5th row: As 1st row.
7th row: As 3rd row.
9th row: K1, *[yf, k2tog] 3 times, k6; rep from * to last 7 sts, [yf, k2tog] 3 times, k1.
11th row: K1, *[k2tog, yf] 3 times, k6; rep from * to last 7 sts, [k2tog, yf] 3 times, k1.
13th row: As 9th row.
15th row: As 11th row.
16th row: Purl.
Rep these 16 rows.

Fancy Openwork

Multiple of 4
Note: Stitches should only be counted after the 2nd and 4th rows.

1st row (right side): K2, *yf, k4; rep from * to last 2 sts, yf, k2.
2nd row: P2tog, *(k1, p1) into the yf of previous row, [p2tog] twice; rep from * to last 3 sts, (k1, p1) into the yf, p2tog.
3rd row: K4, *yf, k4; rep from * to end.
4th row: P2, p2tog, *(k1, p1) into the yf of previous row, [p2tog] twice; rep from * to last 5 sts, (k1, p1) into the yf, p2tog,p2.
Rep these 4 rows.

Bell Lace

Multiple of 8 + 3
1st row (right side): K1, p1, k1, *p1, yon, sl 1, k2tog, psso, yfrn, [p1, k1] twice; rep from * to end.
2nd row: P1, k1, p1, *k1, p3, [k1, p1] twice; rep from * to end.
Rep last 2 rows twice more.
7th row: K1, k2tog, *yfrn, [p1, k1] twice, p1, yon, sl 1, k2tog, psso; rep from * to last 8 sts, yfrn, [p1, k1] twice, p1, yon, sl 1, k1, psso, k1.
8th row: P3, *[k1, p1] twice, k1, p3; rep from * to end.
Rep the last 2 rows twice more.
Rep these 12 rows.

Diamond Rib

Multiple of 9 + 2
1st row (right side): P2, *k2tog, [k1, yf] twice, k1, sl 1, k1, psso, p2; rep from * to end.
2nd and every alt row: K2, *p7, k2; rep from * to end.
3rd row: P2, *k2tog, yf, k3, yf, sl 1, k1, psso, p2; rep from * to end.
5th row: P2, *k1, yf, sl 1, k1, psso, k1, k2tog, yf, k1, p2; rep from * to end.
7th row: P2, *k2, yf, sl 1, k1, k2tog, psso, yf, k2, p2; rep from * to end.
8th row: As 2nd row.
Rep these 8 rows.

Eyelet Rib

Multiple of 11 + 4

1st row (right side): K1, yfrn, p2tog, k1, *p1, k2, yf, sl 1, k1, psso, k1, p1, k1, yfrn, p2tog, k1; rep from * to end.
2nd and every alt row: K1, yfrn, p2tog, *k2, p5, k2, yfrn, p2tog; rep from * to last st, k1.
3rd row: K1, yfrn, p2tog, k1, *p1, k1, yf, sl 1, k2tog, psso, yf, k1, p1, k1, yfrn, p2tog, k1; rep from * to end.
5th row: As 1st row.
7th row: K1, yfrn, p2tog, k1, *p1, k5, p1, k1, yfrn, p2tog, k1; rep from * to end.
8th row: As 2nd row.
Rep these 8 rows.

Moss Lace Diamonds

Multiple of 8 + 1

1st row (right side): K1, *p1, k1; rep from * to end.
2nd row: K1, *p1, k1; rep from * to end.
Rep the last 2 rows once more.
5th row: K1, *yf, sl 1, k1, psso, k3, k2tog, yf, k1; rep from * to end.
6th row: Purl.
7th row: K2, *yf, sl 1, k1, psso, k1, k2tog, yf, k3; rep from * to last 7 sts, yf, sl 1, k1, psso, k1, k2tog, yf, k2.
8th row: Purl.
9th row: K3, *yf, sl 1, k2tog, psso, yf, k5; rep from * to last 6 sts, yf, sl 1, k2tog, psso, yf, k3.
10th row: Purl.
11th row: K1, *p1, k1; rep from * to end.
Rep the last row 3 times more.

15th row: K2, *k2tog, yf, k1, yf, sl 1, k1, psso, k3; rep from * to last 7 sts, k2tog, yf, k1, yf, sl 1, k1, psso, k2.
16th row: Purl.
17th row: K1, *k2tog, yf, k3, yf, sl 1, k1, psso, k1; rep from * to end.
18th row: Purl.
19th row: K2tog, *yf, k5, yf, sl 1, k2tog, psso; rep from * to last 7 sts, yf, k5, yf, sl 1, k1, psso.
20th row: Purl.
Rep these 20 rows.

Scallop Pattern

Multiple of 13 + 2

Note: Stitches should only be counted after the 5th or 6th row of pattern.
1st row (right side): K1, *sl 1, k1, psso, k9, k2tog; rep from * to last st, k1.
2nd row: Purl.
3rd row: K1, *sl 1, k1, psso, k7, k2tog; rep from * to last st, k1.
4th row: Purl.
5th row: K1, *sl 1, k1, psso, yf, [k1, yf] 5 times, k2tog; rep from * to last st, k1.
6th row: Knit.
Rep these 6 rows.

Astrakhan Bobbles

Multiple of 12 + 3

Either side of this stitch may be used.
1st row: K2, *yf, k4, p3tog, k4, yf, k1; rep from * to last st, k1.
Rep this row 5 times more.
7th row: K1, p2tog, *k4, yf, k1, yf, k4, p3tog; rep from * to last 12 sts, k4, yf, k1, yf, k4, p2tog, k1.
Rep this row 5 times more.
Rep these 12 rows.

Chevron Rib

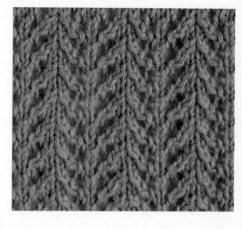

Multiple of 7 + 2

1st row (right side): K2, *k2tog, yf, k1, yf, sl 1, k1, psso, k2; rep from * to end.
2nd row: Purl.
3rd row: K1, *k2tog, yf, k3, yf, sl 1, k1, psso; rep from * to last st, k1.
4th row: Purl.
Rep these 4 rows.

Slanting Eyelets

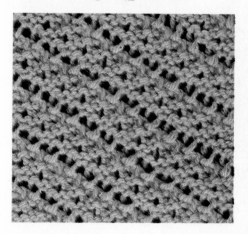

Multiple of 8 + 2

1st row (right side): K1, *yfrn, p2tog, k1, p2tog, yon, k3; rep from * to last st, k1.
2nd row: K6, *p2tog, yon, k6; rep from * to last 4 sts, p2tog, yon, k2.
3rd row: K3, *yfrn, p2tog, k1, p2tog, yon, k3; rep from * to last 7 sts, yfrn, p2tog, k1, p2tog, yon, k2.
4th row: K4, *p2tog, yon, k6; rep from * to last 6 sts, p2tog, yon, k4.
5th row: *P2tog, yon, k3, yfrn, p2tog, k1; rep from * to last 2 sts, k2.
6th row: K2, *p2tog, yon, k6; rep from * to end.
7th row: K2, *p2tog, yon, k3, yfrn, p2tog, k1; rep from * to end.
8th row: *P2tog, yon, k6; rep from * to last 2 sts, k2.
Rep these 8 rows.

All-over Lace Patterns

All-over Eyelets

Multiple of 10 + 1

1st row (right side): Knit.

2nd and every alt row: Purl.

3rd row: K3, *k2tog, yf, k1, yf, sl 1, k1, psso, k5; rep from * to last 8 sts, k2tog, yf, k1, yf, sl 1, k1, psso, k3.

5th row: Knit.

7th row: K1, *yf, sl 1, k1, psso, k5, k2tog, yf, k1; rep from * to end.

8th row: Purl.

Rep these 8 rows.

Snakes And Ladders

Multiple of 8 + 2

1st row (right side): K7, *k2tog, yf, k6; rep from * to last 3 sts, k2tog, yf, k1.

2nd row: K2, *yfrn, p2tog, k6; rep from * to end.

3rd row: K5, *k2tog, yf, k6; rep from * to last 5 sts, k2tog, yf, k3.

4th row: K4, *yfrn, p2tog, k6; rep from * to last 6 sts, yfrn, p2tog, k4.

5th row: K3, *k2tog, yf, k6; rep from * to last 7 sts, k2tog, yf, k5.

6th row: *K6, yfrn, p2tog; rep from * to last 2 sts, k2.

7th row: K1, *k2tog, yf, k6; rep from * to last st, k1.

8th row: K7, *p2tog tbl, yon, k6; rep from * to last 3 sts, p2tog tbl, yon, k1.

9th row: K2, *yf, k2tog tbl, k6; rep from * to end.

10th row: K5, *p2tog tbl, yon, k6; rep from * to last 5 sts, p2tog tbl, yon, k3.

11th row: K4, *yf, k2tog tbl, k6; rep from * to last 6 sts, yf, k2tog tbl, k4.

12th row: K3, *p2tog tbl, yon, k6; rep from * to last 7 sts, p2tog tbl, yon, k5.

13th row: *K6, yf, k2tog tbl; rep from * to last 2 sts, k2.

14th row: K1, *p2tog tbl, yon, k6; rep from * to last st, k1.

Rep these 14 rows.

Eyelet Lace

Multiple of 6 + 2

Note: Stitches should only be counted after the 2nd and 4th row.

1st row (right side): K1, yf, *k2tog tbl, k2, k2tog, yf; rep from * to last st, k1.

2nd row: K1, p5, *p into front and back of next st, p4; rep from * to last 2 sts, p1, k1

3rd row: K2, *k2tog, yf, k2tog tbl, k2; rep from * to end.

4th row: K1, p2, *p into front and back of next st, p4; rep from * to last 4 sts, p into front and back of next st, p2, k1.

Rep these 4 rows.

Travelling Vine

Multiple of 8 + 2

Note: Stitches should only be counted after wrong side rows.

1st row (right side): K1, *yf, KB1, yf, k2tog tbl, k5; rep from * to last st, k1.

2nd row: P5, *p2tog tbl, p7; rep from * to last 6 sts, p2tog tbl, p4.

3rd row: K1, *yf, KB1, yf, k2, k2tog tbl, k3; rep from * to last st, k1.

4th row: P3, *p2tog tbl, p7; rep from * to last 8 sts, p2tog tbl, p6.

5th row: K1, *KB1, yf, k4, k2tog tbl, k1, yf; rep from * to last st, k1.

6th row: P2, *p2tog tbl, p7; rep from * to end.

7th row: K6, *k2tog, yf, KB1, yf, k5; rep from * to last 4 sts, k2tog, yf, KB1, yf, k1.

8th row: P4, *p2tog, p7; rep from * to last 7 sts, p2tog, p5.

9th row: K4, *k2tog, k2, yf, KB1, yf, k3; rep from * to last 6 sts, k2tog, k2, yf, KB1, yf, k1.

10th row: P6, *p2tog, p7; rep from * to last 5 sts, p2tog, p3.

Imitation Crochet

11th row: K1, *yf, k1, k2tog, k4, yf, KB1; rep from * to last st, k1.

12th row: *P7, p2tog; rep from * to last 2 sts, p2.

Rep these 12 rows.

Multiple of 6 + 3

Note: Stitches should *not* be counted after the 1st and 5th row.

1st row (wrong side): K1, *yf, k1; rep from * to end.

2nd row: Knit, dropping yfs of previous row.

3rd row: K1, k3tog, *[yfon] twice (2 sts made), k1, [yfon] twice, sl 2, k3tog, pass both sl sts over; rep from * to last 5 sts, [yfon] twice, k1, [yfon] twice, k3tog, k1.

4th row: K2, *k into front of first loop and back of 2nd loop of double yfon of previous row, k1; rep from * to last st, k1.

5th row: As 1st row.

6th row: As 2nd row.

7th row: K2, *[yfon] twice, sl 2, k3tog, pass both sl sts over, [yfon] twice, k1; rep from * to last st, k1.

8th row: As 4th row.

Rep these 8 rows.

Climbing Leaf Pattern

Multiple of 16 + 1

1st row (right side): K1, *yf, k5, k2tog, k1, k2tog tbl, k5, yf, k1; rep from * to end.

2nd and every alt row: Purl.

3rd row: As 1st row.

5th row: K1, *k2tog tbl, k5, yf, k1, yf, k5, k2tog, k1; rep from * to end.

7th row: As 5th row.

8th row: Purl.

Rep these 8 rows.

Florette Pattern

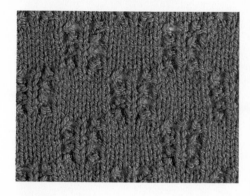

Multiple of 12 + 7

1st row (right side): K1, *p2tog, yon, k1, yfrn, p2tog, k7; rep from * to last 6 sts, p2tog, yon, k1, yfrn, p2tog, k1.

2nd and every alt row: Purl.

3rd row: K1, *yfrn, p2tog, k1, p2tog, yon, k7; rep from * to last 6 sts, yfrn, p2tog, k1, p2tog, yon, k1.

5th row: As 3rd row.

7th row: As 1st row.

9th row: K7, *p2tog, yon, k1, yfrn, p2tog, k7; rep from * to end.

11th row: K7, *yfrn, p2tog, k1, p2tog, yon, k7; rep from * to end.

13th row: As 11th row.

15th row: As 9th row.

16th row: Purl.

Rep these 16 rows.

Gothic Windows

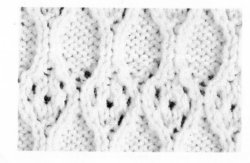

Multiple of 8 + 2

Note: Stitches should *not* be counted after the 3rd, 7th, 9th and 11th rows.

1st row (right side): P4, *k2, p6; rep from * to last 6 sts, k2, p4.

2nd row: K4, *p2, k6; rep from * to last 6 sts, p2, k4.

3rd row: P3, *k2tog, yf, sl 1, k1, psso, p4; rep from * to last 7 sts, k2tog, yf, sl 1, k1, psso, p3.

4th row: K3, *p1, k into back then front of next st, p1, k4; rep from * to last 6 sts, p1, k into back then front of next st, p1, k3.

5th row: P2, *k2tog, yf, k2, yf, sl 1, k1, psso, p2; rep from * to end.

6th row: K2, *p6, k2; rep from * to end.

7th row: K1, *k2tog, yf, k2tog, [yf, sl 1, k1, psso] twice; rep from * to last st, k1.

8th row: P4, *k into front then back of next st, p6; rep from * to last 5 sts, k into front then back of next st, p4.

9th row: K1, *[yf, sl 1, k1, psso] twice, k2tog, yf, k2tog; rep from * to last st, yf, k1.

10th row: K1, KB1, *p6, k into back then front of next st; rep from * to last 8 sts, p6, KB1, k1.

11th row: P2, *yon, k3tog tbl, yf, k3tog, yfrn, p2; rep from * to end.

12th row: K2, *KB1, p1, k into back then front of next st, p1, KB1, k2; rep from * to end.

13th row: P3, *yon, sl 1, k1, psso, k2tog, yfrn, p4; rep from * to last 7 sts, yon, sl 1, k1, psso, k2tog, yfrn, p3.

14th row: K3, *KB1, p2, KB1, k4; rep from * to last 7 sts, KB1, p2, KB1, k3.

Rep these 14 rows.

Simple Lace Rib

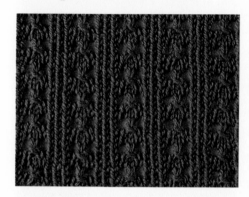

Multiple of 6 + 1

1st row (right side): [KB1] twice, *k3, [KB1] 3 times; rep from * to last 5 sts, k3, [KB1] twice.

2nd row: [PB1] twice, *p3, [PB1] 3 times; rep from * to last 5 sts, p3, [PB1] twice.

3rd row: [KB1] twice, *yf, sl 1, k2tog, psso, yf, [KB1] 3 times; rep from * to last 5 sts, yf, sl 1, k2tog, psso, yf, [KB1] twice.

4th row: As 2nd row.

Rep these 4 rows.

Diamond Diagonal

Multiple of 8 + 2

1st row (right side): K1, *yf, k2tog tbl, k6; rep from * to last st, k1.

2nd row: K1, *yfrn, p2tog, k3, p2tog tbl, yon, k1; rep from * to last st, k1.

3rd row: *K3, yf, k2tog tbl, k1, k2tog, yf; rep from * to last 2 sts, k2.

Wheatear Stitch

4th row: K3, *yfrn, p3tog tbl, yon, k5; rep from * to last 7 sts, yfrn, p3tog tbl, yon, k4.

5th row: K5, *yf, k2tog tbl, k6; rep from * to last 5 sts, yf, k2tog tbl, k3.

6th row: K2, *p2tog tbl, yon, k1, yfrn, p2tog, k3; rep from * to end.

7th row: K2, *k2tog, yf, k3, yf, k2tog tbl, k1; rep from * to end.

8th row: P2tog tbl, *yon, k5, yfrn, p3tog tbl; rep from * to last 8 sts, yon, k5, yfrn, p2tog, k1.

Rep these 8 rows.

Multiple of 8 + 6

1st row (right side): P5, *k2, yf, sl 1, k1, psso, p4; rep from * to last st, p1.

2nd row: K5, *p2, yrn, p2tog, k4; rep from * to last st, k1.

Rep the last 2 rows 3 times more.

9th row: P1, *k2, yf, sl 1, k1, psso, p4; rep from * to last 5 sts, k2, yf, sl 1, k1, psso, p1.

10th row: K1, *p2, yrn, p2tog, k4; rep from * to last 5 sts, p2, yrn, p2tog, k1.

Rep the last 2 rows 3 times more.

Rep these 16 rows.

Flower Buds

Multiple of 8 + 5

1st row (right side): K3, *yf, k2, p3tog, k2, yf, k1; rep from * to last 2 sts, k2.

2nd row: Purl.

Rep the last 2 rows twice more.

7th row: K2, P2tog, *k2, yf, k1, yf, k2, p3tog; rep from * to last 9 sts, k2, yf, k1, yf, k2, p2tog, k2.

8th row: Purl.

Rep the last 2 rows twice more.

Rep these 12 rows.

All-over Lace Patterns

Zigzag Lace

Multiple of 4 + 3

1st row (right side): K4, *k2tog, yf, k2; rep from * to last 3 sts, k2tog, yf, k1.

2nd row: *P2, yrn, p2tog; rep from * to last 3 sts, p3.

3rd row: *K2, k2tog, yf; rep from * to last 3 sts, k3.

4th row: P4, *yrn, p2tog, p2; rep from * to last 3 sts, yrn, p2tog, p1.

5th row: K1, *yf, sl 1, k1, psso, k2; rep from * to last 2 sts, k2.

6th row: P3, *p2tog tbl, yrn, p2; rep from * to end.

7th row: K3, *yf, sl 1, k1, psso, k2; rep from * to end

8th row: P1, *p2tog tbl, yrn, p2; rep from * to last 2 sts, p2.

Rep these 8 rows.

Horizontal Leaf Pattern

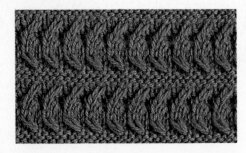

Multiple of 3

1st row (right side): K2, *sl 1 purlwise, k2; rep from * to last st, k1.

2nd row: P3, *sl 1 purlwise, p2; rep from * to end.

3rd row: K2, *C3L; rep from * to last st, k1.

4th row: Purl.

5th row: K2, *yf, k2tog, k1; rep from * to last st, k1.

6th row: Purl.

7th row: K4, *sl 1 purlwise, k2; rep from * to last 2 sts, sl 1 purlwise, k1.

8th row: P1, *sl 1 purlwise, p2; rep from * to last 2 sts, p2.

9th row: K2, *C3R; rep from * to last st, k1.

10th row: Knit.

11th row: Purl.

12th row: Purl.

Rep these 12 rows.

Lace And Cables

Multiple of 11 + 7

1st row (right side): K1, *yf, sl 1, k1, psso, k1, k2tog, yf, k6; rep from * to last 6 sts, yf, sl 1, k1, psso, k1, k2tog, yf, k1.

2nd and every alt row: Purl.

3rd row: K2, *yf, sl 1, k2tog, psso, yf, k8; rep from * to last 5 sts, yf, sl 1, k2tog, psso, yf, k2.

5th row: As 1st row.

7th row: K2, *yf, sl 1, k2tog, psso, yf, k1, C6B, k1; rep from * to last 5 sts, yf, sl 1, k2tog, psso, yf, k2.

8th row: Purl.

Rep these 8 rows.

Wavy Cable Lace

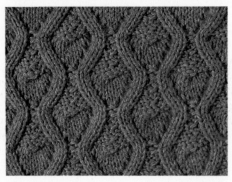

Multiple of 14 + 1

1st row (right side): K1, *yf, k2, p3, p3tog, p3, k2, yf, k1; rep from * to end.

2nd row: P4, *k7, p7; rep from * to last 11 sts, k7, p4.

3rd row: K2, *yf, k2, p2, p3tog, p2, k2, yf, k3; rep from * to last 13 sts, yf, k2, p2, p3tog, p2, k2, yf, k2.

4th row: P5, *k5, p9; rep from * to last 10 sts, k5, p5.

5th row: K3, *yf, k2, p1, p3tog, p1, k2, yf, k5; rep from * to last 12 sts, yf, k2, p1, p3tog, p1, k2, yf, k3.

6th row: P6, *k3, p11; rep from * to last 9 sts, k3, p6.

7th row: K4, *yf, k2, p3tog, k2, yf, k7; rep from * to last 11 sts, yf, k2, p3tog, k2, yf, k4.

8th row: P7, *k1, p13; rep from * to last 8 sts, k1, p7.

9th row: P2tog, *p3, k2, yf, k1, yf, k2, p3, p3tog; rep from * to last 13 sts, p3, k2, yf, k1, yf, k2, p3, p2tog.

10th row: K4, *p7, k7; rep from * to last 11 sts, p7, k4.

11th row: P2tog, *P2, k2, yf, k3, yf, k2, p2, p3tog; rep from * to last 13 sts, p2, k2, yf, k3, yf, k2, p2, p2tog.

12th row: K3, *p9, k5; rep from * to last 12 sts, p9, k3.

13th row: P2tog, *p1, k2, yf, k5, yf, k2, p1, p3tog; rep from * to last 13 sts, p1, k2, yf, k5, yf, k2, p1, p2tog.

14th row: K2, *p11, k3; rep from * to last 13 sts, p11, k2.

15th row: P2tog, *k2, yf, k7, yf, k2, p3tog; rep from * to last 13 sts, k2, yf, k7, yf, k2, p2tog.

16th row: K1, *p13, k1; rep from * to end.

Rep these 16 rows.

Waterfall Pattern

Multiple of 6 + 3

Note: Sts should only be counted after the 4th, 5th and 6th rows.

1st row (right side): P3, *k3, yfrn, p3; rep from * to end.

2nd row: K3, *p4, k3; rep from * to end.

3rd row: P3, *k1, k2tog, yf, k1, p3; rep from * to end.

4th row: K3, *p2, p2tog, k3; rep from * to end.

5th row: P3, *k1, yf, k2tog, p3; rep from * to end.

6th row: K3, *p3, k3; rep from * to end.

Rep these 6 rows.

Lacy Bubbles

Multiple of 6 + 3

1st row (right side): Purl.

2nd row: Knit.

3rd row: Purl.

4th row: K1, p3tog, [k1, p1, k1, p1, k1] into next st, *p5tog, [k1, p1, k1, p1, k1] into next st; rep from * to last 4 sts,

p3tog, k1.
5th row: Purl.
6th row: K1, [k1, p1, k1] into next st, p5tog, *[k1, p1, k1, p1, k1] into next st, p5tog; rep from * to last 2 sts, [k1, p1, k1] into next st, k1.
7th row: Purl.
8th row: Knit.
Rep these 8 rows.

Lacy Diamonds

Multiple of 6+1
1st row (right side): *K1, k2tog, yf, k1, yf, k2tog tbl; rep from * to last st, k1.
2nd and every alt row: Purl.
3rd row: K2tog, *yf, k3, yf, [sl 1] twice, k1, p2sso; rep from * to last 5 sts, yf, k3, yf, k2tog tbl.
5th row: *K1, yf, k2tog tbl, k1, k2tog, yf; rep from * to last st, k1.
7th row: K2, *yf, [sl 1] twice, k1, p2sso, yf, k3; rep from * to last 5 sts, yf, [sl 1] twice, k1, p2sso, yf, k2.
8th row: Purl.
Rep these 8 rows.

Twist Cable And Ladder Lace

Multiple of 7+6
1st row (right side): K1, *k2tog, [yf] twice, sl 1, k1, psso, k3; rep from * to last 5 sts, k2tog, [yf] twice, sl 1, k1, psso, k1.
2nd row: K2, *[KB1, k1] into double yf of previous row, k1, p3, k1; rep from * to last 4 sts, [KB1, k1] into double yf of previous row, k2.
3rd row: K1, *k2tog, [yf] twice, sl 1, k1, psso, knit into 3rd st on left-hand needle, then knit into 2nd st, then knit into 1st st, slipping all 3 sts onto right-hand needle tog; rep from * to last 5 sts, k2tog, [yf] twice, sl 1, k1, psso, k1.
4th row: As 2nd row.
Rep these 4 rows.

Large Lattice Lace

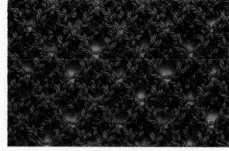

Multiple of 6+2
1st row (right side): K1, p1, *yon, k2tog tbl, k2tog, yfrn, p2; rep from * to last 6 sts, yon, k2tog tbl, k2tog, yfrn, p1, k1.
2nd row: K2, *p4, k2; rep from * to end.
3rd row: K1, p1, *k2tog, [yf] twice, k2tog tbl, p2; rep from * to last 6 sts, k2tog, [yf] twice, k2tog tbl, p1, k1.
4th row: K2, *p1, [k1, p1] into double yf of previous row, p1, k2; rep from * to end.
5th row: K1, *k2tog, yfrn, p2, yon, k2tog tbl; rep from * to last st, k1.
6th row: K1, p2, *k2, p4; rep from * to last 5 sts, k2, p2, k1.
7th row: K1, yf, *k2tog tbl, p2, k2tog, [yf] twice; rep from * to last 7 sts, k2tog tbl, p2, k2tog, yf, k1.
8th row: K1, p2, k2, p1, *[k1, p1] into double yf of previous row, p1, k2, p1; rep from * to last 2 sts, p1, k1.
Rep these 8 rows.

Fuchsia Stitch

Multiple of 6
Note: Stitches should only be counted after the 11th and 12th rows.
1st row (right side): P2, *k2, yfrn, p4; rep from * to last 4 sts, k2, yfrn, p2.
2nd row: K2, *p3, k4; rep from * to last 5 sts, p3, k2.
3rd row: P2, *k3, yfrn, p4; rep from * to last 5 sts, k3, yfrn, p2.
4th row: K2, *p4, k4; rep from * to last 6 sts, p4, k2.
5th row: P2, *k4, yfrn, p4; rep from * to last 6 sts, k4, yfrn, p2.
6th row: K2, *p5, k4; rep from * to last 7 sts, p5, k2.
7th row: P2, *k3, k2tog, p4; rep from * to last 7 sts, k3, k2tog, p2.
8th row: As 4th row.
9th row: P2, *k2, k2tog, p4; rep from * to last 6 sts, k2, k2tog, p2.
10th row: As 2nd row.
11th row: P2, *k1, k2tog, p4; rep from * to last 5 sts, k1, k2tog, p2.

Dewdrop Pattern

Multiple 6+1
1st row (wrong side): K2, *p3, k3; rep from * to last 5 sts, p3, k2.
2nd row: P2, *k3, p3; rep from * to last 5 sts, k3, p2.
3rd row: As 1st row.
4th row: K2, *yf, sl 1, k2tog, psso, yf, k3; rep from * to last 5 sts, yf, sl 1, k2tog, psso, yf, k2.
5th row: As 2nd row.
6th row: K2, *p3, k3; rep from * to last 5 sts, p3, k2.
7th row: As 2nd row.
8th row: K2tog, *yf, k3, yf, sl 1, k2tog, psso; rep from * to last 5 sts, yf, k3, yf, sl 1, k1, psso.
Rep these 8 rows.

Eyelet Check

Multiple of 8+7
1st row (right side): K2, *p3, k5; rep from * to last 5 sts, p3, k2.
2nd row: P2, *k3, p5; rep from * to last 5 sts, k3, p2.
3rd row: K2, *p1, yrn, p2tog, k5; rep from * to last 5 sts, p1, yrn, p2tog, k2.
4th row: As 2nd row.
5th row: As 1st row.
6th row: Purl.
7th row: K6, *p3, k5; rep from * to last 9 sts, p3, k6.
8th row: P6, *k3, p5; rep from * to last 9 sts, k3, p6.
9th row: K6, *p1, yrn, p2tog, k5; rep from * to last 9 sts, p1, yrn, p2tog, k6.
10th row: As 8th row.
11th row: K6, *p3, k5; rep from * to last 9 sts, p3, k6.
12th row: Purl.
Rep these 12 rows.

12th row: K2, *p2, k4; rep from * to last 4 sts, p2, k2.
Rep these 12 rows.

All-over Lace Patterns

Alternating Lace

Multiple of 6+5
1st row (right side): K1, *yf, sl 1, k2tog, psso, yf, k3; rep from * to last 4 sts, yf, sl 1, k2tog, psso, yf, k1.
2nd row: Purl.
Rep the last 2 rows 3 times more.
9th row: K4, *yf, sl 1, k2tog, psso, yf, k3; rep from * to last st, k1.
10th row: Purl.
Rep the last 2 rows 3 times more.
Rep these 16 rows.

Faggotting

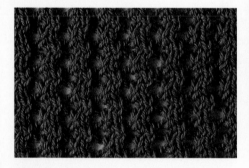

Multiple of 3
Note: Stitches should only be counted after the 2nd and 4th rows.
1st row (right side): *K1, [yf] twice, k2tog; rep from * to end.
2nd row: P1, *purl into first yf of previous row, drop second yf off needle, p2; rep from * to last 3 sts, purl into first yf, drop second yf off needle, p1.
3rd row: *K2tog, [yf] twice, k1; rep from * to end.
4th row: As 2nd row.
Rep these 4 rows.

Lace Check

Multiple of 18+9
1st row (wrong side): Purl.
2nd row: K1, *[yf, k2tog] 4 times, k10; rep from * to last 8 sts, [yf, k2tog] 4 times.
3rd row: Purl.
4th row: *[Sl 1, k1, psso, yf] 4 times, k10; rep from * to last 9 sts, [sl 1, k1, psso, yf] 4 times, k1.
Rep the last 4 rows twice mofe.
13th row: Purl.
14th row: *K10, [yf, k2tog] 4 times; rep from * to last 9 sts, k9.
15th row: Purl.
16th row: K9, *[sl 1, k1, psso, yf] 4 times, k10; rep from * to end.
Rep the last 4 rows twice more.
Rep these 24 rows.

Single Lace Rib

Multiple of 4+1
1st row (right side): K1, *yf, k2tog, p1, k1; rep from * to end.
2nd row: P1, *yrn, p2tog, k1, p1; rep from * to end.
Rep these 2 rows.

Ridged Openwork

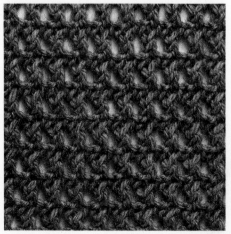

Multiple of 2+1
Note: Stitches should only be counted after the 1st, 3rd or 4th rows of this pattern.
1st row (right side): Purl.
2nd row: *P2tog; rep from * to last st, p1.
3rd row: P1, *purl through horizontal strand of yarn lying between stitch just worked and next st, p1; rep from * to end.
4th row: P1, *yrn, p2tog; rep from * to end.
Rep these 4 rows.

Wavy Eyelet Rib

Multiple of 7+2
1st row (right side): *P2, yon, sl 1, k1, psso, k1, k2tog, yfrn; rep from * to last 2 sts, p2.
2nd row: K2, *p5, k2; rep from * to end.
Rep the last 2 rows twice more.
7th row: *P2, k5; rep from * to last 2 sts, p2.
8th row: As 2nd row.
9th row: *P2, k2tog, yf, k1, yf, sl 1, k1, psso; rep from * to last 2 sts, p2.
10th row: As 2nd row.
Rep the last 2 rows twice more.
15th row: As 7th row.
16th row: As 2nd row.
Rep these 16 rows.

Loose Lattice Lace

Multiple of 8 + 3

Note: Sts should only be counted after the 5th, 6th, 11th and 12th rows.

1st row (right side): K1, *k2tog, k1, yf, k1, sl 1, k1, psso, k2; rep from * to last 2 sts, k2.

2nd and every alt row: Purl.

3rd row: *K2tog, k1, [yf, k1] twice, sl 1, k1, psso; rep from * to last 3 sts, k3.

5th row: K2, *yf, k3, yf, k1, sl 1, k1, psso, k1; rep from * to last st, k1.

7th row: K4, *k2tog, k1, yf, k1, sl 1, k1, psso, k2; rep from * to last 7 sts, k2tog, k1, yf, k1, sl 1, k1, psso, k1.

9th row: K3, *k2tog, k1, [yf, k1] twice, sl 1, k1, psso; rep from * to end.

11th row: K2, *k2tog, k1, yf, k3, yf, k1; rep from * to last st, k1.

12th row: Purl.

Rep these 12 rows.

Fir Cone

Multiple of 10 + 1

1st row (wrong side): Purl.

2nd row: K1, *yf, k3, sl 1, k2tog, psso, k3, yf, k1; rep from * to end.

Rep the last 2 rows 3 times more.

9th row: Purl.

10th row: K2tog, *k3, yf, k1, yf, k3, sl 1, k2tog, psso; rep from * to last 9 sts, k3, yf, k1, yf, k3, sl 1, k1, psso.

Rep the last 2 rows 3 times more.

Rep these 16 rows.

Staggered Eyelets

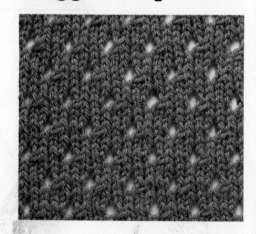

Multiple of 4 + 3

Work 2 rows in st st, starting knit.

3rd row (right side): *K2, k2tog, yf; rep from * to last 3 sts, k3.

Work 3 rows in st st, starting purl.

7th row: *K2tog, yf, k2; rep from * to last 3 sts, k2tog, yf, k1.

8th row: Purl.

Rep these 8 rows.

Layette Stitch

Multiple of 4 + 1

1st row (right side): K2, *p1, k3; rep from * to last 3 sts, p1, k2.

2nd row: P2, *k1, p3; rep from * to last 3 sts, k1, p2.

3rd row: K2tog, yfrn, *p1, yon, k3tog, yfrn; rep from * to last 3 sts, p1, yon, k2tog.

4th row: K1, *p3, k1; rep from * to end.

5th row: P1, *k3, p1; rep from * to end.

6th row: As 4th row.

7th row: P1, *yon, k3tog, yfrn, p1; rep from * to end.

8th row: As 2nd row.

Rep these 8 rows.

Eyelet Chevron

Multiple of 12 + 1

1st row (right side): K4, *k2tog, yf, k1, yf, sl 1, k1, psso, k7; rep from * to last 9 sts, k2tog, yf, k1, yf, sl 1, k1, psso, k4.

2nd and every alt row: Purl.

3rd row: K3, *k2tog, yf, k3, yf, sl 1, k1, psso, k5; rep from * to last 10 sts, k2tog, yf, k3, yf, sl 1, k1, psso, k3.

5th row: K2, *k2tog, yf, k5, yf, sl 1, k1, psso, k3; rep from * to last 11 sts, k2tog, yf, k5, yf, sl 1, k1, psso, k2.

7th row: K1, *k2tog, yf, k7, yf, sl 1, k1,

psso, k1; rep from * to end.

9th row: K2tog, yf, k9, *yf, sl 1, k2tog, psso, yf, k9; rep from * to last 2 sts, yf, sl 1, k1, psso.

10th row: Purl.

Rep these 10 rows.

Tulip Lace

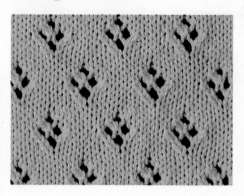

Multiple of 8 + 7

1st row (right side): Knit.

2nd and every alt row: Purl.

3rd row: K3, *yf, sl 1, k1, psso, k6; rep from * to last 4 sts, yf, sl 1, k1, psso, k2.

5th row: K1, *k2tog, yf, k1, yf, sl 1, k1, psso, k3; rep from * to last 6 sts, k2tog, yf, k1, yf, sl 1, k1, psso, k1.

7th row: As 3rd row.

9th row: Knit.

11th row: K7, *yf, sl 1, k1, psso, k6; rep from * to end.

13th row: K5, *k2tog, yf, k1, yf, sl 1, k1, psso, k3; rep from * to last 2 sts, k2.

15th row: As 11th row.

16th row: Purl.

Rep these 16 rows.

Snowdrop Lace

Multiple of 8 + 5

1st row (right side): K1, *yf, sl 1 purlwise, k2tog, psso, yf, k5; rep from * to last 4 sts, yf, sl 1 purlwise, k2tog, psso, yf, k1.

2nd and every alt row: Purl.

3rd row: As 1st row.

5th row: K4, *yf, sl 1 purlwise, k1, psso, k1, k2tog, yf, k3; rep from * to last st, k1.

7th row: K1, *yf, sl 1 purlwise, k2tog, psso, yf, k1; rep from * to end.

8th row: Purl.

Rep these 8 rows.

All-over Lace Patterns

Diagonal Lace

Multiple of 8 + 4

1st row (right side): K2, *yf, sl 1, k1, psso, k1, k2tog, yf, k3; rep from * to last 2 sts, k2.
2nd row: P7, *p2tog tbl, yrn, p6; rep from * to last 5 sts, p2tog tbl, yrn, p3.
3rd row: K4, *yf, sl 1, k1, psso, k1, k2tog, yf, k3; rep from * to end.
4th row: P5, *p2tog tbl, yrn, p6; rep from * to last 7 sts, p2tog tbl, yrn, p5.
5th row: K1, *k2tog, yf, k3, yf, sl 1, k1, psso, k1; rep from * to last 3 sts, k2tog, yf, k1.
6th row: P3, *p2tog tbl, yrn, p6; rep from * to last st, p1.
7th row: K3, *k2tog, yf, k3, yf, sl 1, k1, psso, k1; rep from * to last st, k1.
8th row: P1, *p2tog tbl, yrn, p6; rep from * to last 3 sts, p2tog tbl, yrn, p1.
Rep these 8 rows.

Lacy Rib

Multiple of 3 + 1

1st row (right side): K1, *k2tog, yfrn, p1; rep from * to last 3 sts, k2tog, yf, k1.
2nd row: P3, *k1, p2; rep from * to last 4 sts, k1, p3.
3rd row: K1, yf, sl 1, k1, psso, *p1, sl 1, yon, k1, psso; rep from * to last st, k1.
4th row: As 2nd row.
Rep these 4 rows.

Zigzag Openwork

Multiple of 2 + 1
Note: Stitches should only be counted after the 2nd or 4th rows of this pattern.
1st row (right side): K1, *k2tog; rep from * to end.
2nd row: K1, *M1, k1; rep from * to end.
3rd row: *K2tog; rep from * to last st, k1.
4th row: As 2nd row.
Rep these 4 rows.

Fern Diamonds

Multiple of 10 + 1

1st row (right side): K3, *k2tog, yt, k1, yf, sl 1, k1, psso, k5; rep from * to last 8 sts, k2tog, yf, k1, yf, sl 1, k1, psso, k3.
2nd and every alt row: Purl.
3rd row: K2, *k2tog, [k1, yf] twice, k1, sl 1, k1, psso, k3; rep from * to last 9 sts, k2tog, [k1, yf] twice, k1, sl 1, k1, psso, k2.
5th row: K1, *k2tog, k2, yf, k1, yf, k2, sl 1, k1, psso, k1; rep from * to end.
7th row: K2tog, *k3, yf, k1, yf, k3, sl 1, k2tog, psso; rep from * to last 9 sts, k3, yf, k1, yf, k3, sl 1, k1, psso.
9th row: K1, *yf, sl 1, k1, psso, k5, k2tog, yf, k1; rep from * to end.
11th row: K1, *yf, k1, sl 1, k1, psso, k3, k2tog, k1, yf, k1; rep from * to end.

Hourglass Eyelets

Multiple of 6 + 1

1st row (right side): K6, *p1, k5; rep from * to last st, k1.
2nd row: K1, *p5, k1; rep from * to end.
3rd row: K1, *yf, sl 1, k1, psso, p1, k2tog, yf, k1; rep from * to end.
4th row: K1, p2, *k1, p5; rep from * to last 4 sts, k1, p2, k1.
5th row: K3, *p1, k5; rep from * to last 4 sts, p1, k3.
6th row: As 4th row.
7th row: K1, *k2tog, yf, k1, yf, sl 1, k1, psso, p1; rep from * to last 6 sts, k2tog, yf, k1, yf, sl 1, k1, psso, k1.
8th row: As 2nd row.
Rep these 8 rows.

13th row: K1, *yf, k2, sl 1, k1, psso, k1, k2tog, k2, yf, k1; rep from * to end.
15th row: K1, *yf, k3, sl 1, k2tog, psso, k3, yf, k1; rep from * to end.
16th row: Purl.
Rep these 16 rows.

Garter Stitch Eyelet Chevron

Multiple of 9 + 1

1st row (right side): K1, *yf, sl 1, k1, psso, k4, k2tog, yf, k1; rep from * to end.
2nd row: P2, *k6, p3; rep from * to last 8 sts, k6, p2.
3rd row: K2, *yf, sl 1, k1, psso, k2, k2tog yf, k3; rep from * to last 8 sts, yf, sl 1, k1, psso, k2, k2tog, yf, k2.
4th row: P3, *k4, p5; rep from * to last 7 sts, k4, p3.
5th row: K3, *yf, sl 1, k1, psso, k2tog, yf, k5; rep from * to last 7 sts, yf, sl 1, k1, psso, k2tog, yf, k3.
6th row: P4, *k2, p7; rep from * to last 6 sts, k2, p4.
Rep these 6 rows.

Fern Lace

Multiple of 9 + 4

1st row (wrong side): Purl.

2nd row: K3, *yf, k2, sl 1, k1, psso, k2tog, k2, yf, k1; rep from * to last st, k1.

3rd row: Purl.

4th row: K2, *yf, k2, sl 1, k1, psso, k2tog, k2, yf, k1; rep from * to last 2 sts, k2.

Rep these 4 rows.

Lacy Zigzag

Multiple of 6 + 1

1st row (right side): *Sl 1, k1, psso, k2, yf, k2; rep from * to last st, k1.

2nd row: Purl.

Rep the last 2 rows twice more.

7th row: K3, *yf, k2, k2tog, k2; rep from * to last 4 sts, yf, k2, k2tog.

8th row: Purl.

Rep the last 2 rows twice more.

Rep these 12 rows.

Foaming Waves

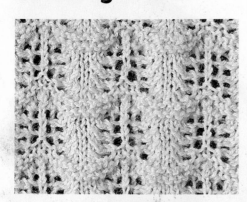

Multiple of 12 + 1

Knit 4 rows.

5th row (right side): K1, *[k2tog] twice, [yf, k1] 3 times, yf, [sl 1, k1, psso] twice, k1; rep from * to end.

6th row: Purl.

Rep the last 2 rows 3 times more.

Rep these 12 rows.

Arrowhead Lace

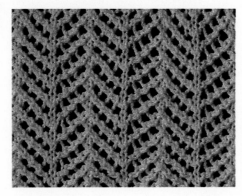

Multiple of 10 + 1

1st row (right side): K1, *[yf, sl 1, k1, psso] twice, k1, [k2tog, yf] twice, k1; rep from * to end.

2nd row: Purl.

3rd row: K2, *yf, sl 1, k1, psso, yf, sl 1, k2tog, psso, yf, k2tog, yf, k3; rep from * to last 9 sts, yf, sl 1, k1, psso, yf, sl 1, k2tog, psso, yf, k2tog, yf, k2.

4th row: Purl.

Rep these 4 rows.

Leafy Lace

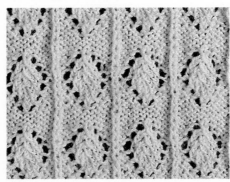

Multiple of 10 + 1

1st row (right side): KB1, *p9, KB1; rep from * to end.

2nd row: P1, *k9, p1; rep from * to end.

Rep the last 2 rows once more.

5th row: KB1, *p2, p2tog, yon, KB1, yfrn, p2tog, p2, KB1; rep from * to end.

6th row: P1, *k4, PB1, k4, p1; rep from * to end.

7th row: KB1, *p1, p2tog, yon, [KB1] 3 times, yfrn, p2tog, p1, KB1; rep from * to end.

8th row: P1, *k3, [PB1] 3 times, k3, p1; rep from * to end.

9th row: KB1, *p2tog, yon, [KB1] 5 times, yfrn, p2tog, KB1; rep from * to end.

10th row: P1, *k2, [PB1] 5 times, k2, p1; rep from * to end.

11th row: KB1, *p1, yon, [KB1] twice, sl 1, k2tog, psso, [KB1] twice, yfrn, p1, KB1; rep from * to end.

12th row: As 10th row.

13th row: KB1, *p2, yon, KB1, sl 1, k2tog, psso, KB1, yfrn, p2, KB1; rep from * to end.

14th row: As 8th row.

15th row: KB1, *p3, yon, sl 1, k2tog, psso, yfrn, p3, KB1; rep from * to end.

16th row: As 6th row.

Rep these 16 rows.

Little Arrowhead

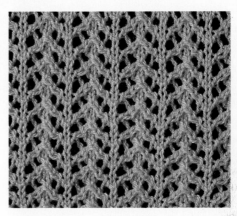

Multiple of 6 + 1

1st row (right side): K1, *yf, sl 1, k1, psso, k1, k2tog, yf, k1; rep from * to end.

2nd row: Purl.

3rd row: K2, *yf, sl 1, k2tog, psso, yf, k3; rep from * to last 5 sts, yf, sl 1, k2tog, psso, yf, k2.

4th row: Purl.

Rep these 4 rows.

Bluebell Ribs

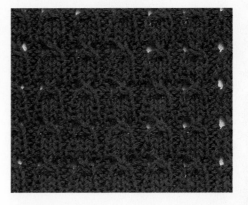

Multiple of 5 + 2

1st row (right side): P2, *k3, p2; rep from * to end.

2nd row: K2, *p3, k2; rep from * to end.

Rep the last 2 rows once more.

5th row: P2, *yon, sl 1, k2tog, psso, yfrn, p2; rep from * to end.

6th row: As 2nd row.

Rep these 6 rows.

All-over Lace Patterns

Purse Stitch

Multiple of 2 sts.
1st row: P1, *yrn, p2tog; rep from * to last st, p1.
Rep this row.

Simple Garter Stitch Lace

Multiple of 4 sts + 2.
1st row: K2, *yfrn, p2tog, k2; rep from * to end.
Rep this row.

Lacy Openwork

Multiple of 4 sts + 1.
1st row: K1, *yfrn, p3tog, yon, k1; rep from * to end.
2nd row: P2tog, yon, k1, yfrn, *p3tog, yon, k1, yfrn; rep from * to last 2 sts, p2tog.
Rep these 2 rows.

Feather Openwork

Multiple of 5 sts + 2.
1st row (right side): K1, *k2tog, yf, k1, yf, sl 1, k1, psso; rep from * to last st, k1.
2nd row: Purl.
Rep these 2 rows.

Chevron and Feather

Multiple of 13 sts + 1.
1st row (right side): *K1, yf, k4, k2tog, sl 1, k1, psso, k4, yf; rep from * to last st, k1.
2nd row: Purl.
Rep these 2 rows.

Alternating Feather Openwork

Multiple of 6 sts + 1.

1st row (right side): K1, *k2tog, yf, k1, yf, sl 1, k1, psso, k1; rep from * to end.
2nd row: Purl.
Rep these 2 rows 5 times more.
13th row: K1, *yf, sl 1, k1, psso, k1, k2tog, yf, k1; rep from * to end.
14th row: Purl.
Rep the last 2 rows 5 times more.
Rep these 24 rows.

Gate and Ladder Pattern

Multiple of 9 sts + 3.
Foundation row (wrong side): Purl.
Commence Pattern
1st row: K1, k2tog, k3, [yf] twice, k3, *k3tog, k3, [yf] twice, k3; rep from * to last 3 sts, k2tog, k1.
2nd row: P6, k1, *p8, k1; rep from * to last 5 sts, p5.
Rep the last 2 rows.

Ridge and Hole Pattern

Multiple of 2 sts + 1.
Note: Stitches should only be counted after the 1st, 3rd or 4th rows of this pattern.
1st row (right side): Purl.
2nd row: *P2tog; rep from * to last st, p1.
3rd row: P1, *purl through horizontal strand of yarn lying between stitch just worked and next st, p1; rep from * to end.
4th row: P1, *yrn, p2tog; rep from * to end.
Rep these 4 rows.

Filet Net

Multiple of 3 sts.

1st row (right side): K2, *sl 2, pass 1st slipped st over 2nd and off needle, sl 1, pass 2nd slipped st over 3rd and off needle, slip the 3rd slipped st back onto left-hand needle, [yf] twice (to make 2 sts), knit the 3rd slipped st in usual way; rep from * to last st, k1 (original number of sts retained).

2nd row: K3, *p1, k2; rep from * to end.

Rep these 2 rows.

Cell Stitch

Multiple of 4 sts + 3.

1st row (right side): K2, *yf, sl 1, k2tog, psso, yf, k1; rep from * to last st, k1. ·

2nd row: Purl.

3rd row: K1, k2tog, yf, k1, *yf, sl 1, k2tog, psso, yf, k1; rep from * to last 3 sts, yf, sl 1, k1, psso, k1.

4th row: Purl.

Rep these 4 rows.

Diagonal Openwork

Multiple of 4 sts + 2.

1st row (right side): *K1, yf, sl 1, k2tog, psso, yf; rep from * to last 2 sts, k2.

2nd and every alt row: Purl.

3rd row: K2, *yf, sl 1, k2tog, psso, yf, k1; rep from * to end.

5th row: K2tog, yf, k1, yf, *sl 1, k2tog, yf, k1, yf; rep from * to last 3 sts, sl 1, k1, psso.

7th row: K1, k2tog, yf, k1, yf, *sl 1, k2tog, psso, yf, k1, yf; rep from * to last 2 sts, sl 1, k1, psso.

8th row: Purl.

Rep these 8 rows.

Grand Eyelets

Multiple of 4 sts.

Note: Sts should not be counted after the 1st row.

1st row: P2, *yrn, p4tog; rep from * to last 2 sts, p2.

2nd row: K3, [k1, p1, k1] into next st, *k1, [k1, p1, k1] into next st; rep from * to last 2 sts, k2.

3rd row: Knit.

Rep these 3 rows.

Little Fountain Pattern

Multiple of 4 sts + 1.

Note: Sts should only be counted after the 3rd and 4th rows.

1st row (right side): K1, *yf, k3, yf, k1; rep from * to end.

2nd row: Purl.

3rd row: K2, sl 1, k2tog, psso, *k3, sl 1, k2tog, psso; rep from * to last 2 sts, k2.

4th row: Purl.

Rep these 4 rows.

Bead Stitch

Multiple of 7 sts.

1st row (right side): K1, k2tog, yf, k1, yf, sl 1, k1, psso, *k2, k2tog, yf, k1, yf, sl 1, k1, psso; rep from * to last st, k1.

2nd row: *P2tog tbl, yrn, p3, yrn, p2tog; rep from * to end.

3rd row: K1, yf, sl 1, k1, psso, k1, k2tog, yf, *k2, yf, sl 1, k1, psso, k1, k2tog, yf; rep from * to last st, k1.

4th row: P2, yrn, p3tog, yrn, *p4, yrn, p3tog, yrn; rep from * to last 2 sts, p2.

Rep these 4 rows.

Lacy Lattice Stitch

Multiple of 6 sts + 1.

1st row (right side): K1, *yfrn, p1, p3tog, p1, yon, k1; rep from * to end.

2nd and every alt row: Purl.

3rd row: K2, yf, sl 1, k2tog, psso, yf, *k3, yf, sl 1, k2tog, psso, yf; rep from * to last 2 sts, k2.

5th row: P2tog, p1, yon, k1, yfrn, p1, *p3tog, p1, yon, k1, yfrn, p1; rep from * to last 2 sts, p2tog.

7th row: K2tog, yf, k3, yf, *sl 1, k2tog, psso, yf, k3, yf; rep from * to last 2 sts, sl 1, k1, psso.

8th row: Purl.

Rep these 8 rows.

All-over Lace Patterns

Little Shell Pattern

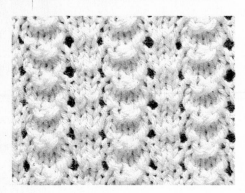

Multiple of 7 sts + 2.
1st row (right side): Knit.
2nd row: Purl.
3rd row: K2, *yfrn, p1, p3tog, p1, yon, k2; rep from * to end.
4th row: Purl.
Rep these 4 rows.

Pillar Openwork

Multiple of 3 sts + 2.
1st row (right side): K1, *yf, sl 1 purlwise, k2, psso the k2; rep from * to last st, k1.
2nd row: Purl.
Rep these 2 rows.

Twisted Openwork Pattern I

Multiple of 4 sts + 1.
1st row (right side): P1, *k3, p1; rep from * to end.

2nd row: K1, *p3, k1; rep from * to end.
3rd row: As 1st row.
4th row: K1, *yfrn, p3tog, yon, k1; rep from * to end.
5th row: K2, p1, *k3, p1; rep from * to last 2 sts, k2.
6th row: P2, k1, *p3, k1; rep from * to last 2 sts, p2.
7th row: As 5th row.
8th row: P2tog, yon, k1, yfrn, *p3tog, yon, k1, yfrn; rep from * to last 2 sts, p2tog.
Rep these 8 rows.

Twisted Openwork Pattern II

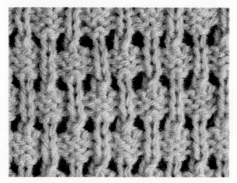

Worked as Twisted Openwork Pattern I, using reverse side as right side.

Little Flowers

Multiple of 6 sts + 3.
1st row (right side): Knit.
2nd and every alt row: Purl.
3rd row: Knit.
5th row: *K4, yf, sl 1, k1, psso; rep from * to last 3 sts, k3.
7th row: K2, k2tog, yf, k1, yf, sl 1, k1, psso, *k1, k2tog, yf, k1, yf, sl 1, k1, psso; rep from * to last 2 sts, k2.
9th and 11th rows: Knit.
13th row: K1, yf, sl 1, k1, psso, *k4, yf, sl 1, k1, psso; rep from * to end.
15th row: K2, yf, sl 1, k1, psso, k1, k2tog, yf, *k1, yf, sl 1, k1, psso, k1, k2tog, yf; rep from * to last 2 sts, k2.

16th row: Purl.
Rep these 16 rows.

Eyelet V-Stitch

Multiple of 12 sts + 1.
1st row (right side): Knit.
2nd and every alt row: Purl.
3rd row: K4, yf, sl 1, k1, psso, k1, k2tog, yf, *k7, yf, sl 1, k1, psso, k1, k2tog, yf; rep from * to last 4 sts, k4.
5th row: K5, yf, sl 1, k2tog, psso, yf, *k9, yf, sl 1, k2tog, psso, yf; rep from * to last 5 sts, k5.
7th row: Knit.
9th row: K1, *k2tog, yf, k7, yf, sl 1, k1, psso, k1; rep from * to end.
11th row: K2tog, yf, k9, *yf, sl 1, k2tog, psso, yf, k9; rep from * to last 2 sts, yf, sl 1, k1, psso.
12th row: Purl.
Rep these 12 rows.

Pine Cone Pattern

Multiple of 10 sts + 1.
1st row (right side): Knit.
2nd and every alt row: Purl.
3rd row: K3, k2tog, yf, k1, yf, sl 1, k1, psso, *k5, k2tog, yf, k1, yf, sl 1, k1, psso; rep from * to last 3 sts, k3.
5th row: K2, k2tog, yf, k3, yf, sl 1, k1, psso, *k3, k2tog, yf, k3, yf, sl 1, k1, psso; rep from * to last 2 sts, k2.
7th and 9th rows: As 3rd row.
11th row: Knit.
13th row: K1, *yf, sl 1, k1, psso, k5, k2tog, yf, k1; rep from * to end.
15th row: K2, yf, sl 1, k1, psso, k3, k2tog,

yf, *k3, yf, sl 1, k1, psso, k3, k2tog, yf; rep from * to last 2 sts, k2.
17th and 19th rows: As 13th row.
20th row: Purl.
Rep these 20 rows.

Raindrops

Multiple of 6 sts + 5.
1st row (right side): P5, *yrn, p2tog, p4; rep from * to end.
2nd row: K5, *p1, k5; rep from * to end.
3rd row: P5, *k1, p5; rep from * to end.
Rep the last 2 rows once more then the 2nd row again.
7th row: P2, yrn, p2tog, *p4, yrn, p2tog; rep from * to last st, p1.
8th row: K2, p1, *k5, p1; rep from * to last 2 sts, k2.
9th row: P2, k1, *p5, k1; rep from * to last 2 sts, p2.
Rep the last 2 rows once more then the 8th row again.
Rep these 12 rows.

Snowflakes I

Multiple of 8 sts + 7.
1st and every alt row (wrong side): Purl.
2nd row: K5, sl 1, k1, psso, yf, k1, yf, k2tog, *k3, sl 1, k1, psso, yf, k1, yf, k2tog; rep from * to last 5 ,sts, k5.
4th row: K6, yf, sl 2, k1, p2sso, yf, *k5, yf, sl 2, k1, p2sso, yf; rep from * to last 6 sts, k6.
6th row: As 2nd row.
8th row: K1, sl 1, k1, psso, yf, k1, yf, k2tog, *k3, sl 1, k1, psso, yf, k1, yf, k2tog; rep from * to last st, k1.
10th row: K2, yf, sl 2, k1, p2sso, yf, *k5,

Snowflakes II

Multiple of 6 sts + 1.
Note: Sts should not be counted after 3rd, 4th, 9th and 10th rows.
1st row (right side): K1, *yf, sl 1, k1, psso, k1, k2tog, yf, k1; rep from * to end.
2nd and every alt row: Purl.
3rd row: K2, yf, *k3, yf; rep from * to last 2 sts, k2.
5th row: K2tog, yf, sl 1, k1, psso, k1, k2tog, yf, *sl 1, k2tog, psso, yf, sl 1, k1, psso, k1, k2tog, yf; rep from * to last 2 sts, sl 1, k1, psso.
7th row: K1, *k2tog, yf, k1, yf, sl 1, k1, psso, k1; rep from * to end.
9th row: As 3rd row.
11th row: K1, *k2tog, yf, sl 1, k2tog, psso, yf, sl 1, k1, psso, k1; rep from * to end.
12th row: Purl.
Rep these 12 rows.

Eyelet Diamonds

Multiple of 16 sts + 11.
1st row (right side): K10, yf, sl 1, k1, psso, k3, k2tog, yf, *k9, yf, sl 1, k1, psso, k3, k2tog, yf; rep from * to last 10 sts, k10.
2nd and every alt row: Purl.
3rd row: K3, k2tog, yf, k1, yf, sl 1, k1, psso, *k3, yf, sl 1, k1, psso, k1, k2tog, yf, k3, k2tog, yf, k1, yf, sl 1, k1, psso; rep from * to last 3 sts, k3.
5th row: K2, k2tog, yf, k3, yf, sl 1, k1, psso,

yf, sl 2, k1, p2sso, yf; rep from * to last 2 sts, k2.
12th row: As 8th row.
Rep these 12 rows.

*k3, yf, sl 1, k2tog, psso, yf, k3, k2tog, yf, k3, yf, sl 1, k1, psso; rep from * to last 2 sts, k2.
7th row: K1, k2tog, yf, k5, yf, sl 1, k1, psso, *k7, k2tog, yf, k5, yf, sl 1, k1, psso; rep from * to last st, k1.
9th row: K2, yf, sl 1, k1, psso, k3, k2tog, yf, *k9, yf, sl 1, k1, psso, k3, k2tog, yf; rep from * to last 2 sts, k2.
11th row: K3, yf, sl 1, k1, psso, k1, k2tog, yf, k3, *k2tog, yf, k1, yf, sl 1, k1, psso, k3, yf, sl 1, k1, psso, k1, k2tog, yf, k3; rep from * to end.
13th row: K4, yf, sl 1, k2tog, psso, yf, *k3, k2tog, yf, k3, yf, sl 1, k1, psso, k3, yf, sl 1, k2tog, psso, yf; rep from * to last 4 sts, k4.
15th row: K9, k2tog, yf, k5, yf, sl 1, k1, psso, *k7, k2tog, yf, k5, yf, sl 1, k1, psso; rep from * to last 9 sts, k9.
16th row: Purl.
Rep these 16 rows.

Swinging Triangles

Multiple of 12 sts + 1.
1st and every alt row (wrong side): Purl.
2nd row: *K10, sl 1, k1, psso, yf; rep from * to last st, k1.
4th row: K9, sl 1, k1, psso, yf, *k10, sl 1, k1, psso, yf; rep from * to last 2 sts, k2.
6th row: *K8, [sl 1, k1, psso, yf] twice; rep from * to last st, k1.
8th row: K7, [sl 1, k1, psso, yf] twice, *k8, [sl 1, k1, psso, yf] twice; rep from * to last 2 sts, k2.
10th row: *K6, [sl 1, k1, psso, yf] 3 times; rep from * to last st, k1.
12th row: K5, [sl 1, k1, psso, yf] 3 times, *k6, [sl 1, k1, psso, yf] 3 times; rep from * to last 2 sts, k2.
14th row: *K4, [sl 1, k1, psso, yf] 4 times; rep from * to last st, k1.
16th row: K1, *yf, k2tog, k10; rep from * to end.
18th row: K2, yf, k2tog, *k10, yf, k2tog; rep from * to last 9 sts, k9.
20th row: K1, *[yf, k2tog] twice, k8; rep from * to end.
22nd row: K2, [yf, k2tog] twice, *k8, [yf, k2tog] twice; rep from * to last 7 sts, k7.
24th row: K1, *[yf, k2tog] 3 times, k6; rep from * to end.
26th row: K2, [yf, k2tog] 3 times, *k6, [yf, k2tog] 3 times; rep from * to last 5 sts, k5.
28th row: K1, *[yf, k2tog] 4 times, k4; rep from * to end.
Rep these 28 rows.

All-over Lace Patterns

Zigzag Eyelets

Multiple of 9 sts.

1st row (right side): K4, *yf, sl 1, k1, psso, k7; rep from * to last 5 sts, yf, sl 1, k1, psso, k3.

2nd and every alt row: Purl.

3rd row: K5, *yf, sl 1, k1, psso, k7; rep from * to last 4 sts, yf, sl 1, k1, psso, k2.

5th row: K6, *yf, sl 1, k1, psso, k7; rep from * to last 3 sts, yf, sl 1, k1, psso, k1.

7th row: *K7, yf, sl 1, k1, psso; rep from * to end.

9th row: K3, *k2tog, yf, k7; rep from * to last 6 sts, k2tog, yf, k4.

11th row: K2, *k2tog, yf, k7; rep from * to last 7 sts, k2tog, yf, k5.

13th row: K1, *k2tog, yf, k7; rep from * to last 8 sts, k2tog, yf, k6.

15th row: *K2tog, yf, k7; rep from * to end.

16th row: Purl.

Rep these 16 rows.

Rhombus Lace

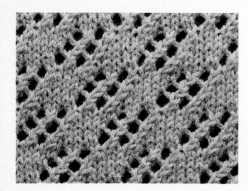

Multiple of 8 sts + 2.

1st row (right side): K1, [k2tog, yf] twice, *k4, [k2tog, yf] twice; rep from * to last 5 sts, k5.

2nd and every alt row: Purl.

3rd row: [K2tog, yf] twice, *k4, [k2tog, yf] twice; rep from * to last 6 sts, k6.

5th row: K1, k2tog, yf, k4, *[k2tog, yf] twice, k4; rep from * to last 3 sts, k2tog, yf, k1.

7th row: K3, [k2tog, yf] twice, *k4, [k2tog, yf] twice; rep from * to last 3 sts, k3.

9th row: K2, *[k2tog, yf] twice, k4; rep from * to end.

11th row: As 1st row.

13th row: K5, [k2tog, yf] twice, *k4, [k2tog, yf] twice; rep from * to last st, k1.

15th row: *K4, [k2tog, yf] twice; rep from * to last 2 sts, k2.

17th row: As 7th row.

19th row: As 5th row.

21st row: K2tog, yf, k4, *[k2tog, yf] twice, k4; rep from * to last 4 sts, k2tog, yf, k2.

23rd row: As 13th row.

24th row: Purl.

Rep these 24 rows.

Diagonal Ridges

Multiple of 5 sts + 2.

1st row (right side): K2tog, yf, *k3, k2tog, yf; rep from * to last 5 sts, k5.

2nd row: P2, *k3, p2; rep from * to end.

3rd row: K4, k2tog, yf, *k3, k2tog, yf; rep from * to last st, k1.

4th row: K1, *p2, k3; rep from * to last st, p1.

5th row: *K3, k2tog, yf; rep from * to last 2 sts, k2.

6th row: K2, *p2, k3; rep from * to end.

7th row: K2, *k2tog, yf, k3; rep from * to end.

8th row: *K3, p2; rep from * to last 2 sts, k2.

9th row: K1, k2tog, yf, *k3, k2tog, yf; rep from * to last 4 sts, k4.

10th row: P1, *k3, p2; rep from * to last st, k1.

Rep these 10 rows.

Lacy Diagonals

Mutliple of 10 sts + 2.

1st row (right side): K7, sl 1, k1, psso, yf, k2tog, yf, *k6, sl 1, k1, psso, yf, k2tog, yf; rep from * to last st, k1.

2nd and every alt row: Purl.

3rd row: *K6, sl 1, k1, psso, yf, k2tog, yf; rep from * to last 2 sts, k2.

5th row: K5, sl 1, k1, psso, yf, k2tog, yf, *k6, sl 1, k1, psso, yf, k2tog, yf; rep from * to last 3 sts, k3.

7th row: K4, sl 1, k1, psso, yf, k2tog, yf, *k6, sl 1, k1, psso, yf, k2tog, yf; rep from * to last 4 sts, k4.

9th row: K3, sl 1, k1, psso, yf, k2tog, yf, *k6, sl 1, k1, psso, yf, k2tog, yf; rep from * to last 5 sts, k5.

11th row: K2, *sl 1, k1, psso, yf, k2tog, yf, k6; rep from * to end.

13th row: K1, sl 1, k1, psso, yf, k2tog, yf, *k6, sl 1, k1, psso, yf, k2tog, yf; rep from * to last 7 sts, k7.

15th row: Sl 1, k1, psso, yf, k2tog, yf, *k6, sl 1, k1, psso, yf, k2tog, yf; rep from * to last 8 sts, k8.

17th row: K1, *k2tog, yf, k6, sl 1, k1, psso, yf; rep from * to last st, k1.

19th row: *K2tog, yf, k6, sl 1, k1, psso, yf; rep from * to last 2 sts, k2.

20th row: Purl.

Rep these 20 rows.

Fish Hooks

Multiple of 8 sts + 1.

1st and every alt row (wrong side): Purl.

2nd row: Knit.

4th row: K2, sl 1, k1, psso, yf, k1, yf, k2tog, *k3, sl 1, k1, psso, yf, k1, yf, k2tog; rep from * to last 2 sts, k2.

6th row: K1, *sl 1, k1, psso, yf, k3, yf, k2tog, k1; rep from * to end.

8th row: K4, sl 1, k1, psso, yf, *k6, sl 1, k1, psso, yf; rep from * to last 3 sts, k3.

10th row: K3, sl 1, k1, psso, yf, *k6, sl 1, k1, psso, yf; rep from * to last 4 sts, k4.

12th row: K2, sl 1, k1, psso, yf, *k6, sl 1, k1, psso, yf; rep from * to last 5 sts, k5.

14th row: K1, *sl 1, k1, psso, yf, k6; rep from * to end.

16th row: Knit.

18th row: As 4th row.

20th row: As 6th row.

22nd row: K3, yf, k2tog, *k6, yf, k2tog; rep from * to last 4 sts, k4.

24th row: K4, yf, k2tog, *k6, yf, k2tog; rep from * to last 3 sts, k3.

26th row: K5, yf, k2tog, *k6, yf, k2tog; rep from * to last 2 sts, k2.

28th row: *K6, yf, k2tog; rep from * to last st, k1.

Rep these 28 rows.

Cogwheel Eyelets

Multiple of 8 sts + 1.

1st row (right side): K2, k2tog, yf, k1, yf, sl 1, k1, psso, *k3, k2tog, yf, k1, yf, sl 1, k1, psso; rep from * to last 2 sts, k2.

2nd and every alt row: Purl.

3rd row: K1, *k2tog, yf, k3, yf, sl 1, k1, psso, k1; rep from * to end.

5th row: K2tog, yf, k5, *yf, sl 1, k2tog, psso, yf, k5; rep from * to last 2 sts, yf, sl 1, k1, psso.

7th row: Sl 1, k1, psso, yf, k5, *yf, sl 2tog knitwise, k1, p2sso, yf, k5; rep from * to last 2 sts, yf, k2tog.

9th row: As 7th row.

11th row: K2, yf, sl 1, k1, psso, k1, k2tog, yf, *k3, yf, sl 1, k1, psso, k1, k2tog, yf; rep from * to last 2 sts, k2.

13th row: K3, yf, sl 1, k2tog, psso, yf, *k5, yf, sl 1, k2tog, psso, yf; rep from * to last 3 sts, k3.

15th row: K1, *yf, sl 1, k1, psso, k3, k2tog, yf, k1; rep from * to end.

17th row: As 11th row.

19th row: As 13th row.

21st row: K3, yf, sl 2tog knitwise, k1, p2sso, yf, *k5, yf, sl 2tog knitwise, k1, p2sso, yf; rep from * to last 3 sts, k3.

23rd row: As 21st row.

25th row: As 3rd row.

27th row: As 5th row.

28th row: Purl.

Rep these 28 rows.

Diamond Trellis

Multiple of 16 sts + 1.

1st row (right side): K2tog, yf, k12, *[k2tog, yf] twice, k12; rep from * to last 3 sts, k2tog, yf, k1.

2nd and every alt row: Purl.

3rd row: K2, yf, sl 1, k1, psso, k9, *[k2tog, yf] twice, k1, yf, sl 1, k1, psso, k9; rep from * to last 4 sts, k2tog, yf, k2.

5th row: K1, *[yf, sl 1, k1, psso] twice, k7, [k2tog, yf] twice, k1; rep from * to end.

7th row: K2, [yf, sl 1, k1, psso] twice, k5, [k2tog, yf] twice, *k3, [yf, sl 1, k1, psso] twice, k5, [k2tog, yf] twice; rep from * to last 2 sts, k2.

9th row: K3, [yf, sl 1, k1, psso] twice, k3, [k2tog, yf] twice, *k5, [yf, sl 1, k1, psso] twice, k3, [k2tog, yf] twice; rep from * to last 3 sts, k3.

11th row: K4, [yf, sl 1, k1, psso] twice, k1, [k2tog, yf] twice, *k7, [yf, sl 1, k1, psso] twice, k1, [k2tog, yf] twice; rep from * to last 4 sts, k4.

13th row: K5, yf, sl 1, k1, psso, yf, k3tog, yf, k2tog, yf, *k9, yf, sl 1, k1, psso, yf, k3tog, yf, k2tog, yf; rep from * to last 5 sts, k5.

15th row: K6, yf, k3tog, yf, k2tog, yf, *k11, yf, k3tog, yf, k2tog, yf; rep from * to last 6 sts, k6.

17th row: K6, [k2tog, yf] twice, *k12, [k2tog, yf] twice; rep from * to last 7 sts, k7.

19th row: K5, [k2tog, yf] twice, k1, yf, sl 1, k1, psso, *k9, [k2tog, yf] twice, k1, yf, sl 1, k1, psso; rep from * to last 5 sts, k5.

21st row: K4, [k2tog, yf] twice, k1, [yf, sl 1, k1, psso] twice, *k7, [k2tog, yf] twice, k1, [yf, sl 1, k1, psso] twice; rep from * to last 4 sts, k4.

23rd row: K3, [k2tog, yf] twice, k3, [yf, sl 1, k1, psso] twice, *k5, [k2tog, yf] twice, k3, [yf, sl 1, k1, psso] twice; rep from * to last 3 sts, k3.

25th row: K2, [k2tog, yf] twice, k5, [yf, sl 1, k1, psso] twice, *k3, [k2tog, yf] twice, k5, [yf, sl 1, k1, psso] twice; rep from * to last 2 sts, k2.

27th row: *K1, [k2tog, yf] twice, k7, [yf, sl 1, k1, psso] twice; rep from * to last st, k1.

29th row: [K2tog, yf] twice, k9, *yf, sl 1, k1, psso, yf, k3tog, yf, k2tog, yf, k9; rep from * to last 4 sts, [yf, sl 1, k1, psso] twice.

31st row: K1, k2tog, yf, k11, *yf, k3tog, yf, k2tog, yf, k11; rep from * to last 3 sts, yf, k2tog, k1.

32nd row: Purl.

Rep these 32 rows.

Inverted Hearts

Multiple of 14 sts + 1.

1st row (right side): P2tog, yon, k11, *yfrn, p3tog, yon, k11; rep from * to last 2 sts, yfrn, p2tog.

2nd row: K1, *p13, k1; rep from * to end.

Eyelet Boxes

Multiple of 14 sts + 11.

1st row (right side): K2, p7, *k3, yf, sl 1, k1, psso, k2, p7; rep from * to last 2 sts, k2.

2nd, 4th, 6th, 8th and 10th rows: P2, k7, *p7, k7; rep from * to last 2 sts, p2.

3rd row: K2, p7, *k1, k2tog, yf, k1, yf, sl 1, k1, psso, k1, p7; rep from * to last 2 sts, k2.

5th row: K2, p7, *k2tog, yf, k3, yf, sl 1, k1, psso, p7; rep from * to last 2 sts, k2.

7th row: K2, p7, *k2, yf, sl 1, k2tog, psso, yf, k2, p7; rep from * to last 2 sts, k2.

9th row: As 1st row.

11th row: P2, k3, yf, sl 1, k1, psso, k2, *p7, k3, yf, sl 1, k1, psso, k2; rep from * to last 2 sts, p2.

12th, 14th, 16th and 18th rows: K2, p7, *k7, p7; rep from * to last 2 sts, k2.

13th row: P2, k1, k2tog, yf, k1, yf, sl 1, k1, psso, k1, *p7, k1, k2tog, yf, k1, yf, sl 1, k1, psso, k1; rep from * to last 2 sts, p2.

15th row: P2, k2tog, yf, k3, yf, sl 1, k1, psso, *p7, k2tog, yf, k3, yf, sl 1, k1, psso; rep from * to last 2 sts, p2.

17th row: P2, k2, yf, sl 1, k2tog, psso, yf, k2, *p7, k2, yf, sl 1, k2tog, psso, yf, k2; rep from * to last 2 sts, p2.

19th row: As 11th row.

20th row: K2, p7, *k7, p7; rep from * to last 2 sts, k2.

Rep these 20 rows.

3rd row: P2, yon, sl 1, k1, psso, k7, *k2tog, yfrn, p3, yon, sl 1, k1, psso, k7; rep from * to last 4 sts, k2tog, yfrn, p2.

4th row: K2, p11, *k3, p11; rep from * to last 2 sts, k2.

5th row: P3, yon, sl 1, k1, psso, k5, k2tog, yfrn, *p5, yon, sl 1, k1, psso, k5, k2tog, yfrn; rep from * to last 3 sts, p3.

6th row: K3, p9, *k5, p9; rep from * to last 3 sts, k3.

7th row: P4, yon, sl 1, k1, psso, k3, k2tog, yfrn, *p7, yon, sl 1, k1, psso, k3, k2tog, yfrn; rep from * to last 4 sts, p4.

8th row: K4, p7, *k7, p7; rep from * to last 4 sts, k4.

9th row: P2, p2tog, yon, k1, yf, sl 1, k1, psso, k1, k2tog, yf, k1, yfrn, p2tog, *p3, p2tog, yon, k1, yf, sl 1, k1, psso, k1, k2tog, yf, k1, yfrn, p2tog; rep from * to last 2 sts, p2.

10th row: As 6th row.

11th row: P1, *p2tog, yon, k3, yf, sl 1, k2tog, psso, yf, k3, yfrn, p2tog, p1; rep from * to end.

12th row: As 4th row.

Rep these 12 rows.

All-over Lace Patterns

Shadow Triangles

Multiple of 10 sts + 3.

1st row (right side): K2, yf, sl 1, k1, psso, k5, k2tog, yf, *k1, yf, sl 1, k1, psso, k5, k2tog, yf; rep from * to last 2 sts, k2.

2nd row: P4, k5, *p5, k5; rep from * to last 4 sts, p4.

3rd row: K3, *yf, sl 1, k1, psso, k3, k2tog, yf, k3; rep from * to end.

4th row: P5, k3, *p7, k3; rep from * to last 5 sts, p5.

5th row: K4, yf, sl 1, k1, psso, k1, k2tog, yf, *k5, yf, sl 1, k1, psso, k1, k2tog, yf; rep from * to last 4 sts, k4.

6th row: P6, k1, *p9, k1; rep from * to last 6 sts, p6.

7th row: K5, yf, sl 1, k2tog, psso, yf, *k7, yf, sl 1, k2tog, psso, yf; rep from * to last 5 sts, k5.

8th row: Purl.

9th row: K4, k2tog, yf, k1, yf, sl 1, k1, psso, *k5, k2tog, yf, k1, yf, sl 1, k1, psso; rep from * to last 4 sts, k4.

10th row: K4, p5, *k5, p5; rep from * to last 4 sts, k4.

11th row: K3, *k2tog, yf, k3, yf, sl 1, k1, psso, k3; rep from * to end.

12th row: K3, *p7, k3; rep from * to end.

13th row: K2, k2tog, yf, k5, yf, sl 1, k1, psso, *k1, k2tog, yf, k5, yf, sl 1, k1, psso; rep from * to last 2 sts, k2.

14th row: P1, k1, *p9, k1; rep from * to last st, p1.

15th row: K1, k2tog, yf, k7, *yf, sl 1, k2tog, psso, yf, k7; rep from * to last 3 sts, yf, sl 1, k1, psso, k1.

16th row: Purl.
Rep these 16 rows.

Little and Large Diamonds

Multiple 12 sts + 1.

1st row (right side): K1, *yf, sl 1, k1, psso, k7, k2tog, yf, k1; rep from * to end.

2nd and every alt row: Purl.

3rd row: K2, yf, sl 1, k1, psso, k5, *k2tog, yf, k3, yf, sl 1, k1, psso, k5; rep from * to last 4 sts, k2tog, yf, k2.

5th row: K3, yf, sl 1, k1, psso, k3, *k2tog, yf, k5, yf, sl 1, k1, psso, k3; rep from * to last 5 sts, k2tog, yf, k3.

7th row: *K1, k2tog, yf, k1, yf, sl 1, k1, psso; rep from * to last st, k1.

9th row: K2tog, yf, k3, *yf, sl 1, k2tog, psso, yf, k3; rep from * to last 2 sts, yf, sl 1, k1, psso.

11th row: K4, k2tog, yf, k1, yf, sl 1, k1, psso, *k7, k2tog, yf, k1, yf, sl 1, k1, psso; rep from * to last 4 sts, k4.

13th row: K3, k2tog, yf, k3, yf, sl 1, k1, psso, *k5, k2tog, yf, k3, yf, sl 1, k1, psso; rep from * to last 3 sts, k3.

15th row: K2, k2tog, yf, k5, yf, sl 1, k1, psso, *k3, k2tog, yf, k5, yf, sl 1, k1, psso; rep from * to last 2 sts, k2.

17th row: As 7th row.

19th row: As 9th row.

20th row: Purl.
Rep these 20 rows.

Eyelet Pyramids

Multiple of 12 sts + 3.

1st row (right side): P2, k11, *p1, k11; rep from * to last 2 sts, p2.

2nd row: K2, p11, *k1, p11; rep from * to last 2 sts, k2.

3rd row: *P3, k2, [yf, sl 1, k1, psso] 3 times, k1; rep from * to last 3 sts, p3.

4th row: K3, *p9, k3; rep from * to end.

5th row: P4, k2, [yf, sl 1, k1, psso] twice, k1, *p5, k2, [yf, sl 1, k1, psso] twice, k1; rep from * to last 4 sts, p4.

6th row: K4, p7, *k5, p7; rep from * to last 4 sts, k4.

7th row: P5, k2, yf, sl 1, k1, psso, k1, *p7, k2, yf, sl 1, k1, psso, k1; rep from * to last 5 sts, p5.

8th row: K5, p5, *k7, p5; rep from * to last 5 sts, k5.

9th row: P6, k3, *p9, k3; rep from * to last 6 sts, p6.

10th row: K6, p3, *k9, p3; rep from * to last 6 sts, k6.

11th row: P7, k1, *p11, k1; rep from * to last 7 sts, p7.

12th row: K7, p1, *k11, p1; rep from * to last 7 sts, k7.

13th row: As 12th row.
14th row: As 11th row.
15th row: K1, [yf, sl 1, k1, psso] twice, k1, p3, *k2, [yf, sl 1, k1, psso] 3 times, k1, p3; rep from * to last 6 sts, k2, yf, sl 1, k1, psso, k2.

16th row: As 9th row.
17th row: K2, yf, sl 1, k1, psso, k1, p5, *k2, [yf, sl 1, k1, psso] twice, k1, p5; rep from * to last 5 sts, k2, yf, sl 1, k1, psso, k1.

18th row: P5, k5, *p7, k5; rep from * to last 5 sts, p5.

19th row: K1, yf, sl 1, k1, psso, k1, p7, *k2, yf, sl 1, k1, psso, k1, p7; rep from * to last 4 sts, k2, yf, sl 1, k1, psso.

20th row: P4, k7, *p5, k7; rep from * to last 4 sts, p4.

21st row: As 4th row.
22nd row: P3, *k9, p3; rep from * to end.
23rd row: As 2nd row.
24th row: As 1st row.
Rep these 24 rows.

Feather and Fan

Multiple of 18 sts + 2.

1st row (right side): Knit.
2nd row: Purl.
3rd row: K1, *[k2tog] 3 times, [yf, k1] 6 times, [k2tog] 3 times; rep from * to last st, k1.
4th row: Knit.
Rep these 4 rows.

2-Coloured Feather and Fan

Worked as Feather and Fan.
Work 4 rows in colour A and 4 rows in colour B throughout.

Ears of Corn

Multiple of 12 sts + 2.

1st row (right side): Knit.

2nd row: Purl.

3rd row: K4, k2tog, k1, yf, *k9, k2tog, k1, yf; rep from * to last 7 sts, k7.

4th row: P8, yrn, p1, p2tog, *p9, yrn, p1, p2tog; rep from * to last 3 sts, p3.

5th row: K2, *k2tog, k1, yf, k9; rep from * to end.

6th row: P10, yrn, p1, p2tog, *p9, yrn, p1, p2tog; rep from * to last st, p1.

Work 2 rows in st st, starting knit.

9th row: K7, yf, k1, sl 1, k1, psso, *k9, yf, k1, sl 1, k1, psso; rep from * to last 4 sts, k4.

10th row: P3, p2tog tbl, p1, yrn, *p9, p2tog tbl, p1, yrn; rep from * to last 8 sts, p8.

11th row: *K9, yf, k1, sl 1, k1, psso; rep from * to last 2 sts, k2.

12th row: P1, p2tog tbl, p1, yrn, *p9, p2tog tbl, p1, yrn; rep from * to last 10 sts, p10.

Rep these 12 rows.

Creeping Vines

Multiple of 22 sts + 3.

1st row (right side): K4, k2tog, k3, [yf, k2tog] twice, *yf, k13, k2tog, k3, [yf, k2tog] twice; rep from * to last 12 sts, yf, k12.

2nd and every alt row: Purl.

3rd row: K3, *k2tog, k3, yf, k1, yf, [sl 1, k1, psso, yf] twice, k3, sl 1, k1, psso, k7; rep from * to end.

5th row: K2, k2tog, [k3, yf] twice, [sl 1, k1, psso, yf] twice, k3, sl 1, k1, psso, *k5, k2tog, [k3, yf] twice, [sl 1, k1, psso, yf] twice, sl 1, k1, psso; rep from * to last 6 sts, k6.

7th row: K1, k2tog, k3, yf, k5, yf, [sl 1, k1, psso, yf] twice, k3, sl 1, k1, psso, *k3, k2tog, k3, yf, k5, yf, [sl 1, k1, psso, yf] twice, k3, sl 1, k1, psso; rep from * to last 5 sts, k5.

9th row: K12, yf, [sl 1, k1, psso, yf] twice, k3, sl 1, k1, psso, *k13, yf, [sl 1, k1, psso, yf] twice, k3, sl 1, k1, psso; rep from * to last 4 sts, k4.

11th row: K7, k2tog, k3, [yf, k2tog] twice, yf, k1, yf, k3, sl 1, k1, psso; rep from * to last 3 sts, k3.

13th row: K6, k2tog, k3, [yf, k2tog] twice, [yf, k3] twice, sl 1, k1, psso, *k5, k2tog, k3, [yf, k2tog] twice, [yf, k3] twice, sl 1, k1, psso; rep from * to last 2 sts, k2.

15th row: K5, k2tog, k3, [yf, k2tog] twice, yf, k5, yf, k3, sl 1, k1, psso, *k3, k2tog, k3, [yf, k2tog] twice, yf, k5, yf, k3, sl 1, k1, psso; rep from * to last st, k1.

16th row: Purl.

Rep these 16 rows.

Horseshoe Print

Multiple of 10 sts + 1.

1st row (wrong side): Purl.

2nd row: K1, *yf, k3, sl 1, k2tog, psso, k3, yf, k1; rep from * to end.

3rd row: Purl.

4th row: P1, *k1, yf, k2, sl 1, k2tog, psso, k2, yf, k1, p1; rep from * to end.

5th row: K1, *p9, k1; rep from * to end.

6th row: P1, *k2, yf, k1, sl 1, k2tog, psso, k1, yf, k2, p1; rep from * to end.

7th row: As 5th row.

8th row: P1, *k3, yf, sl 1, k2tog, psso, yf, k3, p1; rep from * to end.

Rep these 8 rows.

Fancy Horseshoe Print

Multiple of 10 sts + 1.

1st row (right side): K1, *yf, k3, sl 1, k2tog, psso, k3, yf, k1; rep from * to end.

2nd and every alt row: Purl.

3rd row: K2, yf, k2, sl 1, k2tog, psso, k2, *yf, k3, yf, k2, sl 1, k2tog, psso, k2; rep from * to last 2 sts, yf, k2.

5th row: K2tog, [yf, k1] twice, *sl 1, k2tog, psso, [k1, yf] twice, sl 1, k2tog, psso, [yf, k1] twice; rep from * to last 7 sts, sl 1, k2tog, psso, [k1, yf] twice, sl 1, k1, psso.

6th row: Purl.

Rep these 6 rows.

Wave Pattern

Multiple of 14 sts + 3.

1st row (right side): K2, yf, k5, k3tog, k5, yf, *k1, yf, k5, k3tog, k5, yf; rep from * to last 2 sts, k2.

2nd row: Purl.

3rd row: Knit.

4th row: As 1st row.

Rep the last 4 rows once more, then the first 3 rows again.

12th, 13th and 15th rows: Purl.

14th and 16th rows: Knit.

Rep these 16 rows.

Flickering Flames

Multiple of 10 sts + 1.

1st row (right side): K1, *yf, k3, sl 1, k2tog, psso, k3, yf, k1; rep from * to end.

2nd row: Purl.

Rep the last 2 rows 3 times more.

9th row: K2tog, k3, yf, k1, yf, k3, *sl 1, k2tog, psso, k3, yf, k1, yf, k3; rep from * to last 2 sts, sl 1, k1, psso.

10th row: Purl.

Rep the last 2 rows 3 times more.

Rep these 16 rows.

All-over Lace Patterns

Tracery Pattern

Multiple of 12 sts + 1.

1st row (right side): K1, *yf, k2tog, yf, sl 1, k1, psso, k3, k2tog, yf, k3; rep from * to end.

2nd and every alt row: P1, *yrn, p2tog, p10; rep from * to end.

3rd row: K1, *yf, k2tog, yf, k1, sl 1, k1, psso, k1, k2tog, k1, yf, k3; rep from * to end.

5th row: K1, *yf, k2tog, k1, k2tog, yf, k1, yf, sl 1, k1, psso, k4; rep from * to end.

7th row: K1, *yf, [k2tog] twice, k1, [yf, k1] twice, sl 1, k1, psso, k3; rep from * to end.

8th row: As 2nd row.

Rep these 8 rows.

Chalice Pattern

Multiple of 10 sts + 3.

1st row (right side): K2, yf, k1, sl 1, k1, psso, k3, k2tog, k1, *[yf, k1] twice, sl 1, k1, psso, k3, k2tog, k1; rep from * to last 2 sts, yf, k2.

2nd and every alt row: Purl.

3rd row: K3, *yf, k1, sl 1, k1, psso, k1, k2tog, k1, yf, k3; rep from * to end.

5th row: K4, yf, k1, sl 1, k2tog, psso, k1, yf, *k5, yf, k1, sl 1, k2tog, psso, k1, yf; rep from * to last 4 sts, k4.

7th row: K2, k2tog, k1, yf, k3, yf, k1, sl 1, k1, psso, *k1, k2tog, k1, yf, k3, yf, k1, sl 1, k1, psso; rep from * to last 2 sts, k2.

9th row: K1, sl 1, k1, psso, k2, yf, k3, yf, k2, *sl 1, k2tog, psso, k2, yf, k3, yf, k2; rep from * to last 3 sts, k2tog, k1.

11th row: K3, *k2tog, k1, [yf, k1] twice, sl 1, k1, psso, k3; rep from * to end.

13th row: K2, k2tog, k1, yf, k3, yf, k1, sl 1, k1, psso, *k1, k2tog, k1, yf, k3, yf, k1, sl 1, k1, psso; rep from * to last 2 sts, k2.

15th row: K1, sl 1, k1, psso, k1, yf, k5, yf, k1, *sl 1, k2tog, psso, k1, yf, k5, yf, k1; rep from * to last 3 sts, k2tog, k1.

17th row: K3, *yf, k1, sl 1, k1, psso, k1,

k2tog, k1, yf, k3; rep from * to end.

19th row: K3, *yf, k2, sl 1, k2tog, psso, k2, yf, k3; rep from * to end.

20th row: Purl.

Rep these 20 rows.

Clover Pattern

Multiple of 12 sts + 1.

1st row (right side): K2tog, k4, yf, k1, yf, k4, *sl 1, k2tog, psso, k4, yf, k1, yf, k4; rep from * to last 2 sts, sl 1, k1, psso.

2nd and every alt row: Purl.

3rd row: K2tog, k3, [yf, k3] twice, *sl 1, k2tog, psso, k3, [yf, k3] twice; rep from * to last 2 sts, sl 1, k1, psso.

5th row: K2tog, k2, yf, k5, yf, k2, *sl 1, k2tog, psso, k2, yf, k5, yf, k2; rep from * to last 2 sts, sl 1, k1, psso.

7th row: K1, *yf, k4, sl 1, k2tog, psso, k4, yf, k1; rep from * to end.

9th row: K2, yf, k3, sl 1, k2tog, psso, k3, *[yf, k3] twice, sl 1, k2tog, psso, k3; rep from * to last 2 sts, yf, k2.

11th row: K3, yf, k2, sl 1, k2tog, psso, k2, *yf, k5, yf, k2, sl 1, k2tog, psso, k2; rep from * to last 3 sts, yf, k3.

12th row: Purl.

Rep these 12 rows.

Goblet Lace

Multiple of 10 sts + 1.

1st row (right side): K1, *yf, sl 1, k1, psso, k2tog, yf, k1; rep from * to end.

2nd and every alt row: Purl.

Rep the last 2 rows twice more.

7th row: K1, *yf, sl 1, k1, psso, k5, k2tog, yf, k1; rep from * to end.

9th row: K2, yf, sl 1, k1, psso, k3, k2tog, yf, *k3, yf, sl 1, k1, psso, k3, k2tog, yf; rep from * to last 2 sts, k2.

11th row: K3, yf, sl 1, k1, psso, k1, k2tog, yf, *k5, yf, sl 1, k1, psso, k1, k2tog, yf; rep from * to last 3 sts, k3.

13th row: K4, yf, sl 1, k2tog, psso, yf, *k7, yf, sl 1, k2tog, psso, yf; rep from * to last 4 sts, k4.

14th row: Purl.

Rep these 14 rows.

Triangles and Lace

Multiple of 12 sts + 1.

1st row (right side): K1, *yf, sl 1, k1, psso, p7, k2tog, yf, k1; rep from * to end.

2nd row: P3, k7, *p5, k7; rep from * to last 3 sts, p3.

3rd row: K1, *yf, k1, sl 1, k1, psso, p5, k2tog, k1, yf, k1; rep from * to end.

4th row: P4, k5, *p7, k5; rep from * to last 4 sts, p4.

5th row: K1, *yf, k2, sl 1, k1, psso, p3, k2tog, k2, yf, k1; rep from * to end.

6th row: P5, k3, *p9, k3; rep from * to last 5 sts, p5.

7th row: K1, *yf, k3, sl 1, k1, psso, p1, k2tog, k3, yf, k1; rep from * to end.

8th row: P6, k1, *p11, k1; rep from * to last 6 sts, p6.

9th row: K1, *yf, k4, sl 1, k2tog, psso, k4, yf, k1; rep from * to end.

10th row: Purl.

11th row: P4, k2tog, yf, k1, yf, sl 1, k1, psso, *p7, k2tog, yf, k1, yf, sl 1, k1, psso; rep from * to last 4 sts, p4.

12th row: K4, p5, *k7, p5; rep from * to last 4 sts, k4.

13th row: P3, k2tog, k1, [yf, k1] twice, sl 1, k1, psso, *p5, k2tog, k1, [yf, k1] twice, sl 1, k1, psso; rep from * to last 3 sts, p3.

14th row: K3, p7, *k5, p7; rep from * to last 3 sts, k3.

15th row: P2, k2tog, k2, yf, k1, yf, k2, sl 1, k1, psso, *p3, k2tog, k2, yf, k1, yf, k2, sl 1, k1, psso; rep from * to last 2 sts, p2.

16th row: K2, p9, *k3, p9; rep from * to last 2 sts, k2.

17th row: P1,*k2tog, k3, yf, k1, yf, k3, sl 1, k1, psso, p1; rep from * to end.

18th row: K1, *p11, k1; rep from * to end.

19th row: K2tog, k4, yf, k1, yf, k4, *sl 1, k2tog, psso, k4, yf, k1, yf, k4; rep from * to last 2 sts, sl 1, k1, psso.

20th row: Purl.

Rep these 20 rows.

Plumes

Multiple of 11 sts + 2.

1st row (right side): K1, *k2tog, k3, yf, k1, yf, k3, sl 1, k1, psso; rep from * to last st, k1.

2nd and every alt row: Purl.

3rd and 5th rows: As 1st row.

7th row: K1, *k2tog, k2, yf, k3, yf, k2, sl 1, k1, psso; rep from * to last st, k1.

9th row: K1, *k2tog, k1, yf, k5, yf, k1, sl 1, k1, psso; rep from * to last st, k1.

11th row: K1, *[k2tog, yf, k1] twice, yf, sl 1, k1, psso, k1, yf, sl 1, k1, psso; rep from * to last st, k1.

13th row: As 11th row.

15th row: As 9th row.

17th row: As 7th row.

18th row: Purl.

Rep these 18 rows.

Obstacles

Multiple of 14 sts + 1.

1st row (right side): P2, k2tog, k3, yf, k1, yf, k3, sl 1, k1, psso, *p3, k2tog, k3, yf, k1, yf, k3, sl 1, k1, psso; rep from * to last 2 sts, p2.

2nd, 4th, 6th and 8th rows: K2, p11, *k3, p11; rep from * to last 2 sts, k2.

3rd row: P2, k2tog, k2, yf, k3, yf, k2, sl 1, k1, psso, *p3, k2tog, k2, yf, k3, yf, k2, sl 1, k1, psso; rep from * to last 2 sts, p2.

5th row: P2, k2tog, k1, yf, k5, yf, k1, sl 1, k1, psso, *p3, k2tog, k1, yf, k5, yf, k1, sl 1, k1, psso; rep from * to last 2 sts, p2.

7th row: P2, k2tog, yf, k7, yf, sl 1, k1, psso, *p3, k2tog, yf, k7, yf, sl 1, k1, psso; rep from * to last 2 sts, p2.

9th row: K1, *yf, k3, sl 1, k1, psso, p3, k2tog, k3, yf, k1; rep from * to end.

10th, 12th, and 14th rows: P6, k3, *p11, k3; rep from * to last 6 sts, p6.

11th row: K2, yf, k2, sl 1, k1, psso, p3, k2tog, k2, *yf, k3, yf, k2, sl 1, k1, psso, p3, k2tog, k2; rep from * to last 2 sts, yf, k2.

13th row: K3, yf, k1, sl 1, k1, psso, p3, k2tog, k1, *yf, k5, yf, k1, sl 1, k1, psso, p3, k2tog, k1; rep from * to last 3 sts, yf, k3.

15th row: K4, yf, sl 1, k1, psso, p3, k2tog, *yf, k7, yf, sl 1, k1, psso, p3, k2tog; rep from * to last 4 sts, yf, k4.

16th row: P6, k3, *p11, k3; rep from * to last 6 sts, p6.

Rep these 16 rows.

Filigree Lace

Multiple of 16 sts + 2.

1st Foundation row (right side): K6, k2tog, yf, k2, yf, sl 1, k1, psso, *k10, k2tog, yf, k2, yf, sl 1, k1, psso; rep from * to last 6 sts, k6.

2nd Foundation row: P5, p2tog tbl, yrn, p4, yrn, p2tog, *p8, p2tog tbl, yrn, p4, yrn, p2tog; rep from * to last 5 sts, p5.

3rd Foundation row: K4, k2tog, yf, k6, yf, sl 1, k1, psso, *k6, k2tog, yf, k6, yf, sl 1, k1, psso; rep from * to last 4 sts, k4.

4th Foundation row: P3, p2tog tbl, yrn, p4, yrn, p2tog, p2, yrn, p2tog, *p4, p2tog tbl, yrn, p4, yrn, p2tog, p2, yrn, p2tog; rep from * to last 3 sts, p3.

Commence Pattern

1st row: K2, *k2tog, yf, k5, yf, sl 1, k1, psso, k3, yf, sl 1, k1, psso, k2; rep from * to end.

2nd row: P1, *p2tog tbl, yrn, p6, yrn, p2tog, p4, yrn, p2tog; rep from * to last st, p1.

3rd row: K1, sl 1 purlwise, k1, yf, sl 1, k1, psso, k4, yf, sl 1, k1, psso, k2, k2tog, yf, k1, *[sl 1 purlwise] twice, k1, yf, sl 1, k1, psso, k4, yf, sl 1, k1, psso, k2, k2tog, yf, k1; rep from * to last 2 sts, sl 1 purlwise, k1.

4th row: P4, yrn, p2tog, p3, yrn, p2tog, p1, p2tog tbl, *yrn, p6, yrn, p2tog, p3, yrn, p2tog, p1, p2tog tbl; rep from * to last 4 sts, yrn, p4.

5th row: K1, yf, sl 1, k1, psso, k2, yf, sl 1, k1, psso, k4, k2tog, *yf, k4, yf, sl 1, k1, psso, k2, yf, sl 1, k1, psso, k4, k2tog; rep from * to last 5 sts, yf, k5.

6th row: P1, yrn, p2tog, p3, yrn, p2tog, p2, p2tog tbl, *yrn, p5, yrn, p2tog, p3, yrn, p2tog, p2, p2tog tbl; rep from * to last 6 sts, yrn, p6.

7th row: K1, yf, sl 1, k1, psso, k4, yf, sl 1, k1, psso, k2tog, *yf, k6, yf, sl 1, k1, psso, k4, yf, sl 1, k1, psso, k2tog; rep from * to last 7 sts, yf, k7.

8th row: P1, yrn, p2tog, p2, p2tog tbl, yrn, p1, [sl 1 purlwise] twice, p1, yrn, p2tog, *p4, yrn, p2tog, p2, p2tog tbl, yrn, p1, [sl 1 purlwise] twice, p1, yrn, p2tog; rep from * to last 5 sts, p5.

Oriel Lace

Multiple of 12 sts + 1.

1st row (right side): P1, *yb, sl 1, k1, psso, k3, yfrn, p1, yon, k3, k2tog, p1; rep from * to end.

2nd row: K1, *p5, k1; rep from * to end.

Rep the last 2 rows twice more.

7th row: P1, *yon, k3, k2tog, p1, yb, sl 1, k1, psso, k3, yfrn, p1; rep from * to end.

8th row: As 2nd row.

9th row: P2, yon, k2, k2tog, p1, yb, sl 1, k1, psso, k2, *yfrn, p3, yon, k2, k2tog, p1, yb, sl 1, k1, psso, k2; rep from * to last 2 sts, yfrn, p2.

10th row: K2, p4, k1, p4, *k3, p4, k1, p4; rep from * to last 2 sts, k2.

11th row: P3, yon, k1, k2tog, p1, yb, sl 1, k1, psso, k1, *yfrn, p5, yon, k1, k2tog, p1, yb, sl 1, k1, psso, k1; rep from * to last 3 sts, yfrn, p3.

12th row: K3, p3, k1, p3, *k5, p3, k1, p3; rep from * to last 3 sts, k3.

13th row: P4, yon, k2tog, p1, yb, sl 1, k1, psso, *yfrn, p7, yon, k2tog, p1, yb, sl 1, k1, psso; rep from * to last 4 sts, yfrn, p4.

14th row: K4, p2, k1, p2, *k7, p2, k1, p2; rep from * to last 4 sts, k4.

15th row: As 7th row.

16th row: As 2nd row.

Rep the last 2 rows twice more.

21st row: P1, *yb, sl 1, k1, psso, k3, yfrn, p1, yon, k3, k2tog, p1; rep from * to end.

22nd row: As 2nd row.

23rd row: P1, *yb, sl 1, k1, psso, k2, yfrn, p3, yon, k2, k2tog, p1; rep from * to end.

24th row: K1, *p4, k3, p4, k1; rep from * to end.

25th row: P1, *yb, sl 1, k1, psso, k1, yfrn, p5, yon, k1, k2tog, p1; rep from * to end.

26th row: K1, *p3, k5, p3, k1; rep from * to end.

27th row: P1, *yb, sl 1, k1, psso, yfrn, p7, yon, k2tog, p1; rep from * to end.

28th row: K1, *p2, k7, p2, k1; rep from * to end.

Rep these 28 rows.

All-over Lace Patterns

Peacock Plumes

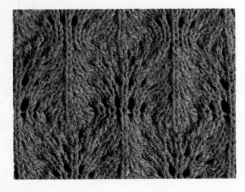

Multiple of 16 sts + 1.

1st and 3rd rows (wrong side): Purl.

2nd row: Knit.

4th row: [K1, yf] 3 times, [sl 1, k1, psso] twice, sl 2, k1, p2sso, [k2tog] twice, *yf, [k1, yf] 5 times, [sl 1, k1, psso] twice, sl 2, k1, p2sso, [k2tog] twice; rep from * to last 3 sts, [yf, k1] 3 times.

Rep the last 4 rows 3 times more.

17th and 19th rows: Purl.

18th row: Knit.

20th row: [K2tog] 3 times, [yf, k1] 5 times, *yf, [sl 1, k1, psso] twice, sl 2, k1, p2sso, [k2tog] twice, [yf, k1] 5 times; rep from * to last 6 sts, yf, [sl 1, k1, psso] 3 times.

Rep the last 4 rows 3 times more.

Rep these 32 rows.

Ornamental Arrow Pattern

Multiple of 12 sts + 1.

1st row (right side): K1, *sl 1, k1, psso, k3, yf, k1, yf, k3, k2tog, k1; rep from * to end.

2nd row: P1, *p2tog, p2, yrn, p3, yrn, p2, p2tog tbl, p1; rep from * to end.

3rd row: K1, *sl 1, k1, psso, k1, yf, k5, yf, k1, k2tog, k1; rep from * to end.

4th row: P1, *yrn, p2tog, p7, p2tog tbl, yrn, p1; rep from * to end.

5th row: K1, *yf, k3, k2tog, k1, sl 1, k1, psso, k3, yf, k1; rep from * to end.

6th row: P2, yrn, p2, p2tog tbl, p1, p2tog, p2, yrn, *p3, yrn, p2, p2tog tbl, p1, p2tog, p2, yrn; rep from * to last 2 sts, p2.

7th row: K3, yf, k1, k2tog, k1, sl 1, k1, psso, k1, yf, *k5, yf, k1, k2tog, k1, sl 1, k1, psso, k1, yf; rep from * to last 3 sts, k3.

8th row: P4, p2tog tbl, yrn, p1, yrn, p2tog,

*p7, p2tog tbl, yrn, p1, yrn, p2tog; rep from * to last 4 sts, p4.

Rep these 8 rows.

Fish-scale Pattern

Multiple of 12 sts.

1st row (right side): *Sl 1, k1, psso, k3, yfrn, p2, yon, k3, k2tog; rep from * to end.

2nd row: *P2tog, p2, yon, k4, yfrn, p2, p2tog tbl; rep from * to end.

3rd row: *Sl 1, k1, psso, k1, yfrn, p6, yon, k1, k2tog; rep from * to end.

4th row: *P2tog, yon, k8, yfrn, p2tog tbl; rep from * to end.

5th row: P1, yon, k3, k2tog, sl 1, k1, psso, k3, yfrn, *p2, yon, k3, k2tog, sl 1, k1, psso, k3, yfrn; rep from * to last st, p1.

6th row: K2, yfrn, p2, p2tog tbl, p2tog, p2, yon, *k4, yfrn, p2, p2tog tbl, p2tog, p2, yon; rep from * to last 2 sts, k2.

7th row: P3, yon, k1, k2tog, sl 1, k1, psso, k1, yfrn, *p6, yon, k1, k2tog, sl 1, k1, psso, k1, yfrn; rep from * to last 3 sts, p3.

8th row: K4, yfrn, p2tog tbl, p2tog, yon, *k8, yfrn, p2tog tbl, p2tog, yon; rep from * to last 4 sts, k4.

Rep these 8 rows.

Lattice Twist with Eyelets

Multiple of 8 sts + 3.

1st row (right side): K3, *k2tog, yf, k1, yf, sl 1, k1, psso, k3; rep from * to end.

2nd and every alt row: Purl.

3rd row: K2, C2F, k3, C2B, *k1, C2F, k3, C2B; rep from * to last 2 sts, k2.

5th row: K1, C2F, k5, *C3R, k5; rep from * to last 3 sts, C2B, k1.

7th row: K2, yf, sl 1, k1, psso, k3, k2tog, yf, *k1, yf, sl 1, k1, psso, k3, k2tog, yf; rep from * to last 2 sts, k2.

9th row: K3, *C2B, k1, C2F, k3; rep from * to end. '

11th row: K4, C3R, *k5, C3R; rep from * to last 4 sts, k4.

12th row: Purl.

Rep these 12 rows.

Filigree Cables Pattern

Multiple of 12 sts + 8.

1st row (right side): P2, *k2, yf, k2tog, p2; rep from * to end.

2nd row: K2, *p2, yrn, p2tog, k2; rep from * to end.

Rep the last 2 rows twice more.

7th row: P2, k2, yf, k2tog, p2, *C4F, p2, k2, yf, k2tog, p2; rep from * to end.

8th row: As 2nd row.

Rep the 1st and 2nd rows 3 times more.

15th row: P2, C4F, p2, *k2, yf, k2tog, p2, C4F, p2; rep from * to end.

16th row: As 2nd row.

Rep these 16 rows.

Cable and Lace Check

Multiple of 12 sts + 8.

1st row (wrong side): K2, p2tog, yrn, p2, k2, *p4, k2, p2tog, yrn, p2, k2; rep from * to end.

2nd row: P2, k2tog, yf, k2, p2, *k4, p2, k2tog, yf, k2, p2; rep from * to end.

3rd row: As 1st row.

4th row: P2, k2tog, yf, k2, p2, *C4B, p2, k2tog, yf, k2, p2; rep from * to end.

5th, 6th and 7th rows: As 1st, 2nd and 3rd rows.

8th row: P2, *C4B, p2; rep from * to end.

9th row: K2, p4, k2, *p2tog, yrn, p2, k2, p4, k2; rep from * to end.

10th row: P2, k4, p2, *k2tog, yf, k2, p2, k4, p2; rep from * to end.

11th row: As 9th row.

12th row: P2, C4B, p2, *k2tog, yf, k2, p2, C4B, p2; rep from * to end.

13th, 14th and 15th rows: As 9th, 10th and 11th rows.

16th row: As 8th row.

Rep these 16 rows.

Meandering Cables with Eyelets

Multiple of 16 sts + 10.

Note: Sts should only be counted after the 1st, 14th, 15th and 28th rows.

1st row (wrong side): K2, *p6, k2; rep from * to end.

2nd row: P2, [k2tog, yf] twice, k2tog, *p2, k6, p2, [k2tog, yf] twice, k2tog; rep from * to last 2 sts, p2.

3rd row: K2, p5, k2, *p6, k2, p5, k2; rep from * to end.

4th row: P2, k1, [yf, k2tog] twice, p2, *C6F, p2, k1, [yf, k2tog] twice, p2; rep from * to end.

5th row: As 3rd row.

6th row: P2, k1, [yf, k2tog] twice, p2, *k6, p2, k1, [yf, k2tog] twice, p2; rep from * to end.

Rep the last 2 rows twice more, then 5th row again.

12th row: As 4th row.

13th row: As 3rd row.

14th row: P2, k2, yf, k1, yf, k2tog, p2, *k6, p2, k2, yf, k1, yf, k2tog, p2; rep from * to end.

15th row: As 1st row.

16th row: P2, k6, p2, *yb, sl 1, k1, psso, [yf, sl 1, k1, psso] twice, p2, k6, p2; rep from * to end.

17th row: K2, p6, k2, *p5, k2, p6, k2; rep from * to end.

18th row: P2, C6F, p2, *yb, [sl 1, k1, psso, yf] twice, k1, p2, C6F, p2; rep from * to end.

19th row: As 17th row.

20th row: P2, k6, p2, *yb, [sl 1, k1, psso, yf] twice, k1, p2, k6, p2; rep from * to end.

Rep the last 2 rows twice more, then 19th row again.

26th row: As 18th row.

27th row: As 17th row.

28th row: P2, k6, p2, *k2, yf, sl 1, k1, psso, yf, k1, p2, k6, p2; rep from * to end.

Rep these 28 rows.

Frost Flower Pattern

Multiple of 34 sts + 2.

1st row (right side): K4, *k2tog, k4, yfrn, p2, [k2, yf, sl 1, k1, psso] 3 times, p2, yon, k4, sl 1, k1, psso, k6; rep from * but ending last rep with k4 instead of k6.

2nd row: P3, *p2tog tbl, p4, yrn, p1, k2, [p2, yrn, p2tog] 3 times, k2, p1, yrn, p4, p2tog, p4; rep from * but ending last rep with p3 instead of p4.

3rd row: K2, *k2tog, k4, yf, k2, p2, [k2, yf, sl 1, k1, psso] 3 times, p2, k2, yf, k4, sl 1, k1, psso, k2; rep from * to end.

4th row: P1, *p2tog tbl, p4, yrn, p3, k2, [p2, yrn, p2tog] 3 times, k2, p3, yrn, p4, p2tog; rep from * to last st, p1.

Rep the last 4 rows twice more.

13th row: K1, *yf, sl 1, k1, psso, k2, yf, sl 1, k1, psso, p2, yon, k4, sl 1, k1, psso, k6, k2tog, k4, yfrn, p2, k2, yf, sl 1, k1, psso, k2; rep from * but ending last rep with k3 instead of k2.

14th row: P1, *yrn, p2tog, p2, yrn, p2tog, k2, p1, yrn, p4, p2tog, p4, p2tog tbl, p4, yrn, p1, k2, p2, yrn, p2tog, p2; rep from * but ending last rep with p3 instead of p2.

15th row: K1, *yf, sl 1, k1, psso, k2, yf, sl 1, k1, psso, p2, k2, yf, k4, sl 1, k1, psso, k2, k2tog, k4, yf, k2, p2, k2, yf, sl 1, k1, psso, k2; rep from * but ending last rep with k3

instead of k2.

16th row: P1, *yrn, p2tog, p2, yrn, p2tog, k2, p3, yrn, p4, p2tog, p2tog tbl, p4, yrn, p3, k2, p2, yrn, p2tog, p2; rep from * but ending last rep with p3 instead of p2.

Rep the last 4 rows twice more.

Rep these 24 rows.

Corona Pattern Stitch

Multiple of 10 sts + 1.

1st row (right side): K3, k2tog, yf, k1, yf, sl 1, k1, psso, *k5, k2tog, yf, k1, yf, sl 1, k1, psso; rep from * to last 3 sts, k3.

2nd, 4th, 6th and 8th rows: Purl.

3rd row: K2, k2tog, yf, k3, yf, sl 1, k1, psso, *k3, k2tog, yf, k3, yf, sl 1, k1, psso; rep from * to last 2 sts, k2.

5th row: K1, *k2tog, yf, k5, yf, sl 1, k1, psso, k1; rep from * to end.

7th row: Knit.

9th row: K6, *insert right-hand needle in first space of 5th row, yrn and draw through to make a long loop which is kept on needle; rep from * into each of remaining 5 spaces of leaf from right to left, k10; rep from * to last 5 sts, take up a long loop as before in next 6 spaces, knit to end.

10th row: P5, purl tog the 6 long loops with the next st, *p9, purl tog the 6 long loops with the next st; rep from * to last 5 sts, p5.

11th row: Knit.

12th, 14th, 16th, 18th and 20th rows: Purl.

13th row: K1, *yf, sl 1, k1, psso, k5, k2tog, yf, k1; rep from * to end.

15th row: K2, yf, sl 1, k1, psso, k3, k2tog, yf, *k3, yf, sl 1, k1, psso, k3, k2tog, yf; rep from * to last 2 sts, k2.

17th row: K3, yf, sl 1, k1, psso, k1, k2tog, yf, *k5, yf, sl 1, k1, psso, k1, k2tog, yf; rep from * to last 3 sts, k3.

19th row: Knit.

21st row: K1, take up a long loop as before in next 3 spaces, k10, *take up a long loop in each of next 6 spaces, k10; rep from * to last st, take up a long loop in each of next 3 spaces.

22nd row: Purl tog the first 3 long loops with the next st, p9, *purl tog the 6 long loops with the next st, p9; rep from * to last st, purl tog the last 3 long loops with the last st.

23rd row: Knit.

24th row: Purl.

Rep these 24 rows.

All-over Lace Patterns

Ornamental Parasols

Multiple of 18 sts + 1.

Note: Sts should only be counted after the 5th, 6th, 11th, 12th, 13th, 14th, 25th, 26th, 27th and 28th rows.

1st row (right side): K1, *[p2, k1] twice, yf, k2tog, yf, k1, yf, sl 1, k1, psso, yf, [k1, p2] twice, k1; rep from * to end.

2nd row: [P1, k2] twice, p9, *k2, [p1, k2] 3 times, p9; rep from * to last 6 sts, [k2, p1] twice.

3rd row: K1, *[p2, k1] twice, yf, k2tog, yf, k3, yf, sl 1, k1, psso, yf, [k1, p2] twice, k1; rep from * to end.

4th row: [P1, k2] twice, p11, *k2, [p1, k2] 3 times, p11; rep from * to last 6 sts, [k2, p1] twice.

5th row: K1, *[p2tog, k1] twice, yf, k2tog, yf, sl 1, k1, psso, k1, k2tog, yf, sl 1, k1, psso, yf, [k1, p2tog] twice, k1; rep from * to end.

6th row: [P1, k1] twice, p11, *k1, [p1, k1] 3 times, p11; rep from * to last 4 sts, [k1, p1] twice.

7th row: K1, *[p1, k1] twice, yf, k2tog, yf, KB1, yf, sl 1, k2tog, psso, yf, KB1, yf, sl 1, k1, psso, yf, [k1, p1] twice, k1; rep from * to end.

8th row: [P1, k1] twice, p13, *k1, [p1, k1] 3 times, p13; rep from * to last 4 sts, [k1, p1] twice.

9th row: K1, *[k2tog] twice, yf, k2tog, yf, k3, yf, k1, yf, k3, yf, sl 1, k1, psso, yf, [sl 1, k1, psso] twice, k1; rep from * to end.

10th row: Purl.

11th row: K1, *[k2tog, yf] twice, sl 1, k1, psso, k1, k2tog, yf, k1, yf, sl 1, k1, psso, k1, k2tog, [yf, sl 1, k1, psso] twice, k1; rep from * to end.

12th row: Purl.

13th row: [K2tog, yf] twice, KB1, yf, sl 1, k2tog, psso, yf, k3, yf, sl 1, k2tog, psso, yf, KB1, yf, sl 1, k1, psso, *yf, sl 1, k2tog, psso, yf, k2tog, yf, KB1, yf, sl 1, k2tog, psso, yf, k3, yf, sl 1, k2tog, psso, yf, KB1, yf, sl 1, k1, psso; rep from * to last 2 sts, yf, sl 1, k1, psso.

14th row: Purl.

15th row: K1, *yf, sl 1, k1, psso, yf, [k1, p2] 4 times, k1, yf, k2tog, yf, k1; rep from * to end.

16th row: P5, [k2, p1] 3 times, k2, *p9, [k2, p1] 3 times, k2; rep from * to last 5 sts, p5.

17th row: K2, yf, sl 1, k1, psso, yf, [k1, p2] 4 times, k1, yf, k2tog, *yf, k3, yf, sl 1, k1, psso, yf, [k1, p2] 4 times, k1, yf, k2tog; rep from * to last 2 sts, yf, k2.

18th row: P6, [k2, p1] 3 times, k2, *p11, [k2, p1] 3 times, k2; rep from * to last 6 sts, p6.

19th row: K1, *k2tog, yf, sl 1, k1, psso, yf, [k1, p2tog] 4 times, k1, yf, k2tog, yf, sl 1, k1, psso, k1; rep from * to end.

20th row: P6, [k1, p1] 3 times, k1, *p11, [k1, p1] 3 times, k1; rep from * to last 6 sts, p6.

21st row: K2tog, yf, KB1, yf, sl 1, k1, psso, yf, [k1, p1] 4 times, k1, yf, k2tog, yf, KB1, *yf, sl 1, k1, k2tog, psso, yf, KB1, yf, sl 1, k1, psso, yf, [k1, p1] 4 times, k1, yf, k2tog, yf, KB1; rep from * to last 2 sts, yf, sl 1, k1, psso.

22nd row: P7, [k1, p1] 3 times, k1, *p13, [k1, p1] 3 times, k1; rep from * to last 7 sts, p7.

23rd row: K1, *yf, k3, yf, sl 1, k1, psso, yf, [sl 1; k1, psso] twice, k1, [k2tog] twice, yf, k2tog, yf, k3, yf, k1; rep from * to end.

24th row: Purl.

25th row: K1, *yf, sl 1, k1, psso, k1, k2tog, [yf, sl 1, k1, psso] twice, k1, [k2tog, yf] twice, sl 1, k1, psso, k1, k2tog, yf, k1; rep from * to end.

26th row: Purl.

27th row: K2, yf, sl 1, k2tog, psso, yf, KB1, yf, sl 1, k1, psso, yf, sl 1, k2tog, psso, yf, k2tog, yf, KB1, yf, sl 1, k2tog, psso, *yf, k3, yf, sl 1, k2tog, psso, yf, KB1, yf, sl 1, k1, psso, yf, sl 1, k2tog, psso, yf, k2tog, yf, KB1, yf, sl 1, k2tog, psso; rep from * to last 2 sts, yf, k2.

28th row: Purl.

Rep these 28 rows.

Crowns of Glory (Cats Paw)

Multiple of 14 sts + 1.

Note: Sts should only be counted after the 7th, 8th, 9th, 10th, 11th and 12th rows.

1st row (right side): K1, *sl 1, k1, psso, k9, k2tog, k1; rep from * to end.

2nd row: P1, *p2tog, p7, p2tog tbl, p1; rep from * to end.

3rd row: K1, *sl 1, k1, psso, k2, [yf] 3 times, k3, k2tog, k1; rep from * to end.

4th row: P1, *p2tog, p2, [k1, p1, k1, p1, k1] into [yf] 3 times making 5 sts, p1, p2tog tbl, p1; rep from * to end.

5th row: K1, *sl 1, k1, psso, k6, k2tog, k1; rep from * to end.

6th row: P1, *p2tog, p7; rep from * to end.

7th row: K2, [yf, k1] 5 times, yf, *k3, [yf, k1] 5 times, yf; rep from * to last 2 sts, k2.

8th row: Purl.

9th and 10th rows: Knit.

11th row: Purl.

12th row: Knit.

Rep these 12 rows.

Ornamental Tulip Pattern

Multiple of 13 sts.

Note: Sts should only be counted after the 1st, 2nd, 9th and 10th rows of this pattern.

1st row (right side): Purl.

2nd row: Knit.

3rd row: P6, [p1, k1] 3 times into next st, *p12, [p1, k1] 3 times into next st; rep from * to last 6 sts, p6.

4th row: K6, p6, *k12, p6; rep from * to last 6 sts, k6.

5th row: P6, k6, *p12, k6; rep from * to last 6 sts, p6.

6th row: As 4th row.

7th row: [P2tog] twice, p2, [k2, yf] twice, k2, *p2, [p2tog] 4 times, p2, [k2, yf] twice, k2; rep from * to last 6 sts, p2, [p2tog] twice.

8th row: K4, p8, *k8, p8; rep from * to last 4 sts, k4.

9th row: [P2tog] twice, [k2tog, yf, k1, yf] twice, k2tog, *[p2tog] 4 times, [k2tog, yf, k1, yf] twice, k2tog; rep from * to last 4 sts, [p2tog] twice.

10th row: K2, p9, *k4, p9; rep from * to last 2 sts, k2.

Rep these 10 rows.

Canterbury Bells

Multiple of 5 sts.

Note: Sts should only be counted after the 1st, 2nd and 10th rows.

1st row (right side): P2, KB1, *p4, KB1; rep from * to last 2 sts, p2.

2nd row: K2, PB1, *k4, PB1; rep from * to last 2 sts, k2.

3rd row: P2, KB1, *p2, turn, cast on 8 sts cable method, turn, p2, KB1; rep from * to last 2 sts, p2.

4th row: K2, PB1, *k2, p8, k2, PB1; rep from * to last 2 sts, k2.

5th row: P2, KB1, *p2, k8, p2, KB1; rep from * to last 2 sts, p2.

6th row: As 4th row.

7th row: P2, KB1, *p2, yb, sl 1, k1, psso, k4, k2tog, p2, KB1; rep from * to last 2 sts, p2.

8th row: K2, PB1, *k2, p2tog, p2, p2tog tbl, k2, PB1; rep from * to last 2 sts, k2.

9th row: P2, KB1, *p2, yb, sl 1, k1, psso, k2tog, p2, KB1; rep from * to last 2 sts, p2.

10th row: K2, PB1, *k1, sl 1, k1, psso, k2tog, k1, PB1; rep from * to last 2 sts, k2.

Rep these 10 rows.

Embossed Leaf Pattern

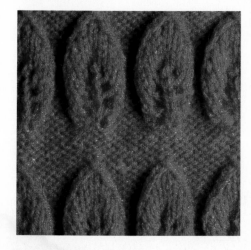

Multiple of 7 sts + 6.

Note: Sts should only be counted after the 15th and 16th rows of this pattern.

1st row (right side): P6, *yon, k1, yfrn, p6; rep from * to end.

2nd row: K6, *p3, k6; rep from * to end.

3rd row: P6, *[k1, yf] twice, k1, p6; rep from * to end.

4th row: K6, *p5, k6; rep from * to end.

5th row: P6, *k2, yf, k1, yf, k2, p6; rep from * to end.

6th row: K6, *p7, k6; rep from * to end.

7th row: P6, *k3, yf, k1, yf, k3, p6; rep from * to end.

8th row: K6, *p9, k6; rep from * to end.

9th row: P6, *sl 1, k1, psso, k5, k2tog, p6; rep from * to end.

10th row: K6, *p7, k6; rep from * to end.

11th row: P6, *sl 1, k1, psso, k3, k2tog, p6; rep from * to end.

12th row: K6, *p5, k6; rep from * to end.

13th row: P6, *sl 1, k1, psso, k1, k2tog, p6; rep from * to end.

14th row: K6, *p3, k6; rep from * to end.

15th row: P6, *sl 1, k2tog, psso, p6; rep from * to end.

16th row: Knit.

17th row: Purl.

Rep the last 2 rows once more then the 16th row again.

Rep these 20 rows.

Hyacinth Blossom Stitch

Multiple of 6 sts + 2.

1st row (wrong side): K1, *p5tog, [k1, p1, k1, p1, k1] into next st; rep from * to last st, k1.

2nd row: Purl.

3rd row: K1, *[k1, p1, k1, p1, k1] into next st, p5tog; rep from * to last st, k1.

4th row: As 2nd row.

5th row: Knit this row winding yarn round the needle 3 times for each st.

6th row: Purl to end dropping extra loops.

Rep these 6 rows.

Mesh Zigzag Stitch

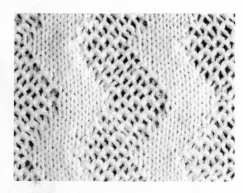

Multiple of 11 sts.

Special Abbreviation

KW5 = knit 5 sts wrapping yarn twice round needle for each st.

1st row (right side): K1, KW5, *k6, KW5; rep from * to last 5 sts, k5.

2nd row: P5, k5 dropping extra loops, *p6, k5 dropping extra loops; rep from * to last st, p1.

3rd row: K2, KW5, *k6, KW5; rep from * to last 4 sts, k4.

4th row: P4, k5 dropping extra loops, *p6, k5 dropping extra loops; rep from * to last 2 sts, p2.

5th row: K3, KW5, *k6, KW5; rep from * to last 3 sts, k3.

6th row: P3, k5 dropping extra loops, *p6, k5 dropping extra loops; rep from * to last 3 sts, p3.

7th row: K4, KW5, *k6, KW5; rep from * to last 2 sts, k2.

8th row: P2, k5 dropping extra loops, *p6, k5 dropping extra loops; rep from * to last 4 sts, p4.

9th row: K5, KW5, *k6, KW5; rep from * to last st, k1.

10th row: P1, k5 dropping extra loops, *p6, k5 dropping extra loops; rep from * to last 5 sts, p5.

11th row: As 7th row.

12th row: As 8th row.

13th row: As 5th row.

14th row: As 6th row.

15th row: As 3rd row.

16th row: As 4th row.

17th row: As 1st row.

18th row: As 2nd row.

Rep these 18 rows.

Wave Stitch

Multiple of 6 sts + 1.

Special Abbreviations

KW2 = knit next st wrapping yarn twice around needle.

KW3 = knit next st wrapping yarn 3 times around needle.

1st row (right side): K1, *KW2, [KW3] twice, KW2, k2; rep from * to end.

2nd row: Knit dropping all extra loops of previous row.

3rd row: KW3, KW2, k2, KW2, *[KW3] twice, KW2, k2, KW2; rep from * to last 2 sts, KW3, k1.

4th row: As 2nd row.

Rep these 4 rows.

All-over Lace Patterns

Vertical Ripple Stripes

Multiple of 4 sts + 3.

Note: Do not count yf and sts resulting from yf as a stitch.

1st Foundation row (right side): K3, *yf, k4; rep from * to end.

2nd, 3rd and 4th Foundation rows: Work 3 rows in st st, starting purl.

Commence Pattern

1st row: *K5, yf; rep from * to last 3 sts, k3.

2nd and every alt row: Purl.

3rd row: K3, *slip next st off left-hand needle and allow it to drop down to the loop made 6 rows below, k5, rep from * to end.

5th row: K3, *yf, k5; rep from * to end.

7th row: *K5, slip next st off left-hand needle as before; rep from * to last 3 sts, k3.

8th row: Purl.

Rep the last 8 rows.

Snow Shoe Pattern

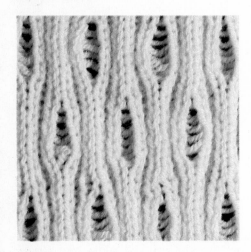

Multiple of 8 sts + 4.

Note: Sts should only be counted after the 8th, 9th, 10th, 18th, 19th or 20th rows.

1st row (right side): K2, M1, *k1, p2, k2, p2, k1, M1; rep from * to last 2 sts, k2.

2nd row: P4, k2, p2, k2, *p3, k2, p2, k2; rep from * to last 4 sts, p4.

3rd row: K4, p2, k2, p2, *k3, p2, k2, p2; rep from * to last 4 sts, k4.

Rep the last 2 rows twice more.

8th row: P2, drop next st down 7 rows, *p1, k2, p2, k2, p1, drop next st down 7 rows; rep from * to last 2 sts, p2.

9th row: K3, p2, *k2, p2; rep from * to last 3 sts, k3.

10th row: P3, k2, *p2, k2; rep from * to last 3 sts, p3.

11th row: K3, p2, k1, M1, k1, p2, *k2, p2, k1, M1, k1, p2; rep from * to last 3 sts, k3.

12th row: P3, k2, p3, k2, *p2, k2, p3, k2; rep from * to last 3 sts, p3.

13th row: K3, p2, k3, p2, *k2, p2, k3, p2; rep from * to last 3 sts, k3.

Rep the last 2 rows twice more.

18th row: P3, k2, p1, drop next st down 7 rows, p1, k2, *p2, k2, p1, drop next st down 7 rows, p1, k2; rep from * to last 3 sts, p3.

19th row: K3, p2, *k2, p2; rep from * to last 3 sts, k3.

20th row: P3, k2, *p2, k2; rep from * to last 3 sts, p3.

Rep these 20 rows.

Reversed Diamonds

Multiple of 12 sts + 1.

1st row (right side): K1, *yf, k3, sl 1, k1, psso, k1, k2tog, k3, yf, k1; rep from * to end.

2nd row: P2, k9, *p3, k9; rep from * to last 2 sts, p2.

3rd row: K2, yf, k2, sl 1, k1, psso, k1, k2tog, k2, yf, *k3, yf, k2, sl 1, k1, psso, k1, k2tog, k2, yf; rep from * to last 2 sts, k2.

4th row: P3, k7, *p5, k7; rep from * to last 3 sts, p3.

5th row: K3, yf, k1, sl 1, k1, psso, k1, k2tog, k1, yf, *k5, yf, k1, sl 1, k1, psso, k1, k2tog, k1, yf; rep from * to last 3 sts, k3.

6th row: P4, k5, *p7, k5; rep from * to last 4 sts, p4.

7th row: K4, yf, sl 1, k1, psso, k1, k2tog, yf, *k7, yf, sl 1, k1, psso, k1, k2tog, yf; rep from * to last 4 sts, k4.

8th row: P5, k3, *p9, k3; rep from * to last 5 sts, p5.

9th row: K5, yf, sl 1, k2tog, psso, yf, *k9, yf, sl 1, k2tog, psso, yf; rep from * to last 5 sts, k5.

10th row: P6, k1, *p11, k1; rep from * to last 6 sts, p6.

11th row: K1, *k2tog, k3, yf, k1, yf, k3, sl 1, k1, psso, k1; rep from * to end.

12th row: As 8th row.

13th row: K1, *k2tog, k2, yf, k3, yf, k2, sl 1, k1, psso, k1; rep from * to end.

14th row: As 6th row.

15th row: K1, *k2tog, k1, yf, k5, yf, k1, sl 1, k1, psso, k1; rep from * to end.

16th row: As 4th row.

17th row: K1, *k2tog, yf, k7, yf, sl 1, k1, psso, k1; rep from * to end.

18th row: As 2nd row.

19th row: K2tog, yf, k9, *yf, sl 1, k2tog, psso, yf, k9; rep from * to last 2 sts, yf, sl 1, k1, psso.

20th row: P1, *k11, p1; rep from * to end.

Rep these 20 rows.

Puff Stitch Check I

Multiple of 10 sts + 7.

Special Abbreviation

K5W = knit next 5 sts wrapping yarn twice around needle for each st.

1st row (right side): P6, k5W, *p5, k5W; rep from * to last 6 sts, p6.

2nd row: K6, p5 dropping extra loops, *k5, p5 dropping extra loops; rep from * to last 6 sts, k6.

Rep the last 2 rows 3 times more.

9th row: P1, k5W, *p5, k5W; rep from * to last st, p1.

10th row: K1, p5 dropping extra loops, *k5, p5 dropping extra loops; rep from * to last st, k1.

Rep the last 2 rows 3 times more.

Rep these 16 rows.

Puff Stitch Check II

Worked as Puff Stitch Check I, using reverse side as right side.

Bluebell Insertion

Worked over 8 sts on a background of reversed st st.

1st row (right side): P2, [k1, p2] twice.
2nd row: K2, [p1, k2] twice.
Rep the last 2 rows once more.
5th row: P1, yon, sl 1, k1, psso, p2, k2tog, yfrn, p1.
6th row: K1, p2, k2, p2, k1.
7th row: P2, yon, sl 1, k1, psso, k2tog, yfrn, p2.
8th row: K2, p4, k2.
Rep these 8 rows.

Little Shell Insertion

Worked over 7 sts on a background of st st.
1st row (right side): Knit.
2nd row: Purl.
3rd row: K1, yfrn, p1, p3tog, p1, yon, k1.
4th row: Purl.
Rep these 4 rows.

Zigzag Insertion

Worked over 5 sts on a background of reverse st st.
1st row: Knit.
2nd and every alt row: Purl.
3rd row: K1, k2tog, yf, k2.
5th row: K2tog, yf, k3.
7th row: Knit.
9th row: K2, yf, sl 1, k1, psso, k1.
11th row: K3, yf, sl 1, k1, psso.
12th row: Purl.
Rep these 12 rows.

Eyelet Lattice Insertion

Worked over 8 sts on a background of st st.
1st row (right side): K1, [k2tog, yf] 3 times, k1.
2nd row: Purl.
3rd row: K2, [k2tog, yf] twice, k2.
4th row: Purl.
Rep these 4 rows.

Eyelet Twist Panel

Worked over 13 sts on a background of st st.
1st and every alt row (wrong side): Purl.
2nd row: K1, [yf, sl 1, k1, psso] twice, k3, [k2tog, yf] twice, k1.
4th row: K2, [yf, sl 1, k1, psso] twice, k1, [k2tog, yf] twice, k2.

6th row: K3, yf, sl 1, k1, psso, yf, sl 1, k2tog, psso, yf, k2tog, yf, k3.
8th row: K4, yf, sl 1, k2tog, psso, yf, k2tog, yf, k4.
10th row: K4, [k2tog, yf] twice, k5.
12th row: K3, [k2tog, yf] twice, k1, yf, sl 1, k1, psso, k3.
14th row: K2, [k2tog, yf] twice, k1, [yf, sl 1, k1, psso] twice, k2.
16th row: K1, [k2tog, yf] twice, k3, [yf, sl 1, k1, psso] twice, k1.
18th row: [K2tog, yf] twice, k5, [yf, sl 1, k1, psso] twice.
Rep these 18 rows.

Braided Lace Panel

Worked over 20 sts on a background of st st.
1st and every alt row (wrong side): Purl.
2nd row: K4, [yf, sl 1, k1, psso] twice, k3, [k2tog, yf] twice, k5.
4th row: K2, [k2tog, yf] twice, k4, [k2tog, yf] twice, k1, yf, sl 1, k1, psso, k3.
6th row: K1, [k2tog, yf] twice, k4, [k2tog, yf] twice, k1, [yf, sl 1, k1, psso] twice, k2.
8th row: [K2tog, yf] twice, k4, [k2tog, yf] twice, k3, [yf, sl 1, k1, psso] twice, k1.
10th row: K2, [yf, sl 1, k1, psso] twice, k1, [k2tog, yf] twice, k5, [yf, sl 1, k1, psso] twice.
12th row: K3, yf, sl 1, k1, psso, yf, sl 1, k2tog, psso, yf, k2tog, yf, k4, [k2tog, yf] twice, k2.
14th row: K4, yf, sl 1, k1, psso, yf, sl 1, k2tog, psso, yf, k4, [k2tog, yf] twice, k3.
16th row: K5, [yf, sl 1, k1, psso] twice, k3, [k2tog, yf] twice, k4.
18th row: K3, k2tog, yf, k1, [yf, sl 1, k1, psso] twice, k4, [yf, sl 1, k1, psso] twice, k2.
20th row: K2, [k2tog, yf] twice, k1, [yf, sl 1, k1, psso] twice, k4, [yf, sl 1, k1, psso] twice, k1.
22nd row: K1, [k2tog, yf] twice, k3, [yf, sl 1, k1, psso] twice, k4, [yf, sl 1, k1, psso] twice.
24th row: [K2tog, yf] twice, k5, [yf, sl 1, k1, psso] twice, k1, [k2tog, yf] twice, k2.
26th row: K2, [yf, sl 1, k1, psso] twice, k4, yf, sl 1, k1, psso, yf, k3tog, yf, k2tog, yf, k3.
28th row: K3, [yf, sl 1, k1, psso] twice, k4, yf, k3tog, yf, k2tog, yf, k4.
Rep these 28 rows.

Lace Panels

Zigzag Panel

Worked over 9 sts on a background of st st.
1st row (right side): K3, sl 1, k1, psso, yf, k2tog, yf, k2.
2nd and every alt row: Purl.
3rd row: K2, sl 1, k1, psso, yf, k2tog, yf, k3.
5th row: K1, sl 1, k1, psso, yf, k2tog, yf, k4.
7th row: Sl 1, k1, psso, yf, k2tog, yf, k5.
9th row: K2, yf, sl 1, k1, psso, yf, k2tog, k3.
11th row: K3, yf, sl 1, k1, psso, yf, k2tog, k2.
13th row: K4, yf, sl 1, k1, psso, yf, k2tog, k1.
15th row: K5, yf, sl 1, k1, psso, yf, k2tog.
16th row: Purl.
Rep these 16 rows.

Zigzag Panel with Diamonds

Worked over 9 sts on a background of st st.
1st row (right side): K2, yf, sl 1, k1, psso, k5.
2nd and every alt row: Purl.
3rd row: K3, yf, sl 1, k1, psso, k4.
5th row: K4, yf, sl 1, k1, psso, k3.
7th row: K5, yf, sl 1, k1, psso, k2.
9th row: K2, yf, sl 1, k1, psso, k2, yf, sl 1, k1, psso, k1.
11th row: K1, [yf, sl 1, k1, psso] twice, k2, yf, sl 1, k1, psso.
13th row: K2, yf, sl 1, k1, psso, k2, k2tog, yf, k1.

15th row: K5, k2tog, yf, k2.
17th row: K4, k2tog, yf, k3.
19th row: K3, k2tog, yf, k4.
21st row: K2, k2tog, yf, k5.
23rd row: K1, k2tog, yf, k3, yf, sl 1, k1, psso, k1.
25th row: K2tog, yf, k3, [yf, sl 1, k1, psso] twice.
27th row: K1, yf, sl 1, k1, psso, k3, yf, sl 1, k1, psso, k1.
28th row: Purl.
Rep these 28 rows.

Eyelet Fan Panel

Worked over 13 sts on a background of st st.
Work 4 rows in garter st (1st row is right side).
5th row: Sl 1, k1, psso, k4, yf, k1, yf, k4, k2tog.
6th, 8th, 10th and 12th rows: Purl.
7th row: Sl 1, k1, psso, [k3, yf] twice, k3, k2tog.
9th row: Sl 1, k1, psso, k2, yf, k2tog, yf, k1, yf, sl 1, k1, psso, yf, k2, k2tog.
11th row: Sl 1, k1, psso, k1, yf, k2tog, yf, k3, yf, sl 1, k1, psso, yf, k1, k2tog.
13th row: Sl 1, k1, psso, [yf, k2tog] twice, yf, k1, [yf, sl 1, k1, psso] twice, yf, k2tog.
14th row: Purl.
Rep these 14 rows.

Lyre Panel

Worked over 21 sts on a background of st st.
1st and every alt row (wrong side): Purl.
2nd row: K1, yf, k2tog, k5, k2tog, yf, k1, yf, sl 1, k1, psso, k5, sl 1, k1, psso, yf, k1.
4th row: K1, yf, k2tog, k4, k2tog, yf, k3, yf,

Pyramid Panel

sl 1, k1, psso, k4, sl 1, k1, psso, yf, k1.
6th row: K1, yf, k2tog, k3, k2tog, yf, k5, yf, sl 1, k1, psso, k3, sl 1, k1, psso, yf, k1.
8th row: K1, yf, k2tog, k2, [k2tog, yf] twice, k3, [yf, sl 1, k1, psso] twice, k2, sl 1, k1, psso, yf, k1.
10th, 12th, 14th, 16th and 18th rows: K1, yf, k2tog, k3, yf, k2tog, yf, sl 1, k1, psso, k1, k2tog, yf, sl 1, k1, psso, yf, k3, sl 1, k1, psso, yf, k1.
20th row: K1, yf, k2tog, k1, k2tog, yf, k9, yf, sl 1, k1, psso, k1, sl 1, k1, psso, yf, k1.
Rep these 20 rows.

Worked over 17 sts on a background of st st.
1st row (right side): [K1, yf, sl 1, k1, psso] twice, p5, [k2tog, yf, k1] twice.
2nd row: P6, k5, p6.
3rd row: K2, yf, sl 1, k1, psso, k1, yf, sl 1, k1, psso, p3, k2tog, yf, k1, k2tog, yf, k2.
4th row: P7, k3, p7.
5th row: K3, yf, sl 1, k1, psso, k1, yf, sl 1, k1, psso, p1, k2tog, yf, k1, k2tog, yf, k3.
6th row: P8, k1, p8.
7th row: K4, yf, sl 1, k1, psso, k1, yf, sl 1, k1, psso, p1, k2tog, yf, k1, k2tog, yf, k4.
8th and every alt row: Purl.
9th row: K5, yf, sl 1, k1, psso, k3, k2tog, yf, k5.
11th row: K6, yf, sl 1, k1, psso, k1, k2tog, yf, k6.
13th row: K7, yf, sl 1, k2tog, psso, yf, k7.
14th row: Purl.
Rep these 14 rows.

Lace Loops

Worked over 20 sts on a background of st st.
1st and every alt row (wrong side): Purl.
2nd row: K2, yf, sl 1, k1, psso, k1, k2tog, yf, k1, yf, sl 1, k1, psso, k10.
4th row: K3, yf, sl 1, k2tog, psso, yf, k3, yf, sl 1, k1, psso, k3, k2tog, yf, k4.
6th row: K4, yf, sl 1, k1, psso, k4, yf, sl 1, k1, psso, k1, k2tog, yf, k1, yf, sl 1, k1, psso, k2.
8th row: K11, yf, k3tog, yf, k3, yf, sl 1, k1, psso, k1.
10th row: K11, k2tog, yf, k5, yf, sl 1, k1, psso.
12th row: K10, k2tog, yf, k1, yf, sl 1, k1, psso, k1, k2tog, yf, k2.
14th row: K4, yf, sl 1, k1, psso, k3, k2tog, yf, k3, yf, k3tog, yf, k3.
16th row: K2, k2tog, yf, k1, yf, sl 1, k1, psso, k1, k2tog, yf, k4, k2tog, yf, k4.
18th row: K1, k2tog, yf, k3, yf, sl 1, k2tog, yf, k11.
20th row: K2tog, yf, k5, yf, sl 1, k1, psso, k11.
Rep these 20 rows.

Ribbed Diamond Panel

Worked over 17 sts on a background of st st.
1st row (right side): K6, k2tog, yf, k1, yf, sl 1, k1, psso, k6.
2nd row: P7, k1, p1, k1, p7.
3rd row: K5, k2tog, yfrn, p1, k1, p1, yon, sl 1, k1, psso, k5.
4th row: As 2nd row.
5th row: K4, k2tog, yf, [k1, p1] twice, k1, yf, sl 1, k1, psso, k4.
6th row: P5, k1, [p1, k1] 3 times, p5.
7th row: K3, k2tog, yfrn, [p1, k1] 3 times, p1, yon, sl 1, k1, psso, k3.
8th row: As 6th row.
9th row: K2, k2tog, yf, [k1, p1] 4 times, k1, yf, sl 1, k1, psso, k2.
10th row: P3, k1, [p1, k1] 5 times, p3.
11th row: K1, k2tog, yfrn, [p1, k1] 5 times, p1, yon, sl 1, k1, psso, k1.
12th row: As 10th row.
13th row: K1, yf, sl 1, k1, psso, [p1, k1] 5 times, p1, k2tog, yf, k1.
14th row: As 10th row.

15th row: K2, yf, sl 1, k1, psso, [k1, p1] 4 times, k1, k2tog, yf, k2.
16th row: As 6th row.
17th row: K3, yf, sl 1, k1, psso, [p1, k1] 3 times, p1, k2tog, yf, k3.
18th row: As 6th row.
19th row: K4, yf, sl 1, k1, psso, [k1, p1] twice, k1, k2tog, yf, k4.
20th row: As 2nd row.
21st row: K5, yf, sl 1, k1, psso, p1, k1, p1, k2tog, yf, k5.
22nd row: As 2nd row.
23rd row: K6, yf, sl 1, k1, psso, k1, k2tog, yf, k6.
24th row: Purl.
Rep these 24 rows.

Moss Stitch Diamond Panel

Worked over 19 sts on a background of st st.
1st row (right side): K8, yf, sl 1, k2tog, psso, yf, k8.
2nd, 4th, 6th and 8th rows: Purl.
3rd row: K7, k2tog, yf, k1, yf, sl 1, k1, psso, k7.
5th row: K6, k2tog, yf, k3, yf, sl 1, k1, psso, k6.
7th row: K5, k2tog, yf, k5, yf, sl 1, k1, psso, k5.
9th row: K4, k2tog, yf, k3, p1, k3, yf, sl 1, k1, psso, k4.
10th row: P9, k1, p9.
11th row: K3, k2tog, yf, k3, p1, k1, p1, k3, yf, sl 1, k1, psso, k3.
12th row: P8, k1, p1, k1, p8.
13th row: K2, k2tog, yf, k3, [p1, k1] twice, p1, k3, yf, sl 1, k1, psso, k2.
14th row: P7, [k1, p1] twice, k1, p7.
15th row: K1, k2tog, yf, k3, [p1, k1] 3 times, p1, k3, yf, sl 1, k1, psso, k1.
16th row: P6, [k1, p1] 3 times, k1, p6.
17th row: K2tog, yf, k3, [p1, k1] 4 times, p1, k3, yf, sl 1, k1, psso.
18th row: P5, [k1, p1] 4 times, k1, p5.
19th row: K2, yf, sl 1, k1, psso, k2, [p1, k1] 3 times, p1, k2, k2tog, yf, k2.
20th row: As 16th row.
21st row: K3, yf, sl 1, k1, psso, k2, [p1, k1] twice, p1, k2, k2tog, yf, k3.

Bishops Mitre Panel

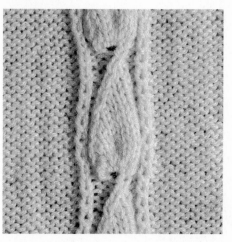

Worked over 9 sts on a background of reverse st st.
Foundation row (wrong side): K1, p1, k5, p1, k1.
Commence Pattern
1st row: P1, KB1, p2, [k1, KB1, k1, KB1, k1, KB1, k1, KB1] into next st, p2, KB1, p1. (16 sts).
2nd row: K1, p1, k2, p8, k2, p1, k1.
3rd row: P1, KB1, p2, k6, k2tog, p2, KB1, p1. (15 sts).
4th row: K1, p1, k2, p7, k2, p1, k1.
5th row: P1, KB1, p2, k5, k2tog, p2, KB1, p1. (14 sts).
6th row: K1, p1, k2, p6, k2, p1, k1.
7th row: P1, KB1, p2, k4, k2tog, p2, KB1, p1. (13 sts).
8th row: K1, p1, k2, p5, k2, p1, k1.
9th row: P1, KB1, p2, k3, k2tog, p2, KB1, p1. (12 sts).
10th row: K1, p1, k2, p4, k2, p1, k1.
11th row: P1, KB1, p2, k2, k2tog, p2, KB1, p1. (11 sts).
12th row: K1, p1, k2, p3, k2, p1, k1.
13th row: P1, KB1, p2, k1, k2tog, p2, KB1, p1. (10 sts).
14th row: K1, p1, k2, p2, k2, p1, k1.
15th row: P1, KB1, p2, k2tog, p2, KB1, p1. (9 sts).
16th row: K1, p1, [k2, p1] twice, k1.
Rep these 16 rows.

Lace Panels

Ascending Arrow Panel

Worked over 13 sts on a background of reverse st st.

1st row (right side): P2, yon, sl 1, k1, psso, k5, k2tog, yfrn, p2.
2nd and every alt row: K2, p9, k2.
3rd row: P2, k1, yf, sl 1, k1, psso, k3, k2tog, yf, k1, p2.
5th row: P2, k2, yf, sl 1, k1, psso, k1, k2tog, yf, k2, p2.
7th row: P2, k3, yf, sl 1, k2tog, psso, yf, k3, p2.
8th row: K2, p9, k2.
Rep these 8 rows.

Twig and Leaf Insertion

Worked over 13 sts on a background of st st.

1st and every alt row (wrong side): Purl.
2nd row: [K1, yf] twice, sl 1, k2tog, psso, k3, k3tog, [yf, k1] twice.
4th row: K1, yf, k3, yf, sl 1, k1, psso, k1, k2tog, yf, k3, yf, k1. (15 sts).
6th row: K1, yf, sl 1, k1, psso, k1, k2tog, yf, sl 1, k2tog, psso, yf, sl 1, k1, psso, k1, k2tog, yf, k1. (13 sts).
8th row: K1, [yf, sl 1, k1, psso, k1, k2tog, yf, k1] twice.
10th row: As 8th row.
Rep these 10 rows.

12th row: Purl.
Rep these 12 rows.

Raised Tyre Track Panel

Worked over 10 sts on a background of st st.

1st row (right side): K4, yf, k1, sl 1, k1, psso, k3.
2nd row: P2, p2tog tbl, p1, yrn, p5.
3rd row: K6, yf, k1, sl 1, k1, psso, k1.
4th row: P2tog tbl, p1, yrn, p7.
5th row: K3, k2tog, k1, yf, k4.
6th row: P5, yrn, p1, p2tog, p2.
7th row: K1, k2tog, k1, yf, k6.
8th row: P7, yrn, p1, p2tog.
Rep these 8 rows.

Vertical Arrow Panel

Worked over 13 sts on a background of st st.
1st row (right side): K1, yf, k4, sl 2tog, k1, p2sso, k4, yf, k1.
2nd and every alt row: Purl.
3rd row: K2, yf, k3, sl 2tog, k1, p2sso, k3, yf, k2.
5th row: K3, yf, k2, sl 2tog, k1, p2sso, k2, yf, k3.
7th row: K4, yf, k1, sl 2tog, k1, p2sso, k1, yf, k4.
9th row: K5, yf, sl 2tog, k1, p2sso, yf, k5.
10th row: Purl.
Rep these 10 rows.

Branch Panel

Worked over 12 sts on a background of reverse st st.

1st row (right side): K2tog, k5, yf, k1, yf, k2, sl 1, k1, psso.
2nd and every alt row: Purl.
3rd row: K2tog, k4, yf, k3, yf, k1, sl 1, k1, psso.
5th row: K2tog, k3, yf, k5, yf, sl 1, k1, psso.
7th row: K2tog, k2, yf, k1, yf, k5, sl 1, k1, psso.
9th row: K2tog, k1, yf, k3, yf, k4, sl 1, k1, psso.
11th row: K2tog, yf, k5, yf, k3, sl 1, k1, psso.

Comb Panel

Worked over 8 sts on a background of reverse st st.
1st row (wrong side): K1, p6, k1.
2nd row: P1, yb, sl 1, k1, psso, k4, yfrn, p1.
3rd row: K1, p1, yrn, p3, p2tog tbl, k1.
4th row: P1, yb, sl 1, k1, psso, k2, yf, k2, p1.
5th row: K1, p3, yrn, p1, p2tog tbl, k1.
6th row: P1, yb, sl 1, k1, psso, yf, k4, p1.
7th row: As 1st row.
8th row: P1, yon, k4, k2tog, p1.
9th row: K1, p2tog, p3, yrn, p1, k1.
10th row: P1, k2, yf, k2, k2tog, p1.
11th row: K1, p2tog, p1, yrn, p3, k1.
12th row: P1, k4, yf, k2tog, p1.
Rep these 12 rows.

Fishtails

Worked over 15 sts on a background of st st.

1st row (right side): K6, yf, sl 1, k2tog, psso, yf, k6.

2nd and every alt row: Purl.

Rep these 2 rows 3 times more.

9th row: [K1, yf] twice, sl 1, k1, psso, k2, sl 1, k2tog, psso, k2, k2tog, [yf, k1] twice.

11th row: K2, yf, k1, yf, sl 1, k1, psso, k1, sl 1, k2tog, psso, k1, k2tog, yf, k1, yf, k2.

13th row: K3, yf, k1, yf, sl 1, k1, psso, sl 1, k2tog, psso, k2tog, yf, k1, yf, k3.

15th row: K4, yf, sl 1, k1, psso, yf, sl 1, k2tog, psso, yf, k2tog, yf, k4.

16th row: Purl.

Rep these 16 rows.

Fountains Panel

Worked over 16 sts on a background of st st.

1st row (right side): K1, yf, k1, sl 1, k1, psso, p1, k2tog, k1, yfrn, p1, yb, sl 1, k1, psso, p1, k2tog, [yf, k1] twice.

2nd row: P5, k1, p1, k1, p3, k1, p4.

3rd row: K1, yf, k1, sl 1, k1, psso, p1, k2tog, k1, p1, yb, sl 1, k2tog, psso, yf, k3, yf, k1. (15 sts).

4th row: P7, k1, p2, k1, p4.

5th row: [K1, yf] twice, sl 1, k1, psso, p1, [k2tog] twice, yf, k5, yf, k1. (16 sts).

6th row: P8, k1, p1, k1, p5.

7th row: K1, yf, k3, yf, sl 1, k2tog, psso, p1, yon, k1, sl 1, k1, psso, p1, k2tog, k1, yf, k1.

8th row: P4, k1, p3, k1, p7.

9th row: K1, yf, k5, yf, sl 1, k1, psso, k1, sl 1, k1, psso, p1, k2tog, k1, yf, k1.

Gardenia Lace Panel

Worked over 12 sts on a background of st st.

Note: Sts should not be counted after 1st row.

1st row (right side): K3, [k2tog, yf] twice, sl 1, k1, psso, k3.

2nd row: P2, p2tog tbl, yrn, p1, inc 1 in next st, p1, yrn, p2tog, p2.

3rd row: K1, k2tog, yf, k6, yf, sl 1, k1, psso, k1.

4th row: P2tog tbl, yrn, p8, yrn, p2tog.

5th row: K1, yf, k3, k2tog, sl 1, k1, psso, k3, yf, k1.

6th row: P2, yrn, p2, p2tog tbl, p2tog, p2, yrn, p2.

7th row: K3, yf, k1, k2tog, sl 1, k1, psso, k1, yf, k3.

8th row: P4, yrn, p2tog tbl, p2tog, yrn, p4.

Rep these 8 rows.

Cascading Leaves

Worked over 16 sts on a background of reverse st st.

1st row (right side): P1, k3, k2tog, k1, yfrn, p2, yon, k1, sl 1, k1, psso, k3, p1.

2nd and every alt row: K1, p6, k2, p6, k1.

3rd row: P1, k2, k2tog, k1, yf, k1, p2, k1, yf, k1, sl 1, k1, psso, k2, p1.

5th row: P1, k1, k2tog, k1, yf, k2, p2, k2, yf, k1, sl 1, k1, psso, k1, p1.

7th row: P1, k2tog, k1, yf, k3, p2, k3, yf, k1, sl 1, k1, psso, p1.

Butterfly Panel

10th row: P4, k1, p2, k1, p8.

Rep these 10 rows.

Worked over 15 sts on a background of reverse st st.

1st row (right side): Yb, sl 1, k1, psso, k4, yf, k3, yf, k4, k2tog.

2nd row: P2tog, p3, yrn, p5, yrn, p3, p2tog tbl.

3rd row: Yb, sl 1, k1, psso, k2, yf, k7, yf, k2, k2tog.

4th row: P2tog, p1, yrn, p9, yrn, p1, p2tog tbl.

5th row: Yb, sl 1, k1, psso, yf, k11, yf, k2tog.

6th row: P1, yrn, p4, p2tog, k1, p2tog tbl, p4, yrn, p1.

7th row: K2, yf, k3, sl 1, k1, psso, p1, k2tog, k3, yf, k2.

8th row: P3, yrn, p2, p2tog, k1, p2tog tbl, p2, yrn, p3.

9th row: K4, yf, k1, sl 1, k1, psso, p1, k2tog, k1, yf, k4.

10th row: P5, yrn, p2tog, k1, p2tog tbl, yrn, p5.

Rep these 10 rows.

Ostrich Plume Panel

8th row: K1, p6, k2, p6, k1.

Rep these 8 rows.

Worked over 13 sts on a background of reverse st st.

1st row (right side): Knit.

2nd row: Purl.

3rd row: K4tog, [yf, k1] 5 times, yf, k4tog.

4th row: Purl.

Rep these 4 rows.

Lace Panels

Lace Diamond Border

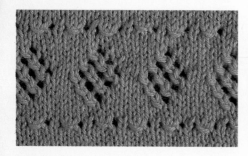

Multiple of 8.
Worked on a background of st st.
1st row (right side): *K1, yf, k3, pass 3rd st on right-hand needle over first 2 sts; rep from * to end.
2nd and every alt row: Purl.
3rd row: Knit.
5th row: K3, *yf, sl 1, k1, psso, k6; rep from * to last 5 sts, yf, sl 1, k1, psso, k3.
7th row: K2, *[yf, sl 1, k1, psso] twice, k4; rep from * to last 6 sts, [yf, sl 1, k1, psso] twice, k2.
9th row: K1, *[yf, sl 1, k1, psso] 3 times, k2; rep from * to last 7 sts, [yf, sl 1, k1, psso] 3 times, k1.
11th row: As 7th row.
13th row: As 5th row.
15th row: Knit.
17th row: As 1st row.

Candelabra Panel

Worked over 13 sts on a background of st st.
1st row (right side): Knit.
2nd and every alt row: Purl.
3rd row: Knit.
5th row: K4, k2tog, yf, k1, yf, sl 1, k1, psso, k4.
7th row: K3, k2tog, yf, k3, yf, sl 1, k1, psso, k3.
9th row: K2, [k2tog, yf] twice, k1, [yf, sl 1, k1, psso] twice, k2.
11th row: K1, [k2tog, yf] twice, k3, [yf, sl 1, k1, psso] twice, k1.
13th row: [K2tog, yf] 3 times, k1, [yf, sl 1, k1, psso] 3 times.
14th row: Purl.
Rep these 14 rows.

Ridged Eyelet Border

Multiple of 2 + 1
Worked on a background of st st.
1st, 2nd and 3rd rows: Knit.
4th row (wrong side): *P2tog, yrn; rep from * to last st, p1.
5th, 6th and 7th rows: Knit.
8th row: Purl.
Rep the first 6 rows once more.

Faggoted Panel

Worked over 9 sts on a st st background.
1st row (right side): P1, k1, k2tog, yf, k1, yf, k2tog tbl, k1, p1.
2nd row: K1, p7, k1.
3rd row: P1, k2tog, yf, k3, yf, k2tog tbl, p1.
4th row: As 2nd row.
Rep these 4 rows.

Diamond Panel

Worked over 11 sts on a background of st st.

1st row (right side): P2, k2tog, [k1, yf] twice, k1, sl 1, k1, psso, p2.
2nd and every alt row: K2, p7, k2.
3rd row: P2, k2tog, yf, k3, yf, sl 1, k1, psso, p2.
5th row: P2, k1, yf, sl 1, k1, psso, k1, k2tog, yf, k1, p2.
7th row: P2, k2, yf, sl 1, k2tog, psso, yf, k2, p2.
8th row: As 2nd row.
Rep these 8 rows.

Parasol Stitch

Worked over 17 sts on a background of st st. (**Note**: Sts should only be counted after the 11th and 12th rows of this pattern.)
1st row (right side): Yf, k1, [p3, k1] 4 times, yf.
2nd and every alt row: Purl.
3rd row: K1, yf, k1, [p3, k1] 4 times, yf, k1.
5th row: K2, yf, k1, [p3, k1] 4 times, yf, k2.
7th row: K3, yf, k1, [p2tog, p1, k1] 4 times, yf, k3.
9th row: K4, yf, k1, [p2tog, k1] 4 times, yf, k4.
11th row: K5, yf, k1, [k3tog, k1] twice, yf, k5.
12th row: Purl.
Rep these 12 rows.

Leaf Panel

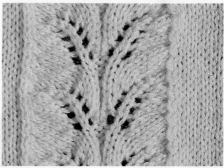

Worked over 24 sts on a background of st st.
1st row (right side): Sl 1, k2tog, psso, k7, yf, k1, yfrn, p2, yon, k1, yf, k7, k3tog.
2nd and every alt row: P11, k2, p11.
3rd row: Sl 1, k2tog, psso, k6 [yf, k1] twice, p2, [k1, yf] twice, k6, k3tog.

5th row: Sl 1, k2tog, psso, k5, yf, k1, yf, k2, p2, k2, yf, k1, yf, k5, k3tog.
7th row: Sl 1, k2tog, psso, k4, yf, k1, yf, k3, p2, k3, yf, k1, yf, k4, k3tog.
9th row: Sl 1, k2tog, psso, k3, yf, k1, yf, k4, p2, k4, yf, k1, yf, k3, k3tog.
10th row: As 2nd row.
Rep these 10 rows.

Fishtail Lace Panel

Worked over 11 sts on a background of st st.
1st row (right side): P1, k1, yf, k2, sl 1, k2tog, psso, k2, yf, k1, p1.
2nd row: K1, p9, k1.
3rd row: P1, k2, yf, k1, sl 1, k2tog, psso, k1, yf, k2, p1.
4th row: As 2nd row.
5th row: P1, k3, yf, sl 1, k2tog, psso, yf, k3, p1.
6th row: As 2nd row.
Rep these 6 rows.

Vandyke Lace Panel I

Worked over 17 sts on a background of st st.
1st row (right side): *K2tog, yf, k1, yf, sl 1, k1, psso*, k3, yf, sl 1, k1, psso, k2, rep from * to * once more.
2nd row: Purl.
3rd row: [K2tog, yf, k1, yf, sl 1, k1, psso, k1] twice, k2tog, yf, k1, yf, sl 1, k1, psso.
4th row: Purl.
5th row: *K2tog, yf, k1, yf, sl 1, k1, psso*, k2tog, yf, k3, yf, sl 1, k1, psso, rep from * to * once more.
6th row: Purl.
Rep these 6 rows.

Vandyke Lace Panel II

Worked over 9 sts on a background of st st.
1st row (right side): K4, yf, sl 1, k1, psso, k3.
2nd and every alt row: Purl.
3rd row: K2, k2tog, yf, k1, yf, sl 1, k1, psso, k2.
5th row: K1, k2tog, yf, k3, yf, sl 1, k1, psso, k1.
7th row: K2tog, yf, k5, yf, sl 1, k1, psso.
8th row: Purl.
Rep these 8 rows.

Bear Paw Panel

Worked over 23 sts on a background of st st.
1st row (right side): K2, [p4, k1] 3 times, p4, k2.
2nd row: P2, [k4, p1] 3 times, k4, p2.
3rd row: K1, yf, k1, p2, p2tog, [k1, p4] twice, k1, p2tog, p2, k1, yf, k1.
4th row: P3, k2, p2, k4, p1, k4, p2, k2, p3.
5th row: K2, yf, k1, p3, k1, p2, p2tog, k1, p2tog, p2, k1, p3, k1, yf, k2.
6th row: P4, k3, p1, k2, p3, k2, p1, k3, p4.
7th row: K3, yf, k1, p1, p2tog, [k1, p3] twice, k1, p2tog, p1, k1, yf, k3.
8th row: P5, k1, p2, k3, p1, k3, p2, k1, p5.
9th row: K4, yf, k1, p2, k1, p1, p2tog, k1, p2tog, p1, k1, p2, k1, yf, k4.
10th row: P6, k2, p1, k1, p3, k1, p1, k2, p6.
11th row: K5, yf, k1, p2tog, [k1, p2] twice, k1, p2tog, k1, yf, k5.
12th row: P9, k2, p1, k2, p9.
13th row: K6, yf, k1, p1, k1, [p2tog, k1] twice, p1, k1, yf, k6.
14th row: P8, k1, p5, k1, p8.
Rep these 14 rows.

Lace And Cable Pattern

Worked over 21 sts on a st st background.
Special Abbreviation
CB4F or CB4B (Cable-Back 4 Front or Back) = slip next 2 sts onto a cable needle and hold at front (or back) of work, knit into the back of next 2 sts on left-hand needle, then knit into the back of sts on cable needle.
1st row (right side): P2, [KB1] 4 times, k1, yf, k2tog tbl, k3, k2tog, yf, k1, [KB1] 4 times, p2.
2nd and every alt row: K2, [PB1] 4 times, k1, p7, k1, [PB1] 4 times, k2.
3rd row: P2, [KB1] 4 times, k2, yf, k2tog tbl, k1, k2tog, yf, k2, [KB1] 4 times, p2.
5th row: P2, CB4F (see Special Abbreviation), k3, yf, sl 1, k2tog, psso, yf, k3, CB4B, p2.
7th row: P2, [KB1] 4 times, k9, [KB1] 4 times, p2.
8th row: As 2nd row.
Rep these 8 rows.

Fan Lace Panel

Worked over 11 sts on a background of st st.
1st row (right side): Sl 1, k1, psso, [KB1] 3 times, yf, k1, yf, [KB1] 3 times, k2tog.
2nd and every alt row: Purl.
3rd row: Sl 1, k1, psso, [KB1] twice, yf, k1, yf, sl 1, k1, psso, yf, [KB1] twice, k2tog.
5th row: Sl 1, k1, psso, KB1, yf, k1, [yf, sl 1, k1, psso] twice, yf, KB1, k2tog.
7th row: Sl 1, k1, psso, yf, k1, [yf, sl 1, k1, psso] 3 times, yf, k2tog.
8th row: Purl.
Rep these 8 rows.

Lace Panels

Lozenge Lace Panel

Worked over 11 sts on a background of st st.

1st row (right side): K1, yf, sl 1, k1, psso, k5, k2tog, yf, k1.
2nd and every alt row: Purl.
3rd row: K2, yf, sl 1, k1, psso, k3, k2tog, yf, k2.
5th row: K3, yf, sl 1, k1, psso, k1, k2tog, yf, k3.
7th row: K4, yf, sl 1, k2tog, psso, yf, k4.
9th row: K3, k2tog, yf, k1, yf, sl 1, k1, psso, k3.
11th row: K2, k2tog, yf, k3, yf, sl 1, k1, psso, k2.
13th row: K1, k2tog, yf, k5, yf, sl 1, k1, psso, k1.
15th row: K2tog, yf, k7, yf, sl 1, k1, psso.
16th row: Purl.
Rep these 16 rows.

Lace Chain Panel

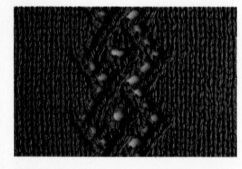

Worked over 10 sts on a background of st st.

1st row (right side): K2, k2tog, yf, k2tog but do not slip from needle, knit the first of these 2 sts again, then slip both sts from needle together, yf, sl 1, k1, psso, k2.
2nd row: Purl.
3rd row: K1, k2tog, yf, k4, yf, sl 1, k1, psso, k1.
4th row: Purl.
5th row: K2tog, yf, k1, k2tog, [yf] twice, sl 1, k1, psso, k1, yf, sl 1, k1, psso.
6th row: P4, k1 into first yf, p1 into 2nd yf, p4.
7th row: K2, yf, sl 1, k1, psso, k2, k2tog, yf, k2.
8th row: Purl.
9th row: K3, yf, sl 1, k1, psso, k2tog, yf, k3.
10th row: Purl.
Rep these 10 rows.

Lace Rib Panel

Worked over 7 sts on a background of reversed st st.

1st row (right side): P1, yon, sl 1, k1, psso, k1, k2tog, yfrn, p1.
2nd row: K1, p5, k1.
3rd row: P1, k1, yf, sl 1, k2tog, psso, yf, k1, p1.
4th row: K1, p5, k1.
Rep these 4 rows.

Openweave Panel

Worked over 11 sts on a background of st st.

1st row (right side): P2, yb, sl 1, k1, psso, yf, k3, yf, k2tog, p2.
2nd row: K2, p7, k2.
3rd row: P2, k2, yf, sl 1, k2tog, psso, yf, k2, p2.
4th row: K2, p7, k2.
Rep these 4 rows.

Arch Lace Panel

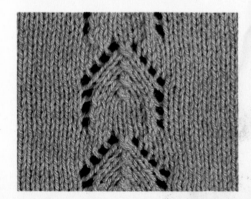

Worked over 11 sts on a background of st st.

1st row (right side): K1, yf, k2tog, k5, sl 1, k1, psso, yf, k1.
2nd and every alt row: Purl.
3rd row: As 1st row.
5th row: As 1st row.
7th row: K1, yf, k3, sl 1, k2tog, psso, k3, yf, k1.
9th row: K2, yf, k2, sl 1, k2tog, psso, k2, yf, k2.
11th row: K3, yf, k1, sl 1, k2tog, psso, k1, yf, k3.
13th row: K4, yf, sl 1, k2tog, psso, yf, k4.
14th row: Purl.
Rep these 14 rows.

Little Lace Panel

Worked on 5 sts on a background of st st.
Note: Sts should not be counted after the 1st or 2nd rows of this pattern.
1st row (right side): K1, yf, k3, yf, k1.
2nd row: Purl.
3rd row: K2, sl 1, k2tog, psso, k2.
4th row: Purl.
Rep these 4 rows.

Quatrefoil Panel

Worked over 15 sts on a background of st st.
Note: Stitches should not be counted after the 6th, 7th, 8th or 9th rows.
1st row (right side): K5, k2tog, yf, k1, yf, sl 1, k1, psso, k5.
2nd row: P4, p2tog tbl, yrn, p3, yrn, p2tog, p4.
3rd row: K3, k2tog, yf, k5, yf, sl 1, k1, psso, k3.

4th row: P2, p2tog tbl, yrn, p1, yrn, p2tog, p1, p2tog tbl, yrn, p1, yrn, p2tog, p2.

5th row: K1, k2tog, yf, k3, yf, k3tog, yf, k3, yf, sl 1, k1, psso, k1.

6th row: P2, yrn, p5, yrn, p1, yrn, p5, yrn, p2.

7th row: [K3, yf, sl 1, k1, psso, k1, k2tog, yf] twice, k3.

8th row: P4, p3tog, yrn, p5, yrn, p3tog, p4.

9th row: K6, yf, sl 1, k1, psso, k1, k2tog, yf, k6.

10th row: P3, p2tog tbl, p2, yrn, p3tog, yrn, p2, p2tog, p3.

Rep these 10 rows.

Eyelet Twigs

Worked over 14 sts on a background of st st.

1st row (right side): K1, yf, k3tog, yf, k3, yf, sl 1, k2tog, psso, yf, k4.

2nd and every alt row: Purl.

3rd row: Yf, k3tog, yf, k5, yf, sl 1, k2tog, psso, yf, k3.

5th row: K5, yf, k3tog, yf, k1, yf, sl 1, k2tog, psso, yf, k2.

7th row: K4, yf, k3tog, yf, k3, yf, sl 1, k2tog, psso, yf, k1.

9th row: K3, yf, k3tog, yf, k5, yf, sl 1, k2tog, psso, yf.

11th row: K2, yf, k3tog, yf, k1, yf, sl 1, k2tog, psso, yf, k5.

12th row: Purl.

Rep these 12 rows.

Diamond Medallion Panel

Worked over 17 sts on a background of st st.

1st row (right side): K6, k2tog, yf, k1, yf, sl 1, k1, psso, k6.

2nd and every alt row: Purl.

3rd row: K5, k2tog, yf, k3, yf, sl 1, k1, psso, k5.

5th row: K4, [k2tog, yf] twice, k1, [yf, sl 1, k1, psso] twice, k4.

7th row: K3, [k2tog, yf] twice, k3, [yf, sl 1, k1, psso] twice, k3.

9th row: K2, [k2tog, yf] 3 times, k1, [yf, sl 1, k1, psso] 3 times, k2.

11th row: K1, [k2tog, yf] 3 times, k3, [yf, sl 1, k1, psso] 3 times, k1.

13th row: [K2tog, yf] 3 times, k5, [yf, sl 1, k1, psso] 3 times.

15th row: K1, [yf, sl 1, k1, psso] 3 times, k3, [k2tog, yf] 3 times, k1.

17th row: K2, [yf, sl 1, k1, psso] 3 times, k1, [k2tog, yf] 3 times, k2.

19th row: K3, [yf, sl 1, k1, psso] twice, yf, sl 1, k2tog, psso, yf, [k2tog, yf] twice, k3.

21st row: K4, [yf, sl 1, k1, psso] twice, k1, [k2tog, yf] twice, k4.

23rd row: K5, yf, sl 1, k1, psso, yf, sl 1, k2tog, psso, yf, k2tog, yf, k5.

25th row: K6, yf, sl 1, k1, psso, k1, k2tog, yf, k6.

27th row: K7, yf, sl 1, k2tog, psso, yf, k7.

28th row: Purl.

Tulip Bud Panel

Worked over 33 sts on a background of garter st.

1st row (wrong side): K16, p1, k16.

2nd row: K14, k2tog, yf, k1, yf, sl 1, k1, psso, k14.

3rd row: K14, p5, k14.

4th row: K13, k2tog, yf, k3, yf, sl 1, k1, psso, k13.

5th row: K13, p7, k13.

6th row: K12, [k2tog, yf] twice, k1, [yf, sl 1, k1, psso] twice, k12.

7th row: K12, p9, k12.

8th row: K11, [k2tog, yf] twice, k3, [yf, sl 1, k1, psso] twice, k11.

9th row: K11, p4, k1, p1, k1, p4, k11.

10th row: K10, [k2tog, yf] twice, k5, [yf, sl 1, k1, psso] twice, k10.

11th row: K10, p4, k2, p1, k2, p4, k10.

12th row: K9, [k2tog, yf] twice, k3, yf, k1, yf, k3, [yf, sl 1, k1, psso] twice, k9. (35 sts)

13th row: K9, p4, k3, p3, k3, p4, k9.

14th row: K1, yf, sl 1, k1, psso, k5, [k2tog, yf] twice, k5, yf, k1, yf, k5, [yf, sl 1, k1, psso] twice, k5, k2tog, yf, k1. (37 sts)

15th row: K1, p2, k5, p4, k4, p5, k4, p4, k5, p2, k1.

16th row: K2, yf, sl 1, k1, psso, k3, [k2tog, yf] twice, k7, yf, k1, yf, k7, [yf, sl 1, k1, psso] twice, k3, k2tog, yf, k2. (39 sts)

17th row: K2, p2, k3, p4, k5, p7, k5, p4, k3, p2, k2.

18th row: K3, yf, sl 1, k1, psso, k1, [k2tog, yf] twice, k9, yf, k1, yf, k9, [yf, sl 1, k1, psso] twice, k1, k2tog, yf, k3. (41 sts)

19th row: K3, p2, k1, p4, k6, p9, k6, p4, k1, p2, k3.

20th row: K4, yf, sl 1, k2tog, psso, yf, k2tog, yf, k7, sl 1, k1, psso, k5, k2tog, k7, yf, sl 1, k1, psso, yf, k3tog, yf, k4. (39 sts)

21st row: K4, p5, k7, p7, k7, p5, k4.

22nd row: K16, sl 1, k1, psso, k3, k2tog, k16. (37 sts)

23rd row: K16, p5, k16.

24th row: K16, sl 1, k1, psso, k1, k2tog, k16. (35 sts)

25th row: K16, p3, k16.

26th row: K16, sl 1, k2tog, psso, k16. (33 sts)

27th row: As 1st row.

Twin Leaf Lace Panel

Worked over 23 sts on a background of st st.

1st row (right side): K8, k2tog, yf, k1, p1, k1, yf, sl 1, k1, psso, k8.

2nd row: P7, p2tog tbl, p2, yon, k1, yfrn, p2, p2tog, p7.

3rd row: K6, k2tog, k1, yf, k2, p1, k2, yf, k1, sl 1, k1, psso, k6.

4th row: P5, p2tog tbl, p3, yrn, p1, k1, p1, yrn, p3, p2tog, p5.

5th row: K4, k2tog, k2, yf, k3, p1, k3, yf, k2, sl 1, k1, psso, k4.

6th row: P3, p2tog tbl, p4, yrn, p2, k1, p2, yrn, p4, p2tog, p3.

7th row: K2, k2tog, k3, yf, k4, p1, k4, yf, k3, sl 1, k1, psso, k2.

8th row: P1, p2tog tbl, p5, yrn, p3, k1, p3, yrn, p5, p2tog, p1.

9th row: K2tog, k4, yf, k5, p1, k5, yf, k4, sl 1, k1, psso.

10th row: P11, k1, p11.

11th row: K11, p1, k11.

12th row: P11, k1, p11.

Rep these 12 rows.

155

Lace Panels

Cockleshells

Worked over 19 sts on a background of garter stitch.

1st row (right side): Knit.

2nd row: Knit.

3rd row: K1, yfrn, yrn, p2tog tbl, k13, p2tog, yrn, yon, k1. (21 sts).

4th row: K2, p1, k15, p1, k2.

5th and 6th rows: Knit.

7th row: K1, yfrn, yrn, p2tog tbl, [yrn] twice, p2tog tbl, k11, p2tog, [yrn] twice, p2tog, yrn, yon, k1. (25 sts).

8th row: [K2, p1] twice, k13, [p1, k2] twice.

9th row: Knit.

10th row: K5, k15 wrapping yarn 3 times around needle for each st, k5.

11th row: K1, yfrn, yrn, p2tog tbl, [yrn] twice, p2tog tbl, [yrn] twice, pass next 15 sts to right-hand needle dropping extra loops, pass same 15 sts back to left-hand needle and purl all 15 sts tog, [yrn] twice, p2tog, [yrn] twice, p2tog, yrn, yon, k1. (19 sts).

12th row: K1, p1, [k2, p1] twice, k3, [p1, k2] twice, p1, k1.

Rep these 12 rows.

Arched Windows

Worked over 13 sts on a background of reverse st st.

Note: Stitches should not be counted after the 3rd, 4th, 7th or 8th rows.

T5R (Twist 5 Right) = slip next 3 sts onto cable needle and hold at back of work, knit next 2 sts from left-hand needle, then p1, k2 from cable needle.

1st row (right side): K2, p2, k2tog, yf, k1,
yf, sl 1, k1, psso, p2, k2.

2nd row: P2, k2, p5, k2, p2.

3rd row: K2, p2, k1, yf, k3, yf, k1, p2, k2.

4th row: P2, k2, p7, k2, p2.

5th row: K2, p2, yb, sl 1, k1, psso, yf, sl 1, k2tog, psso, yf, k2tog, p2, k2.

6th row: As 2nd row.

7th row: T3F, p1, k1, yf, k3, yf, k1, p1, T3B.

8th row: K1, p2, k1, p7, k1, p2, k1.

9th row: P1, T3F, sl 1, k1, psso, yf, sl 1, k2tog, psso, yf, k2tog, T3B, p1.

10th row: K2, p9, k2.

11th row: P2, T3F, p3, T3B, p2.

12th row: [K3, p2] twice, k3.

13th row: P3, T3F, p1, T3B, p3.

14th row: K4, p2, k1, p2, k4.

15th row: P4, T5R, p4.

16th row: Knit.

Rep these 16 rows.

Catherine Wheels

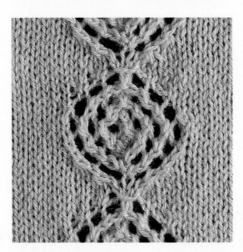

Worked across 13 sts on a background of st st.

Special Abbreviations

Inc 1 (Increase 1) = knit into front and back of next st.

Inc 2 (Increase 2) = knit into front, back and front of next st.

Work 5tog = sl 1, k1, psso, k3tog, pass the st resulting from sl 1, k1, psso over the st resulting from k3tog.

1st and every alt row (wrong side): Purl.

2nd row: K5, sl 3, yf, pass same slipped sts back to left-hand needle, yb, knit 3 slipped sts, k5.

4th row: K3, k3tog, yf, Inc 2, yf, k3tog tbl, k3.

6th row: K1, k3tog, yf, k2tog, yf, Inc 2, yf, sl 1, k1, psso, yf, k3tog tbl, k1.

8th row: [K2tog, yf] 3 times, KB1, [yf, sl 1, k1, psso] 3 times.

10th row: K1, [yf, k2tog] twice, yf, sl 1, k2tog, psso, [yf, sl 1, k1, psso] twice, yf, k1.

12th row: [Sl 1, k1, psso, yf] 3 times, KB1, [yf, k2tog] 3 times.

14th row: K1, Inc 1, yf, sl 1, k1, psso, yf, Work 5tog, yf, k2tog, yf, Inc 1, k1.

16th row: K3, Inc 1, yf, Work 5tog, yf, Inc 1, k3.

Rep these 16 rows.

Frost Flower Panel

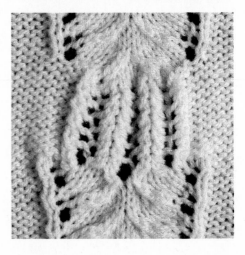

Worked over 18 sts on a background of reverse st st.

1st row (right side): K1, yf, k3, sl 1, k1, psso, k6, k2tog, k3, yf, k1.

2nd row: P1, yrn, p4, p2tog, p4, p2tog tbl, p4, yrn, p1.

3rd row: K2, yf, k4, sl 1, k1, psso, k2, k2tog, k4, yf, k2.

4th row: P3, yrn, p4, p2tog, p2tog tbl, p4, yrn, p3.

Rep these 4 rows twice more.

13th row: P3, [k2, yf, sl 1, k1, psso] 3 times, p3.

14th row: K3, [p2, yrn, p2tog] 3 times, k3.

Rep the last 2 rows 5 times more.

Rep these 24 rows.

Spiral and Eyelet Panel

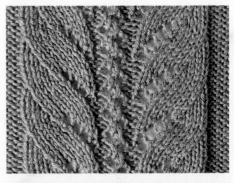

Worked over 24 sts on a background of reverse st st.

1st row (right side): K3, k2tog, k4, yfrn, p2, yon, k2tog, p2, yon, k4, sl 1, k1, psso, k3.

2nd and every alt row: P9, k2, p2, k2, p9.

3rd row: K2, k2tog, k4, yf, k1, p2, k2tog, yfrn, p2, k1, yf, k4, sl 1, k1, psso, k2.

5th row: K1, k2tog, k4, yf, k2, p2, yon, k2tog, p2, k2, yf, k4, sl 1, k1, psso, k1.

7th row: K2tog, k4, yf, k3, p2, k2tog, yfrn, p2, k3, yf, k4, sl 1, k1, psso.

8th row: P9, k2, p2, k2, p9.

Rep these 8 rows.

Patterns for Texture and Colour

Many of these surface textures are very attractive knitted in stripes of more than one colour. We have given examples of these, where applicable, throughout this section.

Knot Pattern

Multiple of 6 + 5

Special Abbreviation

Make knot = p3 tog leaving sts on left-hand needle, now knit them tog, then purl them tog again, slipping sts off needle at end.

Commence Pattern

Work 2 rows in st st, starting knit.

3rd row (right side): K1, *make knot (see Special Abbreviation), k3; rep from * to last 4 sts, make knot, k1.

Work 3 rows in st st, starting purl.

7th row: K4, *make knot, k3; rep from * to last st, k1.

8th row: Purl.

Rep these 8 rows.

Honeycomb Cable Stitch

Mutliple of 4 + 2

1st row (right side): Knit.

2nd row: K2, *p2, k2; rep from * to end. Rep the last 2 rows once more.

5th row: K1, *C2F, C2B; rep from * to last st, k1.

6th row: P2, *k2, p2; rep from * to end.

7th row: Knit.

8th row: As 6th row.

Rep the last 2 rows once more.

11th row: K1, *C2B, C2F; rep from * to last st, k1.

12th row: As 2nd row.

Rep these 12 rows.

Rice Stitch I

Multiple of 2 + 1

1st row (right side): P1, *KB1, p1; rep from * to end.

2nd row: Knit.

Rep these 2 rows.

Rice Stitch II

Worked as Rice Stitch I.

Beginning with the 1st row, worked in stripes of 2 rows in colour A, 2 rows in B and 2 rows in C.

Garter Slip Stitch I

Multiple of 2 + 1

1st row (right side): Knit.

2nd row: Knit.

3rd row: K1, *sl 1 purlwise, k1; rep from * to end.

4th row: K1, *yf, sl 1 purlwise, yb, k1; rep from * to end.

Rep these 4 rows.

Garter Slip Stitch II

Worked as Garter Slip Stitch I.

1st and 2nd pattern rows worked in A, 3rd and 4th rows in B, throughout.

Garter Slip Stitch III

Worked as Garter Slip Stitch I.

Beginning with the 1st row, 2 rows worked in colour A, 2 rows in B and 2 rows in C throughout.

Garter Slip Stitch IV

Worked as Garter Slip Stitch I.

Worked in 1 row each in colours A, B and C throughout.

Patterns for Texture and Colour

Garter Slip Stitch V

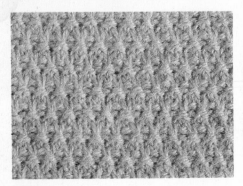

Multiple of 2 + 1
1st row (right side): Knit.
2nd row: Knit.
3rd row: K1, *sl 1 purlwise, k1; rep from * to end.
4th row: K1, *yf, sl 1 purlwise, yb, k1; rep from * to end.
Knit 2 rows.
7th row: K2, *sl 1 purlwise, k1; rep from * to last st, k1.
8th row: K2, *yf, sl 1 purlwise, yb, k1; rep from * to last st, k1.
Rep these 8 rows.

Garter Slip Stitch VI

Worked as Garter Slip Stitch V.
1st, 2nd, 5th and 6th pattern rows worked in A, 3rd, 4th, 7th and 8th rows worked in B throughout.

Garter Slip Stitch VII

Worked as Garter Slip Stitch V.
Beginning with the 1st row 2 rows worked in colour A, 2 rows in colour B and 2 rows in colour C throughout.

Garter Slip Stitch VIII

Worked as Garter Slip Stitch V.
Worked in 1 row each in colours A, B and C throughout.

Bramble Stitch I

Multiple of 4 + 2
1st row (right side): Purl.
2nd row: K1, *(k1, p1, k1) into next st, p3tog; rep from * to last st, k1.
3rd row: Purl.
4th row: K1, *p3tog, (k1, p1, k1) into next st; rep from * to last st, k1.
Rep these 4 rows.

Bramble Stitch II

Worked as Bramble Stitch I.
Beginning with the 2nd row, 2 rows worked in colour A, 2 rows in B, 2 rows in A and 2 rows in C throughout.

Bramble Stitch III

Worked as Bramble Stitch I.
Beginning with the 2nd row, 2 rows worked in colour A, 2 rows in B and 2 rows in C throughout.

Mini Bobble Stitch I

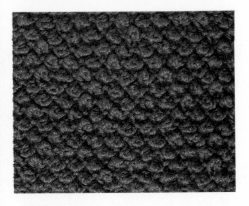

Multiple of 2 + 1
Special Abbreviation
MB (Make Bobble) = work (p1, k1, p1, k1) all into next st, pass 2nd, 3rd and 4th sts over first st.
1st row (right side): Knit.
2nd row: K1, *MB (see Special Abbreviation), k1; rep from * to end.
3rd row: Knit.
4th row: K2, *MB, k1; rep from * to last st, k1.
Rep these 4 rows.

Mini Bobble Stitch II

Worked as Mini Bobble Stitch I.
1st and 2nd pattern rows worked in A, 3rd and 4th rows worked in B throughout.

Mini Bobble Stitch III

Worked as Mini Bobble Stitch I.
Beginning with the 1st row, 2 rows worked in colour A, 2 rows in B and 2 rows in C throughout.

Basket Rib I

Multiple of 2 + 1
1st row (right side): Knit.
2nd row: Purl.
3rd row: K1, *sl 1 purlwise, k1; rep from * to end.
4th row: K1, *yf, sl 1 purlwise, yb, k1; rep from * to end.
Rep these 4 rows.

Basket Rib II

Worked as Basket Rib I
1st and 2nd pattern rows worked in A, 3rd and 4th rows worked in B throughout.

Basket Rib III

Worked as Basket Rib I.
Worked in 1 row each in colours A, B and C throughout.

Woven Cable Stitch I

Multiple of 4
1st row (right side): *C4F; rep from * to end.
2nd row: Purl.
3rd row: K2, *C4B; rep from * to last 2 sts, k2.
4th row: Purl.
Rep these 4 rows.

Woven Cable Stitch II

Multiple of 4
Special Abbreviation
C4 Back or Front (Cable 4 Back or Front) = slip next 2 sts onto a cable needle and hold at back or front of work, knit next 2 sts from left-hand needle using B, then knit sts from cable needle using A.
1st Foundation row: Knit *2A, 2B; rep from * to end.
2nd Foundation row: Purl *2B, 2A; rep

from * to end.
1st Pattern row: *C4 Front (see Special Abbreviation); rep from * to end.
2nd row: Purl *2A, 2B; rep from * to end.
3rd row: K2A, *C4 Back; rep from * to last 2 sts, k2B.
4th row: Purl *2B, 2A; rep from * to end.
Rep these 4 rows.

Candle Flame Stitch

Multiple of 4 + 2
1st row (right side): K2, *p2, k2; rep from * to end.
2nd row: P2, *k2, p2; rep from * to end.
3rd row: K2, *p2, C2F; rep from * to last 4 sts, p2, k2.
4th and 5th rows: As 2nd row.
6th row: As 1st row.
7th row: P2, *C2F, p2; rep from * to end.
8th row: As 1st row.
Rep these 8 rows.

Honeycomb Stitch

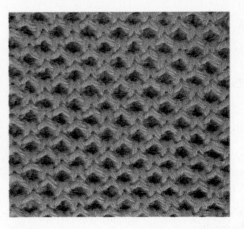

Multiple of 4
1st row (right side): *C2F, C2B; rep from * to end.
2nd row: Purl.
3rd row: *C2B, C2F; rep from * to end.
4th row: Purl.
Rep these 4 rows.

Patterns for Texture and Colour

Orchard Stitch

Multiple of 6 + 5

(**Note**: Stitches should only be counted after the 6th or 12th rows of this pattern.)

1st row (right side): P2, *k into front, back, front and back of next st, p2, k1, p2; rep from * to last 3 sts, k into front, back, front and back of next st, p2.

2nd row: *K2, [k1 winding yarn round needle twice] 4 times, k2, p1; rep from * to last 8 sts, k2, [k1 winding yarn round needle twice] 4 times, k2.

3rd row: P2, *k4 (dropping extra loops), p2, k1, p2; rep from * to last 6 sts, k4 (dropping extra loops), p2.

Rep the last 2 rows once more.

6th row: *K2, p4tog, k2, p1; rep from * to last 8 sts, k2, p4tog, k2.

7th row: P2, *k1, p2, k into front, back, front and back of next st, p2; rep from * to last 3 sts, k1, p2.

8th row: *K2, p1, k2, [k1 winding yarn round needle twice] 4 times; rep from * to last 5 sts, k2, p1, k2.

9th row: *P2, k1, p2, k4 (dropping extra loops); rep from * to last 5 sts, p2, k1, p2.

Rep the last 2 rows once more.

12th row: *K2, p1, k2, p4tog; rep from * to last 5 sts, k2, p1, k2.

Rep these 12 rows.

Trellis Stitch I

Multiple of 6 + 5

1st row (right side): K1, p3, *keeping yarn at front of work sl 3 purlwise, p3; rep from * to last st, k1.

2nd row: P1, k3, *keeping yarn at back of work sl 3 purlwise, k3; rep from * to last st, p1.

3rd row: K1, p3, *k3, p3; rep from * to last st, k1.

4th row: P1, k3, *p3, k3; rep from * to last st, p1.

5th row: K5, *insert point of right-hand needle upwards under the 2 strands in front of the sl sts and knit the next st, then lift the 2 strands off over the point of the right-hand needle (called pull up loop), k5; rep from * to end.

6th row: As 3rd row.

7th row: P1, *keeping yarn at front sl 3 purlwise, p3; rep from * to last 4 sts, sl 3 purlwise, p1.

8th row: K1, *keeping yarn at back sl 3 purlwise, k3; rep from * to last 4 sts, sl 3 purlwise, k1.

9th row: As 4th row.

10th row: As 3rd row.

11th row: K2, *pull up loop, k5; rep from * to last 3 sts, pull up loop, k2.

12th row: As 4th row.

Rep these 12 rows.

Trellis Stitch II

Worked as Trellis Stitch I.

1st and 2nd rows and 7th and 8th rows of pattern worked in contrast colour. Wrong side of fabric becomes the right side.

Speckle Rib I

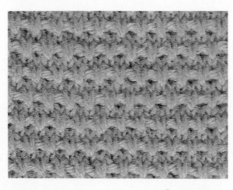

Multiple of 2 + 1

1st row (right side): Knit.

2nd row: Purl.

3rd row: K1, *sl 1 purlwise, k1; rep from * to end.

4th row: K1, *yf, sl 1 purlwise, yb, k1; rep from * to end.

5th row: Knit.

6th row: Purl.

7th row: K2, *sl 1 purlwise, k1; rep from * to last st, k1.

8th row: K2, *yf, sl 1 purlwise, yb, k1; rep from * to last st, k1.

Rep these 8 rows.

Speckle Rib II

Worked as Speckle Rib I.

1st, 2nd, 5th and 6th pattern rows worked in A, 3rd, 4th, 7th and 8th rows worked in B throughout.

Speckle Rib III

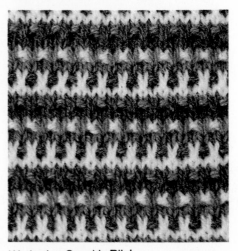

Worked as Speckle Rib I.

Beginning with the 1st row, 2 rows worked in colour A, 2 rows in B and 2 rows in C throughout.

Speckle Rib IV

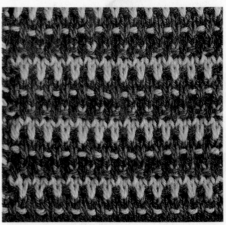

Worked as Speckle Rib I.

Worked in 1 row each in colours A, B and C throughout.

Moss Slip Stitch I

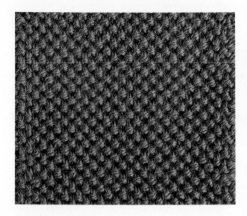

Multiple of 2 + 1

1st row (right side): K1, *sl 1 purlwise, k1; rep from * to end.
2nd row: K1, *yf, sl 1 purlwise, yb, k1; rep from * to end.
3rd row: K2, *sl 1 purlwise, k1; rep from * to last st, k1.
4th row: K2, *yf, sl 1 purlwise, yb, k1; rep from * to last st, k1.
Rep these 4 rows.

Moss Slip Stitch II

Worked as Moss Slip Stitch I.

1st and 2nd pattern rows worked in colour A, 3rd and 4th rows worked in B throughout.

Moss Slip Stitch III

Worked as Moss Slip Stitch I.
Beginning with the 1st row, 2 rows worked in colour A, 2 rows in B and 2 rows in C throughout.

Moss Slip Stitch IV

Worked as Moss Slip Stitch I.
Worked in 1 row each in colours A, B and C throughout.

Twisted Moss I

Multiple of 2 + 1

1st row (wrong side): Knit.
2nd row: K1, *K1B, k1; rep from * to end.
3rd row: Knit.
4th row: K1B, *k1, K1B; rep from * to end.
Rep these 4 rows.

Twisted Moss II

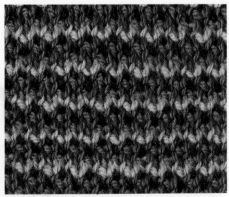

Worked as Twisted Moss I.
Beginning with the 1st row, 2 rows worked in colour A, and 4 rows in colour B throughout.

Twisted Moss III

Worked as Twisted Moss I.
1st and 2nd pattern rows worked in A, 3rd and 4th rows in B throughout.

Garter Stitch Chevron

Multiple of 11
Knit 5 rows in colour A.

6th row (right side): Using colour B, *k2tog, k2, knit into front and back of each of the next 2 sts, k3, sl 1, k1, psso; rep from * to end.
7th row: Using colour B, purl.
Rep the last 2 rows twice more. Work 6th row again using A instead of B.
Rep these 12 rows.

Tweed Stitch

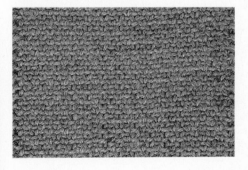

Multiple of 2 + 1

1st row (right side): K1, *yf, sl 1 purlwise, yb, k1; rep from * to end.
2nd row: P2, *yb, sl 1 purlwise, yf, p1; rep from * to last st, p1.
Rep these 2 rows.

Patterns for Texture and Colour

Pillar Stitch I

Multiple of 2
1st row (wrong side): Purl.
2nd row: K1, *yf, k2, pass yf over k2; rep from * to last st, k1.
Rep these 2 rows.

Pillar Stitch II

Worked as Pillar Stitch I.

1st row worked in colour C, then, beginning with 2nd row, 2 rows worked in colour A, 2 rows in B and 2 rows in C throughout.

Eiffel Tower Stitch

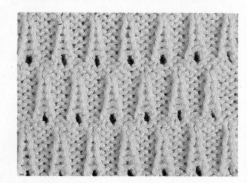

Multiple of 4 + 1
1st row (right side): P4, *yrn, p2tog, p2; rep from * to last st, p1.
2nd row: K4, *p1, k3; rep from * to last st, k1.
3rd row: P4, *k1, p3; rep from * to last st, p1.
Rep these last 2 rows twice more.
8th row: Knit.

9th row: P2, *yrn, p2tog, p2; rep from * to last 3 sts, yrn, p2tog, p1.
10th row: K2, *p1, k3; rep from * to last 3 sts, p1, k2.
11th row: P2, *k1, p3; rep from * to last 3 sts, k1, p2.
Rep the last 2 rows twice more.
16th row: Knit.
Rep these 16 rows.

Cob Nut Stitch

Multiple of 4 + 3
Note: Stitches should only be counted after the 4th, 5th, 6th, 10th, 11th or 12th rows of this pattern.
Special Abbreviation
CN1 (Make 1 Cob Nut) = knit 1 without slipping st off left-hand needle, yf, then k1 once more into same st.
Commence Pattern
1st row (right side): P3, *CN1 (see Special Abbreviation), p3; rep from * to end.
2nd row: K3, *p3, k3; rep from * to end.
3rd row: P3, *k3, p3; rep from * to end.
4th row: K3, *p3tog, k3; rep from * to end.
5th row: Purl.
6th row: Knit.
7th row: P1, *CN1, p3; rep from * to last 2 sts, CN1, p1.
8th row: K1, *p3, k3; rep from * to last 4 sts, p3, k1.
9th row: P1, *k3, p3; rep from * to last 4 sts, k3, p1.
10th row: K1, *p3tog, k3; rep from * to last 4 sts, p3tog, k1.
11th row: Purl.
12th row: Knit.
Rep these 12 rows.

Slip Stitch Rib

Multiple of 2 + 1
1st row (wrong side): Purl.
2nd row: K1, *yf, sl 1 purlwise, yb, k1; rep from * to end.
Rep these 2 rows.

Garter And Slip Stitch

Multiple of 6 + 4
1st row (right side): Knit.
2nd row: K1, *yf, sl 2 purlwise, yb, k4; rep from * to last 3 sts, yf, sl 2 purlwise, yb, k1.
3rd row: K1, *keeping yarn at back sl 2 purlwise, k4; rep from * to last 3 sts, sl 2 purlwise, k1.
Rep the last 2 rows once more.
6th row: As 2nd row.
7th row: Knit.
8th row: K4, *yf, sl 2 purlwise, yb, k4; rep from * to end.
9th row: K4, *keeping yarn at back sl 2 purlwise, k4; rep from * to end.
Rep the last 2 rows once more.
12th row: As 8th row.
Rep these 12 rows.

Garter Stitch Diamonds

Multiple of 8 + 2
1st row (right side): Knit.
2nd row: P4, *keeping yarn at front sl 2 purlwise, p6; rep from * to last 6 sts, sl 2 purlwise, p4.
3rd row: K3, *C2F, C2B, k4; rep from * to last 7 sts, C2F, C2B, k3.
4th row: P3, *keeping yarn at front sl 1 purlwise, yb, k2, yf, sl 1 purlwise, p4; rep from * to last 7 sts, sl 1 purlwise, yb, k2,

yf, sl 1 purlwise, p3.

5th row: K2, *C2F, k2, C2B, k2; rep from * to end.

6th row: P2, *keeping yarn at front sl 1 purlwise, yb, k4, yf, sl 1 purlwise, p2; rep from * to end.

7th row: K1, *C2F, k4, C2B; rep from * to last st, k1.

8th row: P1, keeping yarn at front sl 1 purlwise, yb, *k6, yf, sl 2 purlwise, yb; rep from * to last 8 sts, k6, yf, sl 1 purlwise, p1.

9th row: Knit.

10th row: As 8th row.

11th row: K1, *C2B, k4, C2F; rep from * to last st, k1.

12th row: As 6th row.

13th row: K2, *C2B, k2, C2F, k2; rep from * to end.

14th row: As 4th row.

15th row: K3, *C2B, C2F, k4; rep from * to last 7 sts, C2B, C2F, k3.

16th row: As 2nd row.

Rep these 16 rows.

Stocking Stitch Ridge I

Multiple of 2

Note: Stitches should not be counted after the 2nd row.

1st row (right side): Knit.

2nd row: P1, *k2tog; rep from * to last st, p1.

3rd row: K1, *knit into front and back of next st; rep from * to last st, k1.

4th row: Purl.

Rep these 4 rows.

Stocking Stitch Ridge II

Worked as Stocking Stitch Ridge I.

Worked in stripes of 4 rows in colour A, 4 rows in B and 4 rows in C throughout.

Knot Stitch I

Multiple of 2 + 1

1st row (right side): Knit.

2nd row: K1, *p2tog without slipping sts off needle, then k tog the same 2 sts; rep from * to end.

3rd row: Knit.

4th row: *P2tog without slipping sts off needle, then k tog the same 2 sts; rep from * to last st, k1.

Rep these 4 rows.

Knot Stitch II

Worked as Knot Stitch I.

1st and 2nd pattern rows worked in A, 3rd and 4th rows in B throughout.

Brick Stitch I

Multiple of 4 + 1

1st row (right side): K4, *k1 winding yarn twice round needle, k3; rep from * to last st, k1.

2nd row: P4, *sl 1 purlwise dropping extra loop, p3; rep from * to last st, p1.

3rd row: K4, *sl 1 purlwise, k3; rep from * to last st, k1.

4th row: K4, *yf, sl 1 purlwise, yb, k3; rep from * to last st, k1.

5th row: K2, *k1 winding yarn twice round needle, k3; rep from * to last 3 sts, k1 winding yarn twice round needle, k2.

6th row: P2, *sl 1 purlwise dropping extra loop, p3; rep from * to last 3 sts, sl 1 purlwise, p2.

7th row: K2, *sl 1 purlwise, k3; rep from * to last 3 sts, sl 1 purlwise, k2.

8th row: K2, *yf, sl 1 purlwise, yb, k3; rep from * to last 3 sts, yf, sl 1 purlwise, yb, k2.

Rep these 8 rows.

Brick Stitch II

Multiple of 4 + 1

1st row (right side): K4, *k1 winding yarn twice round needle, k3; rep from * to last st, k1.

2nd row: P4, *sl 1 purlwise dropping extra loop, p3; rep from * to last st, p1.

3rd row: K4, *sl 1 purlwise, k3; rep from * to last st, k1.

4th row: K4, *yf, sl 1 purlwise, yb, k3; rep from * to last st, k1.

Rep the last 4 rows once more.

9th row: K2, *k1 winding yarn twice round needle, k3; rep from * to last 3 sts, k1 winding yarn twice round needle, k2.

10th row: P2, *sl 1 purlwise dropping extra loop, p3; rep from * to last 3 sts, sl 1 purlwise, p2.

11th row: K2, *sl 1 purlwise, k3; rep from * to last 3 sts, sl 1 purlwise, k2.

12th row: K2, *yf, sl 1 purlwise, yb, k3; rep from * to last 3 sts, yf, sl 1 purlwise, yb, k2.

Rep the last 4 rows once more.

Rep these 16 rows.

Brick Stitch III

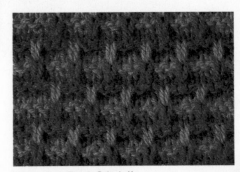

Worked as Brick Stitch II.

1st row worked in colour B then 4 rows in A and 4 rows in B throughout.

Patterns for Texture and Colour

Wheatsheaf Pattern

Multiple of 12+8
Special Abbreviation
CB6 = slip next 3 sts onto a cable needle and leave at back of work, [KB1] 3 times from left-hand needle, then k3 sts from cable needle.
1st row (right side): P7, *k3, [KB1] 3 times, p6; rep from * to last st, p1.
2nd row: K7, *[PB1] 3 times, p3, k6; rep from * to last st, k1.
Rep the last 2 rows once more.
5th row: P7, *CB6 (see Special Abbreviation), p6; rep from * to last st, p1.
6th row: K7, *p3, [PB1] 3 times, k6; rep from * to last st, k1.
7th row: P1, *k3 [KB1] 3 times, p6; rep from * to last 7 sts, k3, [KB1] 3 times, p1.
8th row: K1, *[PB1] 3 times, p3, k6; rep from * to last 7 sts, [PB1] 3 times, p3, k1.
Rep the last 2 rows once more.
11th row: P1, *CB6, p6; rep from * to last 7 sts, CB6, p1.
12th row: K1, *p3, [PB1] 3 times, k6; rep from * to last 7 sts, p3, [PB1] 3 times, k1.
Rep these 12 rows.

Pull Up Stitch I

Multiple of 6+5
Note: Stitches should *not* be counted after the 3rd or 7th rows of this pattern.
Special Abbreviation
Make cluster = k1, insert needle through centre of st 3 rows below next st on needle, yo and pull up a loop, knit st above in the usual way, pull up another loop as before through *same* hole, knit next st from needle, pull up another loop through same hole.

Foundation row (do not repeat this row): Knit.
1st row (right side): Purl.
2nd row: Knit.
3rd row: P1, *make cluster (see Special Abbreviation), p3; rep from * to last 4 sts, make cluster, p1.
4th row: K1, *[p2tog] 3 times, k3; rep from * to last 7 sts, [p2tog] 3 times, k1.
5th row: Purl.
6th row: Knit.
7th row: P4, *make cluster, p3; rep from * to last st, p1.
8th row: K4, *[p2tog] 3 times, k3; rep from * to last st, k1.
Rep these 8 rows.

Pull Up Stitch II

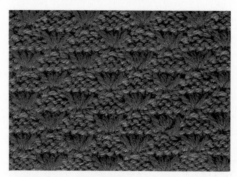

Worked as Pull Up Stitch I.

1st, 2nd, 5th and 6th pattern rows worked in A, 3rd, 4th, 7th and 8th rows worked in B throughout.

Stairway Check

Multiple of 8+4
1st row (right side): *KB1; rep from * to end.
2nd row: [PB1] 4 times, *k4, [PB1] 4 times; rep from * to end.
3rd row: P1, *[KB1] 4 times, p4; rep from * to last 3 sts, [KB1] 3 times.
4th row: [PB1] twice, *k4, [PB1] 4 times; rep from * to last 2 sts, k2.
5th row: P3, *[KB1] 4 times, p4; rep from * to last st, KB1.
6th row: K4, *[PB1] 4 times, k4; rep from * to end.
7th row: As 1st row.

8th row: [PB1] 4 times, *k4, [PB1] 4 times; rep from * to end.
9th row: [KB1] 4 times, *p4, [KB1] 4 times; rep from * to end.
Rep the last 2 rows once more.
12th row: *PB1; rep from * to end.
13th row: P4, *[KB1] 4 times, p4; rep from * to end.
14th row: PB1, *k4, [PB1] 4 times; rep from * to last 3 sts, k3.
15th row: P2, *[KB1] 4 times, p4; rep from * to last 2 sts, [KB1] twice.
16th row: [PB1] 3 times, *k4, [PB1] 4 times; rep from * to last st, k1.
17th row: As 9th row.
18th row: As 12th row.
19th row: P4, *[KB1] 4 times, p4; rep from * to end.
20th row: K4, *[PB1] 4 times, k4; rep from * to end.
Rep the last 2 rows once more.
Rep these 22 rows.

Garter Drop Stitch

Any number of stitches
Work 4 rows in garter stitch (every row knit).
5th row: *K1 winding yarn twice round needle; rep from * to end.
6th row: K to end, dropping the extra loops.
Rep these 6 rows.

Ridged Knot Stitch I

Multiple of 3+2
1st row (right side): Knit.
2nd row: K1, *p3tog leaving sts on needle, yrn, then p same 3 sts together again; rep from * to last st, k1.
3rd and 4th rows: Knit.
Rep these 4 rows.

Ridged Knot Stitch II

Worked as Ridged Knot Stitch I.
1st and 2nd pattern rows worked in A, 3rd and 4th rows in B throughout.

Twisted Check Pattern

Multiple of 8+5
1st row (right side): Purl.
2nd row: K1, *[PB1] 3 times, k5; rep from * to last 4 sts, [PB1] 3 times, k1.
3rd row: P1, *[KB1] 3 times, p5; rep from * to last 4 sts, [KB1] 3 times, p1.
4th row: As 2nd row.
5th row: Purl.
6th row: Knit.
7th row: P5, *[KB1] 3 times, p5; rep from * to end.
8th row: K5, *[PB1] 3 times, k5; rep from * to end.
9th row: As 7th row.
10th row: Knit.
Rep these 10 rows.

Diagonal Knot Stitch I

Multiple of 3+1
Special Abbreviation
Make Knot = P3tog leaving sts on needle, yrn, then purl same 3 sts together again.
1st and every alt row (right side): Knit.
2nd row: *Make Knot (see Special Abbreviation); rep from * to last st, p1.
4th row: P2, *Make Knot; rep from * to last 2 sts, p2.
6th row: P1, *Make Knot; rep from * to end.
Rep these 6 rows.

Diagonal Knot Stitch II

Worked as Diagonal Knot Stitch I.
Beginning with the 1st row, 2 rows worked in A and 2 rows in B throughout.

Cable Fabric

Multiple of 6
1st row: Knit.
2nd and every alt row: Purl.
3rd row: *K2, C4B; rep from * to end.
5th row: Knit.
7th row: *C4F, k2; rep from * to end.
8th row: Purl.
Rep these 8 rows.

Twisted Basket Weave

Multiple of 8+5
1st row (right side): P5, *C3, p5; rep from * to end.
2nd row: K5, *p3, k5; rep from * to end.
Rep the last 2 rows once more.
5th row: P1, *C3, p5; rep from * to last 4 sts, C3, p1.
6th row: K1, *p3, k5; rep from * to last 4 sts, p3, k1.
Rep the last 2 rows once more.
Rep these 8 rows.

Lichen Twist

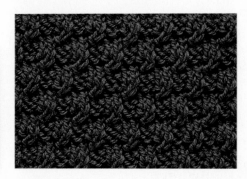

Multiple of 4+2
1st row (right side): *KB1; rep from * to end.
2nd row: *PB1; rep from * to end.
3rd row: P2, *C2F, p2; rep from * to end.
4th row: K2, *p2, k2; rep from * to end.
5th row: As 1st row.
6th row: As 2nd row.
7th row: K2, *p2, C2F; rep from * to last 4 sts, p2, k2.
8th row: P2, *k2, p2; rep from * to end.
Rep these 8 rows.

Ric Rac Pattern

Multiple of 3+1
Special Abbreviation
M1K = pick up horizontal strand of yarn lying between stitch just worked and next stitch and knit into the back of it.
1st row (right side): KB1, *M1K (see Special Abbreviation), k2tog tbl, KB1; rep from * to end.
2nd row: PB1, *p2, PB1; rep from * to end.
3rd row: KB1, *k2tog, M1K, KB1; rep from * to end.
4th row: As 2nd row.
Rep these 4 rows.

Patterns for Texture and Colour

Loaf Pattern

Multiple of 8 + 7

Note: Stitches should only be counted after the 6th and 12th rows of this pattern.

1st row (right side): P7, *(k1, p1, k1) into next st, p7; rep from * to end.

2nd row: K7, *p3, k7; rep from * to end.

3rd row: P7, *k3, p7; rep from * to end.

Rep the last 2 rows once more.

6th row: K7, *p3tog, k7; rep from * to end.

7th row: P3, *(k1, p1, k1) into next st, p7; rep from * to last 4 sts, (k1, p1, k1) into next st, p3.

8th row: K3, *p3, k7; rep from * to last 6 sts, p3, k3.

9th row: P3, *k3, p7; rep from * to last 6 sts, k3, p3.

Rep the last 2 rows once more.

12th row: K3, *p3tog, k7; rep from * to last 6 sts, p3tog, k3.

Rep these 12 rows.

Embossed Lozenge Stitch

Multiple of 8 + 1

1st row (right side): P3, *KB1, p1, KB1, p5; rep from * to last 6 sts, KB1, p1, KB1, p3.

2nd row: K3, *PB1, k1, PB1, k5; rep from * to last 6 sts, PB1, k1, PB1, k3.

Rep the last 2 rows once more.

5th row: P2, *KB1, p3; rep from * to last 3 sts, KB1, p2.

6th row: K2, *PB1, k3; rep from * to last 3 sts, PB1, k2.

7th row: P1, *KB1, p5, KB1, p1; rep from * to end.

8th row: K1, *PB1, k5, PB1, k1; rep from * to end.

9th row: As 7th row.

10th row: As 8th row.

11th row: As 5th row.

12th row: As 6th row.

Rep these 12 rows.

Mock Ribbing

Multiple of 2 + 1

1st row (right side): K1, *p1, k1; rep from * to end.

2nd row: P1, *keeping yarn at front of work sl 1 purlwise, p1; rep from * to end.

Rep these 2 rows.

Double Mock Ribbing

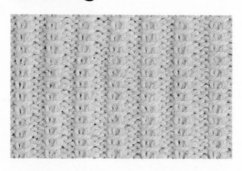

Multiple of 4 + 2

1st row (wrong side): K2, *p2, k2; rep from * to end.

2nd row: P2, *keeping yarn at front of work sl 2 purlwise, p2; rep from * to end.

Rep these 2 rows.

Dash Stitch

Multiple of 6 + 1

1st row (wrong side): K3, *PB1, k5; rep from * to last 4 sts, PB1, k3.

2nd row: P3, *KB1, p5; rep from * to last 4 sts, KB1, p3.

Rep these 2 rows twice more.

7th row: *PB1, k5; rep from * to last st, PB1.

8th row: *KB1, p5; rep from * to last st, KB1.

Rep these 2 rows twice more.

Rep these 12 rows.

Embossed Check Stitch

Multiple of 2 + 1

1st row (right side): *KB1; rep from * to end.

2nd row: K1, *PB1, k1; rep from * to end.

3rd row: P1, *KB1, p1; rep from * to end.

4th row: As 2nd row.

5th row: As 1st row.

6th row: PB1, *k1, PB1; rep from * to end.

7th row: KB1, *p1, KB1; rep from * to end.

8th row: As 6th row.

Rep these 8 rows.

Small Cable Check

Multiple of 12 + 7

1st row (right side): *P1, [KB1] 5 times, [p1, C2F] twice; rep from * to last 7 sts, p1, [KB1] 5 times, p1.

2nd row: *K1, [PB1] 5 times, [k1, p2] twice; rep from * to last 7 sts, k1, [PB1] 5 times, k1.

Rep the last 2 rows twice more.

7th row: *[P1, C2F] twice, p1, [KB1] 5 times; rep from * to last 7 sts, [p1, C2F] twice, p1.

8th row: *[K1, p2] twice, k1, [PB1] 5 times; rep from * to last 7 sts, [k1, p2] twice, k1.

Rep the last 2 rows twice more.

Rep these 12 rows.

Woven Horizontal Herringbone

Multiple of 4

1st row (right side): K3, *yf, sl 2, yb, k2; rep from * to last st, k1.

2nd row: P2, *yb, sl 2, yf, p2; rep from * to last 2 sts, p2.

3rd row: K1, yf, sl 2, yb, *k2, yf, sl 2, yb; rep from * to last st, k1.

4th row: P4, *yb, sl 2, yf, p2; rep from * to end.

Rep the last 4 rows twice more.

13th row: As 3rd row.

14th row: As 2nd row.

15th row: As 1st row.

16th row: As 4th row.

Rep the last 4 rows twice more.

Rep these 24 rows.

Pyramids

Multiple of 15 + 7

1st row (right side): *P1, [KB1] 5 times, p1, k8; rep from * to last 7 sts, p1, [KB1] 5 times, p1.

2nd row: *K1, [PB1] 5 times, k1, p8; rep from * to last 7 sts, k1, [PB1] 5 times, k1.

3rd row: P1, *[KB1] 5 times, p10; rep from * to last 6 sts, [KB1] 5 times, p1.

4th row: K1, *[PB1] 5 times, k10; rep from * to last 6 sts, [PB1] 5 times, k1.

5th row: P2, *[KB1] 3 times, p3, k6, p3; rep from * to last 5 sts, [KB1] 3 times, p2.

6th row: K2, *[PB1] 3 times, k3, p6, k3; rep from * to last 5 sts, [PB1] 3 times, k2.

7th row: P2, *[KB1] 3 times, p12; rep from * to last 5 sts, [KB1] 3 times, p2.

8th row: K2, *[PB1] 3 times, k12; rep from * to last 5 sts, [PB1] 3 times, k2.

9th row: P3, *KB1, p5, k4, p5; rep from * to last 4 sts, KB1, p3.

10th row: K3, *PB1, k5, p4, k5; rep from * to last 4 sts, PB1, k3.

11th row: P3, *KB1, p14; rep from * to last 4 sts, KB1, p3.

12th row: K3, *PB1, k14; rep from * to last 4 sts, PB1, k3.

Rep these 12 rows.

Twisted Knit Tweed

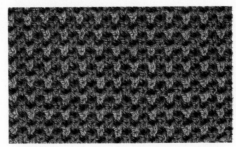

Multiple of 2 + 1

1st and 2nd foundation rows: Using A, knit.

1st row (right side): Using B, k1, *K1B, k1; rep from * to end.

2nd row: Using B, knit.

3rd row: Using A, K1B, *k1, K1B; rep from * to end.

4th row: Using A, knit.

Rep these 4 rows.

Little Birds

Multiple of 14 + 8

1st row (right side): Knit.

2nd row: Purl.

3rd row: K10, *sl 2 purlwise, k12; rep from * to last 12 sts, sl 2 purlwise, k10.

4th row: P10, *sl 2 purlwise, p12; rep from * to last 12 sts, sl 2 purlwise, p10.

5th row: K8, *C3R, C3L, k8; rep from * to end.

6th row: Purl.

Rep 1st and 2nd rows once.

9th row: K3, *sl 2, k12; rep from * to last 5 sts, sl 2, k3.

10th row: P3, *sl 2, p12; rep from * to last 5 sts, sl 2, p3.

11th row: K1, *C3R, C3L, k8; rep from * to last 7 sts, C3R, C3L, k1.

12th row: Purl.

Rep these 12 rows.

Houndstooth Tweed

Multiple of 3

Cast on in A.

1st row (right side): Using A, *k2 sl 1 purlwise; rep from * to end.

2nd row: Using A, knit.

3rd row: Using B, *sl 1 purlwise, k2; rep from * to end.

4th row: Using B, knit.

Rep these 4 rows.

Double Rice Stitch I

Multiple of 2 + 1

1st row (wrong side): P1, *KB1, p1; rep from * to end.

2nd row: Knit.

3rd row: *KB1, p1; rep from * to last st, KB1.

4th row: Knit.

Rep these 4 rows.

Double Rice Stitch II

Worked as Double Rice Stitch I.

1st and 2nd rows worked in A, 3rd and 4th rows in B throughout.

Patterns for Texture and Colour

Little Cable Stitch

Multiple of 6+2
1st row (right side): Knit.
2nd row: Purl.
3rd row: P2, *C2F, C2B, p2; rep from * to end.
4th row: K2, *p4, k2; rep from * to end.
5th row: Knit.
6th row: Purl.
Rep these 6 rows.

Slipped Rib I

Multiple of 4+3
1st row (right side): K1, sl 1 purlwise, *k3, sl 1 purlwise; rep from * to last st, k1.
2nd row: P1, sl 1 purlwise, *p3, sl 1 purlwise; rep from * to last st, p1.
3rd row: *K3, sl 1 purlwise; rep from * to last 3 sts, k3.
4th row: *P3, sl 1 purlwise; rep from * to last 3 sts, p3.
Rep these 4 rows.

Slipped Rib II

Worked as Slipped Rib I.
Work 2 rows in A, 2 rows in B and 2 rows in C throughout.

Knotted Rib

Multiple of 5
(**Note**: stitches should only be counted after the 2nd row.)
1st row (right side): P2, *knit into front and back of next st, p4; rep from * to last 3 sts, knit into front and back of next st, p2.
2nd row: K2, *p2tog, k4; rep from * to last 4 sts, p2tog, k2.
Rep these 2 rows.

Diamond Drops I

Multiple of 4
1st row (right side): Knit.
2nd row: P1, *yrn, p2, pass made st over purl sts, p2; rep from * to last 3 sts, yrn, p2, pass made st over purl sts, p1.
3rd row: Knit.
4th row: P3, *yrn, p2, pass made st over purl sts, p2; rep from * to last st, p1.
Rep these 4 rows.

Diamond Drops II

Worked as Diamond Drops I.
1st and 2nd rows worked in A, 3rd and 4th rows in B throughout.

Smocking Stitch

Multiple of 8+2
1st and every alt row (wrong side): K2, *p2, k2; rep from * to end.
2nd row: P2, *k2, p2; rep from * to end.
4th row: P2, *yb, insert right-hand needle from front between 6th and 7th sts on left-hand needle and draw through a loop, slip this loop onto left-hand needle and knit it tog with the first st, k1, p2, k2, p2; rep from * to end.
6th row: As 2nd row.
8th row: P2, k2, p2, *yb, draw loop as before from between 6th and 7th sts and knit it with 1st st, k1, p2, k2, p2; rep from * to last 4 sts, k2, p2.
Rep these 8 rows.

Cable Squares

Multiple of 12+2
1st row (right side): [P1, k1] twice, p1, k5, *p1, [k1, p1] 3 times, k5; rep from * to last 4 sts, [p1, k1] twice.
2nd row: [K1, p1] twice, k1, p5, *[k1, p1] 3 times, k1, p5; rep from * to last 4 sts, [k1, p1] twice.
3rd row: P1, [k1, p1] twice, *C4B, [k1, p1] 4 times; rep from * to last 9 sts, C4B, k1, [p1, k1] twice.
4th row: As 2nd row.
Rep the last 4 rows twice more.
13th row: Knit.
14th row: Purl.
15th row: K1, *C4B; rep from * to last st, k1.
16th row: Purl.
Rep these 16 rows.

Woven Stitch I

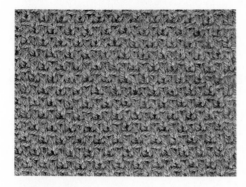

Multiple of 2 + 1
1st row (right side): K1, *yf, sl 1, yb, k1; rep from * to end.
2nd row: Purl.
3rd row: K2, *yf, sl 1, yb, k1; rep from * to last st, k1.
4th row: Purl.
Rep these 4 rows.

Woven Stitch II

Worked as Woven Stitch I.
Work 1st and 2nd rows in A, 3rd and 4th rows in B.

Alternate Bobble Stripe

Multiple of 10 + 5
1st row (right side): P2, k1, *p4, k1; rep from * to last 2 sts, p2.
2nd row: K2, p1, *k4, p1; rep from * to last 2 sts, k2.
3rd row: P2, *MB (Make bobble) as follows: work [k1, p1, k1, p1, k1] into the next st, turn and k5, turn and k5tog (bobble completed), p4, k1, p4; rep from * to last 3 sts, MB, p2.

4th row: As 2nd row.
Rep the last 4 rows 4 times more.
21st row: As 1st row.
22nd row: As 2nd row.
23rd row: P2, *k1, p4, MB, p4; rep from * to last 3 sts, k1, p2.
24th row: As 2nd row.
Rep the last 4 rows 4 times more.
Rep these 40 rows.

Double Woven Stitch I

Multiple of 4
1st row (right side): K3, *yf, sl 2, yb, k2; rep from * to last st, k1.
2nd row: Purl.
3rd row: K1, *yf, sl 2, yb, k2; rep from * to last 3 sts, yf, sl 2, yb, k1.
4th row: Purl.
Rep these 4 rows.

Double Woven Stitch II

Worked as Double Woven Stitch I.
Work 1st and 2nd rows in A, 3rd and 4th rows in B.

Little Cable Fabric

Multiple of 4 + 1
1st row (right side): K1, *sl 1 purlwise, k3; rep from * to end.
2nd row: *P3, sl 1 purlwise; rep from * to last st, p1.
3rd row: K1, *C3L, k1; rep from * to end.
4th row: Purl.
5th row: K5, *sl 1, k3; rep from * to end.
6th row: *P3, sl 1; rep from * to last 5 sts, p5.
7th row: K3, *C3R, k1; rep from * to last 2 sts, k2.
8th row: Purl.
Rep these 8 rows.

Open Check Stitch

Multiple of 2.
1st row (right side): Purl.
2nd row: Knit.
3rd row: K2, *sl 1, k1; rep from * to end.
4th row: *K1, yf, sl 1, yb; rep from * to last 2 sts, k2.
5th row: K1, *yf, k2tog; rep from * to last st, k1.
6th row: Purl.
Rep these 6 rows.

Horizontal Herringbone

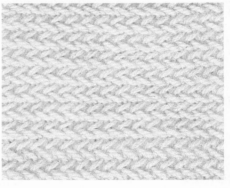

Multiple of 2
1st row (right side): K1, *sl 1, k1, psso but instead of dropping slipped st from left-hand needle, knit into the back of it; rep from * to last st, k1.
2nd row: *P2tog, then purl first st again slipping both sts off needle tog; rep from * to end.
Rep these 2 rows.

Patterns for Texture and Colour

Crosses

Multiple of 12 + 1
1st row (right side): Purl.
2nd row: Knit.
3rd row: P5, *[KB1] 3 times, p9; rep from * to last 8 sts, [KB1] 3 times, p5.
4th row: K5, *p3, k9; rep from * to last 8 sts, p3, k5.
Rep the last 2 rows once more.
7th row: P2, *[KB1] 9 times, p3; rep from * to last 11 sts, [KB1] 9 times, p2.
8th row: K2, *p9, k3; rep from * to last 11 sts, p9, k2.
Rep the last 2 rows once more.
11th row: As 3rd row.
12th row: As 4th row.
Rep the last 2 rows once more.
15th row: Purl.
16th row: Knit.
Rep these 16 rows.

Bordered Diamonds

Multiple of 16 + 2
Note: Slip sts purlwise throughout.
1st row (right side): K6, *p6, k10; rep from * to last 12 sts, p6, k6.
2nd row: P5, sl 1, k6, yf, sl 1, *p8, sl 1, k6, yf, sl 1; rep from * to last 5 sts, p5.
3rd row: K5, *C2L, p4, C2R, k8; rep from * to last 13 sts, C2L, p4, C2R, k5.
4th row: P1, sl 1, p4, sl 1, k4, yf, sl 1, p4, *sl 2, p4, sl 1, k4, yf, sl 1, p4; rep from * to last 2 sts, sl 1, p1.
5th row: K1, *T2F, k3, C2L, p2, C2R, k3, T2B; rep from * to last st, k1.
6th row: P1, k1, yf, sl 1, p4, sl 1, *k2, yf, sl 1, p4, sl 1; rep from *to last 2 sts, k1, p1.
7th row: K1, p1, *T2F, k3, C2L, C2R, k3, T2B, p2; rep from * to last 16 sts, T2F, k3, C2L, C2R, k3, T2B, p1, k1.
8th row: P1, k2, yf, sl 1, *p4, sl 2, p4, sl 1, k4, yf, sl 1; rep from * to last 14 sts, p4, sl 2, p4, sl 1, k2, p1.
9th row: K1, p2, *T2F, k8, T2B, p4; rep

from * to last 15 sts, T2F, k8, T2B, p2, k1.
10th row: P1, k3, yf, sl 1, *p8, sl 1, k6, yf, sl 1; rep from * to last 13 sts, p8, sl 1, k3, p1.
11th row: K1, p3, *k10, p6; rep from * to last 14 sts, k10, p3, k1.
12th row: As 10th row.
13th row: K1, p2, *C2R, k8, C2L, p4; rep from * to last 15 sts, C2R, k8, C2L, p2, k1.
14th row: As 8th row.
15th row: K1, p1, *C2R, k3, T2B, T2F, k3, C2L, p2; rep from * to last 16 sts, C2R, k3, T2B, T2F, k3, C2L, p1, k1.
16th row: As 6th row.
17th row: K1, *C2R, k3, T2B, p2, T2F, k3, C2L; rep from * to last st, k1.
18th row: As 4th row.
19th row: K5, *T2B, p4, T2F, k8; rep from * to last 13 sts, T2B, p4, T2F, k5.
20th row: As 2nd row.
Rep these 20 rows.

Herringbone

Multiple of 7 + 1
Special Abbreviation
K1B Back = From the top, insert point of right-hand needle into back of st below next st on left-hand needle and knit it.
1st row (wrong side): Purl.
2nd row: *K2tog, k2, K1B Back then knit st above, k2; rep from * to last st, k1.
3rd row: Purl.
4th row: K3, K1B Back then knit st above, k2, k2tog, *k2, K1B Back then knit st above, k2, k2tog; rep from * to end.
Rep these 4 rows.

Twisted Check

Multiple of 4 + 2
1st row (right side): Knit all sts through back loops.
2nd row: Purl.

3rd row: [KB1] twice, *p2, [KB1] twice; rep from * to end.
4th row: P2, *k2, p2; rep from * to end.
Rep 1st and 2nd rows once more.
7th row: P2, *[KB1] twice, p2; rep from * to end.
8th row: K2, *p2, k2; rep from * to end.
Rep these 8 rows.

Bobbles

Bobbles may be used to decorate any plain fabric or simple stitch pattern in any arrangement. The example shown is worked over a multiple of 10 + 5 on a background of stocking stitch.
Commence Pattern:
Work 4 rows in st st, starting knit.
5th row: K7, *MB, k9; rep from * to last 8 sts, MB, k7.
Work 5 rows in st st.
11th row: K2, *MB, k9; rep from * to last 3 sts, MB, k2.
Purl 1 row.
Rep these 12 rows.

Bud Stitch

Multiple of 6 + 5
Note: Stitches should only be counted after the 6th or 12th rows.
1st row (right side): P5, *k1, yfrn, p5; rep from * to end.
2nd row: K5, *p2, k5; rep from * to end.
3rd row: P5, *k2, p5; rep from * to end.
Rep the last 2 rows once more.
6th row: K5, *p2tog, k5; rep from * to end.
7th row: P2, *k1, yfrn, p5; rep from * to last 3 sts, k1, yfrn, p2.
8th row: K2, *p2, k5; rep from * to last 4 sts, p2, k2.
9th row: P2, *k2, p5; rep from * to last 4

sts, k2, p2.

Rep the last 2 rows once more.

12th row: K2, *p2tog, k5; rep from * to last 4 sts, p2tog, k2.

Rep these 12 rows.

Mock Cable On Moss Stitch

Multiple of 9 + 5

1st row (right side): [K1, p1] twice, k1, *KB1, p2, KB1, [k1, p1] twice, k1; rep from * to end.

2nd row: *[K1, p1] 3 times, k2, p1; rep from * to last 5 sts, [k1, p1] twice, k1.

Rep these 2 rows once more.

5th row: [K1, p1] twice, k1, *yf, k1, p2, k1, lift yf over last 4 sts and off needle, [k1, p1] twice, k1; rep from * to end.

6th row: As 2nd row.

Rep these 6 rows.

Diagonal Bobble Stitch

Multiple of 6

1st row (right side): *K2, Make Bobble (MB) as follows: [knit into front and back] 3 times into next st, take 1st, 2nd, 3rd, 4th and 5th sts over 6th made st, (bobble completed), p3; rep from * to end.

2nd row: *K3, p3; rep from * to end.

3rd row: P1, *k2, MB, p3; rep from * to last 5 sts, k2, MB, p2.

4th row: K2, *p3, k3; rep from * to last 4 sts, p3, k1.

5th row: P2, *k2, MB, p3; rep from * to last 4 sts, k2, MB, p1.

6th row: K1, *p3, k3; rep from * to last 5 sts, p3, k2.

7th row: *P3, k2, MB; rep from * to end.

8th row: *P3, k3; rep from * to end.

9th row: *MB, p3, k2; rep from * to end.

10th row: P2, *k3, p3; rep from * to last 4 sts, k3, p1.

11th row: K1, *MB, p3, k2; rep from * to last 5 sts, MB, p3, k1.

12th row: P1, *k3, p3; rep from * to last 5 sts, k3, p2.

Rep these 12 rows.

Spaced Knots

Multiple of 6 + 5

Note: Stitches should not be counted after the 5th or 11th rows.

Commence Pattern:

Work 4 rows in st st, starting knit.

5th row: K5, *[k1, p1] twice into next st, k5; rep from * to end.

6th row: P5, *sl 3, k1, pass 3 sl sts separately over last st (knot completed), p5; rep from * to end.

Work 4 rows in st st.

11th row: K2, *[k1, p1] twice into next st, k5; rep from * to last 3 sts, [k1, p1] twice into next st, k2.

12th row: P2, *sl 3, k1, pass sl sts over as before, p5; rep from * to last 6 sts, sl 3, k1, pass sl sts over as before, p2.

Rep these 12 rows.

Bells And Bell Ropes

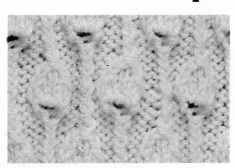

Multiple of 8 + 7

Note: Stitches should only be counted after the 1st, 7th, 8th, 9th, 15th and 16th rows.

1st row (right side): P3, *KB1, p3; rep from * to end.

2nd row: K3, PB1, k3, *[k1, p1, k1, p1, k1] into next st, k3, PB1, k3; rep from * to end.

3rd row: P3, KB1, p3, *k5, p3, KB1, p3; rep from * to end.

4th row: K3, PB1, k3, *p5, k3, PB1, k3; rep from * to end.

5th row: P3, KB1, p3, *sl 1, k1, psso, k1, k2tog, p3, KB1, p3; rep from * to end.

6th row: K3, PB1, k3, *p3, k3, PB1, k3; rep from * to end.

7th row: P3, KB1, p3, *sl 1, k2tog, psso, p3, KB1, p3; rep from * to end.

8th row: K3, *PB1, k3; rep from * to end.

9th row: As 1st row.

10th row: K3, [k1, p1, k1, p1, k1] into next st, k3, *PB1, k3, [k1, p1, k1, p1, k1] into next st, k3; rep from * to end.

11th row: P3, k5, p3, *KB1, p3, k5, p3; rep from * to end.

12th row: K3, p5, k3, *PB1, k3, p5, k3; rep from * to end.

13th row: P3, sl 1, k1, psso, k1, k2tog, p3, *KB1, p3, sl 1, k1, psso, k1, k2tog, p3; rep from * to end.

14th row: K3, p3, k3, *PB1, k3, p3, k3; rep from * to end.

15th row: P3, sl 1, k2tog, psso, p3, *KB1, p3, sl 1, k2tog, psso, p3; rep from * to end.

16th row: As 8th row.

Rep these 16 rows.

Half Brioche Stitch (Purl Version)

Multiple of 2 + 1

1st row (wrong side): Purl.

2nd row: K1, *K1B, k1; rep from * to end.

3rd row: Purl.

4th row: K1B, *k1, K1B; rep from * to end.

Rep these 4 rows.

Garter Stitch Twisted Rib

Multiple of 4

1st row (right side): K1, *C2B, k2; rep from * to last 3 sts, C2B, k1.

2nd row: K1, *yf, C2P, yb, k2; rep from * to last 3 sts, yf, C2P, yb, k1.

Rep these 2 rows.

Patterns for Texture and Colour

Rose Stitch

Multiple of 2 + 1

1st row (wrong side): K2, *p1, k1; rep from * to last st, k1.

2nd row: K1, *K1B, k1; rep from * to end.

3rd row: K1, *p1, k1; rep from * to end.

4th row: K2, *K1B, k1; rep from * to last st, k1.

Rep these 4 rows.

Twisted Stocking Stitch

Any number of stitches

1st row (right side): Knit into the back of every st.

2nd row: Purl.

Rep these 2 rows.

Houndstooth Pattern

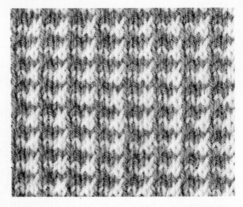

Multiple of 3

Cast on in A.

1st row (right side): Using A, k1, *sl 1 purlwise, k2; rep from * to last 2 sts, sl 1 purlwise, k1.

2nd row: Using A, purl.

3rd row: Using B, *sl 1 purlwise, k2; rep from * to end.

4th row: Using B, purl.

Rep these 4 rows.

Eyelet Knot Stitch

Multiple of 2

Note: Stitches should not be counted after the 1st row.

1st row (right side): K1, *k2tog; rep from * to last st, k1.

2nd row: K2, *M1, k1; rep from * to end.

3rd row: Knit.

4th row: Purl.

Rep these 4 rows.

Whelk Pattern

Multiple of 4 + 3

1st row (right side): K3, *sl 1 purlwise, k3; rep from * to end.

2nd row: K3, *yf, sl 1 purlwise, yb, k3; rep from * to end.

3rd row: K1, *sl 1 purlwise, k3; rep from * to last 2 sts, sl 1 purlwise, k1.

4th row: P1, sl 1 purlwise, *p3, sl 1 purlwise; rep from * to last st, p1.

Rep these 4 rows.

Knotted Cords

Multiple of 6 + 5

Knotted cords can be used singly in Aran patterns. (**Note**: stitches should not be counted after the 3rd row.)

1st row (right side): P5, *k1, p5; rep from * to end.

2nd row: K5, *p1, k5; rep from * to end.

3rd row: P5, *knit into front, back and front of next st, p5; rep from * to end.

4th row: K5, *p3tog, k5; rep from * to end.

Rep these 4 rows.

Little Leaves

Multiple of 6 + 5

Note: Stitches should not be counted after the 3rd – 12th or 19th – 28th rows inclusive.

1st row (right side): P5, *k1, p5; rep from * to end.

2nd row: K5, *p1, k5; rep from * to end.

3rd row: P5, *M1, k1, M1, p5; rep from * to end.

4th row: K5, *p3, k5; rep from * to end.

5th row: P5, *k1, [yf, k1] twice, p5; rep from * to end.

6th row: K5, *p5, k5; rep from * to end.

7th row: P5, *k2, yf, k1, yf, k2, p5; rep from * to end.

8th row: K5, *p7, k5; rep from * to end.

9th row: P5, *k2, sl 2 tog knitwise, k1, p2sso, k2, p5; rep from * to end.

10th row: As 6th row.

11th row: P5, *k1, sl 2tog knitwise, k1, p2sso, k1, p5; rep from * to end.

12th row: As 4th row.

13th row: P5, *yb, sl 2tog knitwise, k1, p2sso, p5; rep from * to end.
14th row: As 2nd row.
15th row: Purl.
16th row: Knit.
17th row: P2, *k1, p5; rep from * to last 3 sts, k1, p2.
18th row: K2, *p1, k5; rep from * to last 3 sts, p1, k2.
19th row: P2, *M1, k1, M1, p5; rep from * to last 3 sts, M1, k1, M1, p2.
20th row: K2, *p3, k5; rep from * to last 5 sts, p3, k2.
21st row: P2, *k1, [yf, k1] twice, p5; rep from * to last 5 sts, k1, [yf, k1] twice, p2.
22nd row: K2, *p5, k5; rep from * to last 7 sts, p5, k2.
23rd row: P2, *k2, yf, k1, yf, k2, p5; rep from * to last 7 sts, k2, yf, k1, yf, k2, p2.
24th row: K2, *p7, k5; rep from * to last 9 sts, p7, k2.
25th row: P2, *k2, sl 2tog knitwise, k1, p2sso, k2, p5; rep from * to last 9 sts, k2, sl 2tog knitwise, k1, p2sso, k2, p2.
26th row: As 22nd row.
27th row: P2, *k1, sl 2tog knitwise, k1, p2sso, k1, p5; rep from * to last 7 sts, k1, sl 2tog knitwise, k1, p2sso, k1, p2.
28th row: As 20th row.
29th row: P2, *yb, sl 2tog knitwise, k1, p2sso, p5; rep from * to last 5 sts, yb, sl 2tog knitwise, k1, p2sso, p2.
30th row: As 18th row.
31st row: Purl.
32nd row: Knit.
Rep these 32 rows.

Chain Stitch

Multiple of of 5 + 4
Cast on in A.
Foundation row (right side): Using B, k1, *yfrn, yrn (2 loops made), sl 2 purlwise, yb, k3; rep from * to last 3 sts, yfrn, yrn, sl 2 purlwise, yb, k1.

1st row: Using B, p1, *yb, [take yarn over top of needle and round to back (called yonb) twice, (2 loops made), sl 2 purlwise, yf, drop the 2 loops made in previous row, p3; rep from * to last 5 sts (including 2 loops made in previous row), yb, [yonb] twice, sl 2, yf, drop 2 loops made in previous row, p1.
2nd row: Using A, k3, drop the 2 loops made in previous row, *k5, drop the 2 loops made in previous row; rep from * to last st, k1.
3rd row: Using A, purl.
4th row: Using A, knit.
5th row: Using A, purl.
6th row: Using B, k1, *yfrn, yrn, place right-hand needle below the 2 B loops at front of work and pick them up, sl next 2 A sts purlwise, lift B loops over the 2 slipped sts and off the needle, yb, k3; rep from * to last 3 sts, yfrn, yrn, pick up the 2 B loops as before, sl next 2 A sts purlwise, lift B loops over the 2 slipped sts and off the needle, yb, k1.
Rep these 6 rows.
For single colour version omit colour changes.

Texture Tweed

Multiple of 4 + 3
1st row: Using A, k1, *sl 1, k3; rep from * to last 2 sts, sl 1, k1.
2nd row: Using A, k1, *yf, sl 1, yb, k3; rep from * to last 2 sts, yf, sl 1, yb, k1.
3rd row: Using B, k3, *sl 1, k3; rep from * to end.
4th row: Using B, k3, *yf, sl 1, yb, k3; rep from * to end.
5th row: As 1st row *but* using C instead of A.
6th row: As 2nd row *but* using C instead of A.
7th row: As 3rd row *but* using A instead of B.
8th row: As 4th row *but* using A instead of B.
9th row: As 1st row *but* using B instead of A.
10th row: As 2nd row *but* using B instead of A.
11th row: As 3rd row *but* using C instead of B.
12th row: As 4th row *but* using C instead of B.
Rep these 12 rows.

Rosehip Stitch

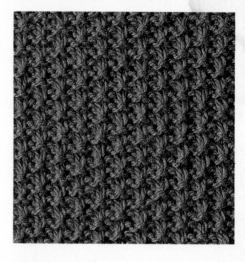

Multiple of 4 + 3
1st row (right side): K3, *sl 1 purlwise, k3; rep from * to end.
2nd row: K3, *yf, sl 1 purlwise, yb, k3; rep from * to end.
3rd row: K1, *sl 1 purlwise, k3; rep from * to last 2 sts, sl 1 purlwise, k1.
4th row: K1, *yf, sl 1 purlwise, yb, k3; rep from * to last 2 sts, yf, sl 1 purlwise, yb, k1.
Rep these 4 rows.

Brick Rib

Multiple of 3 + 1
1st row (right side): *P2, KB1; rep from * to last st, p1.
2nd row: K1, *PB1, k2; rep from * to end.
Rep the last 2 rows once more.
5th row: P1, *[KB1] twice, p1; rep from * to end.
6th row: K1, *[PB1] twice, k1; rep from * to end.
Rep the last 2 rows once more.
9th row: P1, *KB1, p2; rep from * to end.
10th row: *K2, PB1; rep from * to last st, k1.
Rep the last 2 rows once more.
Rep these 12 rows.

Patterns for Texture and Colour

Loop Pattern I

Multiple of 2 sts.
Note: Slip all sts purlwise.
1st row (right side): Knit.
2nd row: *K1, sl 1; rep from * to last 2 sts, k2.
3rd row: Knit.
4th row: K2, *sl 1, k1; rep from * to end.
Rep these 4 rows.

Loop Pattern II

Multiple of 3 sts + 1.
1st row (right side): Knit.
2nd row: *K1, sl 2 purlwise; rep from * to last st, k1.
Rep these 2 rows.

2-Colour Loop Pattern

Multiple of 2 sts + 1.
Note: All slip sts should be slipped purlwise.
1st row (right side): Using A knit.
2nd row: Using A purl.

3rd row: Using B k1, *sl 1, k1; rep from * to end.
4th row: As 3rd row.
5th row: Using B knit.
6th row: Using B purl.
7th row: Using A k2, sl 1, *k1, sl 1; rep from * to last 2 sts, k2.
8th row: Using A p1, k1, *sl 1, k1; rep from * to last st, p1.
Rep these 8 rows.

2-Colour Loop Pattern Variation

Multiple of 4 sts + 1.
Note: All slip sts should be slipped purlwise.
1st row (right side): Using A knit.
2nd row: Using A purl.
3rd row: Using B k1, *sl 3, k1; rep from * to end.
4th row: As 3rd row.
5th row: Using B knit.
6th row: Using B purl.
7th row: Using A k3, sl 3, *k1, sl 3,; rep from * to last 3 sts, k3.
8th row: Using A p2, k1, *sl 3, k1; rep from * to last 2 sts, p2.
Rep these 8 rows.

3-Colour Loop Pattern

Multiple of 2 sts + 1.
1st row (right side): Using A knit.
2nd row: Using A purl.
3rd row: Using B k1, *sl 1, k1; rep from * to end.

4th row: As 3rd row.
5th row: Using B knit.
6th row: Using B purl.
7th and 8th rows: As 3rd row **but** using A instead of B.
9th row: Using A knit.
10th row: Using A purl.
11th and 12th rows: As 3rd row **but** using C instead of B.
13th row: Using C knit.
14th row: Using C purl.
15th and 16th rows: As 3rd row **but** using A instead of B.
Rep these 16 rows.

Bee Stitch

Multiple of 2 sts + 1.
1st row (wrong side): Knit.
2nd row: K1, *K1B, k1; rep from * to end.
3rd row: Knit.
4th row: K2, K1B, *k1, K1B; rep from * to last 2 sts, k2.
Rep these 4 rows.

2-Colour Bee Stitch

Multiple of 2 sts + 1.
1st Foundation row (right side): Using A knit.
2nd Foundation row: Using A knit.
Commence Pattern
1st row: Using B k1, *K1B, k1; rep from * to end.
2nd row: Using B knit.
3rd row: Using A k2, K1B, *k1, K1B; rep from * to last 2 sts, k2.
4th row: Using A knit.
Rep the last 4 rows.

Texture Stitch

Multiple of 2 sts + 1.
1st row (right side): Purl.
2nd row: K1, *yf, sl 1 purlwise, yb, k1; rep from * to end.
Rep these 2 rows.

Knot Ridges I

Multiple of 2 sts + 1.
Using A work 4 rows in st st, starting knit (right side).
5th row Using B k1, [k1, yf, k1] into next st, *sl 1, [k1, yf, k1] into next st; rep from * to last st, k1.
6th row: Using B k1, k3tog tbl, *sl 1, k3tog tbl; rep from * to last st, k1.
Rep these 6 rows.

Knot Ridges II

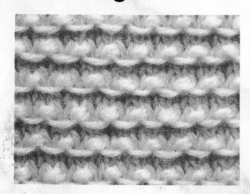

Multiple of 2 sts + 1.
1st row (right side): Using A knit.
2nd row: Using A purl.
3rd row: Using B k1, [k1, yf, k1] into next st, *sl 1, [k1, yf, k1] into next st; rep from * to last st, k1.
4th row: Using B k1, k3tog tbl, *sl 1, k3tog tbl; rep from * to last st, k1.
5th row: Using A knit.
6th row: Using A purl.
7th row: Using B k2, [k1, yf, k1] into next st, *sl 1, [k1, yf, k1] into next st; rep from * to last 2 sts, k2.
8th row: Using B p2, k3tog tbl, *sl 1, k3tog tbl; rep from * to last 2 sts, p2.
Rep these 8 rows.

Knot Ridges with Twists

Multiple of 8 sts + 5.
Note: Slip all stitches purlwise.
1st row (right side): Using A k5, *C3R, k5; rep from * to end.
2nd row: Using A purl.
3rd row: Using B [k1, sl 1] twice, k1, *sl 3, [k1, sl 1] twice, k1; rep from * to end.
4th row: Using B [k1, sl 1] twice, k1, *yf, sl 3, yb, [k1, sl 1] twice, k1; rep from * to end.
Rep these 4 rows.

Thick Woven Blanket Fabric I

Multiple of 4 sts + 1.
Note: Slip all sts purlwise.
Foundation row (wrong side): Using B purl.
Commence Pattern
1st row: Using A k2, sl 1, *k1, sl 1; rep from * to last 2 sts, k2.
2nd row: Using A p1, k1, *yf, sl 1, yb, k1; rep from * to last st, p1.

3rd row: Using B k1, *sl 1, k1; rep from * to end.
4th row: Using B p1, *sl 1, p1; rep from * to end.
5th row: Using C k1, yf, sl 1, yb, sl 1, yf, *sl 3, yb, sl 1, yf; rep from * to last 2 sts, sl 1, yb, k1.
6th row: Using C p1, yb, sl 1, yf, sl 1, yb, *sl 3, yf, sl 1, yb; rep from * to last 2 sts, sl 1, yf, p1.
Rep the first 4 rows once more.
11th row: Using C k1, yf, sl 3, yb, *sl 1, yf, sl 3, yb; rep from * to last st, k1.
12th row: Using C p1, yb, sl 3, yf, *sl 1, yb, sl 3, yf; rep from * to last st, p1.
Rep the last 12 rows.

Thick Woven Blanket Fabric II

Worked as Thick Woven Blanket Fabric I but using one colour throughout.

Plain Triple Slip

Multiple of 6 sts + 5.
Note: Slip all sts purlwise.
1st row (right side): Using A knit.
2nd row: Using A purl.
3rd row: Using B k1, sl 3, *yf, sl 3, yb, sl 3; rep from * to last st, k1.
4th row: Using B p1, sl 3, *yb, sl 3, yf, sl 3; rep from * to last st, p1.
5th row: As 1st row.
6th row: As 2nd row.
7th row: Using B k1, yf, sl 3, yb, *sl 3, yf, sl 3, yb; rep from * to last st, k1.
8th row: Using B p1, yb, sl 3, yf, *sl 3, yb, sl 3, yf; rep from * to last st, p1.
Rep these 8 rows.

Patterns for Texture and Colour

Dotted Triple Slip I

Multiple of 6 sts + 5.
Note: Slip all sts purlwise.
1st row (right side): Using A knit.
2nd row: Using A purl.
3rd row: Using B k1, yf, sl 3, yb, *sl 1, k1, sl 1, yf, sl 3, yb; rep from * to last st, k1.
4th row: Using B p1, yb, sl 3, *yf, sl 1, yb, k1, yf, sl 1, yb, sl 3; rep from * to last st, yf, p1.
5th row: As 1st row.
6th row: As 2nd row.
7th row: Using B [k1, sl 1] twice, *yf, sl 3, yb, sl 1, k1, sl 1; rep from * to last st, k1.
8th row: Using B p1, sl 1, yb, k1, yf, sl 1, *yb, sl 3, yf, sl 1, yb, k1, yf, sl 1; rep from * to last st, p1.
Rep these 8 rows.

Dotted Triple Slip II

Work as Dotted Triple Slip I but using one colour throughout.

Berry Stitch

Multiple of 4 sts + 3.
Note: Sts should only be counted after the 2nd and 4th rows.
1st row (right side): K1, [k1, KB1, k1] into next st, *p3, [k1, KB1, k1] into next st; rep from * to last st, k1.
2nd row: K4, p3tog, *k3, p3tog; rep from * to last 4 sts, k4.
3rd row: K1, p3, *[k1, KB1, k1] into next st, p3; rep from * to last st, k1.
4th row: K1, p3tog, *k3, p3tog; rep from * to last st, k1.
Rep these 4 rows.

Star Stitch Pattern I

Multiple of 4 sts + 1.
Special Abbreviation
Make Star = p3tog leaving sts on needle, yrn, then purl the same 3 sts together again.
1st row (right side): Knit.
2nd row: P1, *Make Star, p1; rep from * to end.
3rd row: Knit.
4th row: P3, Make Star, *p1, Make Star; rep from * to last 3 sts, p3.
Rep these 4 rows.

2-Colour Star Stitch Pattern

Worked as Star Stitch Pattern I.
1st and 2nd rows in colour A, 3rd and 4th rows in colour B throughout.

Star Stitch Pattern II

Multiple of 4 sts + 1.
Special Abbreviation
Make Star = p3tog leaving sts on needle, yrn, then purl the same 3 sts together again.
1st row (right side): P1, *k1, p1; rep from * to end.
2nd row: K1, *Make Star, k1; rep from * to end.
3rd row: As 1st row.
4th row: K1, p1, k1, *Make Star, k1; rep from * to last 2 sts, p1, k1.
Rep these 4 rows.

Textured Acorn Stitch

Multiple of 6 sts + 3.
Note: Sts should only be counted after 1st, 2nd, 7th and 8th rows.
Special Abbreviation
M3 (Make 3) = knit into front, back and front of next st.
1st row (right side): P3, *k3, p3; rep from * to end.
2nd row: K3, *p3, k3; rep from * to end.
3rd row: P1, M3, p1, *sl 1, k2tog, psso, p1, M3, p1; rep from * to end.
4th row: K1, p3, *k3, p3; rep from * to last st, k1.
5th row: P1, k3, *p3, k3; rep from * to last st, p1.
6th row: As 4th row.
7th row: P1, sl 1, k2tog, psso, p1, *M3, p1, sl 1, k2tog, psso, p1; rep from * to end.

8th row: As 2nd row.
Rep these 8 rows.

Diagonal Knot Stitch III

See Diagonal Knot Stitches I and II on page 39 of The Harmony Guide to Knitting Stitches.

Special Abbreviation

MK (Make Knot) = k3tog leaving sts on needle, yf, then knit same 3 sts together again.

Multiple of 4 sts + 1.

1st row (right side): K4, p1, *k3, p1; rep from * to last 4 sts, k4.

2nd row: P4, k1, *p3, k1; rep from * to last 4 sts, p4.

3rd row: P1, *MK, p1; rep from * to end.

4th row: As 2nd row.

5th row: K2, p1, *k3, p1; rep from * to last 2 sts, k2.

6th row: P2, k1, *p3, k1; rep from * to last 2 sts, p2.

7th row: K2, p1, *MK, p1; rep from * to last 2 sts, k2.

8th row: As 6th row.

Rep these 8 rows.

Treble Slip Knot

Multiple of .8 sts + 3.

Note: Stitches should not be counted after 4th, 5th, 12th and 13th rows.

Special Abbreviation

D2 (Draw 2) = yb, insert needle into st 2 rows below next st, yrn and draw through loop, yf, knit into same st dropping st above off needle (2 sts increased).

Work 3 rows in reversed st st, starting knit (1st row is wrong side).

4th row: P1, D2, *p7, D2; rep from * to last st, p1.

5th row: K1, p3, *k7, p3; rep from * to last st, k1.

6th row: P1, yb, sl 2tog knitwise, k1, p2sso, *p7, yb, sl 2tog knitwise, k1, p2sso; rep from * to last st, p1.

Work 5 rows in reversed st st, starting knit.

12th row: P5, D2, *p7, D2; rep from * to last 5 sts, p5.

13th row: K5, p3, *k7, p3; rep from * to last 5 sts, k5.

14th row: P5, yb, sl 2tog knitwise, k1, p2sso, *p7, yb, sl 2tog knitwise, k1, p2sso; rep from * to last 5 sts, p5.

Work 2 rows in reversed st st, starting knit.

Rep these 16 rows.

Ringlet Pillars

Multiple of 5 sts + 1.

1st row (wrong side): Purl.

2nd row: K2, Make Ringlet as follows: p2, [keeping yf slip last 2 sts worked back onto left-hand needle, yb, slip same 2 sts back onto right-hand needle] 3 times (Ringlet completed), *k3, Make Ringlet as before; rep from * to last 2 sts, k2.

Rep these 2 rows.

Flagon Stitch

Multiple of 6 sts + 4.

Note: Slip all sts purlwise.

1st row (wrong side): K1, *p2, k1; rep from * to end.

2nd row: P1, k2, p1, *sl 1, p1, yon, psso the p1 and the yon, p1, k2, p1; rep from * to end.

Rep the last 2 rows 3 times more, then the 1st row again.

10th row: P1, sl 1, p1, yon, psso the p1 and the yon, p1, *k2, p1, sl 1, p1, yon, psso the p1 and the yon, p1; rep from * to end.

11th row: As 1st row.

Rep the last 2 rows twice more, then the 10th row again.

Rep these 16 rows.

Hindu Pillar Stitch

Multiple of 4 sts + 1.

1st row (right side): K1, *p3tog without slipping sts from left-hand needle, knit them tog then purl them tog, k1; rep from * to end.

2nd row: Purl.

Rep these 2 rows.

Drawn Loop Pattern

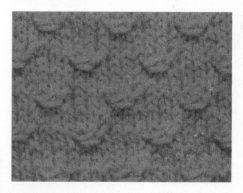

Multiple of 6 sts + 5.

Special Abbreviation

DR (Draw Loop) = insert needle between 3rd and 4th st on left-hand needle, yrn, draw through loop and place on left-hand needle, k2tog tbl (the loop and next st on left-hand needle), k2.

1st row (right side): Knit.

2nd row: Purl.

3rd row: K1, DR, *k3, DR; rep from * to last st, k1.

Work 3 rows in st st, starting purl.

7th row: K4, DR, *k3, DR; rep from * to last 4 sts, k4.

8th row: Purl.

Rep these 8 rows.

Patterns for Texture and Colour

Oyster Pattern

Multiple of 6 sts + 1.

1st row (right side): Knit.

2nd row: P1, *p5 wrapping yarn twice around needle for each st, p1; rep from * to end.

3rd row: K1, *Cluster 5 as follows: pass next 5 sts onto right-hand needle dropping extra loops, pass these 5 sts back onto left-hand needle, [k1, p1, k1, p1, k1] into all 5 sts together wrapping yarn twice around needle for each st, k1; rep from * to end.

4th row: P1, *k5 dropping extra loops, p1; rep from * to end.

5th row: Knit.

6th row: P4, p5 wrapping yarn twice around needle for each st, *p1, p5 wrapping yarn twice around needle for each st; rep from * to last 4 sts, p4.

7th row: K4, Cluster 5 as before, *k1, Cluster 5 as before; rep from * to last 4 sts, k4.

8th row: P4, k5 dropping extra loops, *p1, k5 dropping extra loops; rep from * to last 4 sts, p4.

Rep these 8 rows.

Pique Squares

Multiple of 12 sts + 8.

1st row (right side): K7, [p2, slip these sts onto left-hand needle, yb, slip the 2 sts back onto right-hand needle] 3 times, *k6, [p2, slip these sts onto left-hand needle, yb, slip the 2 sts back onto right-hand needle] 3 times; rep from * to last 7 sts, k7.

2nd row: Purl.

Rep these 2 rows twice more.

7th row: K1, [p2, slip these sts onto left-hand needle, yb, slip the 2 sts back onto right-hand needle] 3 times, *k6, [p2, slip these sts onto left-hand needle, yb, slip the

2 sts back onto right-hand needle] 3 times; rep from * to last st, k1.

8th row: Purl.

Rep these 2 rows twice more.

Rep these 12 rows.

Crowns I

Multiple of 5 sts.

Work 4 rows in garter stitch.

5th row: K1, *k1 winding yarn round needle 3 times; rep from * to end.

6th row: *Sl 5 sts purlwise dropping extra loops, return these 5 sts to left-hand needle then work into these 5 sts together as follows: k1, [p1, k1] twice; rep from * to end.

Work 2 rows in garter stitch.

Rep these 8 rows.

Crowns II

Multiple of 10 sts + 7.

Special Abbreviations

KW5 = knit 5 sts wrapping yarn 3 times round needle for each st.

Twist 5 = slip 5 sts purlwise dropping extra loops, return these 5 sts to left-hand needle, then k1, [p1, k1] twice into same 5 sts tog.

1st row: K6, KW5, *k5, KW5; rep from * to last 6 sts, k6.

2nd row: P6, Twist 5, *p5, Twist 5; rep from * to last 6 sts, p6.

3rd row: Knit.

4th row: K6, p5, *k5, p5; rep from * to last 6 sts, k6.

5th row: K1, KW5, *k5, KW5; rep from * to last st, k1.

6th row: P1, Twist 5, *p5, Twist 5; rep from * to last st, p1.

7th row: Knit.

8th row: K1, p5, *k5, p5; rep from * to last st, k1.

Rep these 8 rows.

Little Crowns

Multiple of 3 sts + 2.

1st row (right side): Knit.

2nd row: Knit.

3rd row: K1, knit to last st wrapping yarn twice around needle for each st, k1.

4th row: K1, *pass next 3 sts to right-hand needle dropping extra loops, pass these 3 sts back to left-hand needle, k1, p1, k1 through 3 sts tog; rep from * to last st, k1.

Rep these 4 rows.

Knotted Boxes I

Multiple of 8 sts + 5.

1st row (right side): Knit.

2nd row: Purl.

3rd row: K1, p3, *k5, p3; rep from * to last st, k1.

4th row: P1, k3, *p5, k3; rep from * to last st, p1.

5th row: K1, yf, k3tog, yf, *k5, yf, k3tog, yf; rep from * to last st, k1.

Work 3 rows in st st, starting purl.

9th row: K5, *p3, k5; rep from * to end.

10th row: P5, *k3, p5; rep from * to end.

11th row: K5, *yf, k3tog, yf, k5; rep from * to end.

12th row: Purl.

Rep these 12 rows.

Knotted Boxes II

Multiple of 6 sts + 5.

1st row (right side): K1, p3, *k3, p3; rep from * to last st, k1.

2nd row: P1, k3, *p3, k3; rep from * to last st, p1.

3rd row: K1, yf, k3tog, yf, *k3, yf, k3tog, yf; rep from * to last st, k1.

4th row: Purl.

5th row: K4, p3, *k3, p3; rep from * to last 4 sts, k4.

6th row: P4, k3, *p3, k3; rep from * to last 4 sts, p4.

7th row: K4, yf, k3tog, yf, *k3, yf, k3tog, yf; rep from * to last 4 sts, k4.

8th row: Purl.

Rep these 8 rows.

Bobble and Ridge Stitch

Multiple of 6 sts + 5.

Special Abbreviation

MB (Make Bobble) = knit into front, back and front of next st, turn and p3, turn and k3, turn and p3, turn and sl 1, k2tog, psso (bobble completed).

1st row (right side): Knit.

2nd row: Purl.

3rd row: K5, *MB, k5; rep from * to end.

4th row: Purl.

5th row: K2, MB, *k5, MB; rep from * to last 2 sts, k2.

6th, 7th and 8th rows: As 2nd, 3rd and 4th rows.

9th row: Purl.

10th row: Knit.

Rep these 10 rows.

2-Colour Bobble and Ridge Stitch

Worked as Bobble and Ridge Stitch but using a second colour for bobbles.

Ridge Stitch

Any number of sts.

Work 3 rows in st st, starting purl (1st row is wrong side).

4th row: Knit into front and back of each st (thus doubling the number of sts).

5th row: *K2tog; rep from * to end (original number of sts restored).

6th row: Knit.

Rep these 6 rows.

Twisted Texture

Multiple of 3 sts + 1.

1st row (wrong side): Purl.

2nd row: P1, *C2B, p1; rep from * to end.

3rd row: K1, *purl into 2nd st on needle then purl first st, slipping both sts off needle at the same time, k1; rep from * to end.

4th row: Knit.

Rep these 4 rows.

Triangle Pleats

Multiple of 10 sts + 4.

1st row (right side): K1, *C2F, k7, p1; rep from * to last 3 sts, C2F, k1.

2nd row: P3, *k2, p8; rep from * to last st, p1.

3rd row: K1, *C2F, k5, p3; rep from * to last 3 sts, C2F, k1.

4th row: P3, k4, *p6, k4; rep from * to last 7 sts, p7.

5th row: K1, *C2F, k3, p5; rep from * to last 3 sts, C2F, k1.

6th row: P3, k6, *p4, k6; rep from * to last 5 sts, p5.

7th row: K1, *C2F, k1, p7; rep from * to last 3 sts, C2F, k1.

8th row: P3, k8, *p2, k8; rep from * to last 3 sts, p3.

Rep these 8 rows.

Granite Stitch

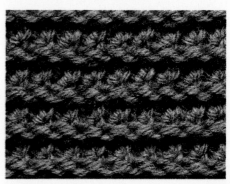

Multiple of 2 sts.

1st row (right side): Knit.

2nd row: *K2tog; rep from * to end.

3rd row: *[K1, p1] into each st; rep from * to end.

4th row: Purl.

Rep these 4 rows.

Patterns for Texture and Colour

Mock Rib Checks I

Multiple of 2 sts.
Foundation row: Purl.
Commence Pattern
1st row (wrong side): *K1, K1B; rep from * to last 2 sts, k2.
Rep this row 5 times more.
7th row: K2, *K1B, k1; rep from * to end.
Rep this row 5 times more.
Rep the last 12 rows.

Mock Rib Checks II

Worked as Mock Rib Checks I, using reverse side as right side.

Blanket Moss Stitch

Multiple of 2 sts + 1.
Note: Sts should only be counted after the 2nd and 4th rows.

1st row (right side): Knit into front and back of each st (thus doubling the number of sts).
2nd row: K2tog, *p2tog, k2tog; rep from * to end (original number of sts restored).
3rd row: As 1st row.
4th row: P2tog, *k2tog, p2tog; rep from * to end.
Rep these 4 rows.

Puff Stitch

Multiple of 4 sts + 3.
1st row (right side): P1, k1, p1, *M5 (make 5) as follows: [k1, yf, k1, yf, k1] into next st, p1, k1, p1; rep from * to end.
2nd row: K1, p1, k1, *D4 (dec 4) as follows: p2tog, p3tog, pass the first of the 2 last sts on right-hand needle over the 2nd and off needle, k1, p1, k1; rep from * to end.
3rd row: P1, M5, p1, *k1, p1, M5, p1; rep from * to end.
4th row: K1, D4, k1, *p1, k1, D4, k1; rep from * to end.
Rep these 4 rows.

Crocus Buds

Multiple of 2 sts + 1.
1st row (right side): K1, *yf, k2; rep from * to end.
2nd row: P1, *p3, pass the 3rd st on right-hand needle over the first 2 sts; rep from * to end.
3rd row: *K2, yf; rep from * to last st, k1.
4th row: *P3, pass the 3rd st on right-hand needle over the first 2 sts on right-hand needle; rep from * to last st, p1.
Rep these 4 rows.

Slip Stitch Stripes

Multiple of 5 sts.
1st row (right side): K2, *p1, k4; rep from * to last 3 sts, p1, k2.
2nd row: K2, *sl 1 purlwise, k4; rep from * to last 3 sts, sl 1 purlwise, k2.
Rep these 2 rows.

Coloured Tweed Stitch

Multiple of 2 sts + 1.
1st row (right side): Using A k1, *yf, sl 1p, yb, k1; rep from * to end.
2nd row: Using A p2, *yb, sl 1p, yf, p1; rep from * to last st, p1.
Rep these 2 rows using B.
Rep these 4 rows.

Slip Stitch Tweed

Multiple of 3 sts + 2.
1st row (right side): Using A k2, *sl 1 purlwise, k2; rep from * to end.
2nd row: Using A knit.
3rd row: Using B k2, *sl 1 purlwise, k2; rep from * to end.
4th row: Using B knit.
Rep these 4 rows.

Pinstripes

Multiple of 2 sts + 1.
Note: Slip all sts purlwise.
1st Foundation row (right side): Using A knit.
2nd Foundation row: Using A purl.
Commence Pattern
1st row: Using B k1, *sl 1, k1; rep from * to end.
2nd row: Using B p1, *sl 1, p1; rep from * to end.
3rd row: Using A k2, sl 1, *k1, sl 1; rep from * to last 2 sts, k2.
4th row: Using A p2, sl 1, *p1, sl 1; rep from * to last 2 sts, p2.
Rep the last 4 rows.

Wide Slip Stitch Stripes

Multiple of 4 sts.
Note: Slip all sts purlwise.
1st Foundation row (right side): Using A knit.
2nd Foundation row: Using A purl.
Commence Pattern
1st row: Using B k3, sl 2, *k2, sl 2; rep from

* to last 3 sts, k3.
2nd row: Using B p3, sl 2, *p2, sl 2; rep from * to last 3 sts, p3.
3rd row: Using A k1, sl 2, *k2, sl 2; rep from * to last st, k1.
4th row: Using A p1, sl 2, *p2, sl 2; rep from * to last st, p1.
Rep the last 4 rows.

Slip Stitch Check Pattern

Multiple of 4 sts.
Note: Slip all sts purlwise.
1st row (wrong side): Using A purl.
2nd row: Using B k3, sl 2, *k2, sl 2; rep from * to last 3 sts, k3.
3rd row: Using B p3, sl 2, *p2, sl 2; rep from * to last 3 sts, p3.
4th row: Using A knit.
5th row: Using C p1, sl 2, *p2, sl 2; rep from * to last st, p1.
6th row: Using C k1, sl 2, *k2, sl 2; rep from * to last st, k1.
Rep these 6 rows.

Tongue and Groove Stitch

Multiple of 6 sts + 2.
Note: Slip all sts purlwise.
Foundation row (wrong side): Using A purl.
Commence Pattern
1st row: Using B k4, sl 1, k1, sl 1, *k3, sl 1, k1, sl 1; rep from * to last st, k1.
2nd row: Using B [p1, sl 1] twice, *p3, sl 1,

p1, sl 1; rep from * to last 4 sts, p4.
3rd row: Using A [k1, sl 1] twice, *k3, sl 1, k1, sl 1; rep from * to last 4 sts, k4.
4th row: Using A p4, sl 1, p1, sl 1, *p3, sl 1, p1, sl 1; rep from * to last st, p1.
5th row: Using B k2, *sl 1, k3, sl 1, k1; rep from * to end.
6th row: Using B *p1, sl 1, p3, sl 1; rep from * to last 2 sts, p2.
7th row: Using A *k3, sl 1, k1, sl 1; rep from * to last 2 sts, k2.
8th row: Using A p2, *sl 1, p1, sl 1, p3; rep from * to end.
9th row: Using B k2, *sl 1, k1, sl 1, k3; rep from * to end.
10th row: Using B *p3, sl 1, p1, sl 1; rep from * to last 2 sts, p2.
11th row: Using A *k1, sl 1, k3, sl 1; rep from * to last 2 sts, k2.
12th row: Using A p2, *sl 1, p3, sl 1, p1; rep from * to end.
Rep the last 12 rows.

Raised Tongue and Groove Stitch

Multiple of 6 sts + 2.
Note: Slip all sts purlwise.
Foundation row (wrong side): Using A purl.
Commence Pattern
1st row: Using B k3, sl 1, *k5, sl 1; rep from * to last 4 sts, k4.
2nd row: Using B k4, yf, sl 1, yb, *k5, yf, sl 1, yb; rep from * to last 3 sts, k3.
3rd row: Using A k6, sl 1, *k5, sl 1; rep from * to last st, k1.
4th row: Using A k1, yf, sl 1, yb, *k5, yf, sl 1, yb; rep from * to last 6 sts, k6.
5th row: Using B k1, sl 1, *k5, sl 1; rep from * to last 6 sts, k6.
6th row: Using B k6, yf, sl 1, yb, *k5, yf, sl 1, yb; rep from * to last st, k1.
7th row: Using A k4, sl 1, *k5, sl 1; rep from * to last 3 sts, k3.
8th row: Using A k3, yf, sl 1, yb, *k5, yf, sl 1, yb; rep from * to last 4 sts, k4.
9th row: Using B *k5, sl 1; rep from * to last 2 sts, k2.
10th row: Using B k2, *yf, sl 1, yb, k5; rep from * to end.
11th row: Using A k2, *sl 1, k5; rep from * to end.
12th row: Using A *k5, yf, sl 1, yb; rep from * to last 2 sts, k2.
Rep the last 12 rows.

Patterns for Texture and Colour

Flecked Tweed

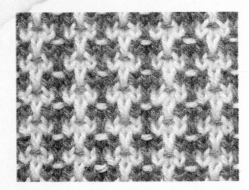

Multiple of 4 sts + 3.
Note: Slip all sts purlwise.
1st row (wrong side): Using A p1, yb, sl 1, yf, *p3, yb, sl 1, yf; rep from * to last st, p1.
2nd row: Using A k1, sl 1, *k3, sl 1; rep from * to last st, k1.
3rd row: Using B p3, *yb, sl 1, yf, p3; rep from * to end.
4th row: Using B k3, *sl 1, k3; rep from * to end.
Rep these 4 rows.

3-Colour Flecked Tweed

Worked as Flecked Tweed.
Beginning with the 1st row work 2 rows in A, 2 rows in B and 2 rows in C throughout.

3-Colour Scottie Tweed

Multiple of 3 sts + 2.
Note: Slip all sts purlwise.
1st row (wrong side): Using A purl.
2nd row: Using B k2, *sl 1, k2; rep from * to end.
3rd row: Using B purl.
4th row: Using C k1, sl 1, *k2, sl 1; rep from * to last 3 sts, k3.
5th row: Using C purl.
6th row: Using A k3, sl 1, *k2, sl 1; rep from * to last st, k1.
Rep these 6 rows.

2-Colour Flecked Garter Stitch

Multiple of 6 sts + 3.
1st row (right side): Using A k3, *p3, k3; rep from * to end.
2nd row: As 1st row.
3rd row: Using B k3, *p3, k3; rep from * to end.
4th row: As 3rd row.
Rep these 4 rows.

T-Square

Multiple of 10 sts + 2.
Note: Slip all sts purlwise.
Foundation row (wrong side): Using A purl.
Commence Pattern
1st row: Using B k4, sl 1, k2, sl 1, *k6, sl 1, k2, sl 1; rep from * to last 4 sts, k4.
2nd row: Using B p4, sl 1, p2, sl 1, *p6, sl 1, p2, sl 1; rep from * to last 4 sts, p4.
3rd row: Using A k5, sl 2, *k8, sl 2; rep from

* to last 5 sts, k5.
4th row: Using A p5, sl 2, *p8, sl 2; rep from * to last 5 sts, p5.
5th row: Using B k2, *sl 1, k6, sl 1, k2; rep from * to end.
6th row: Using B p2, *sl 1, p6, sl 1, p2; rep from * to end.
7th row: Using A k1, sl 1, k8, *sl 2, k8; rep from * to last 2 sts, sl 1, k1.
8th row: Using A p1, sl 1, p8, *sl 2, p8; rep from * to last 2 sts, sl 1, p1.
Rep the last 8 rows.

Blister Check Pattern

Multiple of 6 sts + 2.
Note: Slip all sts purlwise.
1st row (wrong side): Using A purl.
2nd row: Using B k3, sl 2, *k4, sl 2; rep from * to last 3 sts, k3.
3rd row: Using B p3, sl 2, *p4, sl 2; rep from * to last 3 sts, p3.
4th row: As 2nd row.
5th row: Using B purl.
6th row: Using A k5, sl 2, *k4, sl 2; rep from * to last st, k1.
7th row: Using A p1, sl 2, *p4, sl 2; rep from * to last 5 sts, p5.
8th row: As 6th row.
Rep these 8 rows.

Moroccan Pattern

Multiple of 6 sts + 5.
Note: Slip all sts purlwise.

Foundation row (wrong side): Using A purl.
Commence Pattern
1st row: Using B k6, sl 1, *k5, sl 1; rep from * to last 4 sts, k4.
2nd row: Using B k4, yf, sl 1, yb, *k5, yf, sl 1, yb; rep from * to last 6 sts, k6.
3rd row: Using A k3, sl 1, k1, *sl 1, k3, sl 1, k1; rep from * to end.
4th row: Using A k1, yf, sl 1, yb, k3, *yf, sl 1, yb, k1, yf, sl 1, yb, k3; rep from * to end.
5th row: Using B k2, sl 1, *k5, sl 1; rep from * to last 2 sts, k2.
6th row: Using B k2, yf, sl 1, yb, *k5, yf, sl 1, yb; rep from * to last 2 sts, k2.
7th row: Using A [k1, sl 1] twice, *k3, sl 1, k1, sl 1; rep from * to last st, k1.
8th row: Using A [k1, yf, sl 1, yb] twice, *k3, yf, sl 1, yb, k1, yf, sl 1, yb; rep from * to last st, k1.
9th row: Using B k4, sl 1, *k5, sl 1; rep from * to last 6 sts, k6.
10th row: Using B k6, yf, sl 1, yb, *k5, yf, sl 1, yb; rep from * to last 4 sts, k4.
11th row: Using A k1, sl 1, k3, *sl 1, k1, sl 1, k3; rep from * to end.
12th row: Using A k3, yf, sl 1, yb, k1, *yf, sl 1, yb, k3, yf, sl 1, yb, k1; rep from * to end.
Rep the last 12 rows.

Simulated Basketweave

Multiple of 10 sts + 5.
Note: Slip all sts purlwise.
Foundation row (wrong side): Using A purl.
Commence Pattern
1st row: Using B k4, sl 2, *k8, sl 2; rep from * to last 9 sts, k9.
2nd row: Using B p9, sl 2, *p8, sl 2; rep from * to last 4 sts, p4.
3rd row: Using A [k1, sl 1] twice, *k2, sl 1, k1, sl 1; rep from * to last st, k1.
4th row: Using A [p1, sl 1] twice, *p2, sl 1, p1, sl 1; rep from * to last st, p1.
5th row: Using B k9, sl 2, *k8, sl 2; rep from * to last 4 sts, k4.
6th row: Using B p4, sl 2, *p8, sl 2; rep from * to last 9 sts, p9.
7th row: Using A k1, sl 1, *k6, sl 1, k2, sl 1; rep from * to last 3 sts, k3.
8th row: Using A p3, sl 1, *p2, sl 1, p6, sl 1; rep from * to last st, p1.
9th row: As 5th row.
10th row: As 6th row.
11th row: As 3rd row.

12th row: As 4th row.
13th row: As 1st row.
14th row: As 2nd row.
15th row: Using A k3, sl 1, *k2, sl 1, k6, sl 1; rep from * to last st, k1.
16th row: Using A p1, sl 1, *p6, sl 1, p2, sl 1; rep from * to last 3 sts, p3.
Rep the last 16 rows.

Raised Brick Stitch

Multiple of 4 sts + 3.
Note: Slip all sts purlwise.
1st row (right side): K3, *sl 1, k3; rep from * to end.
2nd row: K3, *yf, sl 1, yb, k3; rep from * to end.
3rd row: K1, sl 1, *k3, sl 1; rep from * to last st, k1.
4th row: K1, yf, sl 1, yb, *k3, yf, sl 1, yb; rep from * to last st, k1.
Rep these 4 rows.

3-Colour Ladders

Multiple of 4 sts + 3.
Note: Slip all sts purlwise.
Foundation row (wrong side): Using A purl.
Commence Pattern
1st row: Using B k3, *sl 1, k3; rep from * to end.
2nd row: Using B k3, *yf, sl 1, yb, k3; rep from * to end.
3rd row: Using A k1, sl 1, *k3, sl 1; rep from * to last st, k1.
4th row: Using A p1, sl 1, *p3, sl 1; rep from * to last st, p1.

5th row: Using C as 1st row.
6th row: Using C as 2nd row.
7th row: As 3rd row.
8th row: As 4th row.
Rep the last 8 rows.

2-Colour Ladders

Multiple of 6 sts + 5.
Note: Slip all sts purlwise.
1st row (right side): Using A k2, sl 1, *k5, sl 1; rep from * to last 2 sts, k2.
2nd row: Using A p2, sl 1, *p5, sl 1; rep from * to last 2 sts, p2.
3rd row: Using B k5, *sl 1, k5; rep from * to end.
4th row: Using B k5, *yf, sl 1, yb, k5; rep from * to end.
Rep these 4 rows.

2-Colour Ladders with Twists

Multiple of 6 sts.
Note: Slip all sts purlwise.
1st Foundation row (right side): Using A knit.
2nd Foundation row: Using A purl.
Commence Pattern
1st row: Using B k2, sl 2, *k4, sl 2; rep from * to last 2 sts, k2.
2nd row: Using B k1, p1, sl 2, p1, *k2, p1, sl 2, p1; rep from * to last st, k1.
3rd row: Using A k1, C2F, C2B, *k2, C2F, C2B; rep from * to last st, k1.
4th row: Using A purl.
Rep the last 4 rows.

Patterns for Texture and Colour

Nubbly Tweed I

Multiple of 2 sts + 1.
Note: Slip all sts purlwise.
1st row (wrong side): Using A p1, *k1, p1; rep from * to end.
2nd row: Using B k1, *sl 1, k1; rep from * to end.
3rd row: Using B k1, *p1, k1; rep from * to end.
4th row: Using A k2, sl 1, *k1, sl 1; rep from * to last 2 sts, k2.
Rep these 4 rows.

Nubbly Tweed II

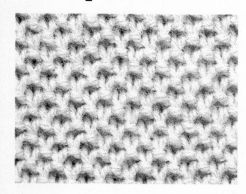

Work as Nubbly Tweed I but using one colour throughout.

Nubbly Tweed III

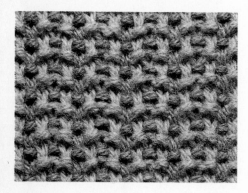

Multiple of 4 sts + 1.
Note: Slip all sts purlwise.
1st row (right side): Using B k4, sl 1, *k3, sl 1; rep from * to last 4 sts, k4.

2nd row: Using B k4, yf, sl 1, yb, *k3, yf, sl 1, yb; rep from * to last 4 sts, k4.
3rd row: Using A k1, *sl 1, k1; rep from * to end.
4th row: Using A k1, *yf, sl 1, yb, k1; rep from * to end.
Rep these 4 rows.

Tweed Checks

Multiple of 10 sts + 9.
Note: Slip all sts purlwise.
Using A work 4 rows in st st, starting knit (1st row is right side).
5th row: Using B k1, sl 1, k1, sl 3, *[k1, sl 1] 3 times, k1, sl 3; rep from * to last 3 sts, k1, sl 1, k1.
6th row: Using B k1, yf, sl 1, yb, k1, yf, sl 3, yb, *[k1, yf, sl 1, yb] 3 times, k1, yf, sl 3, yb; rep from * to last 3 sts, k1, yf, sl 1, yb, k1.
Using A work 2 rows in st st, starting knit.
Rep the last 4 rows twice more then 5th and 6th rows again.
Rep these 18 rows.

Basket Twists

Multiple of 8 sts + 5.
Special Abbreviation
Twist 3 = knit into front of 3rd st on left-hand needle, then knit 2nd st, then knit 1st st, slipping all 3 sts off needle together.
1st row (right side): P5, *Twist 3, p5; rep from * to end.
2nd row: K5, *p3, k5; rep from * to end.
Rep the last 2 rows once more.
5th row: P1, Twist 3, *p5, Twist 3; rep from * to last st, p1.
6th row: K1, p3, *k5, p3; rep from * to last st, k1.
Rep the last 2 rows once more.
Rep these 8 rows.

Slip Stitch Crosses

Multiple of 6 sts.
Note: Slip all sts purlwise.
1st Foundation row (right side): Using A knit.
2nd Foundation row: Using A purl.
Commence Pattern
1st row: Using B k2, *sl 2, k4; rep from * to last 4 sts, sl 2, k2.
2nd row: Using B p2, *sl 2, p4; rep from * to last 4 sts, sl 2, p2.
3rd row: Using A k1, C2F, C2B, *k2, C2F, C2B; rep from * to last st, k1.
4th row: Using A purl.
5th row: Using B k5, sl 2, *k4, sl 2; rep from * to last 5 sts, k5.
6th row: Using B p5, *sl 2, p4; rep from * to last 7 sts, sl 2, p5.
7th row: Using A k4, C2F, C2B, *k2, C2F, C2B; rep from * to last 4 sts, k4.
8th row: Using A purl.
Rep the last 8 rows.

Slip Stitch Zigzags

See Little Cable Fabric on page 43 of the Harmony Guide to Knitting Stitches.
Multiple of 4 sts + 1.
1st row (right side): Using A k1, *sl 1 purlwise, k3; rep from * to end.
2nd row: Using A *p3, sl 1 purlwise; rep from * to last st, p1.
3rd row: Using B k1, *C3L, k1; rep from * to end.
4th row: Using B purl.
5th row: Using A k5, *sl 1, k3; rep from * to end.
6th row: Using A *p3, sl 1; rep from * to last 5 sts, p5.

7th row: Using B k3, *C3R, k1; rep from * to last 2 sts, k2.
8th row: Using B purl.
Rep these 8 rows.

Snowballs

Multiple of 5 sts + 1.
Note: Sts should not be counted after 4th, 5th and 6th rows.
1st row (wrong side): Using A purl.
2nd row: Using A knit.
3rd row: Using A p1, *p1 wrapping yarn twice around needle, p2, p1 wrapping yarn twice around needle, p1; rep from * to end.
4th row: Using B k1, sl 1 (dropping extra loop), k2, sl 1 (dropping extra loop), *[k1, yf, k1, yf, k1] into next st, sl 1 (dropping extra loop), k2, sl 1 (dropping extra loop); rep from * to last st, k1.
5th row: Using B p1, sl 1, p2, sl 1, *yb, k5, yf, sl 1, p2, sl 1; rep from * to last st, p1.
6th row: Using B k1, sl 1, k2, sl 1, *yf, p5, yb, sl 1, k2, sl 1; rep from * to last st, k1.
7th row: Using B p1, sl 1, p2, sl 1, *yb, k2tog, k3tog, pass k2tog st over k3tog st, yf, sl 1, p2, sl 1; rep from * to last st, p1.
8th row: Using A k1, *drop first elongated st off needle, with yb sl 2, drop next elongated st off needle, with left-hand needle pick up first elongated st, pass the slipped sts from right-hand needle back to left-hand needle, then pick up second elongated st on left-hand needle, k5; rep from * to end.
Rep these 8 rows.

Trellis Stitch III

See Trellis Stitches I and II on page 34 of the Harmony Guide to Knitting Stitches.

Multiple of 6 sts + 5.
Special Abbreviation
Pull up loop = insert point of right-hand needle under the 2 strands of B, then knit the next st at the same time slipping the B strands over to the back of the work.
Using A cast on and work 1 row knit, 1 row purl.
Commence Pattern
1st row (right side): Using B p4, *keeping yarn at front sl 3 purlwise, p3; rep from * to last st, p1.
2nd row: Using B k4, *keeping yarn at back sl 3 purlwise, k3; rep from * to last st, k1.
3rd row: Using A knit.
4th row: Using A purl.
5th row: Using A k5, *pull up loop, k5; rep from * to end.
6th row: Using A purl.
7th row: Using B p1, *keeping yarn at front sl 3 purlwise, p3; rep from * to last 4 sts, sl 3 purlwise, p1.
8th row: Using B k1, *keeping yarn at back sl 3 purlwise, k3; rep from * to last 4 sts, sl 3, k1.
9th row: Using A knit.
10th row: Using A purl.
11th row: Using A, k2, *pull up loop, k5; rep from * to last 3 sts, pull up loop, k2.
12th row: Using A purl.
Rep the last 12 rows.

Trellis Stitch IV

Multiple of 6 sts + 5.
Special Abbreviation
Pull up loop = insert point of right-hand needle under the 2 strands of B, then knit the next st at the same time slipping the B strands over to the back of the work.
Cast on using A and work 1 row knit, 1 row purl.
Commence Pattern
1st row (right side): Using B, k4, *yf, sl 3 purlwise, yb, k3; rep from * to last st, k1.
2nd row: Using B p4, *yb, sl 3 purlwise, yf, p3; rep from * to last st, p1.
3rd row: Using A knit.
4th row: Using A purl.
5th row: Using A k5, *pull up loop, k5; rep from * to end.
6th row: Using A purl.
7th row: Using B k1, *yf, sl 3 purlwise, yb, k3; rep from * to last 4 sts, yf, sl 3 purlwise, yb, k1.
8th row: Using B p1, *yb, sl 3 purlwise, yf, p3; rep from * to last 4 sts, yb, sl 3 purlwise, yf, p1.
9th row: Using A knit.
10th row: Using A purl.
11th row: Using A, k2, *pull up loop, k5; rep from * to last 3 sts, pull up loop, k2.
12th row: Using A purl.
Rep the last 12 rows.

Slip Stitch Bubbles I

Multiple of 8 sts + 4.
Note: Slip all sts purlwise.
1st row (right side): Knit.
2nd row: Purl.
3rd row: P1, yb, sl 2, yf, *p6, yb, sl 2, yf; rep from * to last st, p1.
4th row: K1, yf, sl 2, yb, *k6, yf, sl 2, yb; rep from * to last st, k1.
Rep the last 2 rows twice more.
9th row: Knit.
10th row: Purl.
11th row: P5, yb, sl 2, yf, *p6, yb, sl 2, yf; rep from * to last 5 sts, p5.
12th row: K5, yf, sl 2, yb, *k6, yf, sl 2, yb; rep from * to last 5 sts, k5.
Rep the last 2 rows twice more.
Rep these 16 rows.

Slip Stitch Bubbles II

Worked as Slip Stitch Bubbles I, using reverse side as right side.

Patterns for Texture and Colour

Slip Stitch Bubbles with Garter Stitch

Multiple of 6 sts + 4.
Note: Slip all sts purlwise.
1st row (right side): Knit.
2nd row: K1, yf, sl 2, yb, *k4, yf, sl 2, yb; rep from * to last st, k1.
3rd row: K1, sl 2, *k4, sl 2; rep from * to last st, k1.
Rep the last 2 rows once more.
6th row: As 2nd row.
7th row: Knit.
8th row: K4, *yf, sl 2, yb, k4; rep from * to end.
9th row: K4, *sl 2, k4; rep from * to end.
Rep the last 2 rows once more.
12th row: As 8th row.
Rep these 12 rows.

Bubble Pattern I

Multiple of 4 sts + 3.
Special Abbreviation
K5B (Knit 5th St Below) = slip next st off left-hand needle and drop 4 rows down. Insert point of right-hand needle under strands and into the st on the 5th row down, insert left-hand needle under the strands and into the stitch. Knit the st normally catching the strands at the same time.
Cast on and purl 1 row.
Commence Pattern
Work 4 rows in st st, starting knit (1st row is right side).
5th row: K3, *K5B, k3; rep from * to end.
6th row: Purl.
Work 4 rows in st st, starting knit.
11th row: K1, *K5B, k3; rep from * to last 2 sts, K5B, k1.

12th row: Purl.
Rep the last 12 rows.

Bubble Pattern II

Worked as Bubble Pattern I, but using 3 colours.
Cast on and purl 1 row in A.
Commence Pattern
Work 4 rows in B, 2 rows in A, 4 rows in C, 2 rows in A.
Rep the last 12 rows.

Bubble Pattern III

Multiple of 4 sts + 3.
Special Abbreviation
K5B (Knit 5th St Below) = slip next st off left-hand needle and drop 4 rows down. Insert point of right-hand needle under strands and into the st on the 5th row down, insert left-hand needle under the strands and into the stitch. Knit the st normally catching the strands at the same time.
Cast on and knit 1 row in A.
Commence Pattern
Using B work 4 rows in st st, starting knit.
5th row: Using A k3, *K5B, k3; rep from * to end.
6th row: Using A knit.
Using C work 4 rows in st st, starting knit.
11th row: Using A k1, *K5B, k3; rep from * to last 2 sts, K5B, k1.
12th row: Using A knit.
Rep the last 12 rows.

Basket Stitch

Multiple of 10 sts + 7.
Note: Slip all sts purlwise.
Work 3 rows in reversed st st, starting knit (1st row is wrong side).
4th row: K6, sl 5, *k5, sl 5; rep from * to last 6 sts, k6.
5th row: P6. sl 5, *p5, sl 5; rep from * to last 6 sts, p6.
Rep the last 2 rows once more then 4th row again.
Work 3 rows in reversed st st, starting knit.
12th row: K1, sl 5, *k5, sl 5; rep from * to last st, k1.
13th row: P1, sl 5, *p5, sl 5; rep from * to last st, p1.
Rep the last 2 rows once more then the 12th row again.
Rep these 16 rows.

3-Colour Honeycomb I

Multiple of 8 sts + 4.
Note: Slip all sts purlwise.
1st and 2nd rows: Using A knit (1st row is right side).
3rd row: Using B k1, sl 2, *k6, sl 2; rep from * to last st, k1.
4th row: Using B p1, sl 2, *p6, sl 2; rep from * to last st, p1.
Rep the last 2 rows twice more.
9th and 10th rows: Using A knit.
11th row: Using C k5, sl 2, *k6, sl 2; rep from * to last 5 sts, k5.
12th row: Using C p5, sl 2, *p6, sl 2; rep from * to last 5 sts, p5.
Rep the last 2 rows twice more.
Rep these 16 rows.

3-Colour Honeycomb II

Multiple of 8 sts + 4.
Note: Slip all sts purlwise.
1st row (right side): Using A knit.
2nd row: Using A purl.
3rd row: Using B k1, sl 2, *k6, sl 2; rep from * to last st, k1.
4th row: Using B p1, sl 2, *p6, sl 2; rep from * to last st, p1.
Rep the last 2 rows twice more.
9th row: Using A knit.
10th row: Using A purl.
11th row: Using C k5, sl 2, *k6, sl 2; rep from * to last 5 sts, k5.
12th row: Using C p5, sl 2, *p6, sl 2; rep from * to last 5 sts, p5.
Rep the last 2 rows twice more.
Rep these 16 rows.

Brick Pattern I

Multiple of 6 sts + 3.
Note: Slip all sts purlwise.
1st row (right side): Using A knit.
2nd row: Using A purl.
3rd row: Using B k4, sl 1, *k5, sl 1; rep from * to last 4 sts, k4.
4th row: Using B k4, yf, sl 1, yb, *k5, yf, sl 1, yb; rep from * to last 4 sts, k4.
5th row: Using B p4, yb, sl 1, yf, *p5, yb, sl 1, yf; rep from * to last 4 sts, p4.
6th row: As 4th row.
7th row: Using A knit.
8th row: Using A purl.
9th row: Using B k1, sl 1, *k5, sl 1; rep from * to last st, k1.
10th row: Using B k1, yf, sl 1, yb, *k5, yf, sl 1, yb; rep from * to last st, k1.

11th row: Using B p1, yb, sl 1, yf, *p5, yb, sl 1, yf; rep from * to last st, p1.
12th row: As 10th row.
Rep these 12 rows.

Brick Pattern II

Multiple of 16 sts + 7.
Note: Slip all sts purlwise.
1st row (right side): Using A knit.
2nd row: Using A purl.
3rd row: Using B k2, sl 3, *k13, sl 3; rep from * to last 2 sts, k2.
4th row: Using B k2, yf, sl 3, yb, *k13, yf, sl 3, yb; rep from * to last 2 sts, k2.
5th row: Using B p2, yb, sl 3, yf, *p13, yb, sl 3, yf; rep from * to last 2 sts, p2.
Rep the last 2 rows twice more then 4th row again.
Using A work 4 rows in st st, starting knit.
15th row: Using B k10, sl 3, *k13, sl 3; rep from * to last 10 sts, k10.
16th row: Using B k10, yf, sl 3, yb, *k13, yf, sl 3, yb; rep from * to last 10 sts, k10.
17th row: Using B p10, yb, sl 3, yf, *p13, yb, sl 3, yf; rep from * to last 10 sts, p10.
Rep the last 2 rows twice more then 16th row again.
23rd row: Using A knit.
24th row: Using A purl.
Rep these 24 rows.

Surface Quilting Stitch I

Multiple of 10 sts + 7.
Note: Slip all sts purlwise.
Cast on in A and purl 1 row.

Foundation row (right side): Using B k6, sl 2, yf, sl 1, yb, sl 2, *k5, sl 2, yf, sl 1, yb, sl 2; rep from * to last 6 sts, k6.
Commence Pattern
1st row: Using B k6, sl 5, *k5, sl 5; rep from * to last 6 sts, k6.
Using A work 4 rows in st st, starting knit.
6th row: Using B k1, sl 2, yf, sl 1, yb, sl 2, *k2, insert point of right-hand needle upwards under loose strand in B in front of the slipped sts 4 rows down, place onto left-hand needle and knit this loop together with next st on left-hand needle tbl (called pull up loop), k2, sl 2, yf, sl 1, yb, sl 2; rep from * to last st, k1.
7th row: Using B k1, sl 5, *k5, sl 5; rep from * to last st, k1.
Using A work 4 rows in st st, starting knit.
12th row: Using B k3, pull up loop, *k2, sl 2, yf, sl 1, yb, sl 2, k2, pull up loop; rep from * to last 3 sts, k3.
Rep the last 12 rows.

Surface Quilting Stitch II

Multiple of 10 sts + 7.
Note: Slip all sts purlwise.
Cast on with A and purl 1 row.
Foundation row (right side): Using B k6, yf, sl 5, yb, *k5, yf, sl 5, yb; rep from * to last 6 sts, k6.
Commence pattern
1st row: Using B k6, sl 5, *k5, sl 5; rep from * to last 6 sts, k6.
Using A work 4 rows in st st, starting knit.
6th row: Using B k1, yf, sl 5, yb, *k2, insert point of right-hand needle upwards under loose strands in B in front of the slip sts 4 and 5 rows down, place onto left-hand needle and knit these loops together with next st on left-hand needle tbl (called pull up loops), k2, yf, sl 5, yb; rep from * to last st, k1.
7th row: Using B k1, sl 5, *k5, sl 5; rep from * to last st, k1.
Using A work 4 rows in st st, starting knit.
12th row: Using B k3, pull up loops, *k2, yf, sl 5, yb, k2, pull up loops; rep from * to last 3 sts, k3.
Rep the last 12 rows.

Abbreviations

Alt = alternate; beg = begininning; cms = centimetres; dec = decrease; inc = increase; ins = inches; k = knit; m = metres; p = purl; psso = pass slipped stitch over; p2sso = pass 2 slipped sts over; rep = repeat; sl = slip; st = stitch; st(s) = stitch(es); st st = stocking stitch (1 row k, 1 row p); tbl = through back of loop; tog = together; yb = yarn back; yf = yarn forward; yfon = yarn forward and over needle; yfrn = yarn forward and round needle; yo = yarn over; yon = yarn over needle; yrn = yarn round needle.

M1 (Make 1 Stitch) = pick up horizontal strand of yarn lying between stitch just worked and next st and knit into back of it.

MB (Make Bobble) = knit into front, back and front of next st, turn and k3, turn and p3, turn and k3, turn and sl 1, k2tog, psso (bobble completed).

K1B (Knit 1 below) = insert needle through centre of st below next st on needle and knit this in the usual way, slipping the st above off needle at the same time.

Sl 2tog knitwise = insert needle into the next 2 sts on left-hand needle as if to k2tog then slip both sts onto right-hand needle without knitting them.

KB1 = knit into back of next stitch.

PB1 = purl into back of next stitch.

C2B or C2F (Cross 2 Back or Cross 2 Front) = knit into back (or front) of 2nd st on needle, then knit first st, slipping both sts off needle at the same time.

C2L (Cross 2 Left) = slip next st onto cable needle and hold at front of work, knit next st from left-hand needle, then knit st from cable needle.

C2R (Cross 2 Right) = slip next st onto cable needle and hold at back of work, knit next st from left-hand needle, then knit st from cable needle.

C2P (Cross 2 Purl) = purl into front of 2nd st on needle, then purl first st, slipping both sts off needle together.

T2 (Twist 2) = slip next st onto cable needle and hold at back of work, PB1 from left-hand needle then PB1 from cable needle.

T2L (Twist 2 Left) = slip next st onto cable needle and hold at front of work, purl next st from left-hand needle, then KB1 from cable needle.

T2R (Twist 2 Right) = slip next st onto cable needle and hold at back of work, KB1 from left-hand needle, then purl st from cable needle.

T2F (Twist 2 Front) = slip next st onto cable needle and hold at front of work, purl next st from left-hand needle, then knit st from cable needle.

T2B (Twist 2 Back) = slip next st onto cable needle and hold at back of work, knit next st from left-hand needle, then purl st from cable needle.

C3 (Cross 3) = knit into front of 3rd st on needle, then knit first st in usual way slipping this st off needle, now knit 2nd st in usual way, slipping 2nd and 3rd sts off needle together.

C3B (Cross 3 Back) = slip next st onto cable needle and hold at back of work, knit next 2 sts from left-hand needle, then knit st from cable needle.

C3F (Cross 3 Front) = slip next 2 sts onto cable needle and hold at front of work, knit next st from left-hand needle, then knit sts from cable needle.

C3L (Cable 3 Left) = slip next st onto cable needle and hold at front of work, knit next 2 sts from left-hand needle, then knit st from cable needle.

C3R (Cable 3 Right) = slip next 2 sts onto cable needle and hold at back of work, knit next st from left-hand needle, then knit sts from cable needle.

T3B (Twist 3 Back) = slip next st onto cable needle and hold at back of work, knit next 2 sts from left-hand needle, then purl st from cable needle.

T3F (Twist 3 Front) = slip next 2 sts onto cable needle and hold at front of work, purl next st from left-hand needle, then knit sts from cable needle.

T3L (Twist 3 Left) = slip next st onto cable needle and hold at front of work, work [KB1, p1] from left-hand needle, then KB1 from cable needle.

T3R (Twist 3 Right) = slip next 2 sts onto cable needle and hold at back of work, KB1 from left-hand needle, then [p1, KB1] from cable needle.

C4B or C4F (Cable 4 Back or Cable 4 Front) = slip next 2 sts onto cable needle and hold at back (or front) of work, knit next 2 sts from left-hand needle, then knit sts from cable needle.

C4L (Cross 4 Left) = slip next st onto cable needle and leave at front of work, knit next 3 sts from left-hand needle, then knit st from cable needle.

C4R (Cross 4 Right) = slip next 3 sts onto cable needle and leave at back of work, knit next st from left-hand needle then knit sts from cable needle.

T4B (Twist 4 Back) = slip next 2 sts onto cable needle and hold at back of work, knit next 2 sts from left-hand needle, then purl the 2 sts from cable needle.

T4F (Twist 4 Front) = slip next 2 sts onto cable needle and hold at front of work, purl next 2 sts from left-hand needle, then knit sts from cable needle.

T4L (Twist 4 Left) = slip next 2 sts onto cable needle and hold at front of work, k1, p1 from left-hand needle, then knit sts from cable needle.

T4R (Twist 4 Right) = slip next 2 sts onto cable needle and hold at back of work, knit next 2 sts from left-hand needle, then p1, k1 from cable needle.

C5 (Cable 5) = slip next 3 sts onto cable needle and hold at back of work, knit next 2 sts from left-hand needle, then knit sts from cable needle.

C5B or C5F (Cross 5 Back or Cross 5 Front) slip next 3 sts onto cable needle and hold at back (or front) of work, knit next 2 sts from left-hand needle, slip the purl st from point of cable needle back onto left-hand needle, purl this st, then k2 from cable needle.

C5L (Cross 5 Left) = slip next 4 sts onto cable needle and hold at front of work, purl next st on left-hand needle, then knit sts on cable needle.

C5R (Cross 5 Right) = slip the next st onto cable needle and hold at back of work, knit next 4 sts on left-hand needle, then purl the st on cable needle.

T5B (Twist 5 Back) = slip next 2 sts onto cable needle and hold at back of work, knit next 3 sts from left-hand needle, then purl sts from cable needle.

T5F (Twist 5 Front) = slip next 3 sts onto cable needle and hold at front of work, purl next 2 sts from left-hand needle, then knit sts from cable needle.

T5L (Twist 5 Left) = slip next 2 sts onto cable needle and hold at front of work, k2, p1 from left-hand needle, then k2 from cable needle.

T5R (Twist 5 Right) = slip next 3 sts onto cable needle and hold at back of work, knit next 2 sts from left-hand needle, then work [p1, k2] from cable needle.

T5FL (Twist 5 Front Left) = slip next 2 sts onto cable needle and hold at front of work, purl next 3 sts from left-hand needle, then knit the 2 sts from cable needle.

T5BR (Twist 5 Back Right) = slip next 3 sts onto cable needle and leave at back of work, knit next 2 sts from left-hand needle, then purl the 3 sts from cable needle.

C6 (Cross 6) = slip next 4 sts onto cable needle and hold at front of work, knit next 2 sts from left-hand needle, then slip the 2 purl sts from cable needle back to left-hand needle. Pass the cable needle with 2 remaining knit sts to back of work, purl 2 sts from left-hand needle, then knit the 2 sts from cable needle.

C6B or C6F (Cable 6 Back or Cable 6 Front) = slip next 3 sts onto cable needle and hold at back (or front) of work, knit next 3 sts from left-hand needle, then knit sts from cable needle.

T6B (Twist 6 Back) = slip next 3 sts onto cable needle and hold at back of work, knit next 3 sts from left-hand needle, then purl sts from cable needle.

T6F (Twist 6 Front) = slip next 3 sts onto cable needle and hold at front of work, purl next 3 sts from left-hand needle, then knit sts from cable needle.

T6L (Twist 6 Left) = slip next 2 sts onto cable needle and hold at front of work, work k2, p2 from left-hand needle, then knit the 2 sts from cable needle.

T6R (Twist 6 Right) = slip next 4 sts onto cable needle and hold at back of work, knit next 2 sts from left-hand needle, then work p2, k2 from cable needle.

C7F or C7B (Cable 7 Front or Cable 7 Back) = slip next 4 sts onto cable needle and hold at front (or back) of work, knit next 3 sts on left-hand needle, slip purl st from cable needle onto left-hand needle and purl it, then k3 from cable needle.

C8B or C8F (Cable 8 Back or Cable 8 Front) = slip next 4 sts onto cable needle and hold at back (or front) of work, knit next 4 sts from left-hand needle, then knit sts from cable needle.

C9B (Cable 9 Back) = slip next 4 sts onto cable needle and hold at back of work, knit next 5 sts from left-hand needle, then knit sts from cable needle.

C9F (Cable 9 Front) = slip next 5 sts onto cable needle and hold at front of work, knit next 4 sts from left-hand needle, then knit sts from cable needle.

C10B or C10F (Cable 10 Back or Cable 10 Front) = slip next 5 sts onto cable needle and hold at back (or front) of work, knit next 5 sts from left-hand needle, then knit sts from cable needle.

C12B or C12F (Cable 12 Back or Cable 12 Front) = slip next 6 sts onto cable needle and hold at back (or front) of work, knit next 6 sts from left-hand needle, then knit sts from cable needle.

Index